MW00668187

RELUCTANT REVOLUTIONARIES

RELUCTANT REVOLUTIONARIES

NEW YORK CITY AND THE ROAD TO

INDEPENDENCE, 1763–1776

JOSEPH S. TIEDEMANN

Cornell University Press | ITHACA AND LONDON

First published 1997 by Cornell University Press

Printed in the United States of America

This book is printed on Lyons Falls Turin Book, a paper that is totally chlorine-free and acid-free.

Library of Congress Cataloging-in-Publication Data

Tiedemann, Joseph S.
  Reluctant revolutionaries : New York City and the road to independence, 1763–1776 / Joseph S. Tiedemann.
    p.   cm.
  Includes index.
  ISBN 0-8014-3237-5 (acid-free paper)
    1. New York (N.Y.)—History—Colonial period, ca. 1600–1775.
  2. New York (N.Y.)—History—Revolution, 1775–1783.   I. Title.
  F128.4.T54   1997
  974.7′107—DC20   96-35249

Cloth printing   10 9 8 7 6 5 4 3 2 1

To Barbara, Scott, and Michael

Contents

Maps

Acknowledgments

While working on this project, I have become indebted to many people, especially those who so kindly sacrificed their time and shared their expertise to make this a much better book than it would otherwise have been.

In the first place, I want to thank all the New York historians who have previously written on this topic. Without their books and articles this work would not have been possible. A special acknowledgment must go to those with whom I have disagreed. Though the conclusions I have reached may have differed from theirs, their insights led me to clarify my own thoughts and to think more deeply than I otherwise would have about Revolutionary New York City. I hope that I will be able to do the same for those who write on this subject in the years to come.

At key stages in my work several historians read drafts of the manuscript and patiently prodded me to develop and refine my argument. Though they saved me from more errors than I care to admit, I take full responsibility for those that may remain. Gene Fingerhut, Bernard Friedman, Milton Klein, and Neil York all read the entire manuscript, some parts more than once. They generously combed through it for infelicities of style and shared with me their extensive and detailed knowledge of Early American history. Bernard Friedman also allowed me to read an unpublished paper he had written on the New York Sons of Liberty, which along with his published articles broadened my understanding of the role these radicals played in New York between 1763 and 1776.

Friends at Loyola Marymount University also made my task much lighter. Seth Thompson read the manuscript, and he along with Jim Faught and Dave Marple made me much more cognizant of how a social scientist would tackle the subject matter. Larry Jelinek read the Introduction and the Historiographical Essay. Thomas Buckley, S.J., read different parts of the manuscript and was a real source of support throughout; his enthusiasm always revived my lagging spirits. Carla Pestana, a former student and now a faculty member at Ohio State University, read an early draft of Part I of the manuscript and did much to help me to clarify my argument.

Despite my many requests for manuscripts and information, the staffs at the New-York Historical Society, the New York Public Library, the Library of Congress, the City Museum of New York, and Columbia University's Special Collections were ever gracious and helpful. My direct quotations from manuscripts at the New-York Historical Society are by courtesy of the New-York Historical Society, and my direct quotations from manuscripts at the New York Public Library are with the permission of the Rare Book and Manuscripts Division, New York Public Library, Astor, Lenox, and Tilden Foundations. My friends and colleagues in the Charles Von der Ahe Library at Loyola Marymount invariably managed to locate the materials that I was forever requesting on short notice.

While working on this book I benefited from several grants and fellowships. The Arnold L. and Lois S. Graves Award, which I held in the fall of 1986, made it possible for me to do research in Washington, D.C., and New York City. A T. Marie Chilton Chair in the Humanities during the summer of 1987 allowed me to start writing without the usual distractions. Summer grants from Loyola Marymount University in 1988, 1989, and 1994 helped me to continue the work. Indeed, Loyola Marymount provided me with support throughout the entire project.

My family's support was incalculable. My parents fed and housed me during my numerous trips to New York, and my other New York relatives spent considerable time entertaining and encouraging me while I was away from home. Barbara tolerated more than her marriage vows demanded. Scott and Michael had the knack of putting things in perspective by relegating my project to its proper place within the scheme of things.

Finally, there were the family and friends, doctors and nurses, and physical and occupational therapists who were such a fantastic support group while I was recovering from a crushing automobile accident, and who made it possible for me to finish this book.

J. S. T.

Los Angeles, California

RELUCTANT REVOLUTIONARIES

The Birth of a Debate

Historians have long been at pains to explain why New York was the last of the thirteen colonies to declare its independence from Great Britain, in 1776. New York City is especially perplexing, for a decade earlier the opposition of its residents to the Stamp Act had brought the city to the brink of rebellion.

For months, in 1765, partisans had been erecting the stage and collecting the props for the street theater that was to commence as soon as the hated stamp tax became effective, on Friday, November 1. Lt. Gov. Cadwallader Colden, an overzealous royal appointee, had been busy since July readying Fort George, at the southwest tip of Manhattan Island, to withstand a mob's assault. And a "secret unknown party" opposed to the tax had been predicting violence for almost as long. Local patricians knew tumult was inevitable, but the violent tremor that struck on that Friday shook their confidence and convinced them that anarchy had engulfed New York.[1]

The actual drama had begun on Thursday, the day before the Stamp Act was to take effect. After merchants voted to boycott British imports, dissidents roamed the streets, shouting "Liberty" and breaking "thousands of windows."[2] Rumor had it that Maj. Thomas James, a British officer who had bragged that he would "cram the Stamps down their Throats," was to be buried alive.[3] Tension mounted on Friday. As soldiers prepared for the mob's onslaught, marines from warships in the harbor took up defensive positions inside the fort. Garden fences and other structures outside its walls were leveled so that "the Great Guns might play the more freely." And the cannons were loaded with grape shot for greater effect against the mob. Meanwhile, Colden received a note predicting his death if redcoats dared to fire their weapons during the upcoming protests.[4]

At nightfall two crowds formed, ostensibly "in defence of his Majesty's *person* and government."[5] The first met in the town Commons and built a movable gallows from which they hung an effigy of Colden. On his back was a drum, an allusion to a canard that he had been a drummer in the army of the Pretender in Scotland; on his breast was a sign inscribed "*The Rebel Drummer in the Year 1715.*" Like the Pretender, who had lost his claim to the throne because of Stuart pretensions to absolutism, Colden epitomized the popular fear of arbitrary government. By assailing him the crowd was affirming its loyalty to George III yet subtly admonishing the king that he too would forfeit his crown if he tried to establish a tyranny.[6] The second group paraded by candlelight through the streets with its own effigy of Colden, ridiculing him in the same fashion residents mocked criminals and scoundrels. When city magistrates halted the demonstrators and threw their dummy to the ground, mob leaders "ordered it to be taken up again in the most Magisterial manner, and told the Mayor etc, they would not hurt them, provided they stood out of their way." The officials complied, and the crowd proceeded "with the greatest order." The group finally reached Fort George, and Colden's effigy "was brought up within 8 or 10 feet of the Fort Gate with the grossest ribaldry from the Mob." The protesters brazenly broke open the governor's coach house and seized Colden's carriage. They then seated the dummy in the coach and drew it to the Coffee House, where merchants applauded the spectacle.[7]

This second crowd then moved uptown to join the first. Now two thousand strong, the crowd returned to the fort, where rioters hurled bricks and stones over the walls. Some even put their hands atop the ramparts, taunting the troops to fire. Luckily, no one did. Three hundred carpenters stood ready to cut down the fort gate at the first shot, and four hundred seamen were waiting to charge through the opening. A mob leader finally intervened, and the rioters regrouped at Bowling Green, where they burned the lieutenant governor's effigy, gallows, and carriage. "While this was doing," said Colden, "a great number of Gentlemen . . . observe[d] this outrage on their King's Governor." When the church bells tolled, the crowd carried off the remains for burial,[8] and the city's patricians assumed the affair was over. But while spectators were still watching the fire, a "Detachment of Volunteers" had slipped off to Major James's newly refurbished mansion. Imitating what a Boston mob had done to Lt. Gov. Thomas Hutchinson's home in August, the New York rioters "brought out of his house all they could find, drank his liquors, and burnt and destroyed everything else before the door." They then "beat to Pieces all the Doors, Sashes, Window Frames and Partitions in the House, leaving it a mere Shell."[9]

The violence that residents employed in 1765 to dissuade royal officials from enforcing the Stamp Act burnished the city's reputation throughout the thirteen colonies. But a decade later whigs (or patriots) all over America were bemoaning the ambivalence with which New Yorkers were defending their rights against British tyranny. In June 1775, for example, the Provincial Congress, which was acting as New York's extralegal government, learned that Gen. George Washington, the American army's newly appointed commander-in-chief, planned to visit town. Patriots wanted to give him a welcome befitting his rank, and the Provincial Congress ordered Col. John Lasher's newly uniformed battalion to act as honor guard. Congress soon found itself in an awkward spot, however. Early on June 25, it learned that Washington and the colony's British governor, William Tryon, who had been overseas, would both be arriving in town that same day. Lasher's orders were promptly changed. He was to station one company at Paulus Hook, across the Hudson in New Jersey, to greet the general and another at the Ferry, in New York, to meet the governor. The remainder of his unit was to be kept "ready to receive either the General or Governor Tryon, which ever shall first arrive."[10]

In the event, Washington was the first on the scene, arriving in New York at four p.m. to the more lavish reception. As the loyalist (or pro-British) historian Thomas Jones described it, "the volunteer companies raised for the express purpose of rebellion, the members of the Provincial Congress, those of the city committee, [and] the parsons of the dissenting meeting-houses" met him at the beach and then dined in his honor at Lispenard's inn. Toward evening, "nine companies of foot in their uniforms, and a greater number of the principle inhabitants" than had ever before assembled escorted him to Hull's tavern, just north of Trinity Church. Once Washington had retired for the night, onlookers could walk the few short blocks to the foot of Broad Street, where the governor was now ready to land. "His Majesty's Council, the Judges of the Supreme Court, the Attorney General, the Speaker and Members of the General Assembly then in town, the Clergymen of the Church of England, . . . the Governors of King's College, of the Hospital, the members of the Chamber of Commerce, and Marine Society, with a numerous train of his Majesty's loyal and well affected subjects," conducted Tryon "with universal shouts of applause" to a private home, where he spent the night. In the group, said Jones, were people "who had been not five hours before pouring out their adulation and flattery" to Washington. They "now one and all joined in the Governor's train, and with the loudest acclamations, attended him to his lodgings, where, with the utmost seeming sincerity, they shook him by the hand, [and] welcomed him back to the Colony."[11]

That shift in behavior across so critical a decade troubled whigs throughout America. In 1774 Joseph Reed of Pennsylvania had complained of New York's leaders: "While they are attending to the little paltry disputes which their own parties have produced, the great cause is suffering in their hands." In 1776 John Adams asked in exasperation, "What is the Reason, that New York is still asleep or dead, in Politics and War? . . . Have they no sense, no Feeling? No sentiment? No Passions? While every other Colony is rapidly advancing, their Motions seem to be rather retrograde."[12]

New York City, of course, was the key to the colony: its capital, commercial entrepot, and cultural nexus. If the city submitted to British imperialism, the province was likely to do so too. Moreover, the city's influence extended even beyond the colony's borders: the New Jersey Sons of Liberty were "satellites of New York, whence came inspiration and guidance."[13] In 1770, when the city was the first in America to rescind its boycott agreement against the Townshend Duties, the other seaports protested bitterly yet followed suit. Given its strategic location, physically dividing the thirteen colonies in half, New York City was also headquarters for the British army in America. Its harbor was the best on the East Coast, and the Hudson River provided excellent lines of communication with Canada and the American interior. Realistically, if Britain could hold onto New York, the whig cause would be sorely imperiled.

What is striking, given the city's importance, is that there is no modern, full-length history of it for the years between 1763 and 1776. The standard histories for the period are George W. Edwards, *New York as an Eighteenth Century Municipality, 1731–1776*; Oscar Theodore Barck, Jr., *New York City during the War for Independence*; Wilbur C. Abbott, *New York in the American Revolution*; Thomas Jefferson Wertenbaker, *Father Knickerbocker Rebels: New York City during the Revolution*; and Malcolm Decker, *Brink of Revolution: New York in Crisis, 1765–1776*. The first is an institutional history; the second concentrates on the period between 1776 and 1783; the third and fourth, which cover the entire era from 1763 to 1783, are outdated; and the last is a narrative, rather than interpretive, work. More recent studies have been either histories of the province, biographies of its prominent political leaders, or studies of particular groups. These later works have added immeasurably to our knowledge, but they have not satisfactorily answered Adams's questions.[14]

To some historians, New Yorkers were reluctant to rebel because the colony was a hotbed of loyalism. In 1901 Alexander Flick claimed that even after July 4, 1776, "a majority" favored the king; "from first to last New York city was overwhelmingly tory." In 1965 Wallace Brown stated that New York's opposition to British initiatives after 1763 "was vocal and vehement, but, uniquely among the colonies, remained in the hands of moderates and future Loyalists." When "the agitation shifted to outright war and independence, many 'Whigs' became 'Tories,' and the latter party stood forth with a strength rarely equaled in any other part of America."[15] In 1966, however, Bernard Mason argued successfully that "the slow maturation of the New York revolutionary party and the tortuous course of the Whigs" might lead an "unwary observer" to conclude that "the Whigs were a minority." Yet "a searching probe" of the evidence proved that patriots were "a majority of the population." In 1986 Philip Ranlet estimated that "perhaps 15 percent" of New Yorkers were loyalist (or tory), "10 percent were neutral for religious reasons or for personal safety," and the rest "patriots of varying categories of firmness."[16]

But if the whigs were a majority, why were they reluctant to rebel? To answer that question, two key historiographical traditions have emerged.[17] The first, or Progressive School of American History, which took form in 1909 with the publication of Carl Becker's *History of Political Parties in the Province of New York, 1760–1776*, minimized the role of ideas and stressed class and economic issues. The Revolution resulted from "two general movements, the contest for home-rule and independence and the democratization of American politics and society." The latter struggle, the more paramount, pitted the few against the many, the rich against the poor, the powerful against the impotent. The second historiographical tradition, which derives from the Consensus or neo-Conservative School of American History, has "found broad economic and social divisions within the colonies to have been less important" in explaining the Revolution "than the conflicting interests and ambitions of rival groups within the upper strata of society."[18]

Despite their profound disagreements, scholars from both schools have focused their attention on the New York elite, arguing that it was its members who had successfully slowed the pace toward revolution, and that they had done so for any of several reasons: they feared losing political power to the increasingly vocal (and violent) lower classes; they were political opportunists who were too busy exploiting the imperial crises to their own advantage to take time for furthering the cause of liberty; or they were too afraid for their own lives, property, and power to fight for American constitutional rights. But such arguments leave a critical question unanswered. If New York was, as one recent historian has argued, ready by 1774 because of internal reasons "for a thoroughgoing revolution," how was this handful of aristocrats able to confound the will of the people and thus to stem the tide of revolution?[19] The aim of the present close study of New York politics, therefore, is to attempt a new synthesis of the city's history for these years and to reconsider why New Yorkers were reluctant to rebel.

In evaluating the causes of a revolution, scholars generally focus on those who rebel, and on their grievances. Yet the mere existence of an aggrieved people does not mean that a revolution will occur. Three conditions must be met for conflict to emerge: the groups involved "must be conscious of themselves as collective entities," at least one of them must resent its position vis-à-vis the other group, and the dissatisfied party must believe that it can remedy its situation. The question, of course, is when does an oppressed people reach the point where they think they can better their lot by rebelling? Walter Laqueur provided one answer in stating that "most modern revolutions, both successful and abortive, have followed in the wake of war," and these have taken place in both victorious and vanquished nations. That same idea was carefully developed in 1979 in Theda Skocpol's *States and Social Revolutions*. She argued that regimes have survived for long periods of time despite overwhelming popular discontent, even in the face of an organized opposition. For a revolution to erupt, there must also be a crisis or breakdown in the central government, and such a crisis is invariably brought on by international conflict. Caught between the exigencies of war and the demands of domestic interest groups, the government loses the ability to enforce its authority over all or part of its subjects.[20]

To explain the Revolution in New York it is thus imperative to examine what Britain was doing as well as what was happening in the city. When Britain's role in causing the struggle is ignored, inter- and intraclass rivalries in New York appear more significant and determinative of behavior than they actually were. When Britain's role is taken for granted, the Anglo-American conflict mistakenly becomes of almost secondary importance in accounting for why residents acted as they did.[21]

Three propositions, based on Skocpol's analysis of the causes of revolution, will explain the thrust of the argument made in the pages that follow.[22] First, the object of a government (like Great Britain's) in the modern competitive state system is to maintain domestic order and to compete successfully against other nation-states.[23] Second, though a government is often assumed to be "created and manipulated" by its polity's "dominant classes," it can also function as an "autonomous" entity that vies with domestic interest groups for scarce resources. In particular, international imperatives and opportunities can impel a state to pursue policies that clash with or contravene the vital interests of these same groups. The potential for clashes of this sort was especially great in the mainland American colonies, because of the ease with which Britain could sacrifice important groups there in the name of the common good or for the benefit of constituencies elsewhere in the empire.[24] Third, when such a conflict emerges, a regime that can neither preserve order at home nor adapt to the changing international situation will suffer "a loss of legitimacy" in the eyes of the people and will survive only if its coercive institutions "remain coherent and effective." Because the American colonies were united to the British crown by ties of affection and self-interest and not by physical force, Britain's insistence in the 1760s and 1770s on "a full and absolute submission" to parliamentary sovereignty dramatically increased the likelihood of revolution.[25]

In brief, the Seven Years' War and the needs of the competitive state system impelled Britain to embark on three major initiatives to tax the colonies and to exert parliamentary sovereignty over them.[26] Each attempt—the first linked to the Stamp Act, the second to the Townshend Acts, and the third to the Tea Act and the Coercive Acts—provoked a political crisis in New York. The last finally propelled the city and province of New York to join with the other mainland American colonies in a revolution against Britain. Accordingly, this study is divided into three parts. Each will examine what Britain did, why the city reacted as it did, and how New York's political landscape changed as a result. In each of the three crises the situation was complex and the conflicts multifaceted. Where partisans stood on the local political spectrum partially determined how they responded to the imperial crises, and the steps they took to resist Britain in turn influenced how they saw New York politics. For instance, debating how power should be shared in the empire led people to question how it was being exercised in the province. Nonetheless, though the final outcome in New York cannot be explained without considering local politics, it was British imperialism, not political and economic strains in New York, that pushed the city toward independence.

Though every historical event is unique, there are nonetheless certain patterns of behavior that typify conflict situations. Peter Shaw and Paul A. Gilje, for example, have each outlined the traditions that Revolutionary Americans reflected when rioting. But because the situation in New York

City was so multidimensional, the present work also makes use of social-conflict theory to better grasp why New York's polyglot population acted as it did between 1763 and 1776. Scholars in this field examine and compare the causes, evolution, and consequences of group antagonisms to better understand conflict as an integral and essential component of human behavior.[27] The present study has relied particularly on the eight-stage model of conflict elaborated by Louis Kriesberg, a leading practitioner of this interdisciplinary approach, in his *Social Conflicts*. He divided the process into the following stages, analytically: the bases of conflict; how the conflict emerges; initial conduct; escalation; deescalation; termination; outcome; and consequences.[28] For the sake of readability, however, the model has not been superimposed on the text. Instead, references to Kriesberg are limited to those contexts, in the text and the notes, where conflict theory proves to be especially useful in illuminating what was transpiring in a particular situation, or where the dynamics typical of a given stage of conflict clarify how participants were acting at a comparable moment in New York City.

Employing social-conflict theory in the present work is important for three reasons. First, comparing what happened in the city with what has been hypothesized about the nature of conflict, both between and within communities, makes it possible to look at Revolutionary New York from a fresh perspective. Behavior that is puzzling when examined solely in terms of the city's history often becomes more understandable when viewed in the broader context of conflict theory.

Second, given New York's factious and heterogeneous population, a social-conflict approach is especially helpful in analyzing its behavior. Many historians recognize that the great breadth of the city's economic, religious, cultural, and ethnic mix of peoples enlivened its colonial history and fostered the emergence of a sophisticated political culture.[29] Some have argued, too, that this same diversity shaped how the city reacted to the coming of the Revolution, though no one has detailed exactly how.[30] Social-conflict theory helps make that possible. According to one scholar, the homogeneous (voting) populations of New England and the South each quickly reached agreement respecting the strategy to be adopted in opposing the policies Britain pursued after the Seven Years' War. The militants at the Continental Congress thus came overwhelmingly from those two sections.[31] Nonetheless, notwithstanding the remarkable diversity of New York City's population, its residents responded like other eighteenth-century Americans by earnestly and repeatedly seeking to create a consensus over how best to resist British imperialism. If Kriesberg's findings can serve as a guide, the nature of that effort at consensus building markedly influenced the pace and direction of revolutionary activity in the province. Given the sharp differences of opinion and interest so characteristic of New York, it understandably took the city's leaders considerable time to hammer out a course of action acceptable to most people. And the course that finally emerged had to be cautious rather than militant, conservative rather than radical, and inclusive rather than exclusive, in order that as many people as possible might be united behind the revolutionary banner. In the end, the vast majority of New Yorkers espoused independence, though most did so very hesitantly.

Third, although conflict is a normal and necessary part of human existence, under some circumstances a series of conflicts between two antagonists can "spiral" out of control and end in a manner that neither party had intended at the outset.[32] That is exactly what happened in Anglo-American relations between 1763 and 1776. It is also where the works of Skocpol and Kriesberg most effectively buttress one another. The first explains why conflict kept recurring, and the second clarifies why people behaved the way they did in the heat of conflict and how the outcome of one dispute influenced the dynamics of the next.

In sum, by applying the theoretical constructs of Skocpol and Kriesberg, by focusing on the role that British imperialism played in provoking the Revolution, by examining how pluralism shaped the way townspeople responded to the three crises, and by observing residents as they labored to form and to maintain a consensus during very challenging times, this study will endeavor to explain why New Yorkers were such reluctant revolutionaries. In the final analysis, residents behaved the way they did not because most were loyalists (most were not), not because a handful of patrician conservatives was able singlehandedly to dampen the passion for revolution, but because the heterogeneity of the city's population made it very difficult for residents to reach a broad consensus over how to resist British imperialism. The really significant fact is not that they moved so slowly but that in the end they painstakingly constructed a consensus, declared their independence, and became a pivotal state in the new nation.

PART I

THE STAMP ACT CRISIS, 1763–1766

New York City on the Eve of the First Crisis

Situated on Manhattan Island, New York City was "the metropolis and grand mart of the Province."[1] Geography made it so. "Navigation up to the City, from the Sea" was "safe and easy."[2] Washing the island's western shore was the Hudson River, which cut northward in an almost straight line into the colony's interior. A "grand road," the river was generally from seven to twelve feet deep, so that a vessel of sixty tons could with "easy Passage" reach Albany, almost one hundred eighty miles away.[3] One boat, manned by a crew of two or three, could carry into New York City a cargo of greater value "than *forty* Waggons, *One Hundred and Sixty* Horses, and *Eighty* Men, [could] into *Philadelphia*." Because the Hudson formed the eastern boundary of northern New Jersey, and because the Atlantic Ocean provided that colony with ready access to New York, eastern New Jersey was also part of the city's hinterland. But since the Hudson's shoreline often became iced, New York's harbor was located on the opposite shore of Manhattan along the East River, a mile-wide waterway that separated the city from Long Island and opened into Long Island Sound, which stretched for about one hundred twenty miles between that island's north shore and Connecticut's south shore. The Sound offered vessels a sheltered route to the Connecticut River, linking western Connecticut and the rich farmlands of Long Island to the city.[4]

Already one hundred fifty years old, New York was still young, vibrant, and growing. In 1766, 13,000 people lived there; by 1771, almost 22,000. In 1753, there were 2,393 buildings; by 1775, over 4,000.[5] Yet it remained a compact, walkable city. Most townspeople resided within a mile of Fort

Lieutenant Ratzer's map of the City of New York, 1767. (Collection of the New-York Historical Society)

George, which stood at the very tip of Manhattan Island. Peter Kalm, a Swedish visitor in 1750, declared it "extremely pleasant to walk in the town, for it seemed like a garden." Along "the chief streets there are trees planted, which in summer give them a fine appearance, and . . . afford a cooling shade." The roads were "spacious and well built, and most of them . . . paved."[6] A traveler in 1756 remarked, "I had no idea of finding a place in America," so "elegantly built of brick, raised on an eminence and the streets paved and spacious, furnished with commodious keys and warehouses, and employing some hundreds of vessels in its foreign trade and fisheries — . . . very few in England can rival it in its show."[7] By 1775 Dr. Robert Honyman was less enthusiastic. He thought the streets "badly paved" and the homes "built indifferently of Stone, or wood or brick." Still, he "confess[ed]," the city "pleases me better than Philadelphia."[8]

New York was a community of merchants and retailers, artisans and laborers, servants and slaves, making a living by trade. Quite a few prospered. In 1762 residents owned 477 vessels, and about 10 percent of the population shared at least part ownership in one or more of those ships. By 1772, despite adverse economic conditions, the city had added 232 more ships. The variety of products exported was remarkable: pork, beef, bread, butter, peas, rye, cheese, onions, pickled oysters, apples, corn, horses, sheep, boards, and staves to the British and foreign West Indies. On their return, local ships carried sugar, molasses, hides, lumber, silver, and bills of exchange. Trade with Madeira and Tenerife was also substantial; in exchange for wine that was resold in the West Indies, New York offered grain, lumber, and beeswax. Whenever southern Europe suffered a grain shortage, the city's traders exploited that opportunity to import salt, specie, and bills of exchange. A few vessels sailed each year to Africa, where they traded rum and British manufactures for slaves to be sold in the West Indies. By 1774 New York's exports to foreign countries totaled about one hundred fifty thousand pounds sterling per year, and imports amounted to about one hundred thousand pounds sterling. The colony also had a favorable balance of trade with the British West Indies.[9]

These profits were vital, helping New Yorkers to pay for the huge quantities of British dry goods they imported. According to Gov. William Tryon, "more than Eleven Twelfths" of the inhabitants clothed themselves in British textiles and furnished their homes with British manufactures. By 1774 Britain was exporting to New York products worth around five hundred thousand pounds sterling. In return, the mother country imported about one hundred thirty thousand pounds in merchandise, including "pot and pearl ashes, Pig and Bar Iron, Peltries, Beeswax, Masts and Spars, with Timber and Lumber of all kinds." British shipowners annually spent another thirty thousand pounds for vessels built in New York.[10]

Though trade gave people a shared perspective, social values divided them by class, religion, and ethnicity when they visited taverns, attended church, or slept at night.[11] The city had several neighborhoods, each with its own distinct flavor. The hub of activity was at the docks bordering the East River. Along Dock and Queen streets were the homes and warehouses of wholesalers and retailers. Here too could be found the symbols of merchant power. The Exchange, where insurance and bills of exchange were negotiated, was on Broad Street, near Whitehall Slip. The Chamber of Commerce met there regularly after its founding in 1768. The Merchant Coffee House, where traders gossiped and shared the latest news, was at the foot of Wall Street. The waterfront was also the town's worst slum, home to the dives, boarding houses, and whorehouses that seamen frequented. Drinking, fighting, gambling, and gaming were daily activities.

A second slum lay northeast of the waterfront. Starting east of Roosevelt and north of Cherry streets, it continued up Bowery Lane as far as Judith Street. The poor who lived here evidently worked in the nearby distilleries, tanneries, shipyards, rope walks, and pot-baking establishments. A third slum was located in the northwest corner of town, north of Partition Street and west of Broadway. It included not only King's College, but Trinity Church Farm, which was populated by carters, carpenters, gardeners, and laborers. The area also contained quite a few taverns and "infamous houses," where hundreds of prostitutes catered to the soldiers who lived across Broadway in the "upper barracks" near the Fields (or town Commons).[12] Although relations between redcoats and whores could turn violent, more momentous from a political standpoint were the scuffles fought here between soldiers and civilians. It was in the Fields, where the troops exercised, that a Liberty Pole was erected in 1766. During imperial crises redcoats and townspeople engaged in a kind of guerrilla warfare to determine whether this symbol of American freedom would remain standing. On the west side of Broadway, opposite the Fields, were De La Montayne's and Bardin's taverns, which the pro-American Sons of Liberty (or Liberty Boys) frequented and from which they periodically emerged to battle with the soldiers. North of the slum, near the edge of town, at the foot of Warren Street and overlooking the Hudson, stood Vaux Hall, Maj. Thomas James's newly renovated mansion, which would be trashed in the Stamp Act riots.

There was of course another side to New York society. A half-mile walk from Partition Street down tree-lined Broadway brought the pedestrian

Major Holland's map of
the City of New York,
1776. (Collection of the
New-York Historical So-
ciety)

REFERENCES.

A Military Hospital   O St. Pauls.
B Governors House.   P Trinity Church.
C Secretary's Office.   O St. Georges Chapel
D Custom House   R Old Dutch Church.
E Fish Market   S New Dutch Church.
F Old Slip Market.   T Lutheran Church.
G Meat Market.   V Calvinist Church
H Fly Market.   W French Protestant Church
I Pecks Market.   X Quakers Meeting.
K Oswego Market   Y Presbyterian Meeting
L Exchange   Z Baptist Meeting.
M Dutch Free School   a Moravian Meeting
N Engine which suplies   b New Lutheran Meeting
the City with Fresh Water c Jews Synagogue

to Bowling Green, a small park across from Fort George and in one of the city's most exclusive areas. The lots on the west side of Broadway, opposite the Green, extended down to the Hudson and afforded a vista of the Jerseys. On the lot closest to the fort was the mansion of Capt. Archibald Kennedy of the Royal Navy. Next door lived his father-in-law John Watts, a member of the governor's Council. After that was the home of Robert R. Livingston, a justice of the New York Supreme Court. The fourth house was owned by the Van Cortlandt family. The fifth belonged to John Wetherhead (a future loyalist) and was sold by the Commissioners of Forfeiture in 1784 to Livingston.[13] Nearby was the City Arms Tavern, where the wealthy gathered in the Long Room for concerts, lectures, and assemblies.

On Broadway, between the fort and Partition Street, was Trinity Episcopal Church, which the people of "quality chiefly resort[ed] to." Its interior was "ornamented beyond any other place of publick worship" in town, and its 175-foot steeple was a city landmark. There were two other Anglican churches. Saint Paul's Chapel, an "elegant building" reminiscent "of St Martins in the fields in London," stood at Partition and Broadway on the edge of the city's northwest slum. Saint George's Chapel, "a very neat edifice, faced with hewn stone and tiled," had been built in 1752 on the corner of Beekman and Cliff. Situated on the border of a middle-class neighborhood, it was within walking distance of the manufacturing zone.[14] Perhaps, as one historian has said, the Anglican church was "reaching out to the working class."[15] But given that Anglicanism was a faith based on nationality and not class, the two chapels might instead have represented an attempt by prosperous Episcopalians to segregate themselves. Whatever the intent, that was the effect. When poor people passed Trinity on Sunday, they were reminded of their plebeian status. A visitor in 1775 described the scene: "I counted 13 coaches and chariots waiting at the door of this church for their owners, and in truth the number of Equipages in this town, considering the extent of it, is surprising, and most of them exceeding fine ones too."[16]

The elite also favored the area just east of Broadway. Bordered on the southwest by Whitehall Slip and on the east by Dock and Queen streets, the neighborhood continued as far north as King Street, which ran perpendicular to Broadway at Trinity churchyard. Because merchants often lived where they worked, the district was very commercial. At the "Court End," across from the fort, resided prominent members of the powerful Cruger, De Lancey, Morris, and Livingston families. At Broad and Dock was the Queen's Head (or Fraunces) Tavern, where patricians like John Watts, Jr., and John Jay gathered in winter for the Social Club. Located nearby in the early 1760s was the King's Arms Tavern, at which army officers held balls and assemblies. A few blocks farther up Dock Street was Hanover Square, where Hugh Gaine printed his *New York Mercury* and where James Rivington would print his loyalist *Rivington's New York Gazetteer* in the 1770s. If the area was not as exclusive as Bowling Green, its residents were nonetheless politically active. Here lived Theophylact Bache, an Anglican dry-goods merchant, charter member of the Chamber of Commerce and member of the Committee of Fifty-one, which was formed in May 1774 in reaction to the Coercive Acts. So too did Abram Duryee, a Dutch Reformed dealer in dry goods, paints, and oils, who was also on the Committee of Fifty-one; and Samuel Broome, a Presbyterian cutlery merchant, who served on the Committee of One Hundred, which was created in May 1775 after the battles at Lexington and Concord. At the opposite end of the neighborhood, at Wall Street, stood the Presbyterian Church. Built in 1748, it was not as imposing as Trinity. Yet many patricians who worshiped here belonged to the Livingston party, which vied for power with the De Lancey faction, many of whose members prayed at Trinity. Their battles were often fought on Wall Street at City Hall, which housed the provincial legislature, the Supreme Court, the Municipal Court, and the county jail.[17]

A visitor who walked out of City Hall's back door, northward on Nassau Street, entered middle-class New York. In an area bounded on the west by Broadway, on the north by Beekman, and on the east by Queen Street were the modest homes of small shopkeepers and artisans. According to the historian Carl Abbott, "of the 250-odd retailers and makers of consumer goods, metal workers, grocers and druggists, printers, skilled construction workers, and the like for whom a rough location has been found, three-fifths lived" here.[18] Its dissenting churches bespoke the area's social status: the Moravian Church on Fair Street; the Quaker Meeting House on Crown Street; the French Church and New-Scots Church on Little-Queen Street; the German Calvinist Church on Nassau; and the Anabaptist Church on Vandercliff. The Methodists and Baptists shared a building on Smith.[19] The neighborhood was just east of the Liberty Pole, and because the Fields were wedged between a middle-class area on the east and a lower-class slum on the west, partisans could quickly raise a crowd against a British law or policy.

II

But New York's political geography embodied more than its neighborhoods. It also comprised the diverse ethnic and religious groups living there. No other American city had a more polyglot population: English, Dutch, French, German, Scottish, Scotch-Irish, Irish, Swedish, and African. There were Anglicans, Quakers, Presbyterians, Dutch Reformed, Methodists, Moravians, Lutherans, Baptists, German Calvinists, Anabaptists, Huguenots, Jews, and Catholics. Pluralism made New Yorkers "a factious people," especially about religion, for each ethnic group typically worshipped in its own church. The fact that the city's population was growing rapidly merely heightened the tensions.[20]

The Anglican church was the most powerful, though its influence was not based on numbers. William Smith, Jr., an eighteenth-century New York historian and church critic, claimed that "the Episcopalians" were "scarce in the proportion of one to fifteen." The historian George W. Edwards later estimated that they actually constituted one-tenth of the population. Anglicanism's prestige rested on its communicants' social preeminence. Since the church wielded so much power, it attracted wealthy townspeople, whose conversion further enhanced Anglicanism's influence. Thomas Jones, an Anglican, boasted that "the Church of England was the most extensive, of the most influence, and greatest opulence. To this Church the Governor, the Lieutenant-Governor, most of his Majesty's Council, many members of the General Assembly, all the officers of Government, with a numerous train of rich and affluent merchants, and landlords, belonged." Smith complained that because Anglicanism was the established church in England, local Episcopalians "pretend[ed]" that the same arrangement existed in New York. In 1693 the legislature had passed a Ministry Act, requiring residents of New York, Richmond, Queens, and Westchester counties to provide "good Sufficient Protestant" ministers for their parishes. Royal governors interpreted the law to mean that the money raised could be used only for Anglican clergymen. In effect, the act established the church in those counties.[21]

The next most influential denomination just prior to the Revolution was Presbyterianism. It had begun to grow rapidly in the 1740s with the absorption into the fold of several new groups, some of whom detested both the English and the Anglican church: Scottish and Scotch-Irish immigrants, New England and Long Island Puritans, Dutch Reformed converts, and the offspring of marriages between Dutch and Scottish families. Membership came mostly from "the middle rank," though it included "some rich, wealthy, sensible men." Among these were three lawyers—William Livingston, William Smith, Jr., and John Morin Scott—who formed a Whig "triumvirate," the goal of which was to promote Presbyterianism. At their best they were motivated by a belief in religious liberty; at their worst they promoted bigotry to gain power.[22]

Several issues fanned the flames of sectarian discord. Aside from the Ministry Act, Presbyterians were galled most by the charter for King's College.[23] In 1754 Trinity Church had offered the college a gift of land if the school would agree that its president would be Anglican and that religious services would be conducted in the Anglican rite. The college trustees, most of whom were Anglican, accepted the offer, and the governor's Council instructed the attorney general to prepare a charter to be issued by Lt. Gov. James De Lancey, an Anglican. Outraged, the Whig "triumvirate" unleashed a verbal assault in the press. At issue was whether New York would be better served by a nondenominational or a sectarian college, and whether public money could be spent on a school run by a religious minority. In the end, the Anglicans succeeded in giving the college an Episcopalian hue, but Presbyterians saw to it that it was denied public funding.[24] Another issue dividing the two denominations concerned whether the city's Presbyterian church should be granted a charter of incorporation. Yet another was the Anglican campaign to have a bishop appointed for the colonies. Of course, these disputes became even more contentious, for political parties exploited sectarian rivalries to build a base of support, and churches often entered the political fray to advance their own interests.[25]

The third most powerful denomination in the 1760s was the Dutch Reformed church. Jones considered it "next in rank [to the Anglican church], for its riches, its influence, and from the number of its wealthy, opulent, and reputable citizens." Yet it had been declining in numbers and importance since England's conquest of New Amsterdam in the 1660s. Debate over whether ecclesiastical authority must remain with the Classis of Amsterdam or could be exercised by an autonomous American Coetus, whether clerical ordination could take place in America, and whether church services should be conducted in Dutch or English, had by the mid-eighteenth century split the congregation into warring factions and had persuaded many members (like Robert R. Livingston) to worship elsewhere. Despite the church's decline, or perhaps because of it, the denominational leadership had worked out an accommodation with the Episcopal church: the Anglicans allowed the Dutch freedom of worship, and the latter supported the former politically. Hence, despite the Ministry Act, the Dutch were not taxed to support Trinity Church, and their church possessed a charter of incorporation. Dutch church leaders, in turn, backed the Anglicans in their struggle to secure a pro-Anglican charter for King's College.[26]

In *A Perfect Babel of Confusion: Dutch Religion and English Culture in the Middle Colonies*, Randall Balmer has argued that during the eighteenth century two distinct Dutch cultures had emerged in the Middle Atlantic Colonies. One, centered around New York City and Long Island, was influenced greatly by the Church of England and the proselytizing efforts of the Anglican Society for the Propagation of the Gospel in Foreign Parts. The other, centered in New Jersey and the Hudson Valley, was shaped by the evangelical pietism of the Great Awakening. On the whole, the Dutch who had been Anglicized would become loyalists; those who had "assimilated to a culture defined by New Light Presbyterianism and other evangelicals" would become whigs. As important as Balmer's discovery of these two Dutch cultures is, it is essential to realize that the two coexisted in New York City. The stories of three Dutch Reformed merchants, all evidently born in the 1720s, make that clear. John Abeel acted the way Balmer predicted a member of the city's Dutch Reformed church should. He failed to sign a petition by some of his co-religionists in 1754 in favor of using English in church services. Though he did not go to the polls in 1768, he voted for three of the four De Lancey candidates in 1769 and became a loyalist in the 1770s. Evert Bancker had also failed to sign the 1754 petition. Yet he voted for the Livingston party in 1768 and 1769, served on the Committee of One Hundred in 1775, and became a whig delegate to the Second and Third Provincial Congresses, extralegal bodies elected in 1775 and 1776 to spearhead the opposition to British imperialism. Isaac Roosevelt, unlike the other two, had signed the 1754 petition. And, as might be expected, he voted for the Livingston ticket in 1768 and 1769, served on the Committee of One Hundred, and sat as a whig in the First and Third Provincial Congresses.[27] The behavior of these three men underscores how divided the New York City Dutch community had become. And it was this tendency to factionalism that explains why the Dutch Reformed church did not have the impact that the Anglican and Presbyterian churches had on events in the city between 1763 and 1776. But on the whole the Dutch who had become Americanized played a more public role in the 1760s and 1770s than did those who had become Anglicized.

Of the other dissenting denominations in New York just prior to the Revolution, the Lutherans apparently constituted the largest group, and most of them, reportedly, were De Lancéyites in the 1760s. The Quakers—one estimate had about 5,000 living in the colony—had no significant influence on New York City politics. Not only were they a tiny segment of the population (perhaps 3 percent), but the Society of Friends was undergoing a period of "spiritual revitalization" that led Quakers to turn inward upon themselves in order to purify "the life of the Society."[28] There were also some members of several other Protestant denominations, a few Catholics, and some Jews. Whether individually or collectively, however, these smaller groups lacked political muscle. Mostly middle class in membership, they had few powerful patrons to advance their cause. The Presbyterians tried, especially in the late 1760s, to unite the city's Protestant dissenters against the Anglicans, but without much success. Many of these dissenting churches were preoccupied with their own internal quarrels, and they were as jealous of one another and of the Presbyterians as they were of the Anglicans. Hence, when Anglicans and Presbyterians jockeyed for power and place, these smaller groups generally remained on the sidelines. In the crises that led up to the American Revolution, they were for the most part followers rather than leaders, nameless members of the crowd rather than identifiable participants. It is consequently much more difficult to follow their actions or to determine what they thought.

III

Despite religious and ethnic factionalism, indeed because of it, there had emerged by the 1760s a spirit of toleration and a propensity to channel disputes into the political arena. As Milton M. Klein has explained, "The extraordinary diversity of the colony's citizenry compelled its political leadership to build coalitions, court other interest groups, balance tickets, awaken political consciousness, and enlist the support of large numbers of voters."[29] When eighteenth-century New Yorkers referred to their political groupings, they used the terms "party" and "faction" interchangeably. Nonetheless, according to Benjamin H. Newcomb, factions in the Middle Colonies had by 1740 already begun to evolve into "organizations with wider appeal and purpose, taking on the character of political parties." These emerging parties were able to sustain themselves in the legislature for extended periods and to appeal successfully to the electorate for support.[30] The genius and the gusto that New Yorkers exhibited for partisan politics of course underscore the fact that the province was not, at the time of the Revolution, "a political system in decay."[31] Indeed, between 1763 and 1776, residents utilized their formidable political skills to forge a strong consensus concerning how best to resist British imperialism.

If politics was to be the response to both pluralism and tyranny, then the complexity of the governmental structure would require innovation and ingenuity. Politicians had to operate simultaneously on several different playing fields: the city, provincial, and imperial governments, each of

which often entered into partisan disputes. Because New York was headquarters for the British army in America, the military, too, became embroiled in politics. In each of these arenas, class, occupation, religion,
ethnicity, and personality were variables that contestants had to consider
carefully when determining strategy and tactics. Moreover, the different
interest groups had varying degrees of influence on the several governmental levels. Politics was thus a multidimensional chess game, whose outcome was rarely predictable. It is thus necessary to examine New York's
governmental structure to appreciate the institutional difficulties that residents confronted in the three imperial crises between 1763 and 1776.

Closest to the people was the Corporation of the City of New York.
Under the Montgomerie Charter of 1731 the city had several key officials:
mayor, recorder, town clerk, aldermen, and assistant aldermen, the first
three of whom were appointed by the provincial governor.[32] Except for
the town clerk, these officials together constituted the Common Council.
The mayor customarily came from a distinguished family and had an aver-
age tenure in office of about seven years. Holding a post that was more
honorific than powerful, he appointed only minor functionaries, such as
cartmen and marshals. He could not veto acts passed by the Council,
though he could cast a vote in case of a tie. The recorder was the city's
chief legal officer. He often sat on the governor's Council, as well, and
served as a link between the city and provincial governments. The town
clerk kept the minutes of the Common Council and the city courts, forwarded petitions to the provincial government, and filed tax-collector reports. Given the administrative skills the job demanded, there were only
three incumbents between 1692 and 1776.

Power resided in the Common Council and thus in the aldermen and
assistant aldermen who sat in that body. Each of the city's seven wards
annually elected one of each. The two had equal authority, except that
the aldermen were also magistrates. The Council appointed most local
officials and could pass ordinances regulating the municipal docks, market stalls, housing, zoning, and finance. Though these regulations could
remain in force for only a year, unless approved by the governor and his
Council, the Common Council evaded provincial oversight by automatically reenacting them as a whole each year.

A Sisyphean responsibility of the Corporation was to keep the peace.
Officials had to deal not only with the many sailors and seamen in town,
but also with the soldiers stationed there. The newspapers are replete
with accounts of crimes perpetrated by redcoats, often while drunk. Civil
authorities had to contend too with periodic outbreaks of mob violence.
Edward Countryman counted twenty-eight disturbances between 1764

and 1775. The city had minimal means to deter such violence, and in
1762 the Common Council established a paid watch. Whenever the watch
failed to control a situation, city officials could call out the militia, but
since that body was composed of the adult male residents, it would have
been risky to ask it to suppress disturbances for which there was popular
support. In such circumstances the governor (with his Council's consent)
could ask the army to intervene. Here, too, discretion was essential. If the
riot was directed at the military or the imperial government, employing
the army opened the door to insurrection. Hence, on occasion the only
option was for municipal officials, perhaps joined by some patricians, to
walk the streets to calm residents and to counsel prudence.[33]

What gave members of the Common Council courage in such situations was the fact that they sat in the popular branch of city government,
which regularly and effectively adjusted the pedestrian disputes that
emerged among townspeople.[34] Though merchants, lawyers, and large
landowners were overrepresented on the Common Council, artisans,
shopkeepers, and farmers were elected too. Elite representation was
greatest in areas like the Dock and East wards, where the wealthy lived.
In the Montgomery, North, and West wards, where the poor and middle
classes resided, politicians of more modest means often served. Voting in
city and provincial elections was restricted to freeholders and freemen.
The former were white males with estates worth over forty pounds; the
latter, white men who paid a onetime fee for several important privileges:
being a retailer or artisan in the city, holding office, and voting. It was
often for the last reason, especially in the 1760s, when political consciousness among plebeians was growing, that people became freemen. In October 1765, during the Stamp Act crisis, residents were becoming freemen in unprecedented numbers. As a result, by the time of the
Revolution, freemanship had become "a democratic device which
opened the polls to all classes of citizens and gave virtually all the adult
white males the opportunity of exercising the franchise."[35]

Because so many could now vote, the Common Council was sensitive
to public opinion in the imperial crises of the 1760s and 1770s. True, it
often appeared as if the city government were proceeding with routine
business oblivious to the commotion in the streets beyond. Yet, at crucial
moments, usually when law and order were at stake, the Common Council intervened to protect the interests of residents or of a key group in
town. For example, in the Stamp Act crisis, the mayor and Common
Council successfully recommended that the stamps be stored at City Hall
under the city's protection; that intervention averted a riot that might
have become an insurrection. Indeed, in these years, whenever it seemed

as if the provincial government might be justified in calling out the army, the mayor and magistrates usually insisted that the situation was under control and that troops were not needed. Thus, in troubled times, the Common Council acted as a force for social cohesion.

If the city government was responsive to the electorate, it was also answerable to the provincial government. First, because New York was the provincial capital, the governor could monitor affairs closely and intervene at will. Hence, municipal officials in New York probably operated with less autonomy than did those in Albany. Second, since it was the governor who appointed the mayor, recorder, and town clerk, his relationship with them was generally harmonious. Third, it was the provincial legislature that had enacted the Montgomerie Charter into law and would periodically amend it. The city could not even pass a tax on real or personal property without the legislature's approval. But although rural lawmakers were sometimes antagonistic, municipal officials could usually rely on the governor's Council for help: 72 percent of the councillors who held office between 1665 and 1775, and whose residence is known, lived in town.[36]

Conversely, because the city was the colony's capital, its residents had more influence on the provincial government than did other New Yorkers. Issues debated and laws passed were promptly known to interested parties in town, who could react with newspaper articles, broadsides, petitions, mass meetings, and crowd action before rural New Yorkers even knew what had happened. Though the matters for which the municipal government was responsible were essential to the town's well-being, the issues the provincial government tackled in the 1760s and 1770s aroused more controversy. Elections to the provincial Assembly were consequently hotly contested in town, and the proportion of its residents who were politicized was greater than that in rural New York. Because the city was the provincial entrepot, townspeople were better informed, too, about what was happening in the empire, and the port was more directly affected than were farming communities by the new commercial regulations that Britain imposed after 1763. The city was consequently the nerve center of provincial politics and the wellspring of opposition to British policies. Resistance to imperial authority, in turn, involved the city's residents more deeply in provincial politics, for if some branches of the colony's government were responsible to the crown, others represented the popular will. The provincial government thus became directly involved in the crises that divided Britain and New York after 1763.[37]

The governor, lieutenant governor, and Council were crown appointed. The governor could "with the Advice and Consent" of his Council call the Assembly into session; sign a bill into law if it did not contradict "the Laws and Statutes" of Great Britain; veto legislation; grant public land; and "establish such and so many Courts of Judicature and public Justice" as "necessary for the hearing and determining of all Causes as well criminal as civil." The governor could suspend the lieutenant governor or any member of his Council for cause; prorogue or dissolve the Assembly; appoint new councillors if their number fell below seven; and choose judges and other court officials. The lieutenant governor had no lawful responsibilities in the normal course of events; his role was to serve as acting governor whenever the governor was not in the province, or in the event of his incapacitation or death.[38]

The governor had "a Council in Imitation of His Majesty's Privy Council." It consisted of from seven to twelve members "appointed by the Crown during Will and Pleasure" and customarily met with the governor at Fort George.[39] The Council also served as the upper house of the legislature, the Assembly (or "House") being the other. When the Council did so, it met without the governor at City Hall. Its proceedings were "very formal, and . . . imitate the example of the Lords." The governor and Council sat together as a court to hear appeals from the Supreme Court by "writ of error" only. In theory, a councillor's tenure was "extremely precarious," for he served at the king's pleasure; in practice, councillors exercised "considerable" influence. Most came from prominent families, sometimes with important connections in Britain. Indeed, between 1665 and 1775, 60 to 65 percent of the appointees were merchants whose transatlantic business contacts afforded them a hearing in London and even allowed them to challenge an unpopular governor. Politically and economically independent, the councillors were expected to act as a balance between the chief executive and the Assembly and to check the excesses of both. In practice, they sometimes confronted a governor with popular opinion and thereby compelled him to soften the implementation of unpopular ministerial measures. Council minutes were kept, however, and a governor could use these to blacken the reputation of councillors who had challenged him or controverted royal policy.[40]

In 1761, the popularly elected Assembly had twenty-seven members, four of whom represented the city. The Assembly usually sat once or twice a year, and by law elections had to be held at least once every seven years. Because the franchise was broad, the colony's residents revered the House and were prepared in the 1760s to resist parliamentary intrusions upon what they considered to be the Assembly's rights and privileges. Smith recorded that lawmakers invariably followed the procedures used in the British House of Commons. Representation was not equitable, for each county, despite its population, elected two lawmakers. The Hudson Valley manors of Livingston, Rensselaerswyck, and Cortlandt were each entitled to a representative, and the manor lord sometimes determined who held the seat.[41]

If townspeople were unhappy with the provincial government, their dissatisfaction was with the governor. As Smith had explained in 1757 in his *History of the Province of New York*, "Our representatives, agreeable to the general sense of their constituents, are tenacious in their opinion, that the inhabitants of this colony are entitled to all the privileges of Englishmen; that they have a right to participate in the legislative power, and that the session of Assemblies here, is wisely substituted instead of a representation in Parliament." The governors, however, held quite a different view: "All the immunities we enjoy, according to them, not only flow from, but absolutely depend upon, the mere grace and will of the Crown." Given these conflicting opinions, controversy was inevitable.[42]

In theory the governor was quite powerful; in practice the Assembly had the advantage. A visitor explained: "The king appoints the governor according to his royal pleasure; but the inhabitants of the province make up his excellency's salary."[43] Though the governor often came from a prominent British family, he was usually in America to make money. That gave the House leverage, for it could refuse him his salary unless he signed the bills it enacted. The ministry (or cabinet, in London) wanted the Assembly to establish a permanent revenue that the governor and Council would determine how to allocate. But to keep power in its own hands, the House instead made yearly appropriations and stipulated exactly how the money was to be spent. Governors even had problems managing their Council, for councillors understood that they and their families had interests that would outlast any governor, and that he had few resources to hold them in line. He could grant them land, yet once he did, it was theirs forever. He could remove them for cause, though that might create a political uproar and even cause his recall. Smith thus concluded that the provincial government "was weak on all sides, and must be gently touched to save the Appear[ance] of Power to counterbalance the Democratic Scale."[44]

Given this situation, it fell to the British government to hold the legislature in check. Aside from military force, the ministry had several weapons at its disposal. All laws passed by the legislature and signed by the executive had to be forwarded to London, where the crown could disallow those it disliked. The cabinet even began requiring that in specific areas the governor could not sign a bill unless it included a suspending clause delaying its taking effect until the crown approved it. The ministry also issued the governor detailed instructions outlining policies he was to pursue, laws he was to propose, and bills he was to reject. The Council, too, was bound by the governor's instructions and theoretically was to "stand between him and the Assembly" by rejecting acts that violated these directives. The ministry could remove a disobedient governor or councillor, but forcing officials three thousand miles away to act as directed was nonetheless difficult.[45]

Despite these weapons, when Parliament sought after 1763 to tax the colonies and to assert its sovereignty over them, it raised two key issues that would bedevil the imperial relationship until the Revolution. First was the question of how New Yorkers could affect a decision made in Britain. They could write British merchants and politicians or memorialize the crown and Parliament. The Assembly could instruct its colonial agent in London to intercede with the government. But if such pleas were ignored, New Yorkers had no legitimate, effective way to register their complaints. As Governor Tryon explained to the cabinet in 1775, "The Colonies have outgrown the Government anciently set over them which ought to rise in strength and dignity as they increase in wealth and population."[46] In consequence, many inhabitants concluded that they had no choice but to riot, to impose economic sanctions, or to form extralegal committees. These tactics, however, transformed political disputes into constitutional crises.

The second issue raised by Britain's use of its coercive powers was even more basic: when and under what circumstances did parliamentary laws apply to New York? In the Stamp Act crisis the people out of doors (in the streets, not in the halls of power) proclaimed that because they were not represented in Parliament, it could not tax them. A few went so far as to insist that Parliament could pass no legislation whatsoever that was binding on the colonies. In January 1766 a query by "Philalethes" in the *New York Gazette, or, The Weekly Post Boy* asked, "Are any of the Statutes of Great-Britain obligatory upon the Inhabitants of the Colonies, but those which existed previous to their respective Charters, and to which they gave their Consent in the Persons of their Forefathers, who were *actually* represented in Parliament?" In 1773 "A Citizen" declared, "The questions [at issue are], whether we shall be governed by laws, made with our own consent, or by those to which neither we, nor our representatives, have contributed, or consented; whether we shall, in security, possess our lives and properties, or, that they shall be wholly dependent on the will of others, whom we shall have no power, or authority to check, or control; in short, whether we shall be freemen, or slaves."[47]

In essence, once Britain had decided to tax and to assert its sovereignty over the colonies, a conflict developed over how power should be exercised in the empire. But no institutionalized means of collective decision-making or conflict resolution existed, and Britain was unwilling (until too late) to establish any.[48] Parliament and the cabinet had legally accepted lines of communication through which they could make demands on New York. Except for petitions and memorials, then, which could be ignored, residents could resort only to extralegal means to influence the imperial government. Because the political system was not integrated in both directions, periodic crises had become inevitable.

IV

Eighteenth-century New York City's heterogeneity, multilayered governmental structure, and diverse electorate had fostered the emergence of political parties by 1740 and had afforded politicians ample scope for mastering their craft. Yet no one was better able to dominate the scene than James De Lancey, New York's acting governor for all but twenty-two months between October 1753 and his death in July 1760. Though his sudden demise at age fifty-seven cut short a brilliant career, his shadow continued to hang over the city in the 1760s, and his achievements and leadership set a standard by which later aspirants for power could judge their own performance.[49]

The eldest son of Stephen De Lancey, a Huguenot refugee who had arrived in the colony in the 1680s and had acquired a fortune in trade, James enjoyed advantages few New Yorkers of his generation could match. His father had not only converted to the Church of England and thereby solidified his place in the elite, but had also sent James to Britain in 1720 to be educated. In 1728, three years after his return home, James married Anne Heathcote, heiress of Scarsdale Manor and daughter of the late Caleb Heathcote, New York's receiver general. Wealth and high social status, in turn, provided the De Lanceys a path to political power. Stephen had served often in the Assembly for New York City between 1702 and 1737. James's brother Peter represented Westchester from 1750 to 1768, and his brother Oliver sat for the city between 1756 and 1761.

No one in mid-eighteenth-century New York, however, was able to rise so fast or so high as James De Lancey, for he knew better than his competitors that success in Anglo-American politics required a politician "to please the king's ministers at home; and a touchy people here."[50] He also had more resources than most rivals in his quest to master that daunting imperative. His sojourn abroad had introduced him to British politics and had given him political connections that would serve him well for a lifetime. His tutor at Cambridge, Thomas Herring, became Archbishop of Canterbury in 1747 and acquired powerful contacts in government that De Lancey could milk. Nor did the New Yorker neglect to cultivate other ties to the cabinet. His wife's uncle, Sir Gilbert Heathcote, was a director of the Bank of England and an influential London politician. Her cousin, Sir John Heathcote, was one of Sir Robert Walpole's political managers. In 1731, when De Lancey's sister Susannah had married Peter Warren, a British naval officer, James persuaded the Heathcotes to promote the young man's career. Warren's reputation soared after he captured the French fortress at Louisbourg in 1745, and he was made an admiral. De Lancey and Warren then commenced collaborating for their mutual advantage. In 1748 the admiral's private secretary, Robert Charles, was made the Assembly's colonial agent in London, and he thereafter kept De Lancey abreast of British politics. The De Lancey family's commercial agents in England, William and Samuel Baker, were also well-connected. William was a member of Parliament and a principal financier of the government. The Bakers were specialists in American army contracts, and the Duke of Newcastle often sought William's advice on colonial affairs.

De Lancey also exploited his family's wealth and power in New York. Gov. John Montgomerie had appointed him, in 1729, at the age of twenty-six, to the Council and, in 1731, to the New York Supreme Court. In 1735 Gov. William Cosby made him chief justice, one of the most powerful officials in the colony. The Heathcotes and Bakers then used their influence to have his appointment confirmed in London. Adm. George Clinton, governor from 1743 to 1753, was so impressed with James De Lancey that he nominated four De Lanceyites for his Council. Clinton upgraded De Lancey's commission as chief justice such that he then served with a permanent tenure "on good behavior" and not "at the king's pleasure." Clinton even accepted De Lancey's recommendation that the governor's salary be appropriated yearly, thereby increasing the Assembly's power. Meanwhile, De Lancey's English patrons argued that his support of Clinton justified the chief justice's appointment as lieutenant governor. When De Lancey broke with Clinton, he flaunted his British connections to sway New York voters in the 1748 elections, and his party secured a plurality in the Assembly.[51]

Political warfare in New York, especially that between Clinton and De Lancey, finally persuaded the ministry to appoint Sir Danvers Osborne governor. But a few days after his arrival in the province in October 1753, Osborne committed suicide. Lt. Gov. James De Lancey thus became acting governor. His wealth, power, and popularity in New York and his influential British backers had thus combined, with a dose of good luck, to give him control over all three branches of government and to make him New York's preeminent politician. His death in 1760, of course, devastated his party. So too did the demise of George II in the same year, for that succession changed the political equation in Britain and reduced the party's influence in London. James De Lancey's family lobbied to have his brother Oliver named lieutenant governor and his son James made a councillor. But Cadwallader Colden, who as senior member of the Council became acting governor on De Lancey's demise, managed to get himself appointed to the lieutenant governorship, and James, Jr., had to wait until 1769 before being offered a Council seat.[52]

James De Lancey, Jr., had been born in 1732 and, like his father, was British-educated. He served during the French and Indian War as a captain in the British infantry. Groomed to assume leadership of the De Lancey party, he returned to the city upon his father's death. Only twenty-nine years old, he offered himself as a candidate for the Assembly in 1761 but came in last in a field of six. De Lancey spent the next few years managing the family properties and breeding race horses, while his faction sat on the political sidelines. It was not that the interest groups his father had forged into a powerful coalition no longer needed the party. The merchants, artisans, and sailors who made their living by trade still required a forceful voice in London and in New York to advance their interests. Anglicans still wanted help in guarding their privileged status against the Presbyterians, and Dutch Reformed church officials had no reason to forsake their alliance with the Church of England. It was rather that the son, as one historian explained, "lacked his father's subtlety and higher vision as well as his broad popularity."[53] These were qualities that would come only with experience. In 1761 James De Lancey, Jr., was simply not ready to assume his father's mantle.

According to William Smith, the son never developed into a leader, and his conduct in the 1760s was distinguished only by opportunism. True, James, Jr., and his uncle Oliver were doers, not thinkers; politicians, not statesmen; pragmatists, not visionaries. Because they still had powerful friends in Britain, they would at times treat the imperial link as a resource to be milked more than nurtured, and because they were anxious to regain the popularity that was needed to restore their political power, their critics charged that they were not as mindful as they should have been of the dangers inherent in appealing to the crowd. As Smith indignantly wrote, the De Lanceys "dupe the People to gain an Ascendancy in the Assembly and by that rule Gov[erno]rs sway the Ministry and inslave the Colony."[54]

Smith was too harsh. Though James De Lancey wrote little, a close examination of his actions reveals two facts: first, in the 1760s he strove to emulate his father and to use the senior De Lancey's career as a model; second, as he matured as a political leader, he acquired a broader vision and more considered outlook upon affairs. In taking advantage of the Stamp Act crisis to forge an alliance with Isaac Sears and the Sons of Liberty in December 1765, he was not driven simply by opportunism. As a patrician, he knew he had to assume a leadership role and to exert his influence in curbing the excesses of the people. Moreover, his father had made his own popularity in New York a pillar of his power. Because the crisis offered the son the chance to do the same, he seized it. But once calm returned to New York, De Lancey, cosmopolitan by disposition and Anglo-American by training, crafted a policy designed to preserve and promote the empire, the Anglican church, the city's commercial prosperity, and elite rule in the province. The plan would fail, the Liberty Boys would desert him, and De Lancey would head down a path that ended in exile. Nonetheless, his loyalism was neither an accident nor the consequence of opportunism. It was a considered choice based on political and economic beliefs he had espoused throughout the period.

In the years before the Revolution, De Lancey competed politically with the Livingston party, which had coalesced in the 1750s against his father. At issue were the acting governor's partiality toward the Church of England, and his opposition to both Benjamin Franklin's Albany Plan of Union and William Shirley's scheme for a united effort against France in the Seven Years' War. The Livingstons, some of whom lived near Albany, were concerned for their own safety, whereas De Lancey's fear was that a bellicose policy would bring higher taxes, strain the colony's financial resources, and disrupt trade with Canada. De Lanceyites preferred that revenues be raised by taxing land; Livingstonites wanted to tax commerce. More broadly, when the De Lanceys envisioned America's future, they thought in terms of trade and empire. The Livingstons, for their part, placed greater store in "peopling these immense fertile regions (of North America), extending the British empire, and, in the true spirit of economy, advancing the glory of the nation."[55]

Like the De Lanceys, the Livingstons were a coalition of interest groups.[56] The Livingston family, whose members resided in the city and along the Hudson, formed the party's core. Part of the elite, they coveted power for its own sake but also to safeguard the family's economic interests, especially its extensive landholdings. Other large landowners looked to the party not only for protection against the French, but also to ensure that the Assembly would not pass a land tax and that neither the crown nor the colonial government would challenge the legality of their deeds to large tracts of provincial land. Presbyterians also favored the party, since it had taken a determined stand in the 1750s against alleged Anglican encroachments upon religious liberty. The fact that many Presbyterians were Scottish or Scotch-Irish, whereas many Anglicans shared an English background, added ethnic prejudice to religious bigotry. Because the Livingston party also attracted those members of the Dutch Reformed church who had become Americanized, many Livingstonites vainly hoped to unite all dissenters from the Anglican church under their party's banner. The Whig "triumvirate" (William Livingston, William Smith, Jr., and John Morin Scott) provided intellectual leadership and wrote party propaganda. Aside from being aggressively Presbyterian, the three were lawyers. The party accordingly supported the legal fraternity in its demand for judicial independence and in its defense of the common law rights of the individual. Large landowners, of course, expected the legal community to shield them whenever their land titles were challenged. Though this coalition was as one in its desire to unseat the De Lanceys, its constituent groups did not agree on every issue. As Smith put it, "We shall distinguish the opposition [to the De Lanceys] under the name of the Livingston party, though it did not always proceed from motives approved of by that family." Some family members, for example, would be disturbed by the anti-Anglican bigotry the party stirred up in the 1768 and 1769 Assembly elections.[57]

Even though they had forged no unity of opinion, the future seemed bright for the Livingstons in the early 1760s.[58] Four Livingstonites had been among the fifteen new members elected to the Assembly in 1758. De Lancey's death in 1760 had created still more opportunities, and the party's strength in the House rose with the 1761 elections. The Stamp Act crisis, however, became a stumbling block, for party leaders opposed the violence that had been used to defeat the tax, and their demurral undercut their popular appeal. Though committed to defending the people's constitutional liberties and their right to resist tyranny, the Livingstons believed that human nature was basically evil and that people were moved more by passion than by reason. They thus respected government, for its object was to hold men's appetites in check. As Robert R. Livingston explained, "Were mankind governed by the principles of reason and humanity Laws would be unnecessary. . . . But while our passions and prejudices mislead us their malevolent influence must remain restrained to ensure the safety and tranquility of society." William Livingston agreed:

"Government, at best, is a Burden, tho' a necessary one. Had man been wise from his Creation, he would always have been free. We might have enjoyed the Gifts of liberal Nature, unmolested, unrestrained. It is the Depravity of Mankind, that has necessarily introduced Government; and so great is this Depravity, that without it, we could scarcely subsist."[59]

Given the frailty of human nature, maintaining a government worthy of "a Society of Freemen" was arduous. Voters and vote-getters had to eschew self-interest and bribery or risk destroying their liberty. After elections were held, both ruler and ruled had to practice public virtue by putting the common good above "private advantage." As William Livingston warned those called to govern, "That Government was instituted, not to give the Ruler a Power of reigning despotically over the Subject, but to preserve and promote the true Interest and Happiness of both: Thus he will learn, that while he acts agreeable to the true End of his Institution, he justly merits the Love and Obedience of his Subjects, and that he can not deviate from it, without involving both in Misery; and must consequently, forfeit his Right of government."[60] The ideal citizens were "patriots," or "lovers of their country, protectors of liberty, enemies to oppression, and champions for public virtue and human happiness."[61]

The fact that 15 percent of New York's population consisted of African Americans, most of whom were slaves, made many white New Yorkers, especially the Livingstonites, sensitive to what the loss of liberty entailed. In July 1764, when Robert R. Livingston learned that the Stamp Act might be followed by "a duty on negroes," he objected that the latter would be "a poll tax which I think will make negroes of us all." In an "Address to the People of Great Britain," drafted in 1774, John Jay (who married into the Livingston family the same year) wrote that the policies Britain had pursued in America after 1763 were creating "a system of slavery." In 1777 he expanded on the theme in a letter: "Will you ever Madam be able to reconcile yourself to the mortifying Reflection of being the Mother of Slaves? For who are Slaves but those, who in all Cases without Exception are bound to obey the uncontroulable Mandates of a Man— whether stiled King or Peasant." Such arguments led some whigs, including Jay and Gouverneur Morris, to favor the abolition of slavery. Most whigs nonetheless feared that the slaves in New York City might catch the spirit of freedom on their own. In the Militia Act of 1775 the Provincial Congress had explicitly excluded slaves (though not free blacks) from the militia. And a Militia Act passed in August 1776 decreed that a detachment of troops was to be left in town to guard against a slave insurrection.[62]

Their love of liberty, of reason, and of limited government had also led

Livingstonites from the outset to oppose factions and parties. "From the Moment that Men give themselves wholly up to a Party, they abandon their *Reason*, and are led Captive by their *Passions*." Organizing a party might be required, William Livingston conceded, if "a future Governor gave in to Measures subversive of our Liberties." That contingency doubtless had justified his own opposition to the De Lanceys in the 1750s. Still, partisans had to be sure that their cause was just, for "should a Faction be formed . . . without Law or Reason, may the Authors be branded with suitable Infamy." The party spirit led inevitably to rioting: "The great, as well as the little Vulgar, are liable to catch the Spirit of Mobbing; and cluster together to perpetrate a Riot, without knowing the Reason that set them in Motion. The genuine Consequence this, of Party-Rage and Animosity! For when once we suppress the Voice of Reason, by the Clamour of Faction, we are toss'd like a Vessel stripp'd of Sails and Rudder, at the Mercy of Wind and Tide."[63] Hence, though opposition to the Stamp Act in 1765 was imperative, government had to be in the hands of reasonable, propertied men, not at the mercy of a mob. As Smith confessed, "Great Britain has indeed lost the Affection of all the Colonists, and I am very fearful not only of Discontent and partial Tumults amongst them, but that a general Civil War will light up and rage all along the Continent."[64] If a little violence might at times be excused, the Livingstons knew it was a two-edged sword: it could be wielded as easily against the local elite as against unpopular parliamentary legislation.

Many Livingstonites were Real Whigs, who saw politics as an unrelenting struggle of power against liberty, and who consequently believed in a hierarchic society, wherein each class had its rights and responsibilities, and in mixed government, which balanced the interests of monarchy, aristocracy, and democracy against one another and so kept any one of them from gaining the upper hand. Fearful of power and of those who wielded it, they were determined to defend their constitutional rights against the tyranny of an overweening governor, Parliament, or king. Livingston attacks upon Lt. Gov. James De Lancey, in the 1750s, for endangering balanced government by combining executive, judicial, and legislative power in his own hands exemplified their publicly stated commitment to resist oppression from above. The Whig "triumvirate's" assault on the powerful Anglican church expressed their fear of ecclesiastical tyranny.[65]

Livingstonites were adamant, however, that their opposition to tyranny from above not allow the democracy to shatter the bonds of mixed government or to provoke anarchy. Both forms of oppression—tyranny and anarchy—had to be resisted, and it was the special obligation of the British aristocracy and the New York elite to act as a flywheel in government and thus to prevent either abuse. If the British aristocracy claimed its special role by birth, the New York elite's only pretext for its privileged status was the assertion that it acted from reason and the people from passion: "No one has a Right to govern but he that is wise." The Livingstons' ideological outlook thus made them averse, in the 1760s and 1770s, to independence, except as the very last resort in the maintenance of liberty. A constitutionally administered empire would preserve both balanced government and the elite's privileged position; independence would end in anarchy and the elite's loss of status. During the Stamp Act crisis that conviction led the Livingstons, even at the expense of their own popularity, to restrain the crowd, not to lead it.[66]

Besides the Livingstons and the De Lanceys, another group, the Sons of Liberty, had begun to make itself felt in the 1760s. Its leadership came mostly from lesser merchants who had prospered in the war. Ambitious, talented, and successful, they coveted a place among the elite. Though their wealth might have entitled them to such a position, their more modest lineage and upbringing disqualified them. Not surprisingly, they preferred a society where rank was based on merit, not on birth. Colden described them this way: "Many of them have rose suddenly from the lowest Rank of the People to considerable Fortunes, and chiefly by illicit Trade in the last War. They abhor every limitation of Trade and Duty on it, and therefore gladly go into every Measure whereby they hope to have Trade free."[67]

Isaac Sears, the preeminent leader of the group, is a good example. Born in New England in 1729, he became a privateer during the French and Indian War. Not only did he thereby amass a small fortune, but his daring earned him respect on New York's waterfront. Once, while commanding a vessel of fourteen guns, he almost captured a French ship of twenty-four guns. A fearless adventurer and born leader, after the war he became a crowd leader, or "King Sears" to his patrician detractors. Another such man was John Lamb. Born in 1735 of an English father and a Dutch mother, he married a woman of Huguenot descent in 1755. Though trained as an instrument maker, he began importing wine in 1760. A gifted public speaker, fluent in Dutch, French, and German, he became the spokesperson for the Liberty Boys in their contacts with the city's key ethnic groups. Still another such person was Alexander McDougall. An immigrant who had arrived in town in 1738, he first worked as a milkman. Like Sears, he made his fortune as a privateer, and when hostilities ended, he opened a tavern on the waterfront and married a wealthy woman. By 1765 he had become a merchant of considerable means and the Liberty Boy leader who was most comfortable dealing with the elite.[68]

All three were men on the make, devoted to free enterprise at home and abroad. They were joined in the Sons of Liberty by many local artisans and shopkeepers who shared similar aspirations. But postwar British policies hurt them financially and threatened to deny them the status they felt they deserved. For example, the Revenue Act of 1764, which will be examined later, reduced the profits that Sears made on West Indian molasses, ended his business in Madeira wine, and hampered his participation in the intercolonial trade. These men consequently blamed Britain for the economic woes besetting New York, and they sought to liberate themselves from the restrictions Britain had already or might someday impose in the name of the common good. Confident in their own abilities, the Liberty Boys became antimercantilists, trumpeting the right of individuals to pursue their own self-interest. As Sears argued in 1769, "Nor is any Man to blame, for letting his private Interest have some weight, provided it is not inconsistent with the common Interest of the Public." In 1773, "A Citizen" wrote, "It is not to be expected, that any man should be wholly disinterested; indeed self love is the ground of all social connections." And another writer added in 1775, "Tho' a truly patriotic disposition would lead a man to reject every private advantage inconsistent with the good of his country, yet no man is to be supposed so disinterested, as not to include his own interest, in all his endeavors to promote that of others."[69]

Their "demand for self-determination within the empire" was matched by a call "for equality of treatment at home."[70] The Sons of Liberty wanted to share in the political decision-making process, not just to vote. Having acquired wealth, but not social status, they were a "marginal elite" whose "radicalism" challenged the power of New York's patricians. No longer plebeians, they nonetheless remained close enough to their roots to aspire to be popular leaders and to advance causes they thought would benefit ordinary New Yorkers. By playing the role of broker between the classes, they hoped to win political power, protect what they had already gained, and open the doors of opportunity still wider. From this group came the crowd leaders in the Stamp Act crisis. By the mid-1770s their struggle for reduced government interference and greater individual freedom would lead them to espouse independence, republicanism, and the removal of all artificial restraints based on rank, estate, or privilege.[71]

At the same time that Livingstonites, De Lanceyites, and Liberty Boys vied for power in New York, partisans from all three were protesting British policies. Since the three groups represented different constituencies in the city's polyglot population, each had a distinct outlook, and these distinctions complicated politics during the imperial crises of the 1760s and 1770s. If Livingstonites feared the abuse of power, the radicals—the Liberty Boys—detested the abridgment of opportunity. If Livingstonites thought reason the best guide to action, the radicals believed self-interest was the "grand principle" shaping human behavior. If Livingstonites favored a deferential society, radicals wanted one based on the "voluntary, but natural, interaction" of people.[72] If Livingstonites cherished hierarchy, the Liberty Boys espoused equality, "the most radical and ideological force let loose in the Revolution."[73] If Livingstonites feared mob violence, the radicals responded militantly to British imperialism. If Livingstonites looked to the past as their guide, the radicals were the vanguard of the Revolution and the harbingers of nineteenth-century America.

Because neither James nor Oliver De Lancey wrote much, it is difficult to summarize their differences with the Livingstons or the Liberty Boys. Yet their actions indicate that the De Lanceys were whigs who believed in natural rights, balanced government, the rule of law, the idea that the consent of the governed was necessary for legitimate governance, and the principle that no taxation was to be levied without representation. They also exemplified the materialistic outlook so prevalent among New Yorkers. They could join with the Livingstons and the Liberty Boys in decrying the Stamp Act, the Townshend Duties, and the Tea Act. But they did not share the Real Whig fears of arbitrary power and of the dangers of a commercial economy. And they did not share the Liberty Boys' passion for free trade. Instead, they exhibited a zest for exercising power and making money, and they believed that New Yorkers would prosper most by continued membership in Britain's mercantilist empire. Like the Livingstons, they cherished elite rule. Unlike them, they enjoyed mixing with the people and frequenting their taverns. That led Smith to accuse James De Lancey of being a "Demagogue," and Patricia Bonomi to label his party as "popular Whigs."[74] But because so many in the party had been Anglicized and had built fortunes trading within the British empire, they saw themselves as Anglo-Americans, not Americans, and pictured the empire as a commercial network, not a tyranny. They thus found it very difficult to march with the Livingstons and the Liberty Boys into revolution. Indeed, quite a few De Lanceyites became loyalists.[75]

The Onset of Conflict

On July 19, 1763, two years before the stamp riots, New Yorkers had celebrated the end of the Seven Years' War and the return of peace. The exhilaration of victory, however, was tempered by the economic downturn that residents were enduring and by the political acrimony that was plaguing the provincial government.[1] Neither development, nor the two jointly, was capable of causing a revolution. Oppressive tax and policy initiatives by the British government would be necessary for that. Nonetheless, the state of the economy and the political climate were important, for they helped to shape how New Yorkers would respond to the first imperial crisis.

The war had initially benefited the local economy by ending a depression that had beset the colonies from 1750 to 1755. New York City was made the general magazine for the arms and matériel needed to defeat France in America. Though politically connected British merchants were appointed as contractors to purchase these supplies, they usually hired local businessmen as their agents. Provincial forces were raised too, and influential merchants—like Oliver De Lancey; Beverly Robinson, his business partner; and John Cruger, New York's mayor—garnered the contracts to provision these forces. If not everyone profited so directly, other retailers catered to redcoats with hard currency to spend. Rum dealers and tavern owners did especially well. John Watts, a merchant who dealt in spirits and who sat on the governor's Council, estimated that the revenues collected from the New York Duty Act, a provincial tax on most incoming shipping, doubled during the war to about ten thousand pounds per year, partly because the military was "exceedingly publick Spirited in the Consumption of strong Liquors."[2]

Local shipowners and traders also engaged in privateering. Between June 1756 and January 1763, 128 privateers were fitted out, and perhaps twenty thousand seamen sailed from New York aboard these vessels. The rewards could be substantial. Alexander McDougall apparently made seven thousand pounds this way, and Isaac Sears over two thousand pounds. In the first year alone, New Yorkers brought in two hundred thousand pounds sterling in prizes. Competition was so keen that many privateers eventually began smuggling goods to the French West Indies. Such wartime activity stimulated the shipbuilding industry. New York's fleet increased by 320 vessels between 1749 and 1762. And lawyers benefited from an upsurge in maritime litigation caused by ship seizures and captured cargoes.[3]

Those with the capital to exploit these opportunities profited the most, yet all shared in the prosperity. War contracts for matériel provided work for tailors, cordwainers, wagonmakers, cartmen, bakers, and farmers. Soldiers and privateers with money to spend created employment in the retail trades. And shipbuilding opened up jobs for still more artisans. Though merchants struggled to hold down wages, a labor shortage rendered that effort futile. Privateering, for example, attracted so many seamen that the pay for regular voyages trebled. Few consequently enlisted in the provincial forces; and about 90 percent of those who did were foreign-born.[4]

However refreshing the prosperity, in 1760 the war shifted to the Caribbean, and New Yorkers had abruptly to adjust to a postwar economy. War contracts dried up, and redcoats departed to spend their wages elsewhere. The resulting business downturn was exacerbated by other factors that rendered the economy even more perilous. The British navy began cracking down on smuggling between the mainland colonies and the foreign West Indies, further depressing business. The situation was aggravated by a slump in the European sugar market. A decline in prices in Europe and in the consumption of rum in North America eroded the profits that merchants needed to buy British imports. Meanwhile, wholesale prices for British manufactures rose, even though New Yorkers lacked the wherewithal to pay for them. Though sales were down in America, British merchants (who themselves needed specie) demanded payment, forcing some traders into insolvency. With demand in America flagging and with merchants compelled to liquidate inventories, the retail prices for these high-cost goods sank. The droughts of 1761 and 1762 only worsened the situation. Farmers cut back on purchases, and rural shopkeepers ceased paying their urban creditors. Perhaps the best indicator of the overall decline was that between 1761 and 1764 the revenue the provincial government collected from the Duty Act dropped by half.[5]

The repercussions were severe, especially for townspeople who lived day to day. Because it is impossible to compare the incomes of New Yorkers in 1759 and 1763, the human cost of the downturn cannot be measured precisely. Yet debt cases in the Mayor's Court rose sharply. Prior to 1763 fifteen cases per year had been considered high. In the first year of peace forty-six such suits were filed against thirty-six defendants; in 1766 eighty cases were brought against fifty-four persons. Poverty grew apace. The number of paupers jumped fourfold between 1750 and 1775. By 1772, 425 indigents resided in an alms house built for one hundred. The annual expense of caring for these people had climbed from about £667 sterling in the 1750s to almost £1,670 sterling in the 1760s. Rents soared so high "A Herald" complained that they were unconscionable. And firewood cost double what the poor could afford.[6] A father's lament described with emotion what numbers portray with cold logic. He had "hitherto lived comfortably by the Sweat of" his brow and provided his family "with a Competency of the Necessaries of Life." But his situation was now desperate: "I labour'd more diligently, and deny'd myself and Family many of the Comforts of Life we had been accustomed to—but yet I found Want and Poverty approaching me. I labour'd to the utmost of my Strength, and retrench'd my Expenses almost to the bare Necessaries of Life: But alas! I find it all to no Purpose, I am spending my Strength for naught." Why? "The expense of living in the most frugal Way has increased so exorbitantly, that I find it beyond my Ability to support my Family with my utmost Industry. . . . I am going to Ruin, and must starve."[7]

Patricians did what they felt they should for the less fortunate.[8] The elite believed in a well-ordered, hierarchic community: the lower classes were to defer to their betters; the latter were to act for the common good. In 1763 the Assembly passed a lottery bill to raise money to pay for a bounty to encourage the growth of hemp in New York; the aim was to improve the balance of trade, thereby alleviating economic distress. In December 1764 a group of city merchants established "the Society for the Promotion of Arts, Agriculture, and Oeconomy, in the Province of New York." The premise was that the surest way to combat the depression, the dearth of specie, and the reliance on British imports was to nurture home manufacturing and a frugal lifestyle. The hope was that the unemployed could be kept occupied making cloth, not organizing crowds. The society granted premiums for many local products, held fortnightly markets for their sale, and printed pamphlets on manufacturing. But except for fostering the cultivation of flax and the production of linen, the society had no substantive economic effect and was moribund by 1767.[9]

Plebeians were probably impressed more by how patricians lived. Though growing numbers of people were suffering, the elite was expanding in numbers, prestige, and power. Fortunes amassed in the war had elevated quite a few petty merchants and sea captains, including Sears and McDougall, to a higher status. To these entrepreneurs was added the burgeoning number of British officials who staffed the imperial bureaucracy. An account of the mobbing of Maj. Thomas James's home, at the height of the Stamp Act crisis in 1765, affords a revealing glimpse of the lifestyle the privileged enjoyed. The home "had been lately fitted up in an elegant manner, and had adjoining a large handsome Garden stored with both Necessaries and Curiosities,—and had in it several summer houses." The residence "was genteelly furnish'd with good Furniture; contain'd a valuable Library of choice Books, Paper, Accounts, Mathematical Instruments, Draughts, rich Clothes, Linen, etc., and a considerable Quantity of Wine and other Liquors." The rioters "destroy[ed] every individual Article the House contain'd,—the beds they cut open and threw the Feathers abroad; broke all the Glasses, China, Tables, Chairs, Desks, Trunks, Chests; and, making a large Fire at a little Distance, threw in every Thing that would burn."[10] Even if the poor rarely saw the interiors of these homes, they could not avoid contact out of doors with patrician opulence. While the less fortunate were enduring one especially harsh economic spell in 1767, for example, the rich were debating how to alleviate the traffic jams caused by carriages making their way to the John Street theater. Carriages were a status symbol, and by 1770 sixty-two residents together owned twenty-six coaches, thirty-three chariots, and twenty-six phaetons. So common had such vehicles become that the British used them to prove that New Yorkers could afford to pay taxes to the empire. A local writer, however, insisted that imperial officials owned most of them.[11]

The contrast between rich and poor at times caused rancor, for many colonists believed that a maldistribution of wealth enervated liberty and encouraged oligarchy. "A.B.C." asked bitterly whether it was "equitable that 99, or rather 999, should suffer for the Extravagance or Grandeur of one? Especially when it is consider'd that Men frequently owe their Wealth to the Impoverishment of their Neighbours." Another writer suggested that because "the great Creator of the Universe, hath blessed Numbers in this populous City, with comfortable Fortunes, would it not be worth their while to extend their Bounty to such as are the real Objects of Pity and Compassion." The poor were "shut up in a dark and melancholly Dungeon in a manner dead to the World and even deprived of getting Bread by the Sweat of their Brow."[12]

New Yorkers were distressed, too, by their impressment (or forced enlistment) into the British navy. Though illegal since 1708, the practice had continued, and the shortage of manpower during the Seven Years' War had only exacerbated the problem. Naval officers used impressment to replace the many sailors who had deserted because of poor conditions. Probably 60 percent of the adult white males over 16 in New York at any one time were seamen, and they were most directly affected by impressment. Yet the practice touched everyone. At two a.m., on May 20, 1757, naval officials encircled the city by land and water, blocked all escape routes, and corralled eight hundred men. Artisans as well as seamen were caught in the dragnet. Half the group was then impressed into the navy. Most inhabitants had assumed that the return of peace would end impressment, but they were mistaken. On July 10, 1764, the armed sloop *Chaleur* impressed five fishermen off Long Island. The next morning, when the sloop's commander visited New York in a small launch, a crowd seized it. The officer wisely freed the five, but rioters burned his boat anyway. Two residents were promptly arrested, but at a court hearing that afternoon the witnesses lost their memories, and a grand jury subsequently dismissed the charges.[13]

This resentment, the conditions under which the poor were living, and the crowd's furor over the stamp tax raise the question of whether the 1765 riots or the Revolution in New York were at least partly the result of class conflict. Robert R. Livingston predicted that "enforcing the Stamp Act" would provoke a "civil war" that would "be attended with the destruction of all Law Order and Government in the Colonies, and ruin all men of property." Gouverneur Morris's oft-quoted assessment of affairs in 1774 suggests, too, that class consciousness existed: "The mob begin to think and to reason. Poor reptiles! It is with them a vernal morning; they are struggling to cast off their winter's slough, they bask in the sunshine, and ere noon they will bite, depend upon it."[14] Before accepting either statement at face value, however, it should be noted that both men spoke not for the poor but for the elite, which was leery of the lower classes and of mob violence. Moreover, acute economic distress and discontent do not inexorably lead to or cause class conflict. Indeed, this grumbling against the rich can also be ascribed to jealousy and resentment, to the need in a face-to-face society to personalize causation, and to fears that the inequitable distribution of wealth was leading to oligarchy.[15]

Little direct evidence exists to indicate what the participants in specific riots were actually thinking. These people were often politically inarticulate and rarely recorded their thoughts for posterity. Nor is it always clear in a given instance what the profile of the typical demonstrator was, or how it compared to that of the typical city resident. Neither should it be assumed that participants in a riot all shared a common ideology.[16] To offer an example, African Americans constituted about 15 percent of the population, and some mobs were so large that black Americans had to have been active participants. But given the extant record, it is impossible to know what they were thinking or feeling. Were most or at least some so caught up for the moment in the contagion of the mob that their thoughts were indistinguishable from rioters whose ancestry was European? Were most blacks resentful or hopeful upon witnessing the ironic spectacle of slaveholders denouncing tyranny and demanding liberty? Were African American rioters in general more or less militant than white demonstrators?[17] Similar unanswerable questions, of course, can be asked about women. For example, was the behavior of a German female indentured servant during the Stamp Act riots influenced more by her womanhood, her ethnic identity, or her economic status?

Though there were traditions New Yorkers followed when rioting, it would be unwise, without more specific evidence, to lump together all the crowd actions between 1760 and 1776 and to assume that there was a continuity of ideology and membership, or that "King Mob" spoke with one voice over time for the people against the rich.[18] Plainly, New York's middle and lower classes would have a much greater voice in political affairs in 1776 than they had in 1763, but it is also true that they were sharply divided in this period by ethnic, religious, and economic interests, and that they regularly disagreed with one another about politics. In the Revolution, New Yorkers from every class and group could be found on both sides and among the ranks of the neutral.

There were radicals, like Sears, but they did not always articulate the viewpoint of the people, and the people did not necessarily share the radical ideology. Sears has been called "King Sears" because of the power he wielded over the mob that Morris so dreaded and derided. But in December 1769, when Sears broke with the De Lanceys, few followed him. In July 1770, when he opposed rescinding New York's nonimportation agreement (a boycott of British goods), residents voted against him, 794–465, and "King Mob" never rose to reverse the decision. Some people were apolitical; others were "reluctant to venture away from familiar political moorings" and stayed with their old De Lanceyite leaders. More were bound to the De Lanceys by deference, interest, religious prejudice, or the economic pressure that merchants could apply.[19] Whatever the reasons ordinary people sided as they did, they were not puppets. Sometimes they accepted Sears's leadership; other times they did not. Often enough, the people out of doors compelled the city's politicians, including Sears, to see an issue differently or to risk losing political leverage.[20] As shall become clear, if there was any consistent pattern after November 1765, it was that people wanted New Yorkers to move in unison and without violence in opposing British imperialism.

According to R. S. Neale, class consciousness exists only if the objectives of the group involved go beyond "bread and butter" issues to include "the revolutionary overthrow of the existing political order" and the creation of a classless society. That was not the case in New York. There was social strain and economic discontent in this hierarchic society, but not class conflict. For one thing, criticism of the widening economic gap between rich and poor expressed the popular belief that an inequitable distribution of wealth undercut liberty and promoted oligarchy. For another, as Bernard Friedman has ably argued, New York's artisans and farmers "were committed to an acquisitive economy, whether by their personal possession of landed or industrial property, or by virtue of the prevailing system of petty production in which the expectations of property ownership were high." When the propertyless "vented their grievances it was always within the framework of middle-class objectives." Their radicalism was of a "middle-class character," and it sought to abolish the "abridgement of opportunities." It aimed not to overthrow the politico-economic system but to open it wider, so that all could participate more fully in it. New York was a materialistic society, and the resentment ordinary people felt toward the rich was counterbalanced by their own pell-mell rush after riches.[21]

If class consciousness was lacking, economic discontent might have led to the Stamp Act crisis and the Revolution in New York in another way. In 1962 James C. Davies offered a frustration-aggression theory of revolution: "Revolution is most likely . . . when a prolonged period of rising expectations and rising gratifications is followed by a short period of sharp reversal, during which the gap between expectations and gratifications quickly widens and becomes intolerable." His insight helps to explain why New York was so convulsed in 1765: the postwar depression, following a period of prosperity, endangered residents' economic well-being, imperiled their middle-class expectations, and produced bitter frustration. That frustration, in turn, exploded in rioting and brought the city to the brink of insurrection. Britain was an obvious target, for residents believed its trade and taxation policies were causing their economic distress.[22]

Several criticisms of Davies's model can be made, but one is crucial:

frustration does not always end in aggression and by itself cannot cause a revolution. Frustration might explode, as it did in 1765, in a riot, a demonstration, or even a series of disturbances; but without leadership and organization the sustained activity and passion needed to overthrow a government cannot be mounted. In short, discontent was felt among many groups and classes in the mid-1760s; it even influenced how residents saw events between 1763 and 1776. But it did not of itself bring about the Revolution in New York. It was not simply that the strains were not sharp enough, but that discontent alone is an insufficient cause for a successful revolution. Residents' frustration provided the spark that ignited a conflagration in 1765, but fires of that sort burn themselves out. Leaders capable of directing an organizational network of supporters were needed to tend the flames and drive their destructive force toward altering the political environment. Hence, what the city's politicians were doing in the early 1760s is critical for understanding what followed.[23]

II

In reconstructing the years of upheaval and revolution in New York, one can start with Cadwallader Colden, who became acting governor in July 1760 upon James De Lancey's death. An ardent imperialist, Colden had been born in Scotland in 1688 and had graduated from the University of Edinburgh in 1705. He then studied medicine in London before settling in New York in 1718. Tactless, disputatious, inflexible, and arrogant, he had a stormy political career. As Gen. Thomas Gage would put it, "the Old Gentleman th'o Eighty five Years old, does not dislike a little Controversy, which he has been engaged in for the greatest part of his life." As if mimicking the imperial government that had nursed his career, upon becoming acting governor, Colden began provoking crises that would help to launch the spiral of conflict that propelled New York into revolution.[24]

He had entered politics in 1720 upon being appointed surveyor general by Gov. Robert Hunter. In that office Colden became a critic of the colony's large landowners: their huge holdings hindered settlement of the frontier; and their failure to pay quit rents afflicted the crown. Named to the governor's Council in 1721, he became "prime minister" to Gov. George Clinton for a few years, beginning in 1746. But Colden's imperial perspective led him to squabble with the Assembly over its lackluster support of the crown in King George's War. Because lawyers dominated the House, Colden nursed a grudge against lawyers. He once wrote Lord Halifax, President of the Board of Trade, that the lawyers and landowners had become a "faction" that was "dangerous to good Government" and a menace to the "Powers of the Crown." Since the Supreme Court generally protected large landowners, Colden concluded that the chief justice must be a nonresident without political connections in the colony. He also argued that royal officials should be rendered independent by having their salaries paid from the quit rents.[25]

After his tumultuous tour as Clinton's adviser, Colden remained a councillor but retired from politics. It was only De Lancey's death that thrust Colden, senior member of the Council, back into public life. On becoming acting governor in 1760, he might have made himself a champion of the people. They were disturbed by the maldistribution of wealth; he by the elite's power in government. They were suspicious of the law; he distrusted lawyers. But he feared the people and equated their participation in government with anarchy.[26] In truth, he was a placeman whose career was built upon royal favor; his allegiance was to the crown, the royal prerogative, and the Anglican church. Like Gov. Thomas Hutchinson of Massachusetts, both before and after the Seven Years' War, Colden supported government centralization to advance Britain's imperial objectives. That he profited, as a placeman, by these policies only made him more single-mindedly devoted to them. Principle served ambition, and ambition principle. As Watts explained it, "ministerial approbation is the balsam of his soul—next to pelf."[27]

A self-righteous critic of the "frenzied race for economic, social, and political preferment," Colden never comprehended that he, too, exploited his office to advance himself and his family.[28] On August 7, 1760, he wrote the Board of Trade, blazoning his "special regard" for the prerogative. He boasted that he would withstand the political pressures in New York and appoint a new chief justice of the Supreme Court with a commission during his majesty's pleasure and not "during good behavior" (that is, without permanent tenure). And he asked that his son Alexander be put on the Council. On August 11 he obsequiously wrote Lord Halifax of his zeal for the prerogative; he said that he would delay filling the Supreme Court vacancy as long as possible so that the ministry (or cabinet) could do so itself. Once more he requested that his son be made a councillor and pleaded, too, that he himself be allowed to remain acting governor for a time to enjoy the spoils of office. In August he also wrote John Pownall, secretary to the Board of Trade, enclosing an unsealed letter to that official's brother Thomas, suggesting that Thomas might make a good governor of New York. In November Colden reminded the Board of his lifelong devotion to the prerogative and asked to be made lieutenant governor. As events turned out, Colden succeeded in gaining that office for himself, but his son was not put on the Council, and Maj. Gen. Robert Monckton was named governor. Before the general arrived, however, Colden had turned the province into a hornets' nest and had helped to start New York down the road to revolution.[29]

Though the De Lanceys loathed Colden, his chief nemesis at the time was the Livingston faction.[30] The animosity between them dated back at least to the 1740s. By the Seven Years' War it was a power struggle waged on many levels: personality, patronage, class, and constitutional principle. Smith, for instance, once sniffishly complained that Colden "lives cheaply and retired at Flushing"; because of his "want of purse" and "spirit," the acting governor did not comport himself with the "dignity" his office demanded. The Livingstons were infuriated, too, by Colden's efforts to curtail smuggling and to vacate land grants that violated royal instructions.[31]

A crucial battle between Colden and the Livingstons, and one that helped to set the stage on which New Yorkers battled over the Stamp Act, developed over the appointment of De Lancey's successor as chief justice. Should the new chief justice's commission be at the king's pleasure or for an unlimited term on good behavior, as De Lancey's had been? In the Glorious Revolution English judges had won the right to serve during good behavior, and knowledgeable New Yorkers considered that to be their constitutional right. The Board of Trade objected, arguing that American judges lacked proper training and permanent salaries. Colden supported that position; but the Livingstons wanted judges appointed during good behavior so that they might be free from executive interference. To shield their considerable landholdings from judicial scrutiny, however, Livingstonites opposed permanent salaries. The situation had become volatile in 1761 following George II's death and the obligatory Assembly elections. The new House passed a bill that Supreme Court justices should serve during good behavior, but Colden vetoed it. Coaxed by the legal fraternity, the judges then pressed him for new commissions with tenure during good behavior, alleging that the king's death had invalidated their old ones. When Colden demurred, the work of the court ground to a halt. Colden, however, cleverly exposed the limits of his foes' idealism by offering a compromise: he would give the judges the commissions they wanted if the legislature voted them a permanent salary. The House refused. At this point, word arrived that the ministry had named Benjamin Pratt, an accomplished Massachusetts attorney, as chief justice. Colden was delighted, but Pratt lasted just six months. The other justices refused to sit with him, and the Assembly would not grant him a salary.[32]

General Monckton finally assumed office on October 26, 1761, but left in mid-November for a military expedition. The Livingstons quickly took advantage of his departure to underscore how circumscribed Colden's commitment to the prerogative really was by pushing through the Assembly a bill providing salaries for the governor and the judges, but only if the latter's commissions were to hold during good behavior. If Colden vetoed the bill, he forfeited his salary. If he signed it, he would have to answer to his superiors. The Council then rejected the legislation, ostensibly so that Colden would not have to do so himself. The Livingstons had gauged their opponent shrewdly. Constitutional principles aside, Colden craved the money and demanded that the Council approve the bill, so that he could sign it. Colden again offered to sign a bill shielding judges from arbitrary removal if the Assembly voted them a permanent salary. But the damage was done. On June 11, 1762, the Board of Trade rebuked him for approving the salary bill. To make matters worse, in the inaugural issue of the *American Chronicle* on March 20, the Livingstons excoriated him as an executive "intoxicated with the Grandeur of his Election — proud, self-conceited, and all sufficient — impatient of Advice, ignorant of the Constitution — full of himself, imperious, ungracious and forbidding — incapable of Friendship or Sincerity — crafty and rapacious — without Honor — void of Faith — of insatiable Avarice, and abandoned to his passions."[33]

Colden soon received instructions from Britain forbidding governors, on pain of removal, from granting a judge a commission during good behavior. He then threatened the judges with dismissal if they refused to accept new commissions during pleasure. One judge resigned, but two, Daniel Horsmanden and David Jones, bowed to the ultimatum. After Monckton returned in June 1762, he arranged a compromise to oblige his friends the Livingstons. Horsmanden was made chief justice, and two Livingstonites, William Smith, Sr., and Robert R. Livingston, were put on the court. All three received commissions "during the King's pleasure." If having to accept such a commission was a bitter pill, the Livingstons also had to face the fact that they had failed to rouse public opinion against Colden in defense of American rights. The struggle was significant, nonetheless, for it confirmed for Livingstonites that their decades-old antipathy for Colden was justified. For the party's Real Whigs, it proved that power was a genuine threat to liberty so long as this placeman continued in office. Of course, the episode honed Colden's enmity for lawyers, landowners, and Livingstonites, and the next time the two sides clashed, as they surely would, each would be convinced that the other was acting from the basest of motives.[34]

The feud flared again after Monckton left for England in June 1763. This time the quarrel would affect how the people out of doors saw the Stamp Act. The dispute itself had an unlikely beginning. In July 1763, in a quarrel over an unpaid debt, Waddel Cunningham, the creditor, stabbed Thomas Forsey, the debtor, who instituted a civil suit for damages. Sympathy for the debtor was overwhelming, given the troubled economy, and a jury awarded him fifteen hundred pounds in October 1764. The Whig "triumvirate" was involved on both sides: John Morin Scott represented Forsey; William Livingston and William Smith (along with James Duane) represented Cunningham. Once the defense motion for a new trial was denied, Cunningham petitioned the Supreme Court to appeal his case to the governor and Council.[35] By tradition the Council reviewed only errors in court procedure; it never examined the evidence presented in a case or reconsidered a jury's verdict. Because Cunningham was asking the Council to review the facts as well as the law, his lawyers refused to take the case and persuaded almost every other attorney to do likewise. Cunningham had no choice but to appoint, as his counsel, his business partner, Robert Waddell; two rather disreputable attorneys; and a notary public. The last asked the Supreme Court to deliver up the minutes in the case to the Governor in Council. The court sided with the legal fraternity and disallowed the appeal.[36]

Waddell petitioned the acting governor for a writ granting the appeal. A stubborn Colden prepared two writs of his own: one stayed enforcement of the jury's verdict; the other ordered the chief justice to turn over the proceedings in the case to the Council on November 14. Horsmanden refused and on November 19 read to the Council his reasons for rejecting the appeal. He insisted that to have the Council examine the facts of the case would be an innovation "repugnant to the Laws both of England and this Colony" that would endanger a subject's right to a jury trial. Until 1753 the king's instructions had allowed "*appeals in cases of Errors from any of the Courts of Common Law*"; later instructions omitted the words "in cases of Errors" but stated that appeals were to be issued "in the manner which has been usually accustomed." Since the only type ever permitted was a writ of error, Colden's writs were in violation of his instructions.[37]

The lawyers present supported Horsmanden, and Colden later charged that "the whole Body of the Law, Judge and Lawyers, are violently against it, as it will undoubtedly lessen their Power and Influence. Whatever be done in this place, I am very confident I shall have it in my power to humble them, and to curb their Licentiousness after this." To Lord Halifax, Colden added: "From the violent Efforts made at this time by the whole Body of the Profession of the Law, their view appears to me to make the common Law Courts, in effect, the ultimate Resort of Justice in this Province which without doubt must give them an enormous and dangerous influence in it." Thus, the dispute was not merely over appeals; Colden was seeking a victory in his perennial crusade against lawyers. In his view, they coveted only a court they could command; he wanted the governor in Council to act as a provincial court of last resort and the guardian of the imperial interest. Of course, he did not consider himself the aggressor: the lawyers "forced" the issue on him, and he was duty bound to uphold "the King's instructions."[38]

Colden's critics charged that if his proposed form of appellate review were to be accepted, the governor in Council could overturn jury verdicts at his discretion and thus politicize the legal system.[39] It was doubtless for that reason that although Waddell personally visited the Jerseys and Pennsylvania, some of whose attorneys were licensed to practice in New York, he could not get a lawyer from either place to prepare Cunningham's appeal. Yet Colden dismissed such arguments, claiming that though there were no juries in Scotland, justice was administered there as fairly as in England.[40]

Both sides soon broadened the boundaries of the dispute by drawing others into it. Colden sent monotonous missives to London, explaining the controversy and exculpating himself. He claimed that the opposition was spearheaded by large landowners who "know what must be the consequence in suits depending between them and other [of] the Kings Tenants, or the consequence of Informations of Intrusion, which may be justly brought against them etc in case the merits of the Cause be brought before the King and Council."[41] Colden was thus challenging not just lawyers; he wanted a precedent set, so that the governor in Council and the Privy Council (the king's formal advisory body) could review all jury verdicts involving disputed land claims. Livingstonites, in turn, sought to influence London by writing to Monckton. Smith explained that Colden's "unseasonable Effort" to challenge jury verdicts, while Parliament was trying to tax the colonies, "spreads a jealousy that the Crown is aiming to deprive the subject of his most valuable Rights." "People," he avowed, "think their all at Stake." The Livingstons also argued their case in the newspapers. Horsmanden's statement to the Council, which the Whig "triumvirate" had helped to draft, was printed serially in the *New York Gazette* with a preface authored by Scott. In weekly columns published from February 28 to August 29, 1765, "Sentinel" (the Whig "triumvirate") vilified Colden as "a traitor and felon to his country" and pummeled him for "his chicanery, his dissimulation, his doublings and windings, his sophistry and subtilty, his prevarications, and subterfuges." His "scandalous abuse of the King's name and authority" would despoil every resident's right to a jury trial and defile the constitution. "Sentinel" also explained the theory of limited government and asserted the people's right to resist an arbitrary ruler.[42]

At the start of the newspaper campaign Colden had claimed that it was having little effect on public opinion and that "People will quietly submit to the authority of Parliament and his Majesty's determination of the case in dispute relating to appeals." He was too sanguine. In September 1765, after residents had learned that the ministry had instructed him to admit an appeal to the governor in Council in *Forsey v. Cunningham,* John Watts declared that the case had agitated New Yorkers more than the Stamp Act itself; indeed, "the extreme aversion to the old man's person and character" had provided "a noble stock to engraft the stamp act upon, and it flourished accordingly." When Colden informed the Board of Trade about the Stamp Act riots, he explained the mob's animus toward him in terms of his fight over appeals. Smith concurred and wrote Monckton that Colden's stand on appeals had driven the mob to the "pitch of Madness." Even the lieutenant governor's political ally Sir William Johnson agreed "that the Affair of Appeals has incensed your Enemies ag[ain]st You more than anything else."[43]

In the final analysis, the propaganda campaign had helped to politicize and to agitate residents just in time for the Stamp Act crisis. Conversely, the stamp tax sensitized people to the dangers inherent in Colden's interpretation of the law. The two crises thus fed upon each other and intensified the spiral of conflict in New York.

III

The economic, religious, and political cleavages so characteristic of New York, and the success that Livingstonites had had in galvanizing people against an allegedly tyrannical acting governor, although significant, were still insufficient, alone or together, to trigger a revolution. That New Yorkers were still reluctant to rebel in 1776 only underscores that fact. There had to be a crisis in the imperial government itself, and that was brought on by its involvement in the Seven Years' War. The decision following that conflict to tax the colonies and to impose parliamentary sovereignty upon them pushed the city into revolution. "A government facing heavy international burdens may seek to raise taxes or even resort to internal coercion in mobilizing its resources." But "such actions may

be viewed by the populace as a violation of understandings, and they reduce the legitimacy they accord to government leaders. Such withdrawal
[of support] could readily lead to revolutionary goals."[44]

A few British politicians understood the dynamics of the situation and
faulted what Britain was doing in America. In 1768 the Duke of Newcastle
wrote that "the measure of conquering the colonies and obliging them
to submit is become more popular," but "I must in conscience enter my
protest against it; and I hope our friends will well consider before they
give in to so destructive a measure."[45] In 1774, in a speech before Parliament criticizing colonial taxation, Edmund Burke explained:

> Be content to bind America by laws of trade; you have always done it. Let
> this be your reason for binding their trade. Do not burthen them with
> taxes; you were not used to do so from the beginning. Let this be your
> reason for not taxing. . . . But if, intemperately, unwisely, fatally, you
> sophisticate and poison the very source of government, by urging subtile
> deductions, and consequences odious to those you govern, from the un-
> limited and illimitable nature of supreme sovereignty, you will teach
> them . . . to call that sovereignty into question. When you drive him
> hard, the boar will surely turn upon the hunters. If that sovereignty and
> their freedom can not be reconciled, which will they take? They will cast
> your sovereignty in your face. Nobody will be argued into slavery.[46]

To understand why New York City residents became revolutionaries,
one might well begin at the War of the Austrian Succession (1740–1749),
or King George's War as it was known in America. The growth of the
colonies—demographically, geographically, and economically—and Britain's developing awareness of their strategic value were already making
London anxious about American independence. Hence, starting in 1748,
an invigorated Board of Trade under Lord Halifax labored to establish
regular packet-boat service across the Atlantic, to demand that colonial
laws conform to royal instructions; to make chief executives obey their
instructions; to have permanent revenues established in all the colonies;
and to require a suspending clause in an ever-increasing variety of colonial laws. Together, these changes ended the policy of salutary neglect
established by Sir Robert Walpole, the British prime minister from 1721
to 1742, and began a concerted drive to buttress imperial authority in
America.[47]

The Seven Years' War had suspended the Board's reforming activities.
But waging a costly conflict to safeguard British interests in North
America only emphasized the colonies' strategic value and the wisdom of

Halifax's work. The war also brought to the fore thorny issues best left unraised; once advanced, they plagued the empire till independence. The first problem concerned war finance: the cost of the war was enormous, and the cabinet solicited assistance from each province on the basis of its ability to pay. Pennsylvania, Virginia, New York, New Jersey, and Massachusetts together provided about 86 percent of the money raised in America; the other colonies never gave in proportion to their wealth. By war's end Britain's financial situation was acute: the interest on the national debt consumed about 60 percent of the budget. The cabinet consequently looked to its American colonies, which seemed to be lightly taxed, to carry some of the imperial burden. The provinces had spent about £2,500,000 on the war, but Parliament had reimbursed them for about 40 percent of their expenses, and they were fast retiring the debt for the remainder. Moreover, the cost of government in America was low, about £75,000 a year, and reports depicted a society of real opulence.[48]

Another thorny issue was the cabinet's decision to station an army in America at an annual cost of about £225,000. Strategic and political concerns growing out of the war had persuaded the government to take Canada from France. But the potentially hostile population living there mandated the presence of British redcoats, who could also be used to buttress British authority in the other mainland colonies. Since the colonies had contributed to the empire's defense in war, it seemed logical they should also help to support the peacetime establishment. Raising a revenue in America would also reaffirm British sovereignty over the colonies.[49]

Wartime experience led the ministry to conclude that the government's authority in America needed reinvigoration. Central to this decision was the ministry's awareness of wartime smuggling between the colonies and the enemy.[50] During the eighteenth century the northern American provinces had developed an extensive commerce with the British and foreign West Indies, and New York merchants were convinced that the profits from this trade paid for British imports. Britain, however, never collected all the revenues to which it was legally entitled from this traffic, for colonial customs officials routinely colluded with local smugglers. In 1756, as a war measure, the British government prohibited trade with the French West Indies, but smugglers soon began routing contraband to the Spanish port of Monte Cristi on Hispaniola (a few miles from the border of French Haiti), where the goods were reloaded onto enemy vessels.[51]

New Yorkers had participated in the smuggling trade with the connivance of provincial officials, as the case of George Spencer makes manifest. In the fall of 1759 Spencer informed Lt. Gov. James De Lancey of the smuggling that the city's merchants were engaged in. Rumors quickly labeled Spencer a government informer. He was promptly arrested on pretext of debt, paraded about town, and finally thrown in jail in December 1759. New York's attorney general indicted seven merchants allegedly for rioting, though none of them was ever found guilty or otherwise punished. Spencer remained in jail until January 23, 1762, when he was released on condition that he leave the province. In 1763 he apprised the Lords of the Treasury of his ordeal.[52]

In 1760, while Spencer was still imprisoned, the British navy had begun to interdict the illicit trade. Colonial governors had also initiated strict enforcement of the Molasses Act of 1733, believing that payment of the duties would make French molasses and sugar prohibitively expensive and so kill the traffic. The act's enforcement was fairly effective in New York, though residents did not consider complicity in this commerce improper. Watts explained the situation in these words: "We have an odd kind of Mungrell Commerce here called the Mount Trade," which "the Lawyers say . . . is legal and contrary to no Statute, [though] the Men of Warr say it is illegal." British merchant vessels, too, visited Monte Cristi, and New Yorkers could not fathom why the cabinet did not vigorously condemn that commerce as well, or how smuggling by Americans could be more pernicious than that done by Englishmen. The ministry saw matters differently. American disloyalty had aided the enemy and prolonged the war. The trade had also exposed the corruption of customs officials, the reluctance (or inability) of local authorities to enforce the law, and the recalcitrance of the colonial population. The acts of trade would thus have to be enforced rigorously both to affirm colonial dependence and to collect the revenues the Treasury badly needed.[53]

The misunderstanding between the two sides could not easily be resolved. "Groups wittingly and unwittingly define one another as well as themselves," for their identity is shaped partly by how others perceive them. Thus, the more Britain acted as if it feared the colonies wanted independence, the more likely it was that they would seek it, even while denying that they were doing so. In turn, the more autonomy Americans sought, the more resolute the British would be in devising countermeasures.[54]

Ironically, wartime experience had rendered the government's postwar approach to colonial affairs risky to imperial integrity. First, the ministry had given its military commanders in America vast discretionary powers to prosecute the war effectively. Because these officers made military operations their chief priority, they often clashed with civilians, especially over issues like impressment and the quartering of troops in private homes. Many colonists thus became very sensitive to arbitrary rule, and they began to question "whether empire and liberty were compatible."[55] Second, the fact that Britain had invested so much to defend America, and the fact that the colonies had successfully participated in the war, had wrought an attitudinal change among colonists. They not only began to see themselves as "American" and to acquire a "continental" perspective and a "new sense of intercolonial solidarity," but they also developed a spirit of self-sufficiency. Indeed, the struggle against France had given the colonists training in warfare, in statecraft, and in economics. By war's end, they were confident in their ability to govern themselves without much guidance from home.[56]

After the war, New Yorkers came to view the imperial relationship as a reciprocal one. A resident explained: "Without the support of Britain, America must become tributary to some other nation; without America, Britain would cease to be an opulent, powerful nation; their interests are inseparable, and their separation is incompatible with . . . liberty and freedom." To restore harmony, "Britain should confirm to America her original privileges and immunities without blemish; her powers of distinct legislation and taxation, under the immediate control of the Crown and its Governors." "The trade and navigation of America," however, "should be so limited as to make the same mutually useful; America should look to Britain for defense and protection, and for the encouragement of her trade, and good government of her police." America "must abandon her illicit trade" and "by her own special act, bear a proportional part of the expense of Government."[57]

Despite the attitudinal changes taking place in America because of the war, the ministry had already embarked, even before the conflict had ended, on a program to remake the empire. In 1762, "An Act for the further Improvement of His Majesty's Revenue of Customs" became law. A revenue and a trade measure, it granted to a customs official who made a seizure for a trade-law violation half the value of the goods and ships condemned. The king was empowered to employ the navy in peacetime to enforce the acts of trade, and ships' officers and crews were to receive the same proportion of the value of seized cargoes and ships as customs officials on land.[58]

The pace of reform quickened once the financially strapped Grenville ministry came to power in April 1763. On June 1, it issued an Order in Council implementing the Revenue Act of 1762 and sent a circular letter to the colonial governors, demanding compliance. The cabinet also increased the complement of naval vessels stationed in North America. In July, colonial customs officials living in Britain were ordered to be at their station in America by the end of August. In November, a circular letter commanded these same officials to comply fully with their lawful responsibilities or face dismissal. Steps were also taken to start keeping and analyzing records on American trade, wherewith to identify situations where customs officials might be acting in collusion with smugglers.[59]

In 1764 George Grenville, who was prime minister and Chancellor of the Exchequer, proposed that revenue be raised in America by new customs duties and a stamp tax; imposition of the latter was to be delayed, however, for time was needed to draft a bill and to allow for colonial input. Meanwhile, in April, the Sugar or Revenue Act of 1764 became law. Its aim was not to regulate trade but to help to pay for the troops stationed in America. The new act continued the Molasses Act of 1733 but cut the duty on foreign molasses in half, to threepence per gallon, in the belief that the lower rate would make smuggling less attractive. The act also raised the duty on foreign sugar; banned the importation of foreign rum into the colonies; doubled the duties on foreign products reshipped in England to the colonies; set new or higher taxes on non-British coffee, indigo, pimento, textiles, and wines imported into the colonies; and extended the list of enumerated goods that colonists could ship only within the empire.

Equally important were the act's administrative provisions. For instance, a merchant transporting goods from one British colonial port to another had first (if his vessel was to sail more than seven miles offshore) to visit the nearest customs office (no matter how far), file an invoice of what he planned to ship, give bond to pay the duty on any foreign molasses taken aboard, and obtain a customs cocket. Failure to comply could result in the forfeiture of both cargo and ship. According to one historian, "the law was so written as to make it virtually impossible for a merchant who traded along the coastal waterways to avoid some technical violation which would expose him to penalties out of all proportion to the offense."[60]

The Sugar Act also authorized the creation of a new vice-admiralty court in Halifax, Nova Scotia, that was to have concurrent jurisdiction with the vice-admiralty courts already operating in America. The Molasses Act of 1733 had stipulated that violations of that law could be tried either in a vice-admiralty court or in a common law court in the province in which the alleged crime had occurred. Traders generally wanted their cases heard in the latter, where juries were apt to find for the defendant, and not in a juryless vice-admiralty court, where a royally appointed judge rendered the verdict. The Sugar Act of 1764 decreed instead that, at the prosecutor's discretion, any colonial maritime or civil case falling within the jurisdiction of an already existing admiralty court could now be filed in the new court. Improving the odds for conviction would, the cabinet hoped, increase compliance with the act and maximize the revenue produced. But prosecutors could now force defendants to travel to Halifax, a distant venue, or lose their case.[61]

The Currency Act also became law in April 1764. Passed out of fear that colonial legislatures might compel payment of sterling debts owed British creditors in depreciated paper currency, the act forbade both the issuance of paper money as legal tender and the extension of the recall date for outstanding issues. Colonial governors were barred from signing a paper-money bill without a clause suspending its operation until the Privy Council approved it. New Yorkers, however, quickly persuaded themselves that the legislation was only exacerbating the postwar economic downturn. Moreover, the law "served as a constant reminder that the economic well-being of the colonies was subordinate to the desires of the imperial government."[62]

In sum, because of the demands that war and the competitive state system had imposed on Britain, the Grenville ministry had taken forceful steps to check the spirit of autonomy supposedly gaining momentum in America, to reassert parliamentary sovereignty there, and to raise badly needed revenue. Further, Colden's battles both over the tenure of judges and over appeals from jury verdicts must be viewed as a secondary initiative by an imperialist-minded local official to secure the same ends. Colden succeeded chiefly in creating a crisis mentality in New York at the very moment the city was confronted with London's new definition of the empire.[63] The question, then, was not whether New Yorkers would quietly accede but, rather, what specific countermeasures they would take, given the confidence they had gained in the Seven Years' War and the battering and insult they had been enduring in the postwar depression.

CHAPTER THREE

The Stamp Act

If wartime experience had persuaded Britain to enact reforms it thought vital to the empire's survival, New Yorkers considered these same measures an ominous political, economic, and constitutional threat to their well-being. But the city's pluralistic population disagreed mightily over how to seek a redress of grievances, thereby exposing and deepening already existing fissures in the body politic. The rioting on November 1, 1765, only underscored how divided the city actually was. Nonetheless, by year's end, New Yorkers had already begun to overcome their differences. Not only had they nullified the Stamp Act, but they had also begun to alter the political landscape in New York. Remarkably, even though the city's patrician leaders were supposedly moved only by cynicism, and even though "the old order" was allegedly so precarious that it would be ripe "for a thoroughgoing revolution by 1773 or 1774," a community understanding had begun to crystallize by December 1765: British imperialism must be resisted, but not with the violence that had threatened to tear the city apart in November. Indeed, by year's end political power had already begun to flow to those who seemed best able to confront despotism without disrupting the community.[1] Nonetheless, the road to that consensus had been a arduous one.

It had been New York's merchants who had reacted first, in 1764, to the British threat. Upset by news that the Molasses Act of 1733 was to be extended, they embraced a proposal from Boston that they petition Parliament against the duties on foreign molasses and sugar. As a newspaper writer explained: "No impartial, fair, and true State of Trade of her northern Colonies, has ever been laid before the proper" authorities; once that was done, Britain would revise its policies out of self-interest and encourage the colonies "in every branch of Trade to *Europe* and *America*, that does not directly interfere with her own Manufactories."[2] The merchants met on January 27, 1764, and appointed a committee to draft a memorial asking the Assembly to petition Parliament for relief. What transpired at the meeting is unknown, but antimercantilists like Isaac Sears may well have been prodding their colleagues to greater militancy. Shortly afterward, "A.B." wrote John Holt's *New York Gazette*, praising the plan adopted and warning that to "violate the Laws in being, altho' . . . bad Laws, is seditious and injurious to Government, when Redress of Grievances might be obtained by dutiful and regular Representation." Because the Assembly was not in session when the memorial was ready, the governor and Council endorsed it and forwarded it to the Board of Trade. In April, the House approved the memorial and sent it to the colony's agent, Robert Charles.[3]

The petition explained that New York annually imported almost six hundred thousand pounds sterling worth of British products. Because the colony had little to offer in exchange, it had nurtured a lucrative commerce with the British and foreign West Indies, the profits of which paid for the British manufactures. Enforcement of the Molasses Act, however, would impair trade with the foreign West Indies and, in turn, force a cut in the colonial consumption of British goods, for the British West Indies did not produce enough molasses or sugar to meet demand. If the law remained in effect, it would cause "the utter Impoverishment of his Majesty's Northern Colonies," gravely harm "*British* Manufactures and Artificers," and lead to a "great Diminution of the Trade, Power, Wealth, and naval Strength of Great Britain." The act's repeal would render the foreign West Indies "effectually our own, as if they were really subject to the *British* crown."[4]

Meanwhile, more ominous news had begun reaching New York. In March came word that Parliament might ban the use of paper money. Even Colden realized that would cause "hardships which may throw the Colonies into perplexities and confusion." In April rumor said that a stamp tax would be levied in America. By May it appeared that the ministry planned to impose still other external and internal taxes on the colonies.[5] "A.B." objected that because Englishmen were not "affected" by taxes collected so far from home, they had not sought "to prevent the Oppression of such their Distant Countrymen." What the cabinet sowed in America, however, it would reap in Britain. The new laws "were *principally* designed with a View to familiarize and introduce the same sort of

Measures in England, rather than for any Advantage that was expected to be received from America." Once a person was "oppressed, Tax'd without his own Consent—denied the Enjoyment of his natural Rights, Liberty, and Property," he would become "indifferent" to a change of government and might "seek it in hopes of better usage from another."[6]

John Watts was more circumspect, yet events led him to offer his own interpretation on the outcome of the Seven Years' War. It was not that Americans were challenging imperial authority, now that they no longer feared France. Rather, Britain was content to mistreat them, because it no longer needed them to counterbalance French military might in Canada. He believed the colonies were "extremely incensed" and "wish[ed] Canada again French," for "it made them of some Consequence."[7] A local poet agreed:

> Ah! my dear country, curst in peace,
> Why did you wish the war to cease;
> The war in which you strew'd the plain,
> With thousands of your heroes slain.
> When Britain to your bleeding shore
> Impetuous pour'd her squadrons o'er;
> And snatch'd you from the Gallic Brood,
> To drink herself your vital blood![8]

New Yorkers maintained that Britain would only hurt itself by abusing them. Watts wrote that parliamentary taxation would "destroy the very means that enable" the colonies to purchase British imports. Yet that would benefit America, for it would counteract the recent "habits of Luxury" and "oblige us to Cloath ourselves, with the plain Manufactorys of our own Country, and in time may bring the Artists of Britain here for Employment." "A Friend to the Northern Colonies" added that the plan to enforce the Molasses Act was a plot by British West Indian planters to increase their profits by restricting the supply of sugar available to the mainland colonies. Moreover, the scheme would compel farmers to cultivate flax and to shun British textiles. In June, Robert R. Livingston called the ministry "mad" and predicted that the Revenue Act of 1764 would be followed by stamp and land taxes. Already, he said, some New Yorkers would wear only homespun, and others would not drink dutied wine; if a French army landed, people would not oppose it. William Smith wrote Governor Monckton that he feared Britain might use force: "Our People look upon themselves to be absolute Slaves" and would "resist to the last, upon the Presumption that the Contest must be as destructive to Great

Britain as to us; and that when this is felt by them, we shall . . . regain our Liberty."[9]

The depressed economy added a sharp edge to residents' anger. De Lanceyite merchants dreaded bankruptcy, and Livingstonite landowners feared the loss of huge tracts of undeveloped land if these were taxed.[10] Lawyers understood that their best clients were these same merchants and landowners. Artisans and seamen knew that, without trade, demand for their services would vanish. Yet complaints about British policies were motivated by more than selfishness. In 1752 William Livingston had declared, "It is a standing Maxim of *English Liberty*, 'that no Man shall be taxed, but with his own Consent.' " By 1764 writers were defending more than an abstract principle; they were parrying a direct threat to their liberty and their livelihoods.[11] Moreover, because the crisis broke out during the *Forsey v. Cunningham* dispute, New Yorkers were convinced that much more was at stake than matters of economic policy or self-interest. The struggle was over constitutional rights, and that fact justified strong countermeasures.

To fully appreciate the furor, we must focus, too, on the dynamics of the crisis, on the way events were unfolding. Rumor was confused with fact, and the latter crossed the Atlantic wrapped in the former. Apprehension about what might happen was at times as painful as the reality of what residents were being asked to endure. Moreover, it was the sum of British actions, more than any specific act, that made people contemplate resistance. According to one New Yorker, "it is thought the stamp act would not have met with so violent an opposition, if the colonies had not been previously chagrined at the rigorous execution of the laws against their trade." Moreover, because the issues were so fundamental, people were appalled by the apparent disdain with which Britain treated their complaints. British correspondents were warning that colonial opposition would provoke Parliament to enact even harsher measures. In New York, the dilemma was acute: silence would imperil the economy and breach residents' constitutional rights; protest would bring fresh assaults upon American liberty.[12]

Developments elsewhere in America also made townspeople more assertive than they might otherwise have been. Whenever militants in one seaport secured an objective, they generally influenced events up and down the Atlantic Coast.[13] Boston, which had a more homogeneous population and a more depressed economy than New York, often took the lead. Its decision in 1763 to oppose renewal of the Molasses Act had emboldened New York to act. James Otis's *Rights of the Colonies Asserted and Proved*, which rejected Parliament's right to tax America and impugned the distinction between external and internal taxation, convinced colonists everywhere to protest the Revenue Act of 1764 and the proposed stamp duties. When news would reach New York in August 1765 of rioting in Boston, James McEvers would resign as stamp distributor. A decision by Boston merchants in September 1765 to boycott British luxury items would lead other cities, including New York, to take up nonimportation, and once Bostonians put up a Liberty Pole, New York residents would follow suit.[14]

Most important, in 1764, after the Massachusetts House of Representatives had asked the other provinces to petition Britain over the violation of American rights, several patricians asked Colden to convene the Assembly. He acquiesced lest he cause "great disgust."[15] When the House met in September 1764, it followed the Livingston lead. In answering Colden's opening address the lawmakers declared themselves so "depressed with the Prospect of inevitable Ruin" that they could not "attend to Improvements, conducive either to the Interests of our Mother Country, or of this Colony." Because involuntary exactments would reduce them to "the deplorable State of that wretched People," who "can call Nothing their own," they implored him to intercede with the ministry against the Sugar Act and in support of their right "*of being taxed only with our own Consent.*" After failing to persuade the House to temper its reply, Colden wrote the Board of Trade that opposition to parliamentary taxation came from the great landowners, whose fears of a land tax led them to incite the people against all taxation.[16] Ever the faithful placeman, he could readily discern his enemy's greed but could not comprehend their constitutional arguments; he could accuse them of fomenting unrest but could not admit how widespread the opposition was.

Whatever Colden may have thought about Livingstonite motives, the Assembly protested the Revenue Act of 1764 and the proposed stamp tax by sending petitions to the King, Lords, and Commons, prepared respectively by John Morin Scott, William Livingston, and William Smith, Jr. (the Whig "triumvirate"). Though respectful, the memorials were unequivocal assertions of American rights and, according to Bernard Knollenberg, "among the great state papers of the pre-Revolutionary period."[17] They were also a concise statement of Livingston beliefs. The House sought neither to challenge "the Power of the Parliament" nor to seek "Independency." It wished only to protest "the Loss of such Rights as they have hitherto enjoyed, Rights established in the first Dawn of our Constitution, founded upon the most substantial Reasons, [and] confirmed by invariable Usage." New York claimed "an Exemption" from "all Taxes not granted by Themselves." Parliament could not "impose Taxes upon the

Subjects *here*, by Laws to be passed *there*." The Assembly was not pleading for a "*Privilege*" but asserting a "natural Right of Mankind" that "their Ancestors enjoyed in *Great-Britain*." Parliament could impose duties on commerce to regulate trade, but not to raise revenue. "Since all Impositions, whether they be internal Taxes, or Duties paid, for what we consume, equally diminish the Estates upon which they are charged; what avails it to any People, by which of them they are impoverished?" The Sugar Act was thus unconstitutional, for its aim was to raise revenue.

Parliament's ill-advised efforts to sever New York's commerce with the foreign West Indies would prove "equally detrimental to us and *Great-Britain*," for the profits from that trade allowed New Yorkers to buy British manufactures. The Assembly was troubled, too, that recent parliamentary legislation "change[d] the Current of Justice from the common Law, and subject Controversies of the utmost Importance to the Decisions of the Vice-Admiralty Courts," which "proceed not according [to] the old wholesom Laws of the Land, nor are always filled with Judges of approved Knowledge and Integrity." The House also objected to the Currency Act: the province had prudently issued paper money "in every War, since the Reign of King *William* the Third; and without it we could not have co-operated so vigorously in the Reduction of *Canada*." Banning paper money now would disrupt trade and cause "the Ruin of many Families."

II

New York's economy remained in turmoil in 1765. Imports from Britain fell dramatically, and the closing of two sugar houses confirmed the predictions residents had been making about the Sugar Act's ill effects. Poor harvests pushed grain prices higher than the export market would bear, and land prices fell. Traders who could not pay their creditors worried about bankruptcy. One merchant announced that he was retiring to a farm on Long Island. Another complained that "you would imagine the plague had been here, the grass growing in most trading streets; and the best traders[,] so far from wanting the assistance of a clerk, rather want employment for themselves."[18]

In the midst of this economic distress the Stamp Act became law. The first direct tax that Parliament had ever levied on the colonies, it placed an impost on most printed material, including newspapers, broadsides, pamphlets, and many commercial and legal documents. The tax was to be paid in sterling, and the money raised was to be used to support the army stationed in America. Infractions of the law could be tried, at the prosecutor's discretion, in either the vice-admiralty courts or the local common law courts. The tax, by itself, would not have caused severe hardship, but it came during an economic downturn, and the need to use stamps in so many transactions would have been a daily reminder of the power that Parliament claimed over Americans.[19] New Yorkers could also not be sure the tax was not a "Trojan Horse," "an entering wedge or introduction to future oppressions and impositions."[20]

The law antagonized every economic constituency and instantly united the city's heterogeneous population against it. Merchants were incensed because the need for stamps on commercial documents would increase costs and complicate business transactions. The requirement that the tax be paid in specie threatened (following the Currency Act) to kill the very trade upon which the measure aimed to make a revenue. "Publicola" surmised "that two Years at farthest, will effectually drain us of these metals," but he predicted that "when they are gone (the sooner the better) our Troubles on this Score will be at an End, and the downfall of our Credit will be the rise of Industry." Land speculators were vexed by the taxes that were to be levied on their dealings. Lawyers were upset, too, for stamps would have to be affixed to court documents. Printers were appalled, for by inflating the cost of what they printed, the impost threatened to undermine freedom of the press and to destroy their business.[21]

If self-interest was evident, so too was principle. Residents believed that liberty and property were joined; to attack one was to undercut the other. A writer reiterated the Assembly's argument of October 1764: "Since we are agreed in the *Right* of the Colonies, *to be taxed only by their own Consent given by their Representatives*; It follows, that if . . . they are not so represented in Parliament, [then] they have not given, nor can they possibly give their Consent to be there taxed, consequently . . . such a Tax must be arbitrary illegal and oppressive."[22] "Freeman" thought that "it is not the Tax itself," but "the unconstitutional Manner of imposing it, that is the great Subject of Uneasyness to the Colonies. Whatever Justice there may be in their bearing a proportional Charge of the War, they apprehend, that Manner of levying the Money upon them, *without their own Consent*, by which they are deprived of one of the most valuable Rights of British Subjects, *never can be right*." "A.B.C." argued that Americans "should be dealt with as Children of the same Parent, enjoying the same Freedom and Property as our Brethren in England, in Trade and Commerce, and being taxed only by our Legal constitutional Representatives."[23]

British arrogance heightened New York's anguish. When the city learned of the act's passage, it also heard that a member of Parliament had stated, evidently with satisfaction, that the law was harsh, for "where the Colonies stand on such high Pretensions of Independence on the supreme Legislative Authority of Great Britain, there is no moderating anything."[24] Residents were also distressed to learn that Robert Charles, the colony's agent, had considered the Assembly's October 1764 petitions too inflammatory to present to the houses of Parliament. William Smith, who had helped to author them, voiced people's indignation: "When the Americans reflect upon the Parliament's refusal to hear their Representations — when they read abstracts of the speeches within doors, and the ministerial pamphlets without," and when they find "Remonstrances forbidden in time to come," and "when they see the prospects of innumerable loads arising from this connection with an over-burdened nation interested in shaking the weight off of their own shoulders, and commanding silence in the oppressed Beast on which it is cast; what can we expect but discontent for a while, and in the end open opposition."[25]

Though hatred of the Stamp Act was universal, residents were perplexed over how to resist it. One historian has noted how quiet the city was in the months after it learned of the tax. Part of the reason was that people were still preoccupied by *Forsey v. Cunningham.*[26] Yet, beneath the surface calm, politicians were groping to find a way to free New Yorkers from unconstitutional taxation. Over time several alternatives emerged, each of which ultimately played a role in the Stamp Act's eventual defeat.

There are three modes for waging conflict: pure persuasion (that is, by argument alone without threat or promise), reward, and coercion. The first appealed to the Livingston and De Lancey patricians, who knew how much they had to lose (in power and property) if events spun out of control. Because rioting would affect them long after the crisis had passed, they yearned for a pacific resolution.[27] William Livingston urged residents to seek relief by "casting themselves at the king's feet, imploring his royal protection, supplicating . . . the continuation of their rights" in a manner "loyalty approves." Ideologically averse to mob violence, he argued: "Let us oppose arbitrary rule in every shape by every lawful method in our power."[28] "A Colonist" warned against "entering into riots we are ashamed of." If violent measures "prevail, [it is] plain all government is at an end," for "the same people will use the same measures against the most wholesome law, or the mildest government whenever it suits their interest." He urged, "Let us rather seek redress by serious remonstrances; let us calmly and coolly point out to our royal master the circumstance of his faithful colonists."[29]

A logical corollary to this approach was support for the Stamp Act Congress, which Massachusetts had proposed in June. New Yorkers who backed the plan were in a quandary, however, for the New York Assembly was not scheduled to meet until October 15, about a week after the congress was to be convened. The Assembly would thus be unable to appoint delegates. The House's Committee of Correspondence, however, solved the problem by informally selecting its own members as delegates. When the Stamp Act Congress met, its "Declaration of Rights and Grievances" condemned taxation without representation as a violation of American rights. Since colonists were not represented in Parliament, they could be taxed only by their own legislatures. Separate petitions, based on that document, were prepared for the King, Lords, and Commons. Robert R. Livingston sat on the committee that drafted the address to George III; Philip Livingston on the one that memorialized the Lords.[30] In its petition campaign the Stamp Act Congress employed both persuasion and reward. Not only did it seek to educate the government about the evil consequences of its policies, it also promised that if Parliament were to repeal the offending legislation, the colonies would remain loyal to crown and empire.

Livingstonites, realizing that earlier memorials had not moved Parliament, were ready to back petitions with popular action—"Clamor and Noise"—so long as it remained peaceful. In September, John Holt, whom the Livingstons had only recently saved from bankruptcy and whom they now subsidized, reported in his *The New York Gazette, or, The Weekly Post Boy* that "Lady N–th Am—can Liberty" had "died of a cruel *Stamp* on her Vitals" and that "her Remains will not be interred till the First Day of November, 1765, when she is to be buried in the Family Vault under the King's Chapel." "The Funeral will set out at 7 o'clock precisely from the Court-House, when it is hoped all true Lovers of the deceased, and consequently of their Country, will attend." In October, "A Colonist" outlined the Livingston strategy in Holt's paper: "Whenever the stamp-paper arrives, let us not sully our character by any violent measures; let them lie disregarded." Though "a total stagnation of all business will be the consequence, let us wait a few months" and "resolve to suffer, rather than carry the law into execution, by purchasing stampt paper; this will be more eligible than any violent measures."[31]

Livingstonites and De Lanceyites could also espouse another mode of nonviolent coercion: a boycott of British imports. Such a boycott would complement "A Colonist's" plan and convince British merchants to champion American demands. In August 1765, "The Sentinel" (William Livingston) had explained the logic behind forgoing British imports: "Can they injure us with new Impositions? We can more severely Distress them by retrenching our Luxury— And what have we from them that

comes not under that Denomination?" He urged people not to be dis-
couraged by these sacrifices: "They will undoubtedly terminate in our
real Advantage; and however they may tend to render a Ministry odious
at Home, they will only promote Industry and Frugality in the Plantation." On September 12, "Libertas" called for an embargo against British
goods; and on October 31, the day before the Stamp Act was to take
effect, the city's merchants became the first in America to adopt a formal
boycott agreement under which they pledged to instruct their British factors not to send merchandise until the Stamp Act's repeal. Orders made
before October 31 were to be canceled at once; items sent from Britain
upon commission after January 1, 1766, would not be sold. The compact
was to remain in force until revoked at a future meeting of merchants.
On October 31 New York's shopkeepers and retailers also pledged that
as of January 1, 1766, they would not purchase British imports until the
Stamp Act was repealed. Albany soon afterward adopted the same agreement. Philadelphia merchants instituted their own boycott on November
7, and Boston established one in December.[32]

While Livingstonites and De Lanceyites championed petitions, peaceful protests, and a boycott, radicals supported a more militant, even violent, strategy. On June 6, "Freeman" had ridiculed the British argument
that because members of Parliament represented the common good (and
not the people who had elected them), Americans were virtually represented in that body and the Stamp Act was consequently constitutional.
Such reasoning was an "Absurdity . . . so glaring, that it is almost an
Affront to common Sense to use Arguments to expose it; and yet it has
been so much insisted upon, that it seems as if the free Use of common
Sense was to be prohibited, as well as our other common Rights." John
Watts conceded that the piece was "a bold stroke at John Bull"; yet he
thought it "rash," for "it's innocent Work to bait a Minister, but hands
off of edg'd Tools." "Freeman's" next piece was sharper still: "If the Independency which the Colonies are supposed to aim at, means nothing
more, than that they claim the same natural Rights of Liberty and Property, as their Countrymen in England; it is very certain such is their
Claim." So long as Americans "are permitted to have the full Enjoyment
of those Rights which the Constitution entitles them to, they desire no
more, — nor can they be satisfied with less." People "oppressed under a
tyrannical Government, will naturally desire and seek a Change."[33]

What some considered the inevitable outcome of such brazen talk happened on August 14, when a Boston mob forced its stamp agent, Andrew
Oliver, to resign. On August 26 another Massachusetts mob burned the
vice-admiralty court records and ransacked Chief Justice Thomas Hutch-

inson's home. Upon reporting Oliver's resignation in the *New York Gazette*, on August 22, John Holt asked whether every stamp officer in America ought to insure his property against destruction. James McEvers, an Anglican merchant who had accepted appointment as a stamp officer, promptly resigned. If "Caesariensis" applauded the violence, the moderate William Livingston detested it.[34]

On September 21 the sole issue of *The Constitutional Courant* appeared in New York.[35] In one of its two articles "Philoleutherus" declared, "Let the British parliament be treated with all possible respect, while they treat us as fellow-subjects." But "if they transgress the bounds prescribed them by the constitution, if they usurp a jurisdiction, to which they have no right; if they infringe our liberties, and pursue such measures as will infallibly end in a Turkish despotism," he said, "let us boldly deny all such usurped jurisdiction; we owe them no more subjection, in this respect, than the Divan of Constantinople; to seem to acknowledge such a claim, would be to court our chains." "Philo Patriae" insisted that the "guilt" for the rioting at Boston was "chargeable upon the authors and abettors of the Stamp Act." "If the English parliament can lay these burdens upon us, they can also, if they please, take our whole property from us, and order us to be sold for slaves, or put to death." He thought it "better to die in defense of our rights, than to leave such a state as this to the generations that succeed it." He urged people "never" to "acknowledge" that the Stamp Act "is binding upon us, nor pay one farthing in obedience to it, for it was made by a power, that . . . hath no jurisdiction over us."

A shocked Colden tried to ferret out those responsible. What he learned was that James Parker had printed the paper in New Jersey and that postriders had secretly carried it to New York. Though authorship remains unknown to this day, some possible suspects can be ruled out. The De Lanceys were surely not responsible, for they took a patrician attitude toward violence and, following the rioting on November 1, would fear for their own lives and property. And, unlike "Philo Patriae," a Livingstonite would not have argued in print that Parliament could not enact laws for America. John Holt, who sympathized with the radicals, but whom the Livingstons nonetheless subsidized, had refused to print the material and had instead given it to William Goddard, a silent partner in his shop, who set the type for the job in New Jersey.[36]

The Constitutional Courant was doubtless the work of the Liberty Boys. Scholars debate when that band of radicals, who gathered around Isaac Sears and John Lamb and who clandestinely orchestrated popular resistance to the Stamp Act, had come into being. Robert J. Christen, Sears's biographer, believed that the organization of the group never got beyond the talking stage until November 1, and that its leaders did not formalize their association until January 1766. The issue cannot finally be settled here; the event was shrouded in secrecy and probably must remain so. Still, one may logically surmise from the evidence that the Liberty Boys had been meeting as early as September, and that they were responsible for the *Constitutional Courant.*[37] A "Philolutherus" would take up the pen again in December 1765 to support the Liberty Boy agenda; a "Philo-leutheros" would do the same in 1767 and 1773; and "Philo Patriae" would do likewise in both 1769 and 1775.[38]

The group's existence would explain not only the ability of radicals to control the mob so effectively on November 1 (see the Introduction), but also the propaganda that had appeared after September 21, demanding an assertive defense of American rights. On October 17 "Publicus" urged the readers of Holt's *New York Gazette* to conduct business without stamps. In the same issue of the newspaper "the Friends of Liberty and the English Constitution" were asked "to form an Association of all who were not already Slaves, in Opposition to all Attempts to make them so." After the stamps were stored in the fort on October 24, "Vox Populi" warned that "the first Man that either distributes or makes use of Stampt Paper, let him take Care of his House, Person, and Effects." And on October 31 a querist in the *New York Gazette* asked, "May not any Printer, who . . . stops his Press from the mere Panic of the pretended Act, fear the Indignation of the Public, and the Resentment of the Populace; for how will People be made sensible of their Rights, but by the Press?"[39]

III

While the Liberty Boys were plotting against the Stamp Act, Colden was preparing to enforce it. But the radicals could capitalize on people's hatred of him, which Livingstonites had nurtured during *Forsey v. Cunningham*, to mobilize residents against the stamps. Moreover, his stubbornness in handling the Stamp Act crisis would play into the hands of the radicals, making violence a more acceptable option. Colden was too headstrong to appreciate the danger, however, and he had pursued a hard line from the outset. On July 8, he had written Gen. Thomas Gage, asking that troops be stationed at Fort George, for he was worried about mob violence. The general consequently dispatched a company of redcoats to the city.[40]

Trouble began in earnest at the end of August, after McEvers had quit his post, because friends had warned him that "a Storm was Rising." Colden believed that "a design" existed "to destroy the Stamps at their first arrival." Yet he felt confident enough to boast, "I shall not be intimidated."[41] The next day he received a letter from Gage, setting down the terms under which troops could be employed: the governor and his Council had to provide timely notification of their need for military assistance; and "the Civil Magistrates" would have to take responsibility for ordering the troops to fire on civilians. Gage added that the newspapers were "crammed with Treason" and urged Colden to prosecute those responsible. When the governor showed his Council the letter from Gage, on September 4, the four members present refused to authorize the use of troops and asked that the other councillors be summoned to attend. By the time the Council reconvened, on September 7, rioting had occurred again in Boston. The Council nonetheless decided that the garrison had enough soldiers and encouraged Colden "to shew a Confidence in the People." It suggested, too, that the city magistrates be asked for their opinion. When the latter appeared before the Council on September 9, they, too, felt the city was in no danger of rioting. The councillors nonetheless concluded that it would be imprudent to prosecute the authors or printers of seditious publications.[42]

Disdainful of the Council's cowardice, Colden badly misjudged the crisis. On September 23, 1765, he wrote the cabinet that defensive measures had been taken and that the fort was now "secure against any attempt to Insult that was apprehended." He added that several colonies were engaged in a "secret correspondence" to coerce stamp officers into resigning and to seize the stamps. Hotheads had made McEvers quit, "but they have lost all hope of destroying" the stamps, "as they make no doubt of my securing them in the Fort when they arrive." He even boasted, "I shall do everything in my power to have the stamps distributed at the time appointed by the act of Parliament, and if I can have this done, I believe the present Bustle will soon subside." In October, his son David applied to London to be named stamp officer in McEvers's place, arguing that the act would be "quietly" obeyed "in a few months."[43]

On October 22, 1765, the *Edward*, which carried the stamps, arrived off the coast. The next day two warships escorted it into the harbor, but not to the wharf, where two thousand people were awaiting it. When Colden summoned the Council, the three attendees agreed that he should hire a sloop to unload the goods that longshoremen had to remove to reach the stamps. But no one would rent him a boat, and he feared troublemakers were only waiting for him to impress one to begin rioting. The cargo was thus moved onto British warships, and on the night of October 24 the stamps were secretly transferred to Fort George.[44]

"Vox Populi" promptly threatened death to anyone who distributed or used the stamps. "Americanus" traduced Colden as a scoundrel who "tramples upon Liberty, and the most sacred and most inestimable Right of Mankind" in order to "ingratiate himself with a Court." "He, though intrenched within Walls of Stone, and surrounded with Soldiers, Cannon, Mortars, and every necessary Implement for the Destruction of his Enemies, yet is afraid of his own Shadow." John Watts wrote that "the Colony is now more incensed against him than ever; conscious of its dislike and terrified at mobs, which to be sure are wretched masters, he has got the Fort armed beyond whatever you saw in the height of the war." On October 31, a shoemaker warned Colden of plans to riot and to bury Maj. Thomas James alive. The same day "Freeman" admonished the civil and military officials in town to resign before obeying the Stamp Act.[45]

Colden nonetheless seemed impervious to the storm about him and took an oath on October 31 to enforce the act. While merchants were agreeing that same day at Burns's tavern to boycott British goods, residents were gathering outside, asking where the "ceremony of burying liberty" was to be held. They were evidently referring to the September 5 article in Holt's *New York Gazette*, publicizing a demonstration. When nothing happened, they dispersed. But that night a crowd in three squads roamed the streets, shouting "Liberty," smashing street lights and windows, and signaling what homes were to be demolished the next night.[46]

On November 1, frustration over the economy, British trade policies, *Forsey v. Cunningham*, and the Stamp Act exploded in rioting the city would not soon forget. The failure of civil officials to stop the violence or to punish the ringleaders exposed the feebleness of royal authority, for British government in America rested on the consent of the governed. Ironically, though the imperatives of the competitive state system and international warfare had impelled Parliament to enact measures like the Stamp Act, the political realities in America threatened to make those very laws the death blow to the British empire. Moreover, the wanton destruction of Major James's home horrified patricians, for the crowd had exhibited a mind of its own and engaged in activities the elite had not sanctioned. It now seemed as if everyone's property, especially their own, was at risk. Though the elite opposed the Stamp Act, it did not want to stand up to Britain, only to find itself surrendering to the mob.

When New Yorkers awoke on Saturday, November 2, the crisis had not passed. The Stamp Act was still law, the stamps were still in Fort George, and about two hundred redcoats would work throughout the day to prepare the fort for an attack. In the morning Colden showed his Council an anonymous note he had received the day before, threatening his life if soldiers fired on the demonstrators. He added that he had been warned that the fort would be destroyed if the stamps were not put aboard a warship. The councillors ducked responsibility, pleading that they were not military experts. They believed the fort secure but agreed that if anything more was needed to make it so, it ought to be done. They also asked that absentee members be summoned to attend another Council meeting that afternoon. Meanwhile, Isaac Sears was openly boasting in the Coffee House that the inhabitants "will have [the stamps] within four and twenty hours." Privately, he was advising some gentlemen to warn the governor to give up the stamps or to face the consequences.[47]

The mayor and aldermen also assembled that day to consider how they could forestall another night of violence.[48] Because few had any ideas, they sat paralyzed for hours. Finally, Robert R. Livingston, an Anglican Livingstonite, entered the room to volunteer his services. He found some aldermen ready to call out the militia, though most preferred simply to wait for the governor to act. Colden finally notified the group that he would not distribute the stamps, unless someone specifically requested them, and that he would store them aboard a warship if Capt. Archibald Kennedy would take them. Livingston was exasperated, for Colden had told him two weeks past that he had written the ministry that he would not meddle with the stamps without new instructions. If the governor had only "condescended" to announce that publicly, he would now be a hero.

Since Colden would do no more, the group agreed to put his offer in the best possible light and to try to persuade people of the folly of assaulting the fort. James Duane, an Anglican De Lanceyite who had married a Livingston, suggested that the way to reach those who might riot, since many were seamen, was to have a captain of a privateer join them. After several captains refused, Livingston and Duane found one, perhaps Alexander McDougall, who was willing to help. Together they patrolled the streets, trying to restore calm. They eventually came upon a small band who looked dressed for a riot. While the three reasoned with the group, about two hundred more demonstrators appeared. The talking continued until Colden finally announced that he would "do nothing in Relation to the Stamps, but leave it to Sir Henry Moore," who had recently been appointed governor of New York, "to do as he pleases, on his Arrival."[49] Rioting was thus averted that night.

Livingston's victory offered only a brief respite. On Sunday, November 3, "Benevolus" threatened Colden's life, unless he vowed never to distribute the stamps. A letter was also sent to the Customs House officials, promising violence if they did not surrender all the revenues they had already collected and begin clearing out ships as usual. A third missive, signed by "The Sons of Neptune" and posted at the Coffee House, admonished residents to ignore "peaceable orators" and to attack the fort on Tuesday, November 5.

To counter that threat, patricians gathered at the Coffee House on Monday morning. It was time, said Robert R. Livingston, "for those inclined to keep the peace of the City, to rouse their sleeping courage." But the patricians were now as forlorn as the city magistrates had been on November 2. If they did nothing, "Mob government" would rule the city. If they acted, the "secret unknown party" or "Vox Populi" might turn against them. When Livingston urged them to form an association to preserve order, all thought it was a superb idea, yet no one volunteered to join. Some even warned him that he had spoken too freely. Finally, several gentlemen agreed to patrol the streets with him that night to forestall a new outbreak of violence. They also advised Colden to stow the stamps aboard a warship, as he had promised to do on November 2. That evening several sea captains agreed to join Livingston in maintaining order.[50]

The lieutenant governor meanwhile did what he could to afford demonstrators "a warm reception."[51] British regulars had continued readying Fort George for an attack, and on November 3 Colden had ordered all the big guns outside its walls spiked so that rioters could not use them. From a military standpoint that might have been wise; from a public relations perspective it was a blunder that only enraged residents. Meanwhile, Gage sent agents out among the people to see how well armed they were. The spies reported back that mob leaders had distributed weapons to their followers and had even acquired artillery pieces. Fortunately for those inside the fort, the intelligence was erroneous, for Colden did not flinch in his resolve. He was prepared to fight, though he believed the attack would "be attended with much bloodshed, because a great part of the Mob consists of Men who have been Privateers and disbanded Soldiers whose view is to plunder the Town."[52]

Colden's one conciliatory gesture was to agree to transfer the stamps to a warship. He had tried to do so on November 2, but Captain Kennedy had declined to accept them, fearing rioters would make him either surrender the stamps or watch his home at Bowling Green burn.[53] Another futile request was made to Kennedy on November 4. As a result, "to prevent the effusion of blood," the mayor and aldermen asked Colden to give them the stamps. They pledged that the City Council would both guard the stamps and assume financial responsibility for them. Colden hesitated, knowing that the cabinet would demand an explanation. If the "Power of the Corporation alone" was sufficient to defend the stamps, he asked his Council, could not "the same power" be "added to the strength of this Garrison?" The Council could only reply that the city was "in perfect anarchy" and that the "power of Government" was unequal to the challenge facing it.[54] Meanwhile, a crowd had assembled outside City Hall; some were armed, and violence seemed likely if he rejected the offer. Thus, as soon as the Council meeting had ended, he wrote Gage for advice, knowing the general's support would shield him from ministerial rebuke. Fearing the city was near insurrection, Gage approved. That evening five thousand residents accompanied the seven boxes of stamps, weighing almost one and one-half tons, on their trip to City Hall.[55]

The immediate crisis thus ended, and the city was restored to "perfect tranquility."[56] The new governor, Sir Henry Moore, who arrived on November 13, managed affairs more to the public's liking. He began by asking his Council, Colden included, what should be done about the stamps and the fort. When the councillors urged that the latter be restored to its previous condition and that the former not be distributed, Moore agreed.[57] The nine boxes of stamps he had brought with him from home were consequently stored at City Hall, along with the others, and on November 15 the Sons of Liberty lit a bonfire in his honor. Colden complained that the governor was currying popular favor at the crown's expense. But Moore saw affairs differently. "I am obliged to suspend a Power which I am not able to exert," he said, "and to make a merit of acting in a manner which carries no other recommendation with it but that of not exposing the Weakness of our Government."[58] Moore informed the ministry that "as it was not in my power to employ open force, I had no other remedy left but to let the People be sensible of the inconveniences which of course would attend the suspension they so much desired of the Stamp Act, and they begin already to be very severely felt, for all kind of business has stood still since that time." Gage endorsed the strategy, writing home that "when they shall feel the loss of all Business . . . many will soon wish to take the Stamps, tho' all afraid to be the first."[59] Thus, instead of antagonizing residents, Moore's policy was to let them suffer the consequences of their disobedience.

Moore's approach exacerbated relations between the Livingstons and the Liberty Boys. Even before November 1, the radicals had been demanding that business be conducted without stamps.[60] The Livingstons had always objected, for they sought only lawful resistance. They did not want to flout the law, since that could result in prosecution and in the confiscation of their property. And, of course, many Livingstonite patricians and lawyers had sufficient wealth to wait out the British. The Liberty Boys saw matters differently. New York was in depression, and they were concerned about "the Necessities to which the People will be reduced by the Cessation of Business." Radicals feared that, with time, the Livingston approach would, as Moore hoped, cause so much economic distress that it would tempt people to abandon the fight. Logic, too, was on the side of the radicals. If the Stamp Act was unconstitutional, New Yorkers should go about their business and ignore the tax; failure to do so would be an implicit admission of the law's legitimacy.[61] "Philolutherus" insisted, "None in this day of liberty will pretend to say, that duty binds us to yield obedience to any man, or any body of men, which form a part of the *British* constitution, when that man, or body of men, exceeds the limits prescribed by that constitution." "Why then," he asked, "do we pay such a slavish subjection to what we unanimously agree to be not obligatory?"[62]

The Liberty Boys called a public meeting on November 26 to pressure the city's four assemblymen into persuading the House to repeal the stamp tax. Though the Rhode Island Assembly had already passed a resolution directing civil officials there to disobey the Stamp Act, Livingstonites first tried to dissuade the radicals and then tore down the notices for the meeting. When that too failed, the anti-radical forces plotted to seize control of the meeting itself. In the event, they succeeded in appointing a committee composed of Livingstonites and De Lanceyites—men such as William Smith, John Morin Scott, William Livingston, and James De Lancey—to prepare a memorial to the city's four lawmakers. Of course, the committee's petition demanded neither the resumption of business without stamps nor local repeal of the Stamp Act. The defeated Liberty Boys soon publicized their own representation and explained how the city's patricians had outmaneuvered them. Still, it was the more moderate instructions that were presented to the city's assemblymen on November 27.[63]

At a public meeting on December 6 the Liberty Boys retaliated by appointing a committee of twelve to persuade the city's (Livingstonite) lawyers to practice the law without stamps. The civil courts had closed on November 1, and attorneys had promptly ceased engaging in activities requiring stamps. They were not about to leave a paper trail of civil disobedience.[64] Besides, chaos might have resulted if someone later challenged the lawfulness of court papers and legal documents to which stamps had not been affixed. Several of those appointed to the committee on December 6 declined to serve, but James De Lancey agreed to do so. When the committee finally met with the attorneys on December 20, the latter seemingly agreed to resume business. Few did, however, and the Liberty Boys renewed their assault against the lawyers for selfishly disregarding the common good.[65]

If the episode redoubled Sears's distaste for the Livingstons, it also gave him a new respect for James De Lancey, and an alliance between the two blossomed at once. De Lancey had surely seized the moment to recapture the popularity and the power his father had enjoyed in the 1750s. Still, more was involved than the political opportunism that historians have usually stressed. Like other New Yorkers, De Lanceyite merchants detested the Stamp Act and realized that crowd action on behalf of the common good was justified. Many De Lanceyites were nonetheless horrified by what had happened on November 1. Yet that was all the more reason for James De Lancey to get involved. The future would be safer if his party could gain the confidence of mob leaders and thereby temper their excesses. Like the Livingstons, the De Lanceys feared anarchy and believed that patricians should manage public affairs. In this instance, Robert R. Livingston exerted his influence by opposing Sears; James De Lancey by working with the Liberty Boys. Hence, the power base that the Livingstons had started to build in the early 1760s now began to crumble. Since James De Lancey's approach, after December 6, was more subtle, his party's influence rose with that of Sears.[66]

The radicals soon began demanding that the port be reopened for trade without stamps. Many of Sears's supporters were seamen, and "Freeman" reported in mid-December that "great Numbers of our poor People and Seamen [are] without Employment and without Support, — many Families which used to live in comfortable Plenty, daily falling to Decay for Want of Business." Happily for the Sears–De Lancey coalition, resuming trade was a goal that patricians could accept. If the port stayed closed, the city would remain filled with idle seamen who might riot.[67] Because customs officials in Philadelphia had been clearing vessels without stamps since late November, the radicals easily persuaded Andrew Elliot, collector of the customs at New York, to issue unstamped the documents required for trade under the Revenue Act of 1764. But Captain Kennedy refused to let the ships go unless their paperwork was stamped or the governor assumed responsibility for the situation by giving them letpasses to depart. Some Liberty Boys blamed Kennedy for the impasse; others Moore. The latter obviously had no desire to replace Colden as the public's villain, yet he wanted residents to pay a stiff price for resisting Parliament. He assembled the merchants on December 16 and insisted that, even though he would not issue letpasses, he was not to blame for keeping the ships in port. Interestingly, the merchants did nothing to make him relent, and neither he nor they suffered as a result. The next night a crowd burned the effigies of several distant crown officials who were supposedly responsible for the city's plight. But no noteworthy violence took place, no trader's property was destroyed, and Moore was greeted with three cheers. Evidently, James De Lancey's approach to the crisis was already working.[68]

"Freeman" complained bitterly: "Our Business of all Kinds is stopped, our Vessels, ready for Sea, blocked up in our Harbours, as if besieged by an Enemy." Parliament would surely consider Americans "a Herd of mean, despicable Wretches," too afraid to defend their rights. A week later "Philolutherus" made the same point: "We have been blustering for liberty for some months, but when put to the trial, we shrink back in a most dastardly manner, and all our courage evaporates in smoke."[69] At the end of December the Liberty Boys suggested that Moore issue a proclamation offering to name anyone who applied New York's stamp distributor. If no one volunteered (which they knew would be the case), then Moore would issue letpasses. But nothing came of the proposal.[70]

By December, therefore, an equilibrium of sorts had been reached: none dared use stamps, but few would do business without them. Colden was fair game, but radicals would not attack Moore. Livingstonite lawyers could be ostracized for not practicing the law without stamps, but De Lancey merchants went unassailed, though they had failed to make Moore issue letpasses. Violence never seemed far from the surface, but no real rioting took place. On the nights of December 21 and 23, some feared the radicals might destroy the stamps stored at City Hall, "imagining if there were None in the Province, there could be no Pretence to Stop the Ships." The magistrates asked Gage for help, however, and the crisis passed without incident. On December 24, a crowd threatened to wreck Capt. Kennedy's home, yet it remained standing. A few days later threats were made against a naval captain for blocking a merchant ship that had attempted to leave port, but he was not harmed. Violence was averted in part because ships had begun sneaking out at night undetected. And on January 2 the weather forced Kennedy to bring the navy into port for the winter, and that ended the crisis. Vessels wishing to depart could now do so, and angry seamen at last found employment. Nonetheless, what cannot be ignored is the stabilizing influence that James De Lancey's alliance with the Liberty Boys was having on affairs. What was emerging, if the restraint the radicals were now showing is any indication, was a community understanding that British imperialism must be resisted, but that it should (and could) be done without the violence that had rocked the city on November 1. The events of December make it clear that the talent the city's residents had for the art of politics was still alive and that New York was not "a political system in decay."[71]

If the town breathed easier, politicians still had much to ponder in the winter's cold. The city's diverse population had stood as one in its opposition to the Stamp Act but had experienced real trouble in agreeing on a strategy to defeat the tax. In demonstrating how crowd action could be used to nullify the Stamp Act, the Liberty Boys had become a political force. By showing how to contain violence and how to get people of diverse interests and backgrounds to cooperate, the De Lanceys had found a way to regain power. And the Livingstons had lost influence because their approach to the crisis had made them look weak in their opposition to British imperialism. What all that meant for the future, or how affairs would finally turn out, was unclear.

CHAPTER FOUR

The Aftermath

A New York historian has argued that the city "verged on anarchy" from November 1, 1765, until the Stamp Act's repeal in March 1766.[1] Evidence exists to support that assertion if one accepts the judgment of crown officials, military officers, patricians, and merchants. Though their assessment was inaccurate, it is crucial to examine how they depicted affairs, for that shaped their attitude in later years.

From November on, the mob had seemed to be everywhere, and violence was supposedly always a threat. John Watts felt that "the ill boding aspects of things, cramping of trade, suppression of paper money, duties, courts of admiralty, appeals, internal taxes etc, have rendered people so poor, cross, and desperate, that they don't seem to care who are their masters, or indeed for any masters." He expected "to see this City go one day or other, it has looked extremely like it once already, contending for the stamps in the Fort." In January Capt. John Montresor of the British army objected that the town had become so lawless that "Children nightly trampouze the Streets with lanthorns upon Poles and hallowing," and "the Magistry either approve of it, or do not dare to suppress it."[2]

On November 26 Abraham Lott, a Dutch Reformed merchant and clerk of the Assembly, received from "Freedom" a poorly drafted note directing the House to deduct from Cadwallader Colden's salary the cost of repairing the fort and unspiking its guns. The penman further instructed the Assembly to reconsider two laws that were "Rong and take away Liberty." It was time for lawmakers to work "for the Good of the public," not as if "other People know nothing about Government." The

House found the letter "Lybellous, Scandalous, and Seditious," and Gov. Henry Moore offered a reward for the culprit's name. The Liberty Boys proclaimed their innocence and even vowed to help unmask the author.[3]

If "Freedom" was not heard from again, crown officials and patricians still had to contend with the radicals. The next day the Liberty Boys forced the resignation of Colden's grandson, Peter De Lancey, Jr., from a stamp distributorship. The young man, who had been living in London, had been unaware of the depth of colonial opposition to the tax. But the De Lanceys shrewdly minimized the political damage done by making his resignation a ritualistic reaffirmation of the family's opposition to stamps. That same day Moore asked for Isaac Sears's help in preserving order, thereby acknowledging that he felt he had lost control of events. The next day two hundred Liberty Boys visited Flushing, where Maryland's stamp distributor was hiding, and forced him to renounce his commission. On December 2 they made McEvers resign again, this time in public. Captain Montresor complained bitterly that "the Sons of Liberty as they term themselves, [are] openly defying powers, office and all authority. [They are the] sole rulers."[4] His comment underscored just how much these developments distressed the better sort.

On Tuesday, January 7, the *Polly* arrived with about ten packages of stamps for Connecticut. The Liberty Boys met, and the next night an armed band burned the stamps. Broadsides justified the action, but Moore offered a reward for the names of the culprits and threatened to ask Gen. Thomas Gage for troops to restore order. The warning seemingly had the desired effect. Later that month, when more stamps arrived, they were peacefully lodged at City Hall.[5]

On February 6, however, the Liberty Boys pledged to "fight up to their knees in blood" before allowing the use of stamps. Their resolve was soon tested. On February 13, they discovered that Lewis Pintard, a French Protestant merchant, had sent stamped Mediterranean passes to Philadelphia. Pintard was promptly questioned, whereupon it was learned that another merchant, Acheson Thompson, had also used such passes. The next morning, Isaac Sears, John Lamb, and Joseph Allicocke marshaled almost five thousand supporters and demanded that Charles Williams, the Anglican customs official who had issued the passes, surrender any others he might have. The people next made Pintard burn them. Thompson exculpated himself by swearing that he had not known the passes had been stamped. The crowd quieted down but that evening forced open the door to Williams's abode and wrecked some furniture. The house might even have been torn down if crowd leaders had not persuaded the rioters instead to let Williams apologize publicly the next day. On Saturday Williams and Pintard begged the public's pardon before a crowd of several thousand, which then escorted them home, where they confessed anew. The crowd again moved to tear down their houses but was dissuaded from doing so, for James De Lancey owned Williams's residence.[6]

On February 26 the Liberty Boys reportedly agreed that if Britain enforced the Stamp Act, they would put every crown official in town aboard a ship for England. A week later, on March 6, Colden again became a target of abuse. Because he had ordered the cannons spiked in November, a crowd now seated his effigy with a drill in its hand atop a piece of ordnance. While the dummy was being carted about town, marchers visited Gage's headquarters and gave him three cheers. When the salute was not returned, the crowd warned the officers present that "they would have their Hats off yet before [we] were done with them." The protest ended at dusk with the burning of the effigy.[7]

The incidents continued. On March 12 the British warship *Garland* reached port. A few days later, one of the ship's officers, a Lieutenant Hallam, imprudently compared the Liberty Boys to the Scottish rebels of 1745 and boasted that John Holt should "be hanged for publishing what he had, and for his part he would not be against putting a halter about his neck." Twice the Liberty Boys visited the *Garland* in vain to demand a written retraction. Word soon spread that the radicals planned to assault the ship and kill Hallam, and Gage ordered his troops to repulse an attack; munitions were loaded aboard the vessel. The Liberty Boys then brashly visited Gage on March 22 to ask why he was meddling in the affair, and the next day threatened to pull down the abode of an officer who had carried a message between the general and the *Garland's* captain. The dispute ended there, perhaps because news arrived on March 25 that the Stamp Act would soon be repealed.[8]

If radicals declined to take on the navy, army officers ashore were not so lucky. Montresor reported on March 31 that "Five Ruffians or Sons of Liberty" unmercifully beat an officer. The incident might simply have been a waterfront brawl, or it could have been a direct outgrowth of the civil-military rancor caused by the Stamp Act crisis. Montresor saw it as the inevitable consequence of the anarchy unleashed in November. On April 3 he objected that "the Sons or Spawns of Liberty and Inquisition here, [were] still venting threats and Insulting the Crown and Officers under it."[9]

By April reports from Europe indicated that New York would soon receive official confirmation of the Stamp Act's repeal. Yet radicals maintained the pressure and even made fresh demands. Montresor stated that "the Sons of Liberty publickly declare that if the Stamp act is Repealed they will also insist on all Restrictions of Trade being taken off. *No [govern-ment-controlled] Post offices nor [juryless] Courts of Admiralty* as being all in-fringements on the subject, as now is their time, while the Colonies are unanimous." Though nothing overt was done to gain these objectives, the Liberty Boys never slackened in their opposition to the Stamp Act. On April 23 the *Prince George* reached port with goods forbidden by the nonimportation agreement. A group of merchants boarded the vessel and demanded that the captain declare his cargo. The radicals then seized the contraband and reshipped it to England.[10]

The Liberty Boys were supposedly the cause of so much diabolic behav-ior that criminals, victims, and witnesses alike blamed them for every un-toward event. Though it is often impossible to know if they were actually involved in a particular scrape, both patricians and crown officials were in despair. Gage deplored the "Dissolution of all legal Authority" and fretted that people had become "so accustomed to Excess and Riot with-out controul, that it is to be feared it would not be an easy Task to bring them back to their Duty, Should the Wisdom of Parliament ever think proper" to repeal the Stamp Act. Moore wrote home that he was obliged to act alone in the crisis, for the "Power of Governt was too weak." His councillors were of no help because "their apprehensions of future dis-turbances have influenced all the opinions they have given me." As for city officials, "the disorders have become so general that the magistracy are affraid of exerting the powers they have vested with, and dread noth-ing so much as being called upon in these troublesome times for their assistance." Watts thought that "Better Men must be sent from Home to fill [government] offices or all will end in Anarchy." Robert R. Livingston spoke of "Tumults, Rage, and Contempt of Magistracy and Government" and feared New York would "see nothing but the most dreadful confusion arising" if the Stamp Act was not repealed. His father prayed for "peace and tranquility."[11]

The elite even feared for its own survival. In January 1766 Oliver De Lancey had written that "civil war" would follow the Stamp Act's imple-mentation; "all Distinction will then be lost and our family will hardly be unobserved in such a Scene of Confusion and Distress." Robert R. Living-ston informed Robert Monckton that "enforcing the Stamp Act will be attended with the destruction of all Law Order and Government in the Colonies, and ruin all men of property, for such is the temper of people's minds, from one end of the Continent to the other, that whoever carries his opposition to this Act, to the greatest excess, will be most followed, and will force the rest into their measures." After the Pintard affair Moore informed Alexander Colden that enforcing "the Stamp act was now out of the question and only a pretense for a Mobs Collecting in order to plunder" and "that he did not doubt but they would at the rate they went on fix on houses [as] the best plunder."[12]

Crown officials began advocating the use of military force to gain revenge and to restore order. Their reaction was understandable. If the Stamp Act riots had helped to persuade Britain to repeal the tax, they had also psychologically prepared civil and military officials in America of the need to use the troops to teach the colonists a lesson.[13] In September 1765, before the rioting, Colden had already begun taking the steps necessary for the army to enforce the Stamp Act, though neither the city magistrates nor his Council supported him. By December, however, he felt events had vindicated him. When he forwarded to London copies of the Council's minutes for September, he declared confidently that the "Council erred in their Judgment." Though Moore had at first ridiculed Colden for arming the fort, the governor conceded in February that "nothing at present but a superior Force will bring the people to a sense of their Duty."[14]

In January 1766 Gage declared: "I am Sorry to Say, that . . . were there 5000 Troops in the City, that there is no part of the Civil Authority, the Governor excepted, who would have asked their Assistance, to quell any of the Riots." Angered by such cravenness, he told the ministry: "I should be glad of a legal Pretence to collect all the Force I could, into one Body; which might Check in some Measure the Audacious Threats of taking Arms, and in case of extremity enable the King's Servants, and Such as are Friends to Government, to make a respectable Opposition." The same month he wrote Lord Barrington, the secretary of war: "No Requisition has been made of Me for assistance, which I, must acknowledge I have been sorry for, as the disturbances which have happened, have been so much beyond riots, and so like the forerunners of open Rebellion, that I have wanted a pretence to draw the troops together from every post they cou'd be taken from." In February he notified the cabinet that it was imperative to begin quietly collecting an army in the province. Moore concurred but failed to persuade his Council to endorse the idea. In a letter to Barrington in May 1766 Gage suggested that troops be stationed along the coast, chiefly at Philadelphia and New York. Their presence, especially in New York, would permit him "to protect the King's Magazines" and to provide "support to the Civil Government."[15]

Gage's frustration filtered down through the ranks. Captain Montresor thought New York would never have been so rebellious had it had a military government like that in Canada. He later expressed dismay because Moore was not acting decisively to curb the mob. And on July 16 he reported with glee that the Liberty Boys had been quiet ever since troops had arrived in town on June 20. It apparently never dawned on him that the tumult might have ceased because the Stamp Act had been repealed. But his ingrained confidence in the military's ability to resolve the crisis is significant. That conviction, which other officers shared, made the army over the next decade a dangerous, dynamic element in the Anglo-American relationship, one that helped to shape the final outcome. In 1773, for example, Gen. Frederick Haldimand, who was then commanding at New York, would write, "The only remedy for the evils complained of is to form a military government."[16] It is no surprise that British politicians, three thousand miles away, eventually saw the crisis as a military, not a political or constitutional, one.

II

Though events had rankled royal officials and the elite and had noticeably affected their thinking in subsequent years, the situation in New York at the time was not one of anarchy. Despite the appearance of chaos there had been an underlying orderliness to affairs. Colden wrote the cabinet on November 9, 1765, that "the Leaders of the Mob issued their Edicts from time to time by affixing their Placharts in the Merchants Coffee House and on the Corners of the Streets, where they remained whole Days and Nights." Even if it is impossible to describe in detail the dynamic relationship that developed between demonstrators and their leaders, it is clear that the leaders were generally obeyed. When someone had directed the crowd to back away from the fort on November 1, the protesters had quickly reassembled at Bowling Green. When a broadside appeared in the Coffee House on November 6, enjoining further violence, order was restored. Indeed, Colden informed the cabinet on December 13, "After the Packages of stamp'd Papers and Parchments were delivered to the Mayor and Corporation" on November 5, "the City remained quiet and I had the pleasure of delivering up the Administration to Sir Henry Moore on the 13th in as much quietness as could be expected in the present situation of the public affairs." And, in February, when radical leaders instructed the crowd not to demolish Charles Williams's home, they were obeyed.[17]

Complaints about anarchy should thus not be allowed to overshadow the restraint with which the crowd had acted. On the night of November 1, except for Major James's home, which may have been wrecked because he had been responsible for arming the fort and had so arrogantly threatened to use force to implement the Stamp Act, New York rioters "minimized" community and class tensions "by focusing their ire upon an object—like an effigy—which symbolized their grievances." Indeed, demonstrators did not break into the army's ordinance store or Gage's home, both of which lay outside the fort. By thus engaging, for the most part, in ceremonial misrule, the rioters affirmed that their aim was a change in government policy, not anarchy or the overthrow of the existing order. The crowd would not tolerate the use of stamps, but violence was not indiscriminate, nor was it directed against patricians because of their wealth and power. Even though the Liberty Boys were incensed at the legal profession for not practicing the law without stamps, there is no evidence that demonstrators ever physically abused a lawyer or destroyed his property as a result.[18]

Once Governor Moore assumed office, even Colden was safe. He received Moore's permission to absent the procession marking the transfer of power between them because he expected abuse. Still, after he moved out of the fort, he stayed at his son's home in town for days and "walked the Streets several Times, without having the least Disrespect shewn to him by any Person." He then retired to his Long Island farm, about fifteen miles from the city, where he remained "without the least Disturbance in any Shape." A merchant described the period after Moore's arrival as one of "peace and quietness" in which "Happy Unanimity Subsists." A year later the same writer reported that the Stamp Act's repeal had "occasioned almost the same good order and Harmony which we enjoyed before it took place." Nothing untoward happened, for example, when Moore reopened the fort and allowed residents inside its walls.[19]

Though Governor Moore and the patricians had joined together in bewailing the alleged chaos, they could do so only by ignoring the evidence to the contrary. Robert R. Livingston had antagonized radicals by his moderation, yet neither his person nor his property were harmed. In fact, demonstrators had been sufficiently deferential on November 2 to debate with him whether they should riot or go home. Even Captain Montresor, who so relentlessly condemned the Liberty Boys, conceded that the Pintard episode, which took place in mid-February 1766, was "the first instance of this licentiousness in open daylight."[20] Though historians do not know and cannot explain all that happened, it is fair to conclude that the crowd engaged in neither random violence nor class warfare. It instead enforced a standard of behavior that almost everyone in town accepted. The charge that the crowd was out of control arose chiefly from the fact that the traditional power wielders were not in control.

In December 1765 Colden had accused Moore of pandering to the mob, yet the latter's tact had afforded him more influence than the former had ever had. Moore felt secure enough by mid-December to refuse to issue letpasses, thereby keeping ships from leaving port. On December 31 the army even deterred a crowd from molesting the captains of the naval vessels blockading the coast. Several threats had been made, during the crisis, against the stamps stored at City Hall, but except for an incident in January 1766, when rioters burned several packages that had arrived on the *Polly*, the stamps remained untouched and were eventually returned to Britain.[21] Put simply, protesters could stop someone from either enforcing or obeying the Stamp Act, but that was the extent of their power. Popular participation in politics and crowd action caused royal officials and the elite to fear that their world was crumbling around them. Yet losers typically see chaos when what is actually taking place is change.

The alleged anarchy had failed to terrify even the Assembly. It had not only rebuked "Freedom" but had also ignored the radical demand that it repeal the Stamp Act. The resolves it adopted on December 18 were modeled on those the Livingstons had drafted, not on those Sears had sponsored. The House candidly asserted that Americans were "intitled to the same Rights and Liberties which his Majesty's *English* subjects both within and without the Realm have ever enjoyed." Taxation without representation was thus unconstitutional. But the House affirmed that New Yorkers "owe[d] Obedience to all Acts of Parliament not inconsistent with the essential Rights and Liberties of *Englishmen*."[22] If the resolves were pallid for seemingly expecting that words alone would secure a redress of grievances, they were resolute in refusing to succumb to the demands the Liberty Boys were making.

Lawmakers also stood up to the crown in December by declining to obey the Quartering (or Billeting) Act of March 1765. The law required civil authorities in America to house British soldiers stationed in a settled area in barracks, taverns, or vacant buildings, and to provision them. Colonial legislatures were even commanded to provide a daily ration of small beer, cider, or diluted rum. According to one historian, the act was "an abortion" that was unsuited to the situation in America. First, in asking for the legislation, Gage's original concern had been simply the problem of provisioning troops on the move, but the act required the colonies to help support soldiers billeted in settled areas, an expense that had customarily fallen on the crown. Because more troops were generally quartered in New York than elsewhere in America, the province would be forced to bear a disproportionate share of the burden. Second, the act required the colonial assemblies to appropriate funds to support these soldiers. By refusing to do so, a province now had a simple, effective way to flout royal authority. Third, the act again raised the issue of taxation without representation, for Parliament was claiming the right to compel colonial lawmakers, against their own will, to appropriate money.[23] Finally, the ministry never explained why troops had to be stationed in coastal cities in peacetime. The measure thus raised the specter that a standing army, for which the colonists were to be taxed, might someday be used to establish a tyranny over them.

The law became an issue when Gage wrote Moore on December 1, asking the province to appropriate funds for the army under the terms specified in the act. The Assembly did not categorically reject Gage's request; it explained instead that when troops were in barracks belonging to the king, they were ordinarily provisioned without expense to the colony in which they were stationed. Since barracks were available at Albany, no appropriation was needed. If funds were required in the future for army units marching through the province, the Assembly would consider the expense, but only after it had been incurred. Gage was disgruntled, for he had wanted to set a precedent. But the House had steered a middle course between capitulation and contumacy. The general accordingly wrote the cabinet that he would raise the matter again when more troops arrived in New York. The next time, however, he would make sure soldiers were already billeted in the "King's barracks," so that the Assembly would not again have an excuse to evade his request.[24]

If the House functioned well in a period of presumed anarchy, the city also came through the tenant uprising that had begun in Westchester County in the autumn of 1765 and had spread to Albany and Duchess counties by the next spring. Historians disagree over why the tenants rose against their landlords. Some see class conflict as the cause; others focus on New England immigrants who detested the system of landholding prevalent along the Hudson.[25] Regardless, when the rioters marched toward New York City to free some fellow protesters jailed there and to tear down the townhouses of their landlords, they found the entire community, the Liberty Boys included, united against them. Moore reported that "no measure was neglected for the preservation of the City. . . . The Regular Troops as well as the Militia had orders to be in readiness on the Alarm Bell being rung and every other precaution taken which common Prudence would suggest on such an occasion." Why the Liberty Boys opposed these rural rioters is unclear. Most likely, they had little understanding of or sympathy for what the rioters were demanding and viewed the struggle as a wanton assault upon property. If the protesters were mostly from New England, then the prejudice New Yorkers had felt against that region probably militated against an alliance between the two groups.[26]

Whatever the reason, civil authorities functioned efficiently enough to belie the argument that anarchy had engulfed the city. Livingstonites in the Council and the Assembly, on the bar and bench, infused the government with vigor, and the ringleaders were quickly tried and punished.

Most of the claims that anarchy reigned in the city came from persons who had reason to portray affairs that way: royal officials who had to justify capitulating to the mob; army officers who were humiliated by their own impotence; and patricians who could not embrace a future they could not command. Crown officials and the elite never forgot the night of November 1, or their feelings of impotence in the months that followed. Memories of the experience shaped their behavior until well after Independence.

Thomas Jones best articulated the elite's anxious disdain for the combative upstarts who had pushed their way into the political arena. First, there was "King Sears," whose father was "an oyster catcher," and whose father-in-law, Jasper Drake, "kept an alehouse for the entertainment of sailors, boatmen, and vagabonds." "A person of small abilities and no education," Sears was "a troublesome fellow, seditious, rebellious, an enemy to all good government, a low-lived, and a complete black-guard." He was plainly unsuited for a leadership role: "His tune is for mobbing; committees and popular meetings are his delight; his greatest pleasure." John Lamb was the offspring of a convicted thief who had settled in New York and had become an "honest" mathematical instrument maker. But John "longed to be a gentleman." After he failed in trade, "his pride would not suffer him to return to the business of making mathematical instruments." So he lived off "his father, and some of his wife's relations." During the Stamp Act troubles he became "a mighty leader, and haranguer, among the 'mobility.'" Once peace was restored, however, "John's popularity ceased. There was nothing left to keep it up." In the 1770s he again "headed mobs, excited sedition, talked treason, abused the Loyalists, harangued the populace, and damned the Tories." Alexander McDougall was the best of the lot. "The son of a poor industrious milkman," he became a privateer during the Seven Years' War and later operated what was "known among sailors by the name of 'a Slop-Shop.'" He married well and set himself up as a merchant. "Being a strong republican, a rigid presbyterian, extremely ambitious, a dabbler in politics, and having a pretty good genius, and by dint of application having obtained some knowledge in literature, his politics and religion paved the way to an intimacy with the triumvirate, and other leaders of the Republican faction."[27] Given who these three supposedly were, Jones believed that only the irrational passion of the mob could explain their rise to prominence. Small wonder that the elite were unprepared to share power with them and feared that anarchy had overtaken the city and the province.

In retrospect, throughout the Stamp Act ordeal, New Yorkers had been seeking a solution to the crisis that Britain's postwar policies had caused. Almost everyone agreed that the Stamp Act must be nullified. Debate centered on how to achieve that end. While traditional political leaders groped for a solution, the Liberty Boys seized center stage and by using crowd action forever enlarged the voice of the common people in political affairs. The radicals, however, were not as violent as their critics charged and never got their way as readily as has been claimed. Moreover, after November 1, both the Livingston and De Lancey parties worked to contain mob violence. The considerable success they had was due to the force of public opinion, which demanded that Britain's postwar imperial policies be negated without tearing the community asunder; violence was to be shunned and unity preserved.[28] Over the next decade, whenever the Livingstons, De Lanceys, or Sons of Liberty moved outside that consensus, public opinion began nudging them back within the bounds of accepted behavior. Even though New York City's population was multifarious and conflictive, that did not mean residents did not prize a sense of community. In fact, factious heterogeneity made people value community even more.

III

If the Liberty Boys had been more orderly in 1765–1766 than many have assumed, they had also been more organized, and that fact had only enhanced their influence. The Stamp Act crisis not only taught the radicals the power of public opinion, it schooled them in the skills needed for a successful revolution: propaganda, organization, the timely and effective use of force, and the politicization of the apathetic.[29] Propaganda, of course, was the least of their worries. Countless newspaper articles, by partisans of all persuasions, especially the Livingstons, spelled out why the Stamp Act was economically unsound and constitutionally amiss. Though the Liberty Boys explained in print how their strategy for fighting the tax differed from that of the patrician political elite, they did not emphasize their commitment to equality of opportunity. They doubtless saw no reason to publicize their differences with the Livingstons or the De Lanceys in that regard. It was sufficient for the moment to oppose parliamentary taxation as a tyrannical assault upon liberty and property.[30]

Though it is impossible to describe in detail the organization the Liberty Boys built or how it functioned, given the secrecy in which they operated, they clearly managed to use crowd action to rivet public attention on the Stamp Act crisis, to compel Colden to store the stamps at City Hall, and to chastise anyone who obeyed the act. Moreover, the radicals educated lower- and middle-class New Yorkers to the fact that they could be viable participants in the political process.[31]

The longer the crisis lasted, the more effectively the Liberty Boys broadened their power base. Sometime in December 1765 radical leaders became convinced that Britain might send soldiers to enforce the Stamp Act. On December 31, two New York Liberty Boys, Gershom Mott and Hugh Hughes, visited a tavern in New London, Connecticut, where they met six or seven of that community's militants. Hughes and Mott explained that the colonies ought to unite in self-defense. Because the British army would probably attack New York City first, Connecticut must be prepared to march to the city's defense. The two added that they were going next to Norwich and then Windham on the same mission. Meanwhile, two other New Yorkers were on their way to Boston to spread the message there. Before Mott and Hughes departed the next morning for Norwich, they and the New Londoners had adopted the resolutions the New York Liberty Boys had hoped for. Though the document expressed loyalty to George III, the signatories promised that they would "march with the utmost dispatch . . . on the first proper notice . . . to the relief of those that shall, are, or may be in danger from the *stamp-act*, or its promoters or abettors."[32]

This accord, the first step taken on an intercolonial basis to organize an armed resistance to the Stamp Act, indicated how far the crisis had gone. The proliferation of issues in dispute, the rioting on November 1, the emergence of partisan leaders (like Sears) who were prepared to use violence to achieve victory, the politicization of the masses, the rivalry for leadership, the withdrawal of moderate Livingstonites from active participation in the movement, the polarization of the two sides, and the possibility that Britain might use its army had together prepared some New Yorkers to meet force with force rather than to surrender.[33]

On Tuesday night, January 7, 1766, the Liberty Boys held a meeting at William Howard's tavern and adopted five resolves by which they vowed to "go to the last Extremity, and venture our Lives and Fortunes, effectually to prevent the said *Stamp-Act* from ever taking place in this City and Province." This pledge was not a reckless or idle threat made by impulsive hotheads, for the Liberty Boys were working to forge an accommodation with more moderate New Yorkers. It was agreed at the same meeting that anyone who used stamps would "be branded with everlasting Infamy"

and that those who conducted business without them would "be protected to the utmost Power of this Society." Nothing was said, however,
about compelling merchants or lawyers to break the law. Bowing to public
opinion, the Liberty Boys also vowed to keep the "Peace and good Order
of this City." If Britain planned to attack New York, it was time to rally
around principles all could support.[34]

Nor was the effort to reach out to other New Yorkers a mere whim,
made for propaganda purposes or without hope of success, for the January 7 meeting was noteworthy, too, for who attended. Prominent Anglican
De Lanceyites, including John Alsop, William Walton, Gerard Walton,
Theophylact Bache, and James De Lancey, were also present. And, despite
the real possibility of armed conflict, De Lancey patricians would attend
later Liberty Boy meetings. James De Lancey surely hoped by doing so to
benefit from the feud between Liberty Boys and Livingstons. Even so, the
situation was perilous, and he knew it. On January 10, Oliver De Lancey,
sounding not at all like the opportunist, had written his sister Susannah
in England that "If his Majesty's ministers should enforce [the Stamp
Act] by violent means I truly fear the consequences will be a civil war."
Oliver had already begun securing his family's papers against "the ravages
of the population should such hard times come," because "all Distinction
will then be lost and our family will hardly be unobserved in such a Scene
of Confusion and Distress."[35] Thus, it is clear that the De Lanceys knew
bloodshed would result if British troops sought to enforce the Stamp Act
and that Oliver was genuinely horrified by that prospect. Though he
surely hoped that his party, by its presence at these meetings, could help
to control the situation, the Liberty Boys could nevertheless claim elite
support for their military association.

The pace of activity only quickened after the January 7 meeting. The
next day, demonstrators destroyed the stamps that had arrived for Connecticut on the *Polly*. Sears doubtless wanted to signal to his new allies in
New London that New Yorkers would risk a confrontation with the army
to defend the rights of people in neighboring colonies. At a meeting on
February 4 the Liberty Boys established a committee of correspondence
to communicate with the Sons of Liberty throughout America. Everyone
understood the grave implications of what they were doing, for few of
those present would offer their services and thereby hazard their lives
and property if Britain retaliated. Sears and four other radicals finally
volunteered, and the meeting accepted their appointment. Formation of
the committee was crucial, for it gave radicals a network of colonial correspondents to match that which well-to-do merchants already possessed. It
was an organizational technique that Congregationalists and Presbyteri-

ans had used effectively in their struggles against the appointment of an Anglican bishop for the American colonies.[36]

A meeting on February 18 added a sixth resolution to those that had been adopted on January 7: "that we conceive the general safety of the colonies, and the British constitution, to depend on a firm union of the whole," and "we shall ever be ready to the utmost of our power, to assist our fellow subjects in the neighbouring provinces, to repel every attempt that may be made, to subvert or endanger the liberties of America." As the committee of correspondence explained two days later, New York's Liberty Boys "will not be enslaved without opposing force to force." Nor were they alone in their resolve. Quite a few towns in New York, Connecticut, Massachusetts, New Hampshire, New Jersey, Rhode Island, and Maryland also agreed either to establish their own committee of correspondence or to adopt the military association first approved at New London.[37] By April New York radicals were contemplating a "congress of the Sons of Liberty" to coordinate their activities in defense of American liberty.[38]

New York's Liberty Boys had thus accomplished much in five months. If their words and deeds can be taken at face value, the crisis had reached a crossroads. If Britain repealed the Stamp Act, there would be peace; if it enforced the law, there would be armed and organized resistance (not random violence or anarchy). It was the mother country's decision to make.

Though some royal officials in New York had already concluded that the army offered the only solution to the crisis, the cabinet in the end declined to turn the dispute into a martial contest. The Grenville ministry, which had passed the Stamp Act, had fallen from power in July 1765, and a new cabinet headed by the Marquis of Rockingham had succeeded it. Henry Seymour Conway, who had opposed the Stamp Act's passage, was now secretary of state for the Southern Department and thus the cabinet minister responsible for the thirteen colonies. In October he instructed Gage to aid the civil authorities in enforcing the act whenever a governor requested help, yet he admonished the general to temper his conduct "between Caution and Coolness." By December, with ministerial encouragement, London merchants had formed a committee to marshal British public opinion behind repeal. Led by Barlow Trecothick, the merchants disregarded the issue of Parliament's right to tax America and emphasized that the law was detrimental to Anglo-American trade. The act should be repealed, not because of what Americans believed, but because the tax would hurt Britain economically. In effect, the merchants redefined the dispute in a manner that would allow the new administration to end the crisis without having to admit defeat.[39]

When Parliament met in January 1766, Grenville demanded that the army enforce the Stamp Act. But the cabinet, which had been intimidated by the rioting in America and whose members were the political heirs of Sir Robert Walpole (who had practiced salutary neglect), decided to combine the measure's repeal with a declaratory act affirming Parliament's right to legislate for America. Even the king finally agreed that "Repealing [was] infinitely more eligible than Enforcing, which could only tend to widen the breach between this Country and America." Hence, the act was repealed on March 18. Later, when the cabinet discussed Gage's plan to move troops to the coastal cities to support civil government, both Barrington and Conway objected. The former feared it might "unnecessarily provoke" Americans, and the latter warned the general to "weigh that Matter well," for it "will probably be looked upon as an object of Jealousy, and may occasion Difficulties."[40]

On May 20 definitive word reached New York that the Stamp Act had been repealed. The bells tolled, and people celebrated in the streets. They continued rejoicing the next day, when a Liberty Pole was erected in the Fields. And that "Night ended in Drunkeness, throwing of Squibbs, Crackers, firing of muskets and pistols, breaking some windows and forcing off the Knockers off the Doors." On May 25 Governor Moore officially announced the news at the Coffee House, and the next day another celebration was held at Howard's tavern.

This street theater marked the city's return to normalcy. The Liberty Boys promptly put aside their plans for a general congress and for armed resistance in return for the usual pursuits of daily life. Though the strains in the social fabric of the city remained, the Liberty Boys' objective had been to overturn the Stamp Act, not to dismantle the empire or to overthrow the politico-economic power structure in the city. New York was not at this time "a political system in decay." It was a vibrant seaport community, populated by a politically, economically, religiously, and socially diverse population that had managed, despite genuine differences of opinion, to come together and to marshal the resources needed to defeat a British initiative that they believed would have crippled their economy and would have violated their constitutional rights.[41] Unfortunately for the British, the skills the Liberty Boys had honed in the crisis could be drawn upon later if the situation required.[42] Unfortunately for the local elite, the radicals had made themselves a presence in New York and now claimed the right to a major role in the political process.

Given what had happened, the city could not revert politically to what it had been before the crisis. Gage concluded that "*the Province never declared their Sentiments of Independency so openly before.*" He exaggerated. Because he feared the colonies would someday demand freedom, he assumed that that was their objective in 1765–1766. Still, New Yorkers now looked upon the empire from an altered perspective. John Watts informed Robert Monckton that he believed a "New Constitution will be form'd in time between the Mother Country and the Colonys." A New York merchant wrote that he hoped that because of the Stamp Act's repeal the mother country and her colonies would again be "cemented together"; yet he feared that both sides would now keep "*a jealous eye over each other.*" "Cethegus" captured the attitudinal change with these words: "Before the late War, the People of this Country were very little known or considered in England; nor indeed was our Importance fully understood, either by our Fellow Subjects or ourselves, before . . . the Stamp-Act." But "we were then roused out of a supine Inattention to the common Interest and combined Strength of the Continent, and led to form an Estimate of our Powers, to feel our own Consequences, and to impress a new, and that a very high[,] Idea of our Importance to the Mother Country. We exerted ourselves with Vigour and with Unanimity. The Effect was proportioned to our Wishes."[43]

The conflict's outcome was troubling for the empire and the colonies in yet another way. The behavior of New Yorkers in May indicated that they saw the struggle as one that America had won and Britain had lost. But the result had really been a compromise. On the one hand, residents had gained more than anyone could have expected in July 1764: Colden's humiliation and the Stamp Act's repeal. On the other, they had conceded more than they realized: continued enforcement of the new commercial regulations, the Sugar Act, and the Currency Act. The consequences of this implicit compromise would become evident in the next imperial crisis. "Every struggle ends," though "the end is usually the beginning of a new conflict."[44]

IV

The Stamp Act's repeal had left unresolved the underlying issues that had inflamed Anglo-American relations. The government still needed revenue, and many in Britain still wanted to check the spirit of autonomy in the colonies. New Yorkers, for their part, were mindful that if liberty had been preserved for the moment, it remained hostage to a future assault. The Stamp Act crisis thus impelled politicians on both sides of the Atlantic to find a more permanent solution.

Because most British politicians had feared that repeal of the Stamp

Act would erode Parliament's already precarious grip on the colonies, the Rockingham ministry had also sponsored the Declaratory Act, which asserted Parliament's "full power and authority to make laws and statutes of sufficient force and validity to bind the colonies and people of America, subjects of the Crown of Great Britain, in all cases whatsoever." Though the Declaratory Act would become an article of political faith for Rockinghamites, it had also been introduced as a tactical maneuver to win sufficient votes to overturn the troublesome Stamp Act. Members of Parliament could vote for repeal without feeling as if (or allowing others to charge that) they were by default accepting American constitutional arguments. Nonetheless, parliamentary debates in January 1766 had underscored how problematic the Declaratory Act was as a statement of principle. William Pitt and Isaac Barré insisted that Parliament could distinguish (and indeed had already distinguished) the power to tax from other aspects of sovereignty. The Commons, nonetheless, rejected Pitt's motion to strike the words "in all cases whatsoever" from the bill and thereby let stand the implication that Parliament could tax the colonies. When the ministry asked the Attorney General's opinion, however, he replied that the measure would include an assertion of Parliament's right to tax America only if the bill was amended to read: "as well in cases as Taxation, as in all other cases whatsoever." But the text was not altered, for the ministry wanted to avoid the word "taxation" in order to satisfy everyone.[45]

Unlike British politicians of the previous generation, the men who had come to power in the 1760s were legalistic in outlook and dedicated to "the consistent enforcement of law as an end in itself." In 1766, for example, when high prices caused food riots in England, the government suppressed them harshly with military force.[46] The Declaratory Act thus suited their temperament and reflected their inflexible approach to public policy. In the next crisis they would have a parliamentary statute to buttress their constitutional viewpoint. But their rigidity made compromise unlikely. Indeed, the law demonstrated that Britain had not relinquished its long-term objective of making the colonies bend to Parliament's will. The Declaratory Act was thus more than the finale to the first imperial crisis; it was the prelude to the second.

If the ministry was dogmatic, William Smith showed how flexible and resourceful a man steeped in New York's political culture could be. In a document written sometime between 1765 and 1767, allegedly at a time when New York's political system was in decay and its streets were drenched in anarchy, Smith argued that the colonies' growing maturity and their role in the Seven Years' War demanded a redefinition of their status in the empire. The issue was not "what the Constitution was, or is, but what, present Circumstances considered, it ought to be." "The Constitution . . . ought to bend, and *sooner* or *later* will bend; unless it is the Design of Heaven to infatuate and destroy us as a Nation." Because Smith was a Livingstonite and a future loyalist refugee, his argument merits attention. Britain's decision in 1764 to tax America directly was "the Origin of the Controversy." Yet he realized that the colonial assemblies were too parochial in outlook to appreciate imperial imperatives, especially revenue requirements. He thus proposed "that there be a Lord Lieutenant as in Ireland, and a Council of at least Twenty four Members, appointed by the Crown, with a House of Commons, consisting of Deputies chosen by their respective *Assemblies*, to meet at the central Province of New York, as the Parliament of North America." The crown, not Parliament, would make an annual requisition to the American legislature, which would agree on an appropriation and apportion the amount each colony was to pay. The local provincial assemblies would then determine how to raise the money. In return for freedom from parliamentary taxation, the colonies would recognize Parliament's "Legislative Supremacy, in *all Cases* relative to *Life Liberty and Property*, except in the Matter of Taxation for *general Aids*, or the immediate, internal Support of the American Government."[47]

The contrast between Smith's plan and the Declaratory Act (as the ministry interpreted it) showed how far apart the two sides had become and how unlikely it was that a viable solution could be reached at this point. The colonies had matured during the French and Indian War and had become both self-assured and self-conscious. Paradoxically, that same struggle for empire had convinced British politicians not only of America's economic and strategic value but of the need to curb colonial autonomy. Ironically, if Britain's long-term goal was to keep the colonies in subjection, its postwar behavior was endangering that objective. First by provoking the crisis, and then by letting it fester, the government had created an environment in which a faction like the Liberty Boys could emerge, develop a sense of group solidarity, organize, and even contemplate using armed force against Britain. Second, by venturing to curtail colonial autonomy, the government had made its preservation a key American objective. Third, by capitulating to colonial demands that the Stamp Act be repealed, the ministry had fed the confidence that radicals had come to feel in their own abilities and had swelled their reputation among the people. Indeed, their success made it more likely that New York's Liberty Boys would challenge the government again in the future, and the Declaratory Act had thus settled nothing. All that was needed to reignite the flames of discord and to resurrect the fundamental issues in dispute was another onerous Parliamentary initiative.[48] The next time, however, residents would have more experience in building a consensus, and the radicals would be more adept at organizing an opposition and judging when to take action.

PART II

THE TOWNSHEND ACTS CRISIS, 1766–1773

CHAPTER FIVE

Conflict Anew

Confident that it had restored harmony and reaffirmed parliamentary sovereignty, the Rockingham ministry undertook to eliminate the key American economic grievances. Its chief initiative was the Revenue Act of 1766. Drawn up for the most part by British merchants who traded with America (and who drafted the act with the cabinet's concurrence), it reduced the duty on molasses to one penny per gallon. Almost everyone considered that a concession to the colonies, even though the aim was to raise revenue, not to regulate trade: the act required that the impost be paid on molasses imported into the colonies from both the British and the foreign West Indies.[1] From the British perspective the bill had other attractive features, as well. For one thing, William Kelly, a retired New York merchant living in London, had testified before the Commons that despite the lower duty the new measure would dramatically increase the amount of molasses imported and thus enhance revenues. For another, the monies raised were to be used to help maintain the colonial military establishment. And despite American complaints about the rules already in force, the law tightened the administrative procedures established by the Revenue Act of 1764.[2]

The ministry also committed itself to monetary reform. Benjamin Franklin, Pennsylvania's agent, had crafted a bill repealing the Currency Act and creating a colonial paper currency backed by the Bank of England. When it was introduced in the Commons in April 1766, the cabinet pleaded for time to study the issue and promised to offer its own remedy at the next session. But the ministry soon fell from power and thus neither repealed the Currency Act nor devised its own policy.[3]

William Pitt, now the Earl of Chatham, headed the new ministry. The change appeared to bode well for the colonies, for he had opposed the Stamp Act. Pitt's membership in the Lords, however, weakened the ministry in the Commons, and illness diminished his influence. Further, because he was seeking to build a ministry of many talents, not every cabinet member shared his views regarding the Stamp Act and colonial taxation. Charles Townshend, Chancellor of the Exchequer, had concluded in the 1750s, while serving on the boards of Trade and Admiralty, that colonists should be taxed to pay the salaries of crown officials in America. And in January 1765 he had decided that America should pay part of the navy's cost, if only to demonstrate British "supremacy" over the colonies. Economic imperatives and the turmoil in America were also impelling Chatham to reassess his own beliefs. In early 1766 he had said that he would support stiffer measures if the colonies did not demonstrate greater obedience following the Stamp Act's repeal. Three months into office he was already frustrated over colonial affairs. Moreover, heavy taxation in Britain, the crushing deficit, and the need to fund the colonial military establishment made the entire cabinet, Chatham included, contemplate taxing America.[4]

Ideas circulating in New York, however, made it likely that a new crisis would erupt if Britain pressed the issues of taxation or sovereignty. "Philalethes," for example, dismissed the constitutional position Chatham had taken in the Stamp Act crisis and rebuked the American essayists who espoused the colonial cause yet "betrayed the liberties of America." They did so "by granting a sovereign jurisdiction in the Parliament over the Colonies, in all other respects but that of imposing internal taxes."[5]

"Philalethes" was not the only New Yorker with whom the earl would differ. In fact, the city's traders soon suffered a sharp ministerial rebuke for protesting the Revenue Act of 1766. The mercantile community had initially been enthusiastic about the measure, but the mood changed once a copy of it reached town. In a meeting held on November 28, 1766, the merchants prepared a petition roundly criticizing the commercial legislation enacted in the Grenville and Rockingham administrations. The Revenue Act of 1766 was faulted for increasing the "heavy burden" under which Americans "already laboured." Though combative in tone, the petition was moderate in content, for the merchants avoided constitutional issues and emphasized that they were protesting trade legislation. They were also confident the memorial would be effective, for the moving force behind it was William Kelly, back from Britain claiming he had Townshend's support for a petition.[6]

The memorial nonetheless outraged the cabinet. The wounds of resentment that had been opened in the Stamp Act crisis had plainly not healed, and the British obviously wanted assurances that the colonies had accepted the repeal as an act of parental indulgence, not as an admission of defeat or impotence. Chatham called the petition "highly improper" and its arguments "most grossly fallacious and offensive"; New York would draw upon itself a "torrent of indignation in parliament" for its "ingratitude." His reaction revealed much about how Britain saw the imperial relationship. New Yorkers were not, as William Smith believed, adults with a role to play in the empire, but children who must speak only when addressed and who must choose their words carefully, lest they not exhibit a due submissiveness. Certainly there was no thought that the constitution should be modified in recognition of America's growing maturity. To the contrary, the adverse reaction of so many showed that the Stamp Act troubles had caused a hardening, not a rethinking, of British attitudes about the Anglo-American relationship. This stiffening of opinion would make it much easier for the second imperial crisis to "spiral" in intensity and for officials to contemplate taking actions that would have shocked them in 1764.[7]

New York merchants were stunned. Henry and John Cruger thought the ministry's reaction "perfectly astonishing." They protested to a British correspondent about the charge circulating there of New York's "unwillingness" to accept "any subordination." How could the cabinet ignore the fact that merchants were obeying the acts about which they were objecting? Had the colonists not been told repeatedly that they "must humbly petition for relief" and their grievances would be redressed? John Watts wrote Robert Monckton that "tis really beneath the Dignity of a great Government to be so much alarmed and roused at it, be it ever so absurd or ill drawn, when it is considered as coming from only Some Merchants of one Single Trading Town"; if the merchants' "Request [is] unreasonable or Ridiculous, point it out and expose this Folly, but my real Opinion is, it contains too much truth." Isaac Sears would never again sign a petition for a redress of grievances.[8]

Meanwhile, the cabinet was tackling an even more controversial issue: the debt and the need for revenue. In January 1767 Lord Barrington submitted to the Commons an annual budget of £405,607 for the military establishment in America. In the debate that ensued Townshend announced that America should be taxed for these expenses, and that the ministry would submit legislation for that purpose before the session ended. In February Townshend declared that the distinction Americans made between internal and external taxation was fallacious, yet to placate them he would propose a tax on imports into the colonies. In April he decided that part of the revenues collected should be earmarked to pay the salaries of royal officials in the colonies. From an American perspective, that decision made his proposal more alarming, for it threatened to negate the power that colonial assemblies had gained over royal governors by withholding their salaries until they had signed the bills the legislatures deemed necessary. Townshend, of course, understood that. In early May, when colonial agents and some British merchants asked that the troops be withdrawn so that new duties would be unnecessary, he spoke not of his plan to pay the salaries of crown officials but of the need for an army, and of his desire to finance it "in the manner most easy to the people." On May 13, when he presented his taxation scheme to the Commons, he excluded colonial agents from the galleries. His speech ignored the need for funds to pay for keeping troops in America and spoke of his aim "to assert the sovereignty of Parliament." Again, revenue was being raised not only to ease Britain's financial problems but to buttress its authority over supposedly wayward colonies.[9]

As passed, the Townshend Act levied duties on glass, lead, paint, paper, and tea imported into the colonies. The money raised was to be spent both for colonial defense and for defraying the cost of government and the administration of justice in America. A companion measure created an American Board of Customs that reported to the British Treasury Board and had power over all colonial customs officials. A third statute, the New York Restraining Act, suspended that colony's Assembly until it complied with the Quartering Act. Another law, passed the next year, established four new vice-admiralty courts in America, so that persons accused of breaking a trade law no longer had to go to Halifax but could instead have their cases tried in Boston, Philadelphia, or Charleston. Charles Townshend died suddenly on September 4, 1767, and never had to deal with the American reaction to what became known as the Townshend Acts.[10]

II

If budgetary constraints and the desire to assert parliamentary sovereignty over the colonies had impelled Chatham down the path Grenville had trod in 1764, other issues also conspired to widen the Anglo-American rift. Especially egregious was the decision that had been made after the Seven Years' War to keep an army in America. If the government was concerned about defending newly acquired territory, it also wanted those troops handy "to secure the Dependence" of the colonies.[11] But the Stamp Act crisis had quickly exposed the pitfalls of that decision. As soon as Colden espied resistance, he asked Gen. Thomas Gage for help. Though redcoats had never fired on the crowd during the November riots, Colden had opened a Pandora's box. By threatening to use the army, he had made it a public enemy. The troops, in turn, despised the people. The more the two groups mistrusted each other, the more the colonists defined themselves in anti-army terms. If the soldiers were British, New Yorkers were American. If the redcoats were instruments of oppression, residents were the guardians of liberty. These deepening contrasts did not bode well for Anglo-American unity. Equally important, the aversion that civil officials had felt to using force angered many army officers, convincing some that the military alone could uphold parliamentary supremacy and even the score against a foe.[12]

In February 1766 Gage had begun moving troops to the coastal cities to "support" the civil authorities and to ensure political stability.[13] But he underestimated the resentment the army might cause. Soldiers and civilians had not cooperated well in the Seven Years' War, and many Americans considered the military a threat to freedom. By taking the steps he did, Gage made the army a convenient target for enmity and attack, ran the risk that colonists would object to the unconstitutionality of a standing army in peacetime, and gambled that he would not be plagued by the civil-military disputes that typically occur in such situations. Worse, the fact that redcoats were quartered in town increased the chance they would someday be employed against residents; the mere availability of a mode of coercion makes it more probable it will someday be used, even should that be inadvisable.[14]

Fresh troops arrived in New York in June 1766, and newspaper reports make it clear that their presence pummeled the army's reputation. One evening several inebriated officers smashed a street lamp. When an innkeeper upbraided them, they wounded him with their swords. Escorted by two armed redcoats, the officers then proceeded down Broadway, demolishing street lamps along the way. When the city's watchmen overtook them, a scuffle ensued, and several in the watch were injured, two badly. One officer was arrested, but the others escaped. After collecting about a dozen soldiers, including those guarding the general's quarters, the officers who had escaped marched to City Hall to free their jailed compatriot. Another melee ensued, and several more watchmen were hurt. The offending officers were finally arrested the next day.[15] As the example indicates, liquor was often a problem, and drunken soldiers could be destructive of property and vicious to anyone whom they imagined had offended them. On another occasion, late one evening, a gang of redcoats forced their way into a poor cartman's abode. They "wounded him in a terrible Manner" and then proceeded to a stable where they hamstrung his horse, his "only Means" of "Subsistence." City magistrates repeatedly warned townspeople that the law forbade the sale of strong liquor to soldiers between sunset and sunrise, yet drinking, fighting, and crime persisted.[16]

A law-enforcement problem had soon became politicized. Gov. Henry Moore charged that "no means has been left untried by the Populace" to provoke the troops "to committ some action, for which public censure might be drawn of them." If that was the plan, it succeeded. On Sunday night, August 10, 1766, soldiers cut down the Liberty Pole. According to a newspaper, it was done "by Way of Insult to the Town" and caused "great Uneasiness." The next day, Isaac Sears led two thousand people to the Commons, where soldiers were training, to demand an apology. A fight ensued, and both sides later disagreed over who had caused it. Montresor alleged that demonstrators had used the "most scurrilous and abusive language"; the newspapers claimed "the Soldiers were intirely the Aggressors."[17] Whoever had started it, brickbats were soon flying, and the troops defended themselves with bayonets. When the regiment's commanding officer and Gage's aide-de-camp pushed their way through the crowd to stop the fighting, they were insulted the entire way. Someone even tried to pull one of the officers off his horse. The officer drew his sword but refrained from using it when civilians began brandishing pistols. Army officers finally restored order, but the damage was done. A newspaper reported that residents were "very uneasy that such a Number of arm'd Men, without any visible Occasion for them, are station'd among us, and suffer'd to patrol the Streets, as in a Military or conquer'd Town."[18]

On Tuesday Liberty Boys boasted that they would not let redcoats "beat their Retreat and Tattoo through the Streets [except] at their peril." That afternoon radicals erected a new Liberty Pole in honor of "George, Pitt, and Liberty."[19] When a drummer boy made some scurrilous remarks, the mob verbally abused him. At this point accounts of the incident diverge. According to a civilian, the crowd released the culprit and went about its business, until a gang of redcoats appeared and assaulted the people with bayonets. According to Gage, a mob chased the drummer and another soldier to the barracks, where they were reinforced by twenty or thirty soldiers who drove the rioters back to the Commons. City magistrates rushed to the scene, and British officers ordered the troops back to their quarters. Angry residents then surrounded the barracks and dispersed only when it was clear that the soldiers would not be provoked.[20]

If Montresor is to be believed, the city did not return to normal for a week. On Wednesday Liberty Boys heckled troops parading in the Fields, arguing that the area belonged to residents. The next day soldiers were abused in the streets, and authorities had to curtail all contact between the two sides. On Friday the Liberty Boys organized a petition drive demanding the army's withdrawal from town. But no patrician would sign it, and someone tore down the petitions posted about town. On Saturday redcoats were jeered while exercising in the Fields. On Sunday radicals urged vendors in the public markets not to sell to army personnel. On Monday the Liberty Boys demanded that the commander-in-chief prohibit off-duty soldiers from carrying arms. The same day two writs were served on an army commander for five thousand pounds in damages, for which his soldiers were supposedly responsible. The next day a crowd hurled insults and a stone into the officer's home. City magistrates failed to restore order until Gage agreed to surrender to civil authorities any soldier who rioted.[21]

Moore explained the cause of the unrest: "The great objection here is that of having any Troops at all[,] for while they continue in this town, those licentious Assemblies of the People (who call themselves the Sons of Liberty . . .) must be suppressd and the hands of the magistrates so far strengthened that the Laws of the Country must again take Place." True, the army could not quash a civil disturbance without authorization from the governor and his Council, and they never gave it. But redcoats had been acting on their own as a counterforce to the Liberty Boys, who could no longer be sure they commanded the streets. Try as they might, however, the radicals could not drive the army out of New York, for public opinion opposed that. Demanding that the crown not barrack troops in town seemed too provocative a break with past practice, especially when the Liberty Boys shared some responsibility for the unrest. Moreover, though people detested the military, it brought hard currency and jobs into the community in a period of economic stagnation. Hence, when the Liberty Pole was cut down again on September 23, it caused "a good deal of Disturbance." But the Liberty Boys bowed to the public consensus and the next day erected another pole without provoking a fight with the army.[22]

There matters stood until the annual celebration of the Stamp Act's repeal on Wednesday, March 18, 1767, at the King's Arms Tavern near the upper barracks. The next morning, when the town awoke, it found its Tree of Liberty felled again. Acceding to public opinion, the Sons of Liberty responded with restraint and erected a new pole before sunset. For protection it was encased in iron. Soldiers snuck back to the Fields on Thursday night. They sought first to cut down the pole and, when that failed, to dig it out of the ground. Learning what was afoot, the Liberty Boys assembled in force. A battle might have ensued if officers had not ordered the soldiers away. On Saturday night a gang of redcoats returned and tried in vain to topple the symbol of New York's triumph over the Stamp Act. On Sunday night radicals posted a guard, which soldiers declined to challenge. On Monday evening a detachment of redcoats marched past the spot where civilian guards had stood the night before, and fired into Bardin's tavern, a radical haunt operated by the Anglican Edward Bardin. Fortunately, no one was killed. The next afternoon another abortive attempt was made against the Liberty Pole. This time the governor, the general, and city magistrates took "effectual measures" to end the trouble.[23]

Civil-military relations nonetheless remained strained. In August a group of regulars parading in the Fields assaulted several spectators. When fresh troops reached port in September, they disembarked from their ship armed; they were entering "an enemy's country" and wanted to be able to repel an attack. A year later, in October 1768, while Gage was preparing to send troops to Boston, "A North-American" would condemn the presence in the colonies of a standing army whose purpose was to eradicate liberty; he would call for a boycott of British goods until colonial grievances were redressed. And New York merchants would refuse to let Gage hire vessels to transport troops to Boston.[24]

If the army failed to act as an impartial police force, it was problematic in another way, too. In March 1768 Moore would write Lord Shelburne, the secretary of state for the Southern Department, of the difficulty he was having restoring the prestige of civil government. Gage was claiming "by Virtue of his Instructions a Superiority over all the Governors of America *upon all occasions.*" Gage called the affair "a trifling dispute" but wrote Amherst and Barrington for support.[25] The feud had been festering at least since the June 4, 1766, celebration of the king's birthday. Gage had refused to join in the festivities until Moore had sent two councillors to apologize, because Moore had waited upon his Council and the city magistrates before paying his respects to the commander-in-chief. By May 1767 rumors had begun circulating that Lady Moore and Mrs. Gage were feuding over who should take precedence at public events. The prickly issue resurfaced on June 4, 1767, when Moore sent two of his councillors to ask the general to join him in commemorating the king's birthday. Gage refused, since Moore had not invited him in person. The argument reached a crisis in February 1768 when several army officers sought to settle the matter by inviting both men to a party and giving "Precedence to General Gage." In the event, Moore promptly retired from the group.

The next day Gage sent a copy of his instructions to the governor and had the king's Order in Council of December 17, 1760, giving the military commander-in-chief precedence over governors, read to his officers.[26] Moore provided the general with an extract of his own instructions, requiring "all Officers and Ministers *Civil and Military* and all other Inhabitants of the Province . . . to be *obedient, aiding and assisting*" him.[27]

The dispute was not, as Gage had argued, "ridiculous." Moore feared that civilians believed the general's claim was a "step towards the total abolition of the Civil Power in order to introduce a Military Government." Gage insisted that he had tried to ignore the dispute but found that doing so created "a Doubt amongst some of the Officers, whether they should obey me." Trained in the art of war, habituated to a harsh discipline that subordinated personal freedom to the attainment of military objectives, and unaccustomed to acting as a police force over a restive population, these officers had been humiliated by the indignities to which the army had been subjected since 1765.[28] Civil officials accordingly became their scapegoat, and Gage objected to how civil magistrates handled the mob: these officials "depend so much upon [the mob] for their Elections into the Magistracy or General Assembly, that they act with Timidity, and even Suffer themselves to be insulted." Captain Montresor reported that Moore had stood by more than once while the crowd insulted the crown, and that he, Montresor, wished New York were ruled, as Canada was, by a military government. Morale, if Gage judged correctly, was quite low. Asserting, indeed demanding, the general's right to take precedence over the governor was a symbolic gesture to reestablish the army's dignity.[29]

On May 14, 1768, Lord Hillsborough, who was secretary of state for the American Department (a cabinet position created that year), would admonish Moore that the "contest" should be "amicably adjusted" between the two "without it becoming necessary for Government at Home to interfere." In June 1768, on the king's birthday, Moore would be at Albany, and "an elegant entertainment" would be "given [in New York City] by general Gage." Though the controversy thus cooled, subsequent governors would not let it die. In 1770 Lord Dunmore would ask the cabinet to settle the issue before he assumed the New York governorship. The argument would flare again in 1772 while William Tryon was governor. And it was Colden, who had again served as acting governor between September 1769 and October 1770, who had persuaded Tryon to protest. Gage wrote Barrington that he was "sorry" the "idle talk" about "how to place People" at official functions had resurfaced. Yet everyone understood that one's place bespoke one's power. In March 1775, Tryon would ask the ministry to clarify the proper relationship between civil and military officials, for he believed the military's authority had been unwisely expanded at the civil government's expense. And in September he would write that to bolster the dignity of civil government "the governor in his province [must] take the preeminence of all others except the blood royal on every occasion not merely military."[30]

From an American perspective, Tryon's assessment was correct. The memorial the First Continental Congress sent to the king in 1774 had protested that "the Authority of the commander in chief, and, under him, of the brigadiers general has in time of peace, been rendered supreme in all the civil governments in America."[31] The Declaration of Independence charged that the king "has affected to render the Military independent of and superior to the Civil Power." Indeed, as John Shy has explained, the "presence of regular troops in any colony automatically introduced a center of authority that lay outside the political structure of the colony, and reduced the prestige of the governor accordingly." Not once after 1763 did the commander-in-chief lose an argument with a governor. The army also gave the cabinet an alternate source of information about how colonial affairs should be handled. In consequence, "military centralization" ultimately persuaded British officials to opt for a martial solution to what was a political problem.[32]

In sum, keeping an army in the colonies had long-term consequences that British officialdom never fully understood. Maintaining the army complicated the budgetary crisis and required repeated efforts to raise a revenue in the colonies; it raised constitutional questions about stationing a peacetime army in America; it provoked disputes between military and civil officials over which should take precedence; it created in the officer corps a voluble circle antagonistic to civil government in the colonies, a corps cocksure that force was the only credible option left in Anglo-American relations; and it handed radicals a potentially explosive issue to exploit. American opposition, in turn, further persuaded Britain that the spirit of independence was waxing stronger and that more forceful steps would be required to sustain parliamentary supremacy. The dynamic was a volatile one.

III

While civil-military relations were causing problems, so too was the Currency Act. The Assembly had protested the law in its 1764 petition to the House of Commons, yet in 1766 New York was still waiting for

Parliament to reconsider the act. Frustrated, several lawmakers requested the governor's help. Because his instructions obliged him to veto all paper-money bills, even those bills that did not contravene the Currency Act, Governor Moore wrote home in March 1766, asking for new instructions. The timing could not have been better. Before his letter reached London, the Rockingham ministry had already agreed to introduce legislation at Parliament's next session to revise the Currency Act. And in June the Privy Council decided that Moore could sign a paper-currency bill under certain specified conditions: the measure could not contravene the Currency Act by making paper money legal tender; it could not authorize an emission of more than £260,000 or for longer than five years; it must create a sinking fund to redeem the money; and it had to include a clause suspending its operation until the crown approved it.[33]

Although New York's economic plight was palpable, the House refused to pass the act in the form the cabinet required. The lawmakers explained to Moore on November 13 that they were "determined to bear our Distress as well as we are able," unless Moore agreed "to pass a Bill without such an unusual Clause." James Duane felt the House would "never" accept a suspending clause. Peter R. Livingston reported that Moore thought the ministry had made the demand knowing the Assembly would not comply. New Yorkers were nonetheless optimistic that they would get what they wanted without a suspending clause. The *Mercury* had reported in July 1766 that Parliament would enact legislation enabling the colonies to emit paper money and that the provincial assemblies would even have an opportunity to preview the bill. By December New York's agent Robert Charles had sent the Assembly a draft of a currency bill, and on December 11 the Assembly petitioned Parliament to enact a law allowing the colonies to issue paper money as legal tender in all cases except "in discharge of British Debts."[34]

The optimism of December wilted quickly, however. People learned in April how angry official London was over the merchants' protest against the Revenue Act of 1766, and in May they learned that Parliament would neither repeal the Currency Act nor let the Assembly issue paper money. That fall, news of the Townshend Duties acted like rain against the autumn's foliage. Complaints about New York's economic predicament became frequent. "A Tradesman" lamented, "What a dismal Prospect is before us! a long Winter, and no work; many unprovided with Fire-wood, or Money to buy it; House-rent, and Taxes high; our Neighbors daily breaking, their Furniture at Vendue." "Probus" urged that "in this time of great distress," the wealthy should "spontaneously" settle their accounts. Even if the sums involved were "trifling" to the rich, they were of "great consequence" to artisans of limited means.[35]

Well-to-do merchants, however, were suffering their own financial embarrassments. In November 1766 James Beekman wrote two British creditors, grumbling how the shortage of paper money had kept his debtors from making payment, so that he could not make "remittances for all the goods" he had "this fall Imported." Because of the "Scarcety of Cash" in New York, "we daily have many Bankrupts." A year's time would bring no relief. In September 1767 he would tell another creditor: "I exspected to have made you remittance for the ballence of what I owe you, but the Dullness of Trade and the Scarcity of Cash has prevented me." He would send money when he could, though he doubted that would be soon. Hopefully, Parliament would allow "us to Emit a Paper Currency."[36]

The discouraging news from England and the harsh business climate at home led "A Tradesman" to urge residents to emulate Boston by agreeing to patronize local artisans instead of buying imported manufactured items.[37] A writer in John Holt's *New York Journal* asked the city to issue one hundred thousand pounds in five- and ten-pound "Notes of Hand" at 5 percent interest. That would satisfy the need for a circulating medium, and the venture would earn about fifty thousand pounds to help finance the city's budget and to create jobs. "Amicus" wanted the well-to-do to open a bank and loan office and to use the profits to promote commerce and manufacturing.[38] "Phileleutheros" reminded residents of the good that the Society for Promoting the Arts in New York had accomplished in the Stamp Act crisis and exhorted the city to encourage manufacturing. A "strict economy, both in our dress and living," he insisted, would improve "the public welfare" and safeguard "freedom." The society soon began meeting regularly, and by early 1768 would establish a program of premiums and awards to foster local manufacturing.[39]

When the Assembly convened in November 1767, it sought to circumvent the restrictions the Privy Council had imposed by asking Moore to sign legislation establishing a loan office that could issue at interest a sum equal to one-half the amount allowed in his instructions; the bill did not include a suspending clause. But it was not alone the scarcity of money that troubled the Assembly. In September Abraham de Peyster, the provincial treasurer, had died. When his accounts were examined, the House found that he had misappropriated fifty thousand pounds. Even after his estate was settled, about thirty thousand pounds remained outstanding. The aristocratic de Peyster had been linked by marriage to many New York patricians, who relished neither a close inspection of their financial dealings with him nor the imposition of new taxes to cover the shortfall.

Thus the money raised by the proposed loan office would both offset the embarrassing shortage in funds and help to defray the cost of the troops stationed in New York without hiking existing imposts or levying a land tax.[40]

Unable to sign the bill, Moore begged the ministry to grant New York relief. Assembly elections were near, and the next session would be marked by "returns of duty and submission" if Britain was more forthcoming. Hillsborough replied that if the House would not add a suspending clause to the bill, Moore could send a draft of it to London for approval before its passage in New York. Moore did so in May 1768, and Hillsborough promised to lay the measure before the Board of Trade. Meanwhile, in the summer of 1768, the shortage of specie became even more acute, after the new American Board of Customs at Boston instructed Andrew Elliot, Collector of the Customs at New York, to accept only specie in payment of the duties. Previously, because of the economy's woes, Elliot had taken paper money or extended credit. Moore wrote London at once, but the ministry refused to ask the Treasury to alter the policy. Worse, Hillsborough never sent New York's paper-money bill to the Board of Trade, and the matter continued to bedevil New York politics and the imperial relationship after the elections.[41]

IV

While seeking permission to emit paper money, the Assembly was also grappling with the predicament created by General Gage's persistent efforts to enforce the Quartering Act. Once again, the way the Livingstons parried these initiatives refutes the charge that their behavior in this period was marked only by "cynicism" and a readiness "to exploit imperial issues for party advantage."[42]

When Gage had asked for an appropriation in December 1765, three years prior, the House had evaded compliance, arguing that Britain had heretofore supplied soldiers quartered in the king's barracks at Albany without expense to the colony. Outfoxed, the general decided he would make sure that the next time he requested aid all the royal barracks would be occupied.[43] New York would thus be forced to set a precedent the other provinces would be obliged to follow. But if Gage had wanted a confrontation in 1766, the Assembly was determined to avoid one. In December 1765 the colonies and Britain had been divided by the Stamp Act; it had been a time to draw lines and stake out positions. By May 1766 the crisis was over, and it was now time to restore harmony and to mute discordant notes. Moreover, tenant farmers in the Hudson Valley were rioting, and events had reached the point where the governor and Council needed the army's assistance. Gage, of course, expected that in return the House would obey the Quartering Act. Important, too, was the political situation. If Livingstonite lawmakers (and landowners) were to comply with the Quartering Act, that would give the De Lanceys a potent issue at the next Assembly elections, which by law had to be held by early 1768.[44]

When Governor Moore asked the Assembly on June 13, 1766, to appropriate money to furnish "Quarters, Bedding, Utensils, etc." for soldiers about to arrive in town, Livingstonites groped for a way out of the dilemma. The troops were even left aboard sloops for two days in "heavy Rains" before the governor could persuade the House to answer his message.[45] When it finally responded on June 19, its reply was evasive, but it did offer Gage a compromise. The Assembly explained that it had already given a considerable amount and would continue to contribute its fair share by providing "for a proportionable Part of the Troops with the Rest of the Colonies," but its commitment could not be open-ended. In this particular instance, however, if the king's service would suffer because the Assembly could not comply with the general's request, £3,990 had already been earmarked in the provincial treasury for the commander-in-chief, and he could spend it at his own discretion.[46]

The Assembly thus refused compliance with the Quartering Act but offered Gage money if he really required it. This was a pragmatic compromise, devised by William Smith, that let the province cooperate without conceding that Parliament could require it to allocate funds. On June 20, however, Moore sent the House a second message. This one included an extract of a letter from Gage pointing out that his predecessor had returned the said £3,990, since it had not been needed at the time. Gage would now accept the funds but wanted to know whether it was the Assembly's "Intent" that he "should draw" the money "according to the Act of Parliament for quartering His Majesty's Forces in North America." His aim was "to require a categorical answer" concerning the Assembly's willingness "to shew that obedience which was due to an Act of Parliament." The House evaded the trap by voting on June 23 to furnish the barracks at New York and Albany with "Beds and Bedding, Fire Wood, Candles, and Utensils" for two battalions and an artillery company. It declined, however, to mention or to comply with the Quartering Act. Though the law required the legislature to appropriate funds for small beer, cider, salt, and vinegar, the House refused, for these items were not supplied to troops stationed in Europe. At this point Gage decided that he had extracted all he could from the Assembly, and Moore signed the bill on July 3.[47]

The controversy, then, had been finessed, not resolved. Lord Shelburne, the secretary of state for the Southern Department in the new Chatham administration, sent Moore a stern letter on August 9, 1766, underscoring the cabinet's determination to settle the dispute by coercion rather than by persuasion or reward. It was the "duty" of the American colonists "to obey the acts of the Legislature of Great Britain." Hence, it could "not be doubted that . . . New York after the Lenity of Great Britain so recently extended to America will not fail duly to carry into execution the Act of Parliament . . . for quartering His Majestys Troops in the full extent and meaning of the Act." On November 17 the governor sent the Assembly a copy of Shelburne's letter, but the lawmakers were unmoved. After spending a month pondering "the Form in which their refusal should appear," they declined to grant any funds, arguing that the burden was too much to bear. Moore considered dissolving the legislature and holding elections, but decided against it: "the same members would have been returned again, a Flame would have been lighted up throughout the Country, and not a single advantage derived from it."[48]

Why did the Livingston-led Assembly take a more resolute stand in November than it had in the summer? Circumstances had changed, and the House was reacting accordingly. Order had been restored in the Hudson Valley, euphoria over the Stamp Act's repeal had subsided, and people were beginning to examine critically the other measures Britain was pursuing. News had already reached the city about the Revenue Act of 1766 and the demand for a suspending clause in currency legislation. Moreover, when Parliament had repealed the Stamp Act, it had recommended that the colonial assemblies compensate the victims of mob violence. Consequently, on December 19, 1766, the House granted Major James, whose house had been so thoroughly despoiled, over £1,745 and the other sufferers about £580. Though it ignored Cadwallader Colden's losses, the sum granted to James and the others was considerable, and doubtless influenced how much the Assembly had been prepared to give Gage in the same session.[49]

The situation was an ever shifting one, however, and the resolute affirmation of colonial rights that had seemed appropriate in November 1766 was not in the best interests of New York or the Livingstons seven months later. Hence, when Moore again requested funds for the army on May 27, 1767, the Assembly quickly agreed to allocate three thousand pounds. It even made the appropriation a blanket one, so that Gage could purchase whatever supplies he wanted, including small beer, cider, salt, or vinegar. The House could nonetheless console itself that it had not conceded principle, for it had scrupulously avoided acknowledging the Quartering Act. The general was unhappy, but practical considerations persuaded him to accept the bill as being the best he could expect for the moment, and Moore signed it. As painful as it must have been, the Assembly had had good reason for making the appropriation. First, the province had a boundary dispute with Massachusetts pending before the Privy Council, and now was not the time to antagonize London. Second, ominous news was reaching town that the cabinet was infuriated by New York's behavior and planned to send an army to the province. Under the circumstances, the lawmakers concluded that their best course was to calm the waters.[50]

Nor had they misjudged the situation. In January 1767 Gage had written Barrington complaining that the Assembly had refused to allocate money for the army, at its session just past. He concluded with a warning: "The Colonists are taking large strides towards Independency," and the ministry must "shew them that these provinces are British Colonies dependent on her, and that they are not independent States." At a cabinet meeting on March 12 Shelburne advocated replacing Moore with a military governor empowered to use force when needed and to billet troops in private homes whenever the Assembly ignored the Quartering Act. Conway proposed levying a special port duty at New York to defray the cost of stationing troops there. It was finally agreed that Parliament should enact a law restraining the New York Assembly from passing any legislation after October 1, 1767 until it complied with the Quartering Act. And on March 26 the Privy Council disallowed the appropriations bill the province had passed in June 1766, because it violated the Quartering Act. When Townshend then outlined the administration's policy before Parliament on May 13, he explained that New York was being singled out for having completely defied the Quartering Act; making an example of the province would dissuade other colonies from pursuing a similar course.[51]

The New York Restraining Act was adopted soon after the Townshend Duties became law. According to Merrill Jensen, this act was the most drastic action Parliament would take against the colonies until 1774, and was a stunning encroachment on the royal prerogative. Prior to the enactment of that law, it had been the royal governors who had been responsible for calling, proroguing, and dissolving colonial assemblies, and the crown had been responsible for approving or disallowing legislation passed in the colonies. Parliament was now asserting its ultimate authority over those decisions. Thomas Pownall, a former Massachusetts governor, considered the measure "arbitrary and despotic." If a colonial assembly was "a legislative, deliberative body, . . . it must have a right to deliberate, it must have a right to decide; if it has the free will to say Aye, it must have the same power of will to say No. You may properly order an executive power to execute; but how, and with what propriety can you order this deliberative body to exert its will in only one prescribed direction?"[52]

The outward calm with which residents greeted the Restraining Act, which could be invoked in New York by the governor for cause, was striking. At its next session the Assembly allocated fifteen hundred pounds for the army before Moore even asked for money. As always, the situation was complex, and the Assembly was carefully balancing several factors. To begin with, it had previously refused to compensate Colden for his losses in the Stamp Act riots, claiming that he had been personally responsible for what had happened. Colden retaliated by having a pamphlet privately printed and distributed to key British politicians; it erroneously blamed the Livingstons for orchestrating the rioting in 1765. Understandably, then, the party did not want to draw more attention to itself in 1767 by refusing to make an appropriation for the troops stationed in New York. Further, the Livingstons were alarmed by New York's precarious financial situation. Depressed economic conditions had reduced the revenue the colony was collecting from existing taxes, and this was the House's first meeting following de Peyster's death. Yet the Assembly did not want to refuse an appropriation for the troops on the grounds that it lacked funds. At the cabinet's behest Moore had been investigating the quitrent situation in New York. Although the revenue due from the quitrents totaled £1,800 sterling per annum, less than £500 had been collected each year, and over £18,500 were in arrears in 1767. The governor was preparing a map of all New York land grants, and the attorney general was drafting a law to expedite the collection of back taxes. Landowners, of course, wanted neither a close inspection of their land titles nor the prompt payment of the quitrents due on real estate they held for speculation.[53]

The Livingstons were walking a tightrope, for they did not want the governor to invoke the Restraining Act or a crowd to riot over the loss of the Assembly. Governor Moore came to their rescue on both counts. In a letter to Lord Shelburne, the secretary of state for the Southern Department, on August 21, 1767, he had said that he had almost vetoed the Assembly bill of June 1767, which had granted three thousand pounds for the army, for "it was intended the money should appear to have been granted only upon a Requisition made by me as Governor of the Province and not in obedience to what was prescribed by the Act of Parliament." He had signed the act only because the troops badly needed supplies. Yet,

on October 5, after receiving the Restraining Act, Moore reversed himself
and informed Shelburne that he had not immediately imposed the penalties set down in that measure because the June appropriation furnished
the soldiers "with all the articles mentioned in the act of Parliament in as
full and ample a manner as if they had been particularly specified in the
bill." And he would later fail to tell Shelburne that he had arranged matters beforehand, so that in December the Assembly was able to appropriate money for the army before he requested it. In effect, he had con-
nived with the Livingstons so that they could again evade the Quartering
Act. He then wrote the ministry that the Assembly's noncompliance was
in fact capitulation. By doing so, he may have forestalled an outbreak of
mob violence in the city. And the Livingstons, whom he favored, could
stand for reelection in early 1768 without ever having obeyed the Quartering Act. Though money had been appropriated and a purist might
argue that, in spirit, the Livingstons had compromised their beliefs, the
Assembly was still meeting, the Quartering Act would not haunt the party
in the 1768 elections, and the Livingstons could rightly claim they had
not once violated their constitutional principles.[54]

What is more, the opposition could not single out the Livingstons for
attack at election time for having granted the army money, for the De
Lanceys had joined in the compromise. Though Consensus historians
have charged that New York's politicians in the late 1760s acted only from
self-interest, and Edward Countryman has charged that the political system in New York was in decay, both parties knew how crucial it was to rise
above partisanship and to display real political leadership. A few politicians, at first, were "for an absolute Refusal, going without a Legislature,
and risking the Wrath of the Mother Country," but most wanted neither
to obey the Quartering Act nor to suffer enforcement of the Restraining
Act. Accordingly, a select group from the Council and Assembly gathered
secretly to devise a solution, which both houses then approved in a joint
session at City Hall. Because the meetings were extralegal, no entries were
made in the journal of either body. Oliver De Lancey, John Watts, and
Daniel Horsmanden represented the De Lanceys. To save the Assembly,
the participants agreed "to give £1500, and make the Money issuable by
the Governor, with the Advice of the Council, by an Act, without any
Preamble, or the least Reference *in Terms* either to the Mutiny [that is,
the Quartering] or the suspending Act." Moore delayed his request for
funds until the necessary bill had been passed. He then signed it and
presented it to the ministry in the best light possible.[55]

Another factor, too, might help to explain the calm with which the city
reacted both to the Restraining Act and to the Townshend Duties. Gov.

Francis Bernard of Massachusetts claimed that radicals in Boston and New York had made a secret compact whereby the former would take the lead in opposing these measures and in advocating a nonimportation agreement. New York could thus take a back seat, and the ministry would have to find a new scapegoat. Whether or not a pact existed, that is exactly what happened, and New York became the "quintessence of moderation." Massachusetts took the lead, and the *New York Journal* reprinted the protest articles that were appearing in Boston newspapers. In brief, the writers charged Britain with violating the rights of all Americans, not just of New Yorkers. If Parliament had the power it claimed over the New York Assembly, then the Massachusetts legislature was no more than "a poor contemptible air castle." To take a determined stand "in support of those Rights which God and nature" had bestowed upon every American, the colonies must realize that "strength consists in union," and that they must cut "imports from E[nglan]d and S[cotlan]d."[56]

Thus, as 1767 came to a close, a second Anglo-American crisis was at hand. Britain again bore primary responsibility, not only because of the laws Parliament had passed (the Revenue Act of 1766, the Townshend Duties, and the New York Restraining Act), but also because the cabinet had failed to address forthrightly the problems created by actions taken before 1766 (the Currency Act, the Quartering Act, and the stationing of a standing army in the city).[57] Put simply, budgetary problems created by waging war and looking to the imperatives of the competitive state system had again persuaded British politicians to adopt policies that in the long run would be detrimental to the empire. The Rockingham ministry had at least tried—by repealing the Stamp Act, by passing the Declaratory Act, by revising the Revenue Act of 1764, and by advocating monetary reform—to achieve its objectives through persuasion and reward. But the Chatham administration succumbed to the appeals of coercion, especially in devising the Restraining Act. Moreover, Britain's haughty reaction to the petition by New York City merchants against the Revenue Act of 1766 typified the needless rigidity with which crown officials responded to events in the province.

New Yorkers certainly bore some culpability for the imperial crisis. In 1766 and 1767, self-interest had played a part in determining how local politicians reacted to British initiatives. What was more remarkable, however, was the efforts the Livingston-led Assembly made to effect compromise and to pursue a moderate course. Though the Livingstons were not prepared either to risk mob violence or to violate their constitutional beliefs by conceding the legitimacy of the Quartering Act, they were willing to reach an accommodation with Gage if only he had been ready to cooperate. The manner in which both political parties handled the Restraining Act was also a demonstration that New York politicians were responsible leaders who sought to avoid an explosive confrontation, who had no desire for independence, and who were ready to work within the public consensus that had developed, a consensus that the colony's best course was to resist British imperialism without violence.

Urban Politics and
the Imperial Crisis

As required by New York's Septennial Act, Gov. Henry Moore dissolved the Assembly on February 6, 1768. By now, the currents of local politics were creating a treacherous undertow in the storm-tossed waters of imperial affairs. With an election in the offing, De Lanceyites were especially eager to regain the power they had wielded in the 1750s. At a meeting of the Liberty Boys held soon after the Stamp Act's repeal, Isaac Sears had overcome strong opposition and had persuaded the radicals to support James De Lancey in the next election for one of the city's four House seats. Even the Livingstons now considered De Lancey unbeatable.[1]

Joining De Lancey on his party's ticket were two wealthy merchants, Jacob Walton and James Jauncey. The opposition ran Philip Livingston and John Morin Scott. The first was an incumbent with enviable credentials: prominent merchant; delegate to the Stamp Act Congress; elder in the Dutch Reformed church; and brother of Robert Livingston, Jr., third lord of Livingston Manor. Philip was the overwhelmingly popular candidate in the field. Scott, a member of the Whig "triumvirate," was a silver-tongued attorney whose outspoken moderation in the Stamp Act crisis had antagonized radicals.[2]

The candidates campaigned most over issues that seemed only tangential to imperial affairs. De Lanceyites urged voters not to elect a lawyer: "As a Maritime City, our Chief Dependence is upon Trade, for which Reason Merchants . . . are the properest Persons to represent us"; lawyers made it their "sole Study . . . not to increase the Wealth of the State, but to divide the Gain of the industrious Merchant and Mechanick if possible among themselves."[3] Lawyers served the colony's great landowners, who selfishly blocked enactment of a land tax and demanded that revenues be raised instead by excises on trade. The city's attorneys had also put self-interest above the common good by opposing a bill that would have made the legal system more affordable by empowering justices of the peace to try cases under five pounds. Many De Lanceyites avowed that they were not against lawyers per se; only that New York attorneys had forfeited the right to sit in the House by not vigorously resisting the Stamp Act. Indeed, little the city's attorneys had done pleased De Lanceyites. When a Livingston reminded voters that in 1764 lawyers had drafted the Assembly's memorials to the King, Lords, and Commons, a De Lanceyite objected that they had probably demanded a fee. Another argued that the people's elected representatives could have done it themselves had they so desired.[4]

There was logic to the De Lancey strategy. The party conceded that Philip Livingston merited election. The De Lanceys consequently offered a three-candidate ticket and directed their fire at Scott, a lawyer burdened by heavy political baggage. As a Livingstonite, he had espoused moderation in the Stamp Act crisis. He had even argued publicly with Sears over strategy and tactics and had openly opposed the Virginia Resolves, which asserted (in the version that reached the city) that only the General Assembly had the power to tax Virginians. Many New Yorkers had considered those resolutions radical in 1765, but now that the crisis had passed it was easy to upbraid Scott, who had also reportedly said that attorneys should use the stamps, and the public be damned.[5] By censuring Scott's conduct in 1765, De Lanceyites were trumpeting their own militancy without having to explain how they would counter more recent British challenges to American rights. By disparaging a lawyer's ability to represent a mercantile community, they were implying that they could handle the Townshend Duties more effectively than the Livingstons could. By stressing trade, they were emphasizing what united New Yorkers rather than what divided them.

Livingstonites fought back, but their vindication of the legal fraternity never matched their opponents' incriminations. Declaring that moderation was essential in 1765 or that it was prudent to have men "skilled in the Law" in the Assembly may have been sensible, but such talk lacked the impact that charges of greed and corruption had on the public mind. Arguing that every group had its own interests and that each should be represented in the House to check the others had merit, yet it was an idea better defended in a learned treatise than in a campaign broadside.[6]

If Livingstonites were ratiocinative in their defense of lawyers, they exploited sectarian jealousies. Religion had a volatile history in New York, and controversy had continued into the 1760s.[7] In 1766 the city's Presbyterians had petitioned Britain for the fifth time for a church charter. But the Privy Council refused one in August 1767 on the advice of New York's Anglican-dominated governor's Council. That infuriated Presbyterians, and Livingstonites felt it might also rally many non-Anglicans against the De Lanceys, especially since other Protestant churches had suffered the same indignity. The Livingstons also hoped to win the support of dissenters who had been incensed by Thomas Bradbury Chandler's *An Appeal to the Public in Behalf of the Church of England in America*, which in 1767 called for an American episcopate. Livingstonites opposed the idea in principle but also saw it as a marvelous campaign issue. They consequently charged that James De Lancey, who was in England, was there lobbying for an Anglican bishop for the colonies.[8]

If the Livingstonites assumed they could unite dissenters behind their party, because Philip Livingston was Dutch Reformed, they were sadly mistaken. Indeed, religion failed as a campaign issue. First, if stirring religious passions attracted some voters, it antagonized others. Though the Livingstons genuinely feared Anglicanism, many New Yorkers saw bigotry instead. Second, the emphasis De Lanceyites placed, in a period of economic dislocation, on the need for commercially minded men to sit in the Assembly appealed to more voters than did talk of church charters and bishops. The dissenting tradition remained strong among artisans, but feeding one's family was important too. Third, the De Lanceys made sure the Livingston assault upon Anglicanism did not undercut the genuine distrust that other dissenting denominations had for Presbyterianism. The party pointed out that the latter's charter had been refused for good cause, and that other churches had received one. The De Lanceys conceded that Anglicans had requested an American bishop but explained that they wanted one with only spiritual powers and had no wish to set up church courts in New York. That explanation evidently satisfied many dissenters, for James Jauncey was Presbyterian. Finally, because the De Lanceys were allied with Sears, they had the support of voters committed to his brand of political and economic radicalism.[9] In sum, the Livingstons lost by running a campaign designed to divide New Yorkers along religious lines; the De Lanceys won by accentuating issues on which people could find common ground in a time of crisis.

De Lanceyites had also left little to chance. Party leaders stood on street corners at election time wooing voters. Merchants pressured the artisans they patronized to vote the right way. The treasurer of Trinity Church, who was responsible for leasing church lands, did likewise with his tenants. When the votes were counted, Livingston came in first with 1,320. De Lancey was close behind with 1,204. He was followed by Walton and Jauncey with 1,175 and 1,052 votes, respectively. Scott collected only 870 votes. He contested the election, accusing Jauncey of fraud, but to no avail. Still, the De Lancey victory was no rout. Except for Robert R. Livingston's defeat in Dutchess County, the Livingstons won all the seats north of Westchester. The party thus retained sufficient strength to make Philip Livingston Speaker of the new House.[10]

II

The Assembly did not meet until October. Meanwhile, residents had time to ponder the Townshend Duties. Economic hardship had already led to the holding of a public meeting on December 29, 1767. A committee was appointed, and it presented its report on February 2, 1768. Although most of the proposals were unexceptional, residents were asked to sign a "Subscription-Roll" pledging as of June 1 not to buy any of a list of proscribed imports. Disregarding the Townshend Duties, the committee stressed how the "State of Poverty" and the "Decline of Commerce" demanded "Frugality and Industry." The meeting adopted the report, though it is unknown how many signed the document or if those who did indeed bought fewer imports.[11]

Merchants could not continue ignoring the Townshend Duties, especially after Boston invited New York to adopt a nonimportation agreement to protest them. Merchants' enthusiasm for a boycott was not great, however. They held a meeting on March 31, 1768, to consider Boston's proposal, but for lack of attendance no decision was reached. Several traders told Governor Moore that they resented being drawn into a dispute between Bostonians and their governor, yet they feared rioting if they refused to participate. Moore concluded that he could defeat the proposed boycott by promising protection to traders who continued importing. But William Smith warned him not to meddle, lest the merchants feel compelled to side with Massachusetts. In the event, Moore kept his peace, Sears championed nonimportation, and the traders agreed to economic sanctions. If a boycott did not force Britain to repeal the Townshend Duties, merchants could at least unload stale merchandise. Hence, in early April they voted not to deal in products shipped from Britain after October 1 unless the Townshend Duties were removed. The only stipulation was that Boston and Philadelphia must do likewise. The April agreement was never implemented, however, for Philadelphia rejected nonimportation. The anguish that the city's merchants felt about the wretched state of their economy had overcome the concerns that popular leaders had for American constitutional rights.[12]

Opposition to the Townshend Duties kept growing, however, and Boston's merchants agreed on August 1 to cease importing most British products on January 1, 1769. It was at this juncture that the American Board of Customs directed Andrew Elliot to accept only species in payment of the duties. Hence, on August 27, New York City's merchants voted to cancel all orders sent to Britain after August 16 and to refuse exports from Britain after November 1 unless the duties were rescinded. Only items that could not be made in America were exempted. The next week the city's artisans voted not to patronize anyone who sold merchandise imported contrary to the August 27 agreement. On March 13, 1769, about the time the spring shipment of goods usually reached port, the merchants set up a committee of inspection to enforce the association and to correspond with the other colonies.[13]

Nonimportation was not the only way Massachusetts induced New Yorkers to elevate their militance. In February 1768 its House of Representatives had approved a circular letter denouncing the Townshend Duties and asking the other colonial assemblies to petition Parliament against taxation without representation. Lord Hillsborough, the secretary of state for America, retaliated on April 21 by sending a dispatch to the royal governors, condemning the circular and commanding them to dissolve any assembly that endorsed it. Reports also reached New York that Parliament would not repeal the Townshend Duties. If America resisted, Britain would "send Men of War to all trading Towns on the Continent, and stop all your Trade, — and likewise a Number of Soldiers to humble you."[14]

By the time the New York Assembly met in October, the atmosphere was tense, and Livingstonites cautious. Despite their electoral setback, they still wielded considerable power in the House. Why support the circular letter and risk new elections, if they could finesse the situation the way the Pennsylvania Assembly had done it? Hence, at the start of the session, after reading a circular letter from Virginia comparable to that from Massachusetts, the Assembly appointed a committee to draft petitions to the King, Lords, and Commons. The House could thus champion colonial rights without forcing a dissolution. If that alternative was unpopular within or without the Assembly, the Livingstons at least hoped to postpone discussion of the Massachusetts letter until the end of the session, after all other business had been transacted.[15]

But party leaders underestimated the ability of the city's three De

Lancey lawmakers to disrupt their plans. When the Livingstons tried to skirt the Quartering Act by again granting money before Moore requested it, the three demanded that the House wait for the governor to ask for an appropriation. Moore consequently sent a request on November 9. The next day James De Lancey agreed to an appropriation so long as it was accompanied by resolutions affirming New York's right to be free from taxation without representation, to petition the king at will, to correspond with the other colonies, and to have the unconstitutional Restraining Act repealed. Meanwhile, the Liberty Boys harassed the Livingstons by working out of doors "to disturb the tranquility of the City." On the night of November 14 demonstrators marched to the Coffee House to hear speeches praising the Massachusetts Circular Letter and protesting the stationing of troops in Boston. The crowd dispersed only after effigies of Gov. Francis Bernard and the sheriff of Boston were burned. When Moore offered a reward for information leading to the conviction of the instigators, the Livingston-dominated Assembly backed him, but De Lanceyites on the Council refused. Moore concluded that the "Rioters were set up by People of Property," who wanted "to destroy the Harmony subsisting between the several Branches by intimidating the Assembly."[16]

Pressure on the Livingstons continued to mount. On November 17 a newspaper writer, who claimed that lawmakers who obeyed Hillsborough were defying "the Purposes for which they were chosen," demanded to know why the Assembly had not answered the Massachusetts Circular Letter. The next day merchants appeared before the House "to ask what was become of the Boston Letters." De Lanceyites then embraced a tactic Philadelphia's popular leaders had already employed and drew up instructions, ostensibly on voters' behalf, for the city's lawmakers, demanding that no more grants be made for quartering British troops and that the Massachusetts Circular Letter be approved. Branding Hillsborough's April 21 letter a "most daring Insult," the instructions asserted that colonial unity was the "only Bulwark and Defense against the late Measures to oppress and enslave" America. When Liberty Boys went about town canvassing for signatures, they approached Philip Livingston, who answered, "Let them that would choose Tools to Instruct them."[17]

But the opposition would not be silent, and James De Lancey repeatedly threatened to introduce the Massachusetts Circular in the Assembly. Finally, Philip Schuyler, an Albany Livingstonite, called his bluff by moving that the House adopt one of three alternatives: discuss the letter the next day, disregard it, or delay reading it until all other business had been concluded. The House "was thrown into the utmost Confusion," and De

Lancey was "thunderstruck." Denied the honor of introducing the measure himself, he now had to oppose it, since he did not want a dissolution, especially under the circumstances. Now that De Lancey had been embarrassed, Schuyler agreed to defer consideration of his motion for several days. The House eventually put off discussion of the matter till the end of the session and turned to other business. On December 23 it voted £1,800 for quartering the troops lodged in New York. The De Lanceys also accepted the petitions to the King, Lords, and Commons. At last, on December 31, without assigning anyone credit for introducing the subject, the House read the Massachusetts Circular Letter and passed four resolutions (three unanimously) introduced by Schuyler that were similar to but more temperately worded than those De Lancey had offered earlier in the session. The House also directed the Speaker to answer the circular letter.[18]

In essence, by using coercive threats, not persuasion and reward, Hillsborough had united the two parties in a candid statement of rights they would not otherwise have made. When the governor's Council met on January 2, the four De Lanceyites present opposed dissolving the legislature. Moore thus acted alone and called for new elections later in January.[19] Though New Yorkers had again joined hands, the need for another electoral campaign made consensus building very difficult. Indeed, the whipsaw effect created by the imperial relationship and the imperatives of local politics only worsened the crisis.

III

Because James De Lancey was not the prolific writer some Livingstonites were, it is not always possible to explain his intentions. In 1768 he had been more militant in the Assembly than his opponents had. Yet it is unlikely he orchestrated a dissolution, believing his party would thereby win control of the next House, for the situation was volatile, and no one could predict how elections might turn out. The De Lancey strategy was thus circumscribed: avoid antagonizing public opinion and provoke Livingstonites into blundering politically.[20] Residents favored answering the Massachusetts Circular Letter, and the Livingstons did not. The more De Lanceyites prodded the House to support Massachusetts, the more Livingston moderation would be exposed. The opposition's readiness to resist popular pressure in 1765 suggested that they would again stand firm. As a result, when New Yorkers demanded to know why the Massachusetts letter had gone unanswered, the De Lanceys could point an accusing finger at their adversaries and win the next election. Livingstonites, of course, understood the game being played. Smith charged "that De Lancey Walton and Jauncey were fearful of a Dissolution and only wanted to gain Credit with the Sons of Liberty as Friends to the Instructions and yet wished they might be overruled for the Sake of exposing others to the popular Odium."[21]

If James De Lancey had indeed plotted a dissolution, his conduct after January 2 is inexplicable. When the Livingstons suggested a coalition ticket with the Anglicans and dissenters, each nominating two, he sensibly rejected the plan.[22] Since Philip Livingston had already announced he would not seek reelection, there was no need to concede a single seat. But instead of trying to wrest political advantage from the situation, De Lancey proposed that the four incumbents run together to avoid a contentious election. De Lancey's prudence was not matched by the Speaker's realism, however. When De Lancey made his offer, he did so in a way calculated to emphasize his sincerity: the emissary chosen to convey the message was James Duane, a De Lanceyite married to Philip Livingston's niece. Duane told his "uncle" that he could head the ticket and that De Lancey would personally make him the offer "*at any time and place He should appoint.*" Because the Speaker again declined to run, the De Lanceys shrewdly added to their ticket John Cruger, New York's mayor in 1765 when the City Council had persuaded Cadwallader Colden to surrender the stamps. The Livingstons nominated two Dutch Reformed merchants, the seemingly reluctant Philip Livingston and Theodorus Van Wyck, and two Presbyterians, John Morin Scott (a lawyer) and Peter Van Brugh Livingston (a merchant). Philip then announced that he would not campaign but would serve if elected. John Jay accused him of playing "a double Game."[23] Its apparent aim was to provide a pretext so that the Livingstons could run four candidates and improve their numbers in the next Assembly. Though the party's moderation had been out of step with public opinion in 1768, Livingstonites in the city still felt they could win by a handsome margin. In fact, as late as January 23, after the polling had already begun, they still thought they could take at least two seats.[24]

During the campaign, both parties were again reticent about Anglo-American affairs. While each claimed credit for the Assembly's resolves supporting the Massachusetts Circular Letter, neither candidly discussed the imperial relationship. The Livingstons naturally did not relish trumpeting their own moderation. And the De Lancey line was that the city's lawmakers had obeyed the instructions townspeople had given them in 1768 and so merited reelection. In avowing that they would ever abide by the popular will, the De Lanceys evidently saw no need to delve into specifics; once the people had spoken on an issue, their assemblymen would act accordingly.[25] The more the De Lanceys clarified their views, the greater the chance that the Liberty Boys and merchants would focus on their differences. But could artisans and laborers be sure the party would represent them as well as it had represented wealthy merchants? The De Lanceys unexpectedly found an occasion to show that their candidates were of that caliber. During the campaign the king appointed James De Lancey to the governor's Council. He promptly refused the honor the crown had bestowed for one he hoped the people would confer. His decision shocked the elite but had broad popular appeal.[26]

How could the Livingstons defeat a party that had united the producers of wealth and resisted British assaults upon liberty and property? Opposite such a parlay, Philip Livingston's optimism appears foolhardy. With large landowners and lawyers constituting two of his party's key constituencies, it could not claim to better represent the city's economic interests. Nor could it allege that its leaders were more responsive to the popular will, not after they had taken so decided a stand against the Stamp Act rioters. But if his party was so vulnerable, why was Philip so sanguine? There can be only one explanation: he again expected sectarian prejudice to split the artisan vote and to secure victory for his party's candidates. After the 1768 elections William Livingston had continued the assault on Anglicanism in his "The American Whig" column, which appeared in James Parker's *New-York Gazette* until July 1769. The De Lanceys retaliated with "Timothy Tickle's" "A Whip for the American Whig," which was authored by three Anglican clergymen—Samuel Seabury, Thomas Bradbury Chandler, and Charles Inglis—and was published in Hugh Gaine's *New-York Gazette and Weekly Mercury*. The Livingstons responded in kind with "Sir Isaac Foot's" "A Kick for the Whipper," which Parker printed until January 1770.[27]

In the event, however, the religious issue hurt the Livingstons. Not only did sectarian bitterness again cost them votes, but townspeople were still troubled primarily by the economy. And in those cases where voters were not swayed by the claim that the De Lancey party could better protect the city's commercial interests, De Lanceyites allegedly "threatened" wage earners "with the loss of Employment, and to arrest them for Debt, unless they gave their Voices as they were directed."[28] From another perspective, it can be seen that James De Lancey had simply outfoxed Philip Livingston. If De Lancey and Walton were Anglican, Jauncey was Presbyterian and Cruger had been raised Dutch Reformed, though he was apparently not a churchgoer in the 1760s. Thus, in a period of imperial unrest, while the Livingstons were seeking to pit dissenters and Anglicans against one another, the De Lancey ticket appeared ecumenical both in fact and in spirit. When a penman assailed the Presbyterian church, the De Lancey candidates promptly apologized, insisting he did not reflect their views.[29] All the commotion about religion, De Lanceyites argued, was a ruse that self-seekers were using to win office.[30] A dissenter could thus vote in his own economic interest and for harmony in the community without feeling that he was abandoning his church.

Following the election, two facts stood out: fewer people had gone to the polls in 1769 than in 1768, and the De Lancey ticket had swept the field.[31] Nonetheless, contemporaries and historians have debated why the electorate voted as it did. James Duane blamed his uncle Philip for the Livingston defeat: Philip had been at the height of his popularity but threw it away by refusing De Lancey's offer and by alienating the Anglicans and their Dutch and German friends. In 1963, Roger Champagne described the 1768 and 1769 elections as a victory of one opportunistic aristocratic family over another, both of which exploited "imperial issues for . . . local purposes." Two years later Bernard Friedman argued instead that these two political campaigns marked "the disruption of family politics," for "the radical role in these elections was decisive." The Liberty Boys had made "adherence to the American cause in the Constitutional crisis, rather than the customary family, financial, and denominational ties, the principle test of popularity." But in 1979, in *The Urban Crucible*, Gary Nash credited the De Lancey victory in 1769 to the fact that, unlike Philadelphia and Boston, New York lacked the secret ballot. Many people had voted for the De Lancey ticket because of the pressure the party had exerted on artisans and laborers, who were dependent on wealthy De Lanceyites for jobs and housing. These same tactics had also persuaded about one-fourth of those members of the laboring class who were enfranchised to stay away from the polls to avoid being coerced.[32]

We have, then, no shortage of interpretations, but the extant evidence makes it impossible to know precisely what motivated voters. Take an Anglican craftsman who voted a straight De Lancey ticket in 1769. Did he feel obliged to defer to his betters? Did he appreciate that the party protected his church? Did he rent from a De Lanceyite landlord? Did he fear for his job if he voted the wrong way? If his livelihood was dependent on trade, did he believe that the party would best represent his economic interests in the Assembly? Did he support the radical agenda and vote for the De Lancey ticket because Sears had urged him to do so? It is impossible to know. Probably he was moved by a combination of factors. Take, now, another Anglican artisan who had voted a straight De Lancey ticket in 1768, but who failed even to go to the polls in 1769. Had the De

Lanceys antagonized him between the two elections? If he felt coerced by his economic dependency, why were other mechanics and laborers paying money to become freemen in January and February 1769, so that they could vote? Had he become politically apathetic because he was so busy eking out a living in a time of economic hardship? Or was he alienated by the acridity of the campaign? Again, it is impossible to tell.[33]

Graham Russell Hodges's study of the city's cartmen demonstrates how difficult it is to interpret the electoral results. Despite the "traditional bonds between merchants and cartmen," the latter "split their vote almost evenly without a clear favorite among the eight candidates in 1769." Thirty-two carters voted a straight De Lancey ticket, while 26 did the same for the Livingstons. The cartmen turnout was also lower in 1769 than it had been in 1768, when they had "voted heavily" for the De Lancey candidates. Occupation, class, and the lack of a secret ballot were evidently not the key or the only factors determining if or how cartmen voted in this period. Surely some were moved by religious belief or prejudice, while others ignored politics to focus on their own economic survival. Sill others may have been repelled by the partisanship that threatened to disunite the city in the midst of an imperial crisis. Hodges's findings are a reminder, too, that it should not be assumed that because ordinary people were gaining a greater political voice in this period, they were necessarily anti-rich or radical in outlook.[34]

The complexity of the city's population made it as difficult for politicians of the period, as it is for historians today, to decipher the results. James De Lancey may have believed that the city's voters, regardless of class, shared a common economic interest and that that was why his party had won so resounding a triumph. Or he may have concluded, as did Gary Nash, that the economic dependency of wage earners upon the mercantile community had determined the outcome. If De Lancey interpreted the returns in either way, that might well explain why he would break with the radicals in the fall of 1769 over whether the Assembly should appropriate funds to quarter British troops in New York in exchange for permission to issue paper money. His reading of the election returns may explain, too, why the city's merchants would desert the Liberty Boys and would vote in July 1770 to end their anti–Townshend Act boycott of British imports. The radicals, for their part, may have assessed the election results more as Friedman would. They would (and did), therefore, vigorously oppose the De Lanceys on both the appropriations bill and nonimportation.

Thus, even at the time, the outcome of the 1769 election was open to alternate interpretations. How politicians construed the returns shaped their subsequent political behavior, and they would soon begin to suffer political reversals for which their own analysis of the election had not prepared them.

IV

Though the Restraining Act and Lord Hillsborough had impelled New Yorkers to seek common ground, the hotly contested elections of 1768 and 1769 had divided the city's pluralistic population and had led politicians to exaggerate their differences. In the process, wounds were opened that would not easily heal, and bitter partisanship would continue after the elections. With the city polarized over local issues, cooperating on the imperial front would prove more difficult.

The Livingstons were more optimistic following their defeat than circumstances warranted, for Philip would still be in the Assembly (after the election Peter R. Livingston—Robert Livingston's son and the representative for Livingston Manor since 1761—let Philip take his seat). Livingstonites also felt that they could exploit the Quartering Act to good effect. If the Assembly granted new funds, the Liberty Boys might well defect from the De Lancey camp, especially since British troops now occupied Boston. If the De Lanceys refused an appropriation, Governor Moore would doubtless call for new elections before invoking the Restraining Act.[35] To ready themselves for another political campaign the Livingstonites organized a Society of Dissenters to unite all non-Anglican Protestants against religious tyranny and "for the Preservation of their common and respective, civil and religious *Rights* and *Privileges*." The initiative, which was both politically motivated and ideologically sincere, was unsuccessful, particularly because many Dutch Reformed residents refused to join the Society's ranks. Still, the decision to create the organization signaled that the Livingstons planned to escalate the fight, not to admit defeat. The fact that as many as 171 New Yorkers enrolled as freemen on January 31 and that 74 more did so in February indicates that people took the Livingstons seriously and were prepared to enter the fray with their votes.[36]

Even if Livingstonites were too sanguine about new elections, the Quartering Act offered them their best hope. On March 16, "A Countryman," who was evidently a Liberty Boy, asked the people to instruct their lawmakers not to grant any more funds for "a Standing Army," since it was in town only to "over-awe" residents into "blind Submission." Instead of being pestered for money, the House should be granted "the long wish'd for Leave for permitting the issuing [of] Bills of Credit as formerly." The writer made De Lanceyites uneasy, for they knew Moore would surely ask for more money. If assemblymen were indeed the agents of their constituents (as the four De Lancey candidates had argued), and if voters demanded that Moore's request be rejected, then the House would have to do so. The piece disturbed Philip Livingston, too, for the writer also urged the Assembly not to seat anyone elected from a place where he was not a resident: if "a Person" recently defeated in New York City took a seat controlled by a manor lord, outside the city, then the House should enforce the law barring nonresident electors.[37]

The political maneuvering began as soon as the Assembly convened on April 4. The Livingstons proposed bills designed to embarrass their enemies and to force new elections. De Lanceyites tried to forestall a dissolution by ridding the House of irksome opponents. Westchester residents petitioned the Assembly to overturn the electoral results there, because the victor, Lewis Morris, was not a resident. He was, however, a Livingstonite. (Livingstonites could not have been too shocked; they had tried in vain to expel two De Lancey legislators in 1768.) Philip Livingston countered by asking permission to introduce a bill for printing £120,000 in paper money. He was given leave to do so, but the bill would not pass. And Morris moved successfully that the House open its doors to spectators. The idea, a popular one, had been endorsed by the De Lanceys in the elections, and it would now compel them to cope in public with the traps their opponents set for them.[38]

On April 6 Morris futilely introduced a bill to free Protestant dissenters in the counties of lower New York from a provision of the Ministry Act requiring them to pay taxes to support the Anglican clergy serving their communities. The next morning De Lancey successfully urged that the previous House's petitions to the King, Lords, and Commons be entered on the Assembly's *Journals*. A few days later Philip Livingston succeeded in getting the House to thank the merchants for adopting nonimportation. Two days later John Thomas of Westchester moved that Livingston be denied his seat, since he did not live in Livingston Manor. After the House agreed to consider the matter on April 27, Livingston vainly asked the body to adopt the previous Assembly's resolutions endorsing the Massachusetts Circular Letter and thus to force the governor to dissolve the body.[39]

De Lanceyites held the upper hand. Not only did the House elect John Cruger Speaker, but it voted on April 20 to unseat Morris and on May 12 to expel Livingston.[40] Though the De Lanceys had wounded the opposition, they still feared that Robert R. Livingston, a Supreme Court Justice who had represented Dutchess County from 1761 to 1768, would be elected for Livingston Manor. On the day Philip was dismissed from the Assembly, James De Lancey publicly challenged the manor's right to representation. But the outcry was so great and the manor's right so secure that the governor issued writs for a new election the next morning. The De Lanceys then advised Peter R. Livingston that they would not object if he again held the seat. On May 17 the Assembly adopted the position Boston radicals had taken against the plural-officeholder Thomas Hutchinson and resolved that "no Judge of the Supreme Court shall be allowed to sit" in the Assembly.[41] Robert R. Livingston, not Peter, was nonetheless elected for the manor. In November, when he tried to take his seat, the House refused to permit him. He was reelected four times in the next few years and each time denied his seat. Though Livingstonites complained that the judge and Livingston Manor were being treated the way a tyrannical British government handled John Wilkes and the Middlesex electors, the De Lanceys controlled the Assembly. Peter R. Livingston was finally elected in the judge's stead and admitted to the Assembly on February 21, 1774.[42]

The De Lanceyites had little time to savor their triumphs in the Assembly, however, before having to navigate the treacherous shoals of imperial politics. On April 4, the opening day of the Assembly, Moore had asked the House for a new appropriation for the army. When Schuyler drafted an answer, he made it a categorical refusal to grant any money whatsoever. But the De Lanceys would not risk a dissolution, and the reply they finally adopted was evasive: "The repeated Application of Monies" for the military "would effectually ruin a Colony, whose Trade by unnatural Restrictions, and the Want of a Paper Currency to supply the almost total Deficiency of Specie, is so much declined, and still declining." The House would nonetheless give the request its "most serious Consideration." On April 14 the De Lanceys relented, and the House appropriated eighteen hundred pounds.[43]

The De Lancey defense was artful. Since no one knew if Parliament had renewed the Quartering Act, no one could accuse the House of obeying it. Moreover, granting money upon Moore's request would refute any argument the cabinet might make to justify compulsory taxation of the colonies. In effect, by appropriating funds the House was advancing the American cause. Explanations aside, party leaders promised the Liberty Boys that the appropriation would be the last, and Sears was made inspector of potash in an effort to quiet him. James De Lancey had thus dodged a political bullet, yet he knew he had only delayed a showdown. On May 29 Moore wrote the cabinet that the legislature had granted eighteen hundred pounds and that "the Assembly expect[ed] that about the latter end of the year, a farther sum will be demanded for the support of His Maj[es]ty's Troops here."[44]

What did De Lancey plan to do when the Assembly met again? Moore's letter provides the answer. On May 6 the House had passed a bill authorizing the issuance of £120,000 in bills of credit to be retired over a fourteen-year period. Traders and artisans would thus have the paper money they desperately sought. The bills of credit would be issued at 5 percent interest; and the money accrued would pay for quartering the redcoats. Moore's instructions required him to veto the bill, but he asked that he be allowed to sign it. De Lancey no doubt believed that he had fashioned a realistic compromise benefiting ministers, merchants, and mechanics alike. The cabinet would surely agree, for it needed the funds. And New Yorkers would be relieved, since the provincial treasury had begun in November 1768 to retire the paper money issued in the Seven Years' War. The next meeting of the Assembly would thus bring the party accolades, not adversity.[45]

V

On September 11, 1769, before the Assembly had reconvened and before London had decided the fate of the House's currency bill, Moore died and Colden, now over 80, again became acting governor. As chess masters surprised by an unexpected move in tournament play, New York's politicians had quickly to reassess their board positions, shore up their defenses, and prepare to exploit whatever opportunities opened before them.

The Livingstons felt the change immediately. Moore's private secretary, Philip Livingston, the son of Peter Van Brugh Livingston, traveled to Long Island on September 11 to tell the lieutenant governor of Moore's demise. Colden informed him at once that his services as secretary were no longer required.[46] The De Lanceys fared better, however. About September 12 Colden met several times with his Council and a select group of assemblymen led by Speaker Cruger. Afterward, Colden wrote the cabinet that he "had assurances from them of their disposition to make my administration easy to me" and thus believed he could maintain "the Province in tranquility." Though the details are sketchy, the De Lanceys and Colden had agreed to put aside years of enmity and to strike a bargain. Colden promised not to dissolve the legislature but to sign a paper-money bill and to provide the De Lanceys with patronage. They assured him, for their part, that he would enjoy a peaceful administration, that he would be paid his salary promptly, and that the Assembly would appropriate more money for the army.[47]

It is not difficult to surmise why the De Lanceys entered the agreement. Not only had James De Lancey, Sr., upon becoming lieutenant governor in 1753 reached an accommodation with Colden, but an alliance in 1769 would keep alive the hope of a political settlement acceptable to the ministry, the radicals, and the mercantile community. In the balance hung the city's economic well-being and the party's fate. There were reasons, too, why so inflexible a man as Colden had suddenly become so pragmatic. The ordeal of 1765–1766 had taught him practical lessons in statecraft that had earlier eluded him. He had retreated from the city in 1766, broken in health and spirit, but with the solitude necessary to assess his predicament. It was less his humiliation by the mob than how London had treated him that rankled. Though he felt that he had vigorously supported the royal prerogative and that no crown official had done more to uphold the Stamp Act, the ministry had forced him to defend himself for having stated on November 4 that he would do nothing with the stamps until Moore arrived. He had never catered to the mob, though he believed Moore had; yet it was he, not his successor, who had to explain himself. Nor did the British government do enough after the crisis to reward a faithful servant. It had not taken a resolute stand when the Assembly refused, until 1768, to pay him the compensation he was owed for his last two months as acting governor. Worse, the House had never reimbursed him for his losses in the November riots. Britain had paid lip service to his cause but had not budged the Assembly or granted relief itself. Colden was now going to make sure he got his due.[48]

Pivotal to the agreement was the expectation that the crown would approve the paper-money bill the House had passed in May 1769. If London let the lieutenant governor sign it, the De Lanceys could justify a new grant for the army, and Colden would not have to dissolve the Assembly. The political calm that would ensue would persuade the cabinet (or so Colden thought) to keep him in office for a time to compensate him for his "Losses and Sufferings" in 1765. Still, the Liberty Boys were a problem. The British army's occupation of Boston in October 1768 and the refusal of Massachusetts and South Carolina to grant the military the funds required by the Quartering Act had convinced New York radicals that the Assembly should never again vote the army money in peacetime. The De Lanceys, moreover, had promised the Liberty Boys in the spring that the House would not again make such a grant; and the same pledge had been repeated at the start of the new session. Still, paper money was popular, and the De Lanceys evidently hoped the radicals would eventually conclude that the party had struck a good deal.[49]

Part of the agreement played out as planned. When they had met on September 11, Colden had promised the younger Philip Livingston he could remain as Registrar of the Prerogative Court. But a few days later the acting governor appointed Goldsbrow Banyar, a De Lanceyite, to that office. Colden also replaced the sheriffs of Westchester and Dutchess counties and made Thomas Jones, James De Lancey's brother-in-law, Recorder of New York City. But the De Lanceys waited in vain for word from London that New York could issue paper money. Inexplicably, Moore had not sent a copy of the proposed act home, and Lord Hillsborough had been obliged, on July 15, 1769, to request one. Colden delayed convening the Assembly as long as possible while he awaited London's decision. The press of business finally forced his hand, and he called the legislature into session on November 21.[50]

Despite their promises to the Liberty Boys, the De Lanceys persisted in the view that the way out of their dilemma was to pass both a paper-currency bill and an appropriation for the army. In a letter on December 4 Colden prepared London. Good news was interspersed with the bad, and the best face was put on what would ruffle the cabinet. He reported that the merchants had summarily rejected a proposal from Boston to continue nonimportation until Parliament removed all the duties laid on items imported into the colonies. He also expressed the frustration New Yorkers felt at not hearing about the fate of their currency bill. The House had already introduced a new bill to issue £120,000 in currency; it would be one of the first measures passed, and the Council would surely approve it. He explained that "the greatest number of the present Assembly [i.e., the De Lanceys]" knew how vital it was "to have the mutual Confidence" between Britain and America "restored." But since these lawmakers were unsure about how Parliament would treat their petitions, they were "carefull not to lose their popularity." They had, therefore, approved a resolution supporting the Virginia Resolves of May 1769, which had declared that the right to tax Virginians resided solely in that colony's governor and legislature.[51]

On December 16 Colden wrote Hillsborough that the House had voted the army an appropriation, but a debate was raging over how to fund it. The De Lanceys wanted it to come from the treasury; the opposition, from "the Money to be emitted on Loan." A campaign was being waged to sway public opinion, and he could not predict the outcome. Either Colden did not know, or he wanted the cabinet to learn of events by bits and pieces. But the day before, in a closed-door session of the Assembly made possible by Speaker Cruger's absence, the De Lanceys accepted a compromise. Of the £2,000 appropriated, half was to come from the treasury and half from the interest earned on the £120,000 to be issued as bills of credit.[52]

Colden had little choice but to disregard his instructions and to sign the currency bill, though that might cause his dismissal from office. He wrote the ministry that it was "absolutely necessary" to approve the measure. The appropriations bill had been carried by only a few votes and would have failed if he had not assured the "friends of administration" that he would "assent to the Bill for emitting Bills of Credit." A clause in the latter act provided that paper money could not be issued until June 10, 1770. That proviso, he argued, served as "a Suspending Clause" by giving the crown ample time to veto the measure if it was so inclined.[53]

Even if the cabinet accepted that argument, Colden and the De Lanceys had badly misjudged public opinion. The fact that Massachusetts and South Carolina had recently defied the Quartering Act had made funding the army anathema in New York, especially among radicals. On November 1, about three weeks before the Assembly was to convene, the Liberty Boys had resolved "not to surrender their Rights to arbitrary Power" and had prayed that the example of South Carolina and Massachusetts would "be universally adopted in North America." After the Assembly convened, Cruger asked Sears if the House should vote the army money. Sears said that he "was averse to granting Money to the Troops in Time of Profound Peace, and was always against the former Assemblies for doing it." When the Speaker admitted that that was "hard" to accept, Assemblyman Jauncey inquired what "the People's Sentiments in general were, out of doors." Sears replied that "People I have talked with, seem to be willing Money should be given," but only after "a Money-Bill should be passed, and the Money struck and issued."[54] It was apparently with that statement in mind that the De Lanceys agreed on December 15 that one-half the money appropriated for the army should come from the interest generated by the issuance of the bills of credit.

The failure of Sears, Cruger, and Jauncey to hammer out a compromise at once was significant. Dissension in a coalition's leadership over goals is often a first sign that a conflict (in this case that between New York and Britain) is about to deescalate. That is especially true when part of the coalition wants to limit the struggle, believing that the cost has become too high. In this instance De Lancey merchants not only were suffering financially from the boycott, but they also valued paper money more than their alliance with the radicals. What typically follows in such situations is a heightened rivalry between the competing factions in the coalition, a split in the leadership, and accusations of disloyalty being hurled at the less militant for selling out.[55]

De Lanceyites quickly learned the price of their actions. On December 16, using the pseudonym "A Son of Liberty," Alexander McDougall published a broadside *To the Betrayed Inhabitants of the City and Colony of New York*. A Liberty Boy and a Scotch Presbyterian who had sided with the Livingstons in 1765, McDougall was less militant than Isaac Sears or John Lamb were. But the broadside, a beautifully crafted piece of Livingston propaganda, propelled McDougall to the forefront of the American cause. Arguing that "the minions of tyranny and despotism" were setting traps "to enslave a free people," he said that the Assembly had "betray[ed] the trust committed to" it by voting funds for the army. True, half the money was to come from the interest on the bills of credit; yet if the crown disapproved that act, the province would still have to pay the full amount appropriated. New York should instead have emulated Massachusetts and South Carolina, for Britain hoped that the "distressed circumstances" would divide Americans, so that the ministers "may carry their designs against the colonies." If those two colonies "did right (which every sensible American thinks they did)," then "we have done wrong, very wrong." The troops were in New York "not to protect but enslave us." Who had betrayed New York? First, that old scoundrel Cadwallader Colden. To procure his salary, he had signed the currency bill, knowing it would not "obtain the royal assent." Second, the De Lancey leaders. Because of "their ambitious designs, to manage a new Governor," they had formed "a coalition" with Colden "to secure to them the sovereign lordship" over New York.[56]

McDougall still had to persuade the public, especially the artisans, that disobeying the Quartering Act would benefit the community. Because people were hurting economically, he had to make sure they did not decide that De Lancey had cleverly exchanged a grant of two thousand pounds for the relief that paper money would bring. On December 18, "A Son of Liberty" issued another broadside, *Union, Activity, and Freedom, or Division, Supineness, and Slavery*.[57] Since the city was headquarters for the British army, he argued, the colony would forever be asked to pay a disproportionate share of the cost of keeping troops in America. New Yorkers would thus have to pay higher taxes than colonists elsewhere, and that would inflate prices. But if the Assembly refused to make any further grants, Britain would need to ship hard currency to the city to support the troops, thereby helping to alleviate New York's financial woes. Thus principle and interest should together persuade New York to stand united with the other colonies on so vital an issue.

The broadside also summoned residents to meet at eleven a.m. that day at the Liberty Pole. The De Lanceys, the Livingstons, and other prominent members of the elite were asked to stay home and not give "people any unease." Perhaps McDougall wanted to signal that more was at stake than the rivalry of two warring aristocratic factions. Perhaps he feared that many New Yorkers were still too deferential or economically dependent to ignore a patrician's advice. Whatever his motives, his request was a declaration that the people out of doors deserved a voice in public affairs.

It rankled the De Lanceys to suffer such scorn for crafting a program that would aid the economy without violating residents' constitutional rights. "A Citizen" carefully explained in a December 18 broadside that the Assembly, not the De Lanceys, had voted the money; the only argument had been over how to fund the grant. The city's lawmakers had supported the measure because it was the "Mode by which alone they could obtain the passing of the Bill for emitting a Paper Currency." Had people so changed "that they would rather have the Duty Acts continue in full Force, and be forever deprived of a Paper Currency, than grant one Half of the Sum which was given the last year; when they had more Reason to object against Money being granted then they possibly can have at this Time?"[58]

The public consensus had changed, however. And the De Lanceys had violated it when they broke with Massachusetts, South Carolina, and the Liberty Boys by granting the military more money. British troops had occupied Boston in October 1768. The inevitable civil-military clashes had begun almost at once, and the militants there had initiated an intercolonial propaganda campaign against the army. McDougall's broadsides should therefore be read in the context of this larger campaign, the effect of which was immediately evident at the December 18 meeting. The multilingual John Lamb served as moderator. After recounting what the Assembly had done, he asked the fourteen hundred people present, "Whether they approved of the Vote of the House of Assembly, for granting the Money to support the Troops?" At most six voted yes, so he asked the group, "Whether they were for giving any Money to the Troops, on any Consideration whatsoever?" Again, the question was carried heavily in the negative. A committee of ten, which included McDougall, Sears, and Lamb, was then appointed to apprise the city's four lawmakers of "the Whole of this Transaction."[59]

It is impossible to date when Sears and Lamb first joined forces with McDougall. In 1768 McDougall had supported the instructions the merchants had drafted on residents' behalf for the city's assemblymen. Yet on March 18, 1769, the two sides celebrated the Stamp Act's repeal in separate taverns. And when one of McDougall's Livingstonite friends visited the Sears-Lamb group, suggesting that each side toast the other, the offer was rejected. Several hours later, when someone else from McDougall's camp made a like proposal, the radicals debated whether he should be "*shown*" the "Way out of a *Window*." The rapprochement between the two groups perhaps began in July 1769 when the "United Sons of Liberty" formed to help enforce nonimportation and to work for repeal of the Townshend Duties.[60] By December 18, in any case, the three Liberty Boys had clearly settled their differences, and they all served on the committee that met the next day with the city's assemblymen. In the event, the lawmakers treated the delegation with "Decency" but insisted that a "Majority" was "disposed to give Money to support the Troops." Nor did the De Lanceys waver in the Assembly. On December 20 the military-appropriations bill passed its second reading; and on December 30 it passed a third time.[61]

The Assembly also sought revenge against the still anonymous "A Son of Liberty." On December 18 it found the penman guilty of "a false, seditious, and infamous Libel." Colden offered a reward of one hundred pounds for the culprit's identity, and John De Noyelles, an Orange County De Lanceyite, accused Lamb of abetting the libel by chairing the meeting in the Fields. Lamb was ordered to appear before the House. But seven members of the December 18 committee wrote De Noyelles that Lamb had acted in a manner that was "the undoubted Right and Privilege of every *Englishman*." If he had committed a crime, they were in the "same Predicament" and should also be summoned to answer for their "conduct in a constitutional Manner." The inference, of course, was that if the meeting had been illegal, then residents could not instruct their representatives, something the De Lanceys had insisted upon in the 1769 elections. De Lancey party leaders quickly realized the trap into which De Noyelles had put them. Hence, no new summons were issued, and Lamb appeared alone. When he arrived, De Noyelles suddenly took ill and fled the chamber. Once Lamb declared that he did not know who the author of the libel was, he was dismissed, and the matter was dropped.[62]

VI

As often happens, the controversy McDougall's broadside had stirred up grew in scope as each side sought victory through escalation. On December 20 John Thomas moved that Stephen Sayre, an American living in London, be named to assist Robert Charles, New York's colonial agent. Not only had Charles been appointed because of his ties to the De Lancey family, but he had failed to defend the American cause in 1765. The De Lanceys refused to accept Sayre, who was a friend of Isaac Sears and a graduate of the Presbyterian College of New Jersey. De Lanceyites also found themselves on the defensive for again denying Robert R. Livingston his Assembly seat in May 1770. Sears now castigated that act as an injustice "without Law."[63]

The two parties clashed, too, over a proposed balloting bill. Given the arm-twisting the De Lanceys had supposedly engaged in during the 1768 and 1769 elections, the issue afforded Livingstonites another chance to portray themselves as defenders of the public interest against the tyrannical De Lancey faction. On December 22 John Thomas introduced a bill to conduct elections by secret ballot, not viva voce voting. On December 28 several "judicious Friends to Liberty" sponsored a meeting at the Liberty Pole. Because De Lancey partisans tore down the posters for the event, few attended, and the meeting was rescheduled for the next day. Despite raw weather and another low turnout, the group appointed a committee—one that included Isaac Sears, John Lamb, and Alexander McDougall—to instruct the city's lawmakers that the voters wanted the ballot measure enacted.[64]

The De Lanceys called their own meeting for January 5 to prove that the allegation that voters had been intimidated was a politically motivated falsehood.[65] When both De Lanceyites and Livingstonites attended, the event turned disorderly; and participants later argued over the fairness of the proceedings and even about what had happened. Unruffled, the De Lanceys prepared a petition in favor of viva voce voting and arranged a door-to-door campaign to collect signatures. In the end, it did not matter that no one really knew what the public wanted. When Thomas's measure came up in the Assembly, it was defeated, thirteen to twelve. He then asked permission to bring in a bill "that no Assembly hereafter shall continue any longer than three Years at one Time." That proposal, too, failed.[66]

Despite all the political maneuvering, arguing that party leaders were motivated only by crass self-interest obscures rather than illuminates what was happening. While in power, Livingstonites had sought, without forsaking their principles or hurting their popularity, to find compromises to resolve the imperial crisis. Defeated in 1769 and afforded the luxury of opposition, the party strove to regain power (and thereby to advance its strategic objectives) by arguing that its opponent's actions undercut liberty for short-term economic gain. De Lanceyites, by contrast, had always been less ideological. But they too had sought compromises that would reduce New York's economic distress without eroding either American constitutional rights or their own popularity. The party had rejected the Quartering Act; the Assembly had endorsed the Virginia Resolves of May 1769; and the merchants had strictly enforced the nonimportation agreement.[67] In sum, if the two parties pursued power by exaggerating their political differences, they also sought workable solutions to the imperial crisis that did not repudiate their fundamental beliefs. They were pragmatic politicians, not unprincipled opportunists.

Nor could either party mastermind events, and British soldiers added an especially volatile dimension to the situation. That became clear on Saturday night, January 13, 1770. Angered by the public outcry over the army-appropriations bill, they attempted to destroy the Liberty Pole. When a passerby alerted the patrons of De La Montayne's tavern and a crowd formed, the soldiers chased the civilians back into the building and wrecked the place. On Monday redcoats again attacked the Liberty Tree, but this time an alderman stopped them. The next day "Brutus" charged that "the Army is not kept here to protect, but to enslave us." He urged residents not to hire redcoats. "Is it not enough," he asked, "that you pay Taxes for Billeting Money to support the Soldiers, and a Poor Tax, to maintain many of their Whores and Bastards in the Work-House, without giving them the Employment of the Poor?" He scheduled a noontime meeting on Wednesday at the Liberty Pole "to bear a Testimony against a literal Compliance with the Mutiny Act." On Tuesday night soldiers made two more attempts to cut down the Liberty Tree, and succeeded on the second try. They then sawed the pole into pieces, dumping them at the door of a tavern the Liberty Boys frequented. The next day about three thousand townspeople met in the Fields, where radicals admonished them to put aside their differences and warned employers not to hire soldiers. When the meeting agreed to petition the City Council to demolish the army barracks in the Fields, redcoats standing nearby drew their weapons and dared the people to do it themselves. At that point army officers and city magistrates intervened to prevent a riot. Meanwhile, seamen went along the docks and chased away the soldiers working there.[68]

On Friday, January 19, redcoats distributed a broadside of their own, explaining their side of the story.[69] It began with a poignant piece of verse expressing their dismay:

> God and a Soldier, all Men doth adore,
> In Time of War, and not before;

> When the War is over, and all Things righted
> God is forgotten, and the Soldier slighted.

The poem called the Liberty Boys "enemies to society" and "pretended" heroes who "thought their freedom depended in a piece of wood." When Sears and Walter Quackenbush, a Dutch baker, caught seven regulars posting the handbill near the Fly Market, the two radicals grabbed two of the soldiers and dragged them before Mayor Whitehead Hicks, an attorney who had been appointed to his office by Governor Moore in October 1766. While Hicks was deciding what to do, about twenty redcoats appeared with drawn cutlasses and bayonets. The civilians present armed themselves with wooden rungs from nearby sleighs. Before violence could break out, however, the mayor ordered the troops back to their barracks. When they marched off, a crowd followed. Eventually, the retreating redcoats reached Golden Hill, where they were joined by reinforcements. Drawing their weapons, the soldiers charged the civilians, taunting them, "Where are your Sons of Liberty now?" Several people on both sides were injured before army officers restored order. Violence continued throughout the night and into the next day, and peace was reestablished only after the City Council and the army agreed that the soldiers would remain in their quarters unless accompanied by a noncommissioned officer.[70]

Though the "Battle of Golden Hill" may have set the stage for the Boston Massacre, its immediate import for New York became evident once James Parker's *New York Gazette* printed the first account of the skirmish. The governor's Council was convened hastily on January 22, and some councillors suggested that the printer be prosecuted. Smith warned against it: why attempt what many would consider an attack on freedom of the press, when Mayor Hicks felt the violence was abating? The idea was dropped, and Smith proposed that a commission or a special court be set up to determine whether the rioting could be suppressed. If not, and Smith evidently thought that to be the case, Gen. Thomas Gage should remove the troops from town in order to restore order. Smith was not condoning violence, but he was voicing the radical belief that the army was the real threat to peace. The De Lancey–dominated Council rejected the plan, and the soldiers remained in town. De Lanceyites saw the army as a counterweight to the Liberty Boys and were pleased it had got the better of residents at Golden Hill. Roger Morris, a De Lanceyite councillor, told Smith "he was for letting the Disease cure itself and the Sons of Liberty get a Dressing."[71]

A committee of radicals that included Sears, Lamb, and McDougall soon asked Mayor Hicks's permission to erect a new Liberty Pole on the

Commons. They doubtless wanted to clothe the symbol of liberty (and their cause) with a legitimacy it had not previously had. If the regulars violated the pole again, they would be insulting the city government itself. After a heated debate the De Lancey–dominated City Council refused permission, in order to remove the "cause" of the violence. That did not deter Sears, who bought a lot just north of the Fields and closer to the barracks than the original site had been. Leaving nothing to chance, the radicals made the Liberty Pole almost indestructible. Forty-six feet long, it was encased in "Iron bars, laid length wise, rivited thro' with large flat Rivits, and laid close together, so as entirely to cover the Mast for about two thirds of its Length, and over these Bars were driven large Iron Hoops, near half an Inch thick, at small Distances, from Bottom to Top." Drawn from the docks by a team of thirty horses, it was placed in a 12-foot hole. At its top a 22-foot mast and a gilt weather vane were added. The new Liberty Pole would survive until the city fell to British forces in 1776.[72] For the moment, the crowd of thousands that had gathered for the occasion could revel, and Sears could rejoice that the redcoats had rashly handed him a potent issue to exploit in his fight against British imperialism. Nonetheless, the power struggle between De Lanceyites and Liberty Boys was not over.

CHAPTER SEVEN

"Liberty and Trade"

On February 7, 1770, the day after the Liberty Pole festivities, Lt. Gov. Cadwallader Colden ordered James Parker, deputy postmaster general and publisher of the *New York Gazette*, to appear before his Council. A journeyman in Parker's shop, bitter for having been dismissed, had informed the authorities that Parker had printed *To the Betrayed Inhabitants of New York*. Parker, an old friend of Benjamin Franklin and a prominent eighteenth-century American printer, was accepting any work he could get, at this late stage in his life, just to keep body and soul together. At first he denied the allegation, but two apprentices from his shop confirmed the journeyman's story and said Alexander McDougall had edited the proofs. Parker quickly admitted to the De Lancey–controlled Council that the Liberty Boy had brought him the manuscript and had paid three pounds to have it printed. McDougall was arrested and arraigned the next day, at which time he demanded a jury trial. Upon refusing to put up bail, he was jailed.[1]

If De Lanceyites thought that they could so easily discredit an opponent who had publicly ridiculed their solution to the imperial crisis, they had badly miscalculated. Intelligent (but stubborn), methodical in thought (yet passionate in conviction), and capable of speaking with tolerable ease (though he had a noticeable speech impediment), McDougall became a martyr to the American cause. In the 1768 and 1769 elections De Lanceyites had committed their party to defending colonial rights. Now the opposition was determined to judge them accordingly. Livingstonites shrewdly compared McDougall's mistreatment to that of the celebrated

John Wilkes, who had been imprisoned in Britain in 1763 for publishing an attack upon a speech by George III to Parliament. Because Wilkes's libel was printed in "Number 45" of the *North Briton*, that number now symbolized McDougall's cause. On one occasion he was presented with a side of venison stamped with the number forty-five. On the forty-fifth day of the year, forty-five gentlemen visited him; together they ate forty-five pounds of steak from a forty-five-months-old steer. Another time forty-five virgins proceeded to the jail to sing the Forty-fifth Psalm.[2]

Trouble next developed over the annual celebration of the Stamp Act's repeal on March 18. When the Liberty Boys advertised that they planned to gather at De La Montayne's tavern, the De Lanceyite proprietor replied that the "Friends to Liberty and Trade" had already made reservations for that day. Isaac Sears, Alexander McDougall, John Morin Scott, and several well-to-do residents, therefore, bought a building on Broadway near the Liberty Pole and christened the new meeting place Hampden Hall, to honor the seventeenth-century British hero in the fight against arbitrary taxation. March 18 thus indicated how much the political landscape had changed in a few short years. De Lanceyite "Friends to Liberty and Trade" toasted Cadwallader Colden, whom the Liberty Boys of 1765 had despised. Radicals saluted the imprisoned McDougall, for whom they had had scant respect five years earlier. The key difference between the two groups was the De Lancey faction's dual commitment to trade and liberty. That platform would eventually impel the party to balance its opposition to British tyranny against its quest for economic recovery. The radicals, by contrast, valued liberty more than any commercial advantage to be gained by compromising on constitutional issues.[3]

The newspapers became a battleground. Well versed in wielding the pen as a weapon, the Livingstons published "The Watchman" series, which spared no venom in assailing the enemy, whom they likened to the despotic Stuart monarchs. The De Lanceys responded with the "Dougliad" articles, authored anonymously by James Duane, who heaped scorn on McDougall and the "greedy Livingston family," comparing them to the "Independents," who had been responsible for the excesses of the Commonwealth Period. Denying that McDougall was capable of authoring *To the Betrayed Inhabitants*, Duane claimed it had been written by a Livingston partisan who lacked the courage (as did Duane!) to identify himself.[4] De Lanceyites argued repeatedly that the Livingstons and the Liberty Boys had been enemies in 1765 and that until December 1769 Sears had considered McDougall "a rotten headed Fellow." De Lancey writers emphasized Sears's previous association with their party, claiming he had become a turncoat, only because he had felt poorly rewarded for his part in the 1769 election.[5] Stung, Sears declared, "It is the Measures I look at and not the Men: But if they [the Livingstons] should ever lose Sight of supporting the Liberties of their Country, I shall be as ready to leave them as I have the others." James De Lancey had "kick[ed] down the Ladder of Liberty," which he had climbed with the help of the Liberty Boys, once he had secured "the Chair of Honour and Power."[6]

Partisanship even touched the judiciary, for a grand jury had to determine if McDougall should be indicted. At issue was whether the jury could be impartial. John Holt's *New York Journal* reported in February that "some say all the Sons of Liberty ought to be excluded as Parties too deeply interested in the Event." Radicals thought otherwise. According to Thomas Jones, a prosecutor in the case, Sears had "applied to the Sheriff, and desired that himself and several of his particular friends" might be appointed; but the officer had "summoned a grand jury consisting of the most impartial, reputable, opulent, and substantial gentlemen." McDougall now had good reason to worry. Of the twenty-four selected, fifteen had voted a straight De Lancey ticket in 1769, and only one had picked all four Livingston candidates. James Rivington, a future loyalist, counted just three jurors "likely to shew any tenderness for one who flagitiously flies into the face of government."[7] The defense made elaborate preparations anyway. Since the case turned on whether his broadside was libelous, the *New York Journal* printed the record of John Peter Zenger's 1735 trial, in which the jury had been allowed to decide not only the facts of publication, but also whether the allegedly slanderous statements were true and thus not criminal. The Liberty Boys even advertised for material printed in New York that could be presented to the jury as examples of libel. The more such examples, the easier it would be to prove that McDougall was being politically persecuted. But the preparations were for naught. When the grand jury met in April, Chief Justice Horsmanden ruled that the jurors could decide only if McDougall had authored the broadside, not the truth of what was alleged. Eight days later the jury indicted McDougall for libel.[8]

The political theater continued, for McDougall's attorney, John Morin Scott, asked that the defendant be allowed to plead to the indictment in person. When the prisoner made his way on April 28 from the jail to City Hall, he was escorted, Thomas Jones reported, by "two or three hundred of the rabble of the town, headed by some of the most zealous partisans of the republican faction." McDougall pleaded innocent and was released on bail. The case never came to trial, however: James Parker had moved to New Jersey, where he died suddenly. Because the government now lacked sufficient evidence to prosecute, the charges against McDougall were dismissed.[9]

II

In the brief time it had taken to indict McDougall, the political climate had changed dramatically. His broadside had protested the Quartering Act; by April, attention had shifted to whether New York should end nonimportation. Behind that development were decisions the Grafton and North ministries had made in 1769 and early 1770, once it had become manifest that events across the ocean required a policy change. The Townshend Duties were not generating the revenues expected, and American resistance to Parliament had again raised the specter of colonial independence.[10]

Lord Hillsborough, the secretary of state for America, favored a hard line. Having sat on the Board of Trade between 1763 and 1765, he shared Lord Halifax's imperial perspective. In February 1769 Hillsborough offered a draconian plan to punish colonies that challenged parliamentary supremacy. New York was given special attention. First, the four councillors who had voted in January 1769 not to dissolve the Assembly were to be cashiered. Second, Parliament would either censure the House for approving the Massachusetts Circular Letter or pass a law disqualifying from office "the mover or seconder of such Questions, the Speaker, Chairman, or other Person who puts them, and the Clerk or other Person who enter them upon the Journal." The secretary also wanted to invoke the Restraining Act if New York again disobeyed the Quartering Act. Hillsborough's plan was never implemented, for George III feared troops might be needed to enforce such "odious" measures.[11]

In March Lord Barrington asked Parliament to amend the Quartering Act, so that soldiers could be billeted in private homes whenever a legislature refused support. Both the cabinet and the opposition rejected the idea, but a compromise was devised: if an assembly passed a bill that would provide suitable funding for the army, that province would be exempt from the billeting provisions of the Quartering Act. Though less harsh than Barrington's plan, the new law was nonetheless based on the premise that colonial legislatures must appropriate money whenever Parliament required it. The ministry also cautiously backed away from the Townshend Duties. In May Hillsborough notified the colonial governors that at Parliament's next session the cabinet would recommend repeal of all the Townshend Duties, except the one on tea. They were being withdrawn not because of American protests but because taxation of British manufactures violated mercantilism. The impost on tea would remain, to demonstrate Parliament's right to tax America. Though the Grafton ministry fell in January 1770, Parliament passed the necessary legislation in April. The new North administration hoped repeal would divide the colonies and derail the nonimportation movement.[12]

Lord North also moved to accommodate New York's demand for monetary reform. In December 1769 the Privy Council had examined the Assembly bill passed while Moore was still alive, authorizing the printing of £120,000 in paper money. The concern was that the law violated the Currency Act by making the bills legal tender at the public loan office and the provincial treasury, though not in private transactions. The Privy Council consequently requested an opinion from the Board of Trade, which refused to recommend approval. Meanwhile, Colden had signed the De Lancey measure, linking an appropriation for the army to the emission of paper currency. Again, the Board advised that the law be disallowed. On April 24, 1770, however, Robert Charles petitioned Parliament for legislation allowing the colony to print £120,000 in paper money that would be legal tender at the treasury and the loan office. A bill was quickly passed, and the crown approved it in May.[13]

In sum, by repealing all but one of the Townshend Duties and by letting New York issue paper money, Britain had changed the modes it was using to wage the conflict: the offering of rewards had replaced the use of coercion. A long stride had thus been taken to divide American opinion and thus to allow the ministry to play factions, and even colonies, against one another. By so doing, the ministry would extinguish whatever was left of the De Lancey–Liberty Boy coalition, for the costs and benefits of continuing nonimportation were now different for the two groups.[14]

III

Before New Yorkers knew that the Townshend Acts would be repealed, or that the province would be allowed to issue paper money, support for a boycott remained firm. It was not simply that Boston had adopted nonimportation; more important was the public's consensus that a boycott was the best way to check the most recent British challenges to liberty. Following the 1765 rioting, many residents had concluded that the city's diverse population had to eschew violence and to act as one in upholding American rights. In May 1766 Gen. Thomas Gage had noted that "the better sort" feared that if the Stamp Act was not soon repealed, "the Inhabitants wou'd rise and attack each other." In 1770 Colden declared that "All Men of Property are now so sensible of their Danger from Riots and Tumults that they will not rashly be induced to enter into Combinations which may promote Disorder for the future."[15]

It was not just the wealthy who had come to feel that way. In 1769, "Cethegus" had encouraged all residents to heed the example of the United Netherlands in opposing arbitrary government, but not in "resisting, like them, onto blood." He even reprimanded the Liberty Boys for using force to secure their objectives. "Demagogues" were "hot headed violent zealots, who gain the ascendancy over the populace, by indulging their licentious disposition, and engaging them in enterprises, great, daring, and violent." Rioting was ill-advised, for "there is no appointing bounds to a mob beforehand, and saying, thus far you shall go and no further." Such admonitions plainly reflected public opinion. Of the twenty-eight riots that Edward Countryman documented in the city between 1764 and 1775, only three took place in the period from 1768 to 1775. Although residents abjured violence, they understood, too, that sending more memorials to Britain would be futile. As "Cethegus" explained, petitions "have been tried" and "have proved ineffectual." Indeed, Britain's indignant reaction to earlier efforts at persuasion (for that is what the petitions really were) had become another colonial grievance.[16]

Given the objections both to violence and to petitions, New Yorkers of all political persuasions had eventually turned to nonimportation (or nonviolent coercion) as the best defense against the Townshend Duties. A boycott would compel Britain to rescind the duties and would benefit New York by spurring home manufacturing and slashing the trade imbalance. In fact, cutting the city's dependence on British imports would afford residents their best long-term weapon against arbitrary rule. As one writer declared, "the Helmet of Defense against any mistaken Acts, is in your own Hands, I mean the Spinning Wheel."[17]

The mercantile community had consequently established a boycott in August 1768 and had set up a committee of inspection to enforce it, on March 13, 1769. Isaac Low—an Anglican, De Lanceyite merchant and future loyalist who believed that Americans had to respect "the just Rights of our Mother Country"—was a member; so too was Isaac Sears. In time the committee functioned like an extralegal government. According to General Gage, it "contrive[d] to exercise the Government they have set up, to prohibit the Importation of British Goods, appoint Inspectors, tender Oaths to the Masters of Vessels, and enforce their Prohibitions by coercive Measures." The general was galled "that British Manufactures were prohibited in British Provinces, by an illegal Combination of People, who at the same Time, presume to trade under the Protection of the British Flagg in most Parts of the World."[18] Of course, the lessons New Yorkers had learned at this time would later be applied with good effect, in 1775 and 1776. Indeed, each crisis became a repository of experience upon which to draw in subsequent disputes.

Because the committee of inspection had such broad support, local officials failed to protect those who refused to respect its authority. Simeon Cooley, an affluent silversmith from Britain, was among the first to break the boycott. Though having subscribed to the agreement, he nonetheless failed to countermand his orders from home. When the merchandise arrived, he said he had ordered it before nonimportation had gone into effect but would store it until the crisis ended. He later got permission to visit the storehouse to polish his wares, but he abused the indulgence by removing and selling the articles. When a second shipment arrived, he declined to turn it over to the committee and boasted of his earlier deception. A public meeting was held on July 21, 1769, and emissaries were sent to demand his attendance. Though guaranteed his safety, Cooley said that he would address the crowd only from his window and got a British officer to assign a "File of Soldiers" to protect him. But after some "superior Officers" removed the guard, because the civil authorities had not authorized it, Cooley fled to the fort, where the governor ignored his plea for assistance. The next day the silversmith appeared in the Fields, acknowledged his crimes, and begged forgiveness.[19]

General Gage, who was out of town, later castigated "the Civil Power." "All the troops were ready" and "had this Man been supported the Association must have been broken to Pieces."[20] Yet Gage was much too sanguine about the army's ability to shield Cooley and to smash the boycott. The general's repeated exhortations that a political crisis be turned into a military one only further polarized the two sides and made armed conflict more likely. Civil officials, such as the governor and mayor, had at least had the good sense to swallow their pride, to accept what they must, and to wait out the storm.

Because the legitimate authorities were stymied, the committee of inspection was able to interpret the scope of its extralegal authority rather broadly. In September 1769 it investigated complaints that some shopkeepers were charging more for each item than they had been accustomed to charge, since they had fewer to sell. The committee later reported in the *New York Journal* that, on the contrary, most goods were actually cheaper than they were before the boycott. But "Paracelsus," who was ever suspicious of merchants, charged that the committee was suppressing evidence and that most of its members in fact disagreed with the report. In February 1770 the committee determined that the retail price of Bohea Tea was excessive and ordered dealers to sell it at a specified price for the boycott's duration. How rigorously the decision was enforced is unknown. Perhaps no more was involved than moral suasion. At least one trader, Jacobus Van Zandt, advertised the tea at the official price, but others continued to overcharge.[21]

The committee could even be compassionate in carrying out its duties. Thomas Richardson, a jeweler recently from London, began displaying imported jewelry in his shop window. When questioned, he confessed that he needed the sales to make ends meet. The committee offered to help him secure a loan to cover any losses he might suffer by closing his business. When he refused the compromise, he was branded "an Enemy to the glorious Cause of Liberty." Residents "legally convened" and erected a scaffold near the Liberty Pole, where they made him ask pardon and vow not to retail his merchandise. They then escorted him home "with Safety."[22]

One controversial committee ruling concerned the disposition of items that reached port contrary to the nonimportation agreement. Usually, either a local importer had ordered the articles in violation of the agreement or a British trader had sent them on his own initiative. Sometimes a merchant agreed to return the items at his own expense, but normally the committee was satisfied if the contraband was stored in a locked warehouse under the committee's control. "Paracelsus," however, objected. Boycotted products would continue to pour into town because the committee had not prohibited importers from making remittances to Britain. At some point, "the Detainers of them will be threatened with a Process, if they do not deliver on Demand, — and the *Bubble will burst in an Instant.*" Though the committee tried to appease "Paracelsus" by letting merchants reexport the goods in question, the essayist was not satisfied: merchants were "Wolves in Sheep's Clothing" who could not be trusted.[23]

"Paracelsus" had support, especially after Philadelphia's nonimportation committee, which that city's popular leaders now controlled, agreed on August 2 to return all boycotted goods to Britain. What did it matter to the British, "A. B." asked, whether "we store or use the Goods we import?" Either way, "their Ends are answered." British workers will keep their jobs, the items will be sold once the boycott ends, and British manufacturers and merchants will make their profits. Worse, those who had obeyed the boycott will suffer, for they will have nothing to sell when the port reopens. The only viable option was to reship all contraband on arrival, so that violators would be penalized by having to pay the return freight. "A. B." also complained that merchandise was being secretly removed from the warehouse. Gage reported that articles put there were "delivered soon after to the Owner." In September 1769 John Wetherhead, an English immigrant, Anglican merchant, and future loyalist, wrote Sir William Johnson that committeemen "had several Times got their own Goods clandestinely out of the Store and were daily Selling them by little and little." Wetherhead secured for Johnson items that had been "Stored by order of" the committee; he simply persuaded a disgruntled nonassociator "to break open the Store in the Dead of the Night and take the Goods . . . and return the empty Packages."[24] But these allegations must be kept in perspective: they were few in number; and in almost every case they were made privately by men averse to nonimportation.

What is remarkable is that the boycott was enforced more rigorously in New York than elsewhere. Though historians have called party leaders opportunists and argued that New York's "political system [was] in decay," British exports to the city fell from £482,930 in 1768 to £74,918 in 1769; the duties paid on European imports declined from "some Hundreds Sterling" in the fall of 1768 to forty shillings the next spring. Community support and committee vigilance were crucial, for some people went to great lengths to outwit the boycott. In June 1769 the committee learned that Alexander Robertson had smuggled merchandise into New York. Confronted with the evidence, he denied knowingly violating the boycott and agreed to return the items. The committee accepted his explanation. But Robertson hid the goods and reshipped empty casks. Upon being caught, the cheater was forced "to implore the Pardon of the Public" and promise never again to "Act contrary to the true Interest and Resolutions of a People zealous in the Cause of *Virtue* and *Liberty*."[25]

How the committee treated boycott violators is instructive, for the purpose was not to persecute offenders. Though Robertson, Richardson, and Cooley could have been physically beaten or expelled from town, their ritual humiliation served three objectives. One, the aim was to "deter others." Two, mass rallies were a way to build the group solidarity and consciousness needed for the struggle ahead. Three, public recantations were meant to reaffirm the community's and the committee's moral authority. The best way to achieve these aims was to have violators confess and acknowledge their allegiance to the ideals New Yorkers were upholding. Virtue must triumph over vice. Ritual humiliation was thus as much a form of persuasion as it was a mode of coercion.[26]

IV

Even though the city was in turmoil in late 1769 and early 1770 over the McDougall case, the balloting bill, and the Battle of Golden Hill, radicals and De Lanceyites continued cooperating on the committee of inspection. But it was inevitable that the grounds of their rivalry would eventually extend to the boycott. Once antagonists resort to coercion, what typically results is polarization, a decrease in communication, a heightened suspicion, and a progressive inability to cooperate on issues not originally in dispute.[27]

Working outside the committee, Sears and five other radicals wrote the "Friends of Just Liberty in Philadelphia" on March 10, 1770, for evidence to refute rumors that the merchants there planned to forsake nonimportation. The six penmen claimed to be a committee representing New York's "Friends of America" who had entered into an "Association" to uphold the boycott and who wanted Philadelphia's popular leaders to do likewise. On March 18, when the Liberty Boys assembled at Hampden Hall to commemorate the Stamp Act's repeal, they toasted the "Continuance of the Non-importation Agreement, until the Revenue Acts are repealed." Meanwhile, De Lanceyites drank to "Trade and Navigation, and a speedy Removal of their Embarrassments."[28]

On April 20, Colden informed his Council that the king had vetoed the bill for emitting £120,000 in paper currency, but that the cabinet would ask Parliament to change the law to permit New York to issue paper money. In early May definitive word reached town that Parliament had finally repealed all the Townshend Duties, except the one on tea. It was at this point that the ultimately irreconcilable objectives of the two coalition partners began to manifest themselves. First, the boycott had been costly. Although it had initially allowed shopkeepers to clear out old stock, the longer it lasted, the less goods they had to sell, and the harder it was to make ends meet.

Second, evidence had accumulated that Boston was cheating on nonimportation. General Gage summed up the situation well: "New York has kept up to the Agreement with the most punctuality, and is consequently the greatest Sufferer by it; Some rich Merchants have made Advantage, but the Traders in general are greatly hurt. Many testify their Dissatisfaction, and the Country People begin to complain of the dearness of the Commodities, they stand in Need of."[29]

Third, as the pain of the boycott increased, differences over strategy and objectives became more acute. Both the De Lanceys and the Liberty

Boys loathed the Townshend Duties, for neither wanted unconstitutional taxation or the establishment of a permanent revenue that would free crown officials from local oversight. Unlike the De Lanceys, the Liberty Boys also opposed the Townshend Duties, because they detested all restraints on trade. If the boycott had persuaded Britain to stop taxing paper, paint, lead, and glass, why not seek a grander victory and persevere until the tea duty was rescinded too? If continued resistance were to result in the removal of all mercantilist restrictions on trade, so much the better.[30] De Lanceyites were more pragmatic. Though they were loath to repudiate accepted whig principles, they were amenable to compromise. If Britain had rescinded all the Townshend Duties except that on tea, why not end nonimportation against all items but tea? Their moderation was grounded in an ideological and self-interested commitment to the empire. They wanted to make mercantilism work, not to undermine it. American rights must be secured, yet prudence was needed to preserve long-term relationships and to protect the city's economy. They might be in tactical alliance with Real Whigs like "Cethegus" and radicals like Sears, yet they could not join with the first in assailing trade as an obstacle to "economy" or with the second in reviling mercantilism. Instead, they hoped their ability to mediate between Britain and the province would lead to an equitable solution to the imperial crisis, to economic prosperity, and to political power for their party.[31]

Radicals were incensed that the De Lanceys might abandon the consensus that New Yorkers had crafted over how best to resist unconstitutional taxation. On May 10 Nathaniel Rogers, a Bostonian who had not signed that city's boycott agreement, came to New York. A crowd of about a thousand burned his effigy in the Fields. On May 15 "A Son of Liberty" explained in a broadside that continuing nonimportation was the only sure way to secure repeal of the tea tax. On May 17 the Liberty Boys published a letter from South Carolina's General Committee, calling for a comprehensive agreement so that the association would operate uniformly throughout America.[32] But De Lancey merchants would not be dissuaded. On May 16 the committee of inspection had written the merchants of Boston and Connecticut that the partial repeal of the Townshend Duties was a gesture of reconciliation that ought to be met in kind; the colonies should limit nonimportation to items like tea upon which Parliament levied a tax to raise a revenue in America. On May 18 the committee held a meeting of the subscribers to the nonimportation agreement. Though some favored lifting the boycott at once, the members present agreed to wait a few weeks in the hope that the tea tax would be rescinded.[33]

The radicals meanwhile mobilized public opinion. "Brutus" (McDougall) argued, "Nothing can be more flagrantly wrong than the Assertion of some of our mercantile Dons, that the Mechanics have no Right to give their Sentiments about the Importation of *British* Commodities." In 1768, when the merchants had adopted the boycott agreement, "they not only requested a similar Association of the Mechanics, but by frequent Meetings, conspired with them in support of the important Compact" against importation. McDougall now called upon "Freemen, of all Ranks, from the Man of Wealth, to the Man whose only Portion is Liberty" to "Suffer not a few interested, parricidical and treacherous Inhabitants, to gratify their Avarice at the Expense of our common Interests." Another writer protested, "How unreasonable! . . . are the Suggestions of those that say, none but the Importers have a Right to give their Voice on the Subject of breaking or continuing the Agreement." Should "the Advantage of a few . . . be put in Competition by Englishmen with their Freedom?"[34] And letters (purportedly from London) appeared in the newspapers to add weight to that opinion. One claimed that the ministry kept the duty on tea as a "Test of American Liberty"; and that America's "conduct at this juncture will, in great measure determine" its "future fate."[35]

News that Newport's merchants had deserted the boycott intensified the conflict. Though New York's committee of inspection condemned that city on May 29, the radicals held a public meeting the next day to push their own agenda: a boycott of Newport for hurting "the Cause of Liberty"; and the continuation of nonimportation until the Townshend Duties were "totally" repealed.[36] The next day the committee of inspection announced that it was disbanding because of the public meeting, and it asked residents to assemble at eleven o'clock on June 1. In the event, the anti-boycott forces tried to elect a new committee composed entirely of their own supporters. But the meeting, wanting to restore a consensus in the community, reappointed the original group and "determined strictly to adhere to" nonimportation. The next day the committee wrote its counterparts elsewhere in America, asking them to poll their residents and to appoint six delegates each to attend a congress at Norwalk, Connecticut, on June 18 "to adopt one general solid System for the whole," so that "all share equally the same Fate."[37]

McDougall, recipients of the letter, and some historians have argued that De Lancey merchants proposed the plan so that they could secure, at an intercolonial congress, what they could not obtain at a meeting of their own townspeople. Sears, however, signed the letter too. That persuaded Robert J. Christen, for one, that the Liberty Boy had proposed or had at least supported the idea. In truth, both sides had good reason to endorse the plan for a hastily summoned Congress. At the end of May a pamphlet had appeared in New York with estimates of the British manufactures imported into America between December 25, 1767, and December 25, 1769. The numbers confirmed what many had known all along: Boston was cheating on nonimportation. And, if New York merchants could not tolerate their counterparts in Massachusetts taking advantage of the situation, New York radicals feared the boycott would quickly fall apart now that Newport had abandoned it. Moreover, on May 31, the *New York Journal* printed fresh intelligence from Britain that the tea tax would not be removed. Under the circumstances, if the Norwalk congress could be persuaded to accept South Carolina's proposal, which called for the adoption of a comprehensive nonimportation agreement, the radicals would be satisfied; the boycott would survive, and De Lanceyites could no longer claim that they could, on their own initiative, terminate nonimportation. And since public opinion in New York still strongly supported nonimportation, merchants could take comfort from the fact that it would be uniformly enforced throughout the colonies. Of course, if the other cities promptly refused to appoint delegates, or if the meeting accomplished nothing, the merchants understood that their case for ending the boycott would thereby be strengthened.[38]

Unfortunately for New York, Philadelphia rejected the idea of a congress on June 5, and Boston followed suit on June 8. Now that the plan for a congress was dead, the De Lanceys resumed their campaign to lift the boycott. On June 11 a group of merchants and mechanics asked the committee to approve a plan to ascertain public opinion by having people in each ward collect the signatures of those who favored modifying the nonimportation agreement. By conducting a poll the anti-boycott forces could argue that the community, and not the merchants, had made the decision. Why a subscription list and not a public meeting? The De Lanceys knew that they could better influence how artisans sided in one-on-one encounters, where deference and economic dependence would come into play, than at an open meeting, where passions might be swayed by inflammatory rhetoric. De Lanceyites could also limit participation to legal voters, thus keeping Sears from mobilizing the unfranchised.[39]

When the committee concluded that it "could not with any propriety interfere" with the proposal, the group interpreted that as license to proceed and that evening organized a poll. Caught off guard, the Liberty Boys marshaled their forces quickly, and on the morning of June 12 both sides began collecting signatures. The radicals hastily called a midday meeting in the Fields of those opposed to reopening trade. People were urged not to sign the merchants' petition before the meeting (at which the unfranchised could participate) reached a decision. In the end, those against nonimportation gathered about twelve hundred names.[40] When the tallies of the pro-boycott forces failed to come close, the merchants claimed victory and "sent off expresses to Boston and Philadelphia for their concurrence."[41]

When the committee of inspection met on June 14, it nonetheless failed to ratify the De Lancey victory. A majority wanted to end the boycott, but Sears deftly exploited their genuine desire to forge a consensus on the issue. He protested that he had not had enough time to collect signatures and accused several members of impropriety: they had worked openly on June 12 to amend the association, even though they were responsible for enforcing it. To cause more confusion, Sears and Peter Vandervoort, a radical Dutch shopkeeper, resigned from the committee, claiming that they could no longer work with "men who are using every Effort to counteract the very Design of our Appointment."[42] "A Son of Liberty" insisted that the boycott should be continued, since those for lifting it did "not amount to above one third of the inhabitants of this city."[43]

New Yorkers heatedly debated what the poll signified and why Sears had resigned, but the merchants were determined to end the impasse. On June 16 they asked Boston and Philadelphia to poll their residents at once. If New York's importers hoped in that way to spread responsibility for ending the boycott, they were sadly disappointed. On June 18 Philadelphia's committee, which that city's popular leaders still controlled, replied that it was "determined to adhere to the Agreement as it now stands." The letter sarcastically declared that by initiating nonimportation New Yorkers had "made a glorious Stand, which cannot fail of being recorded with Honour in the Annals of Posterity, provided they do not Tarnish their past Conduct by precipitate Measures in Time to come."[44]

Nor were New York's pro-boycott forces idle. "A Member of the Church of England and a Son of Liberty" argued that "no *particular city*" could "break ground, *or to shrink back in the least,* from the grand and *sacred cause of universal Liberty.*" He revived the idea of a congress as the best way to proceed. So that the other side could not piously avow that resuming trade would help the poor, he proposed, "Let us . . . petition our assembly, to grant a *reasonable sum,* for the relief of sufferers; — We have the strongest reason to trust, that *money* would cheerfully be granted." In short, if De Lanceyites had the city's best interest at heart, let the Assembly, which they controlled, come to the rescue.[45]

The battle soon turned violent. On June 26 residents learned that David Hill of Boston was in town selling goods he had acquired contrary to that city's nonimportation agreement. When the committee questioned him, he agreed to store his wares temporarily at the home of Jonas Platt, a Presbyterian who had voted for three of the four Livingston candidates in 1769 and had signed the subscription list to continue nonimportation. That evening a crowd visited Platt's house and proceeded directly into the room where the goods had been "*confidentially*" cached. The contraband was then taken outside and burned. Indignant, the committee called the act a "high Insult." The next day the committee charged that the rioters had acted "from the natural Malignity of their Hearts, or for the sake of *Plunder,* or from a false Zeal to acquire the Title of Sons of Liberty." But Peter T. Curtenius, a committee member and Dutch Reformed merchant who had voted for the Livingston ticket in 1769, objected strongly: what had happened had resulted from "intemperate Zeal," not "from a real malignity of Heart."[46] Of course, the activities of Platt and Curtenius underscore how closely the radicals and Livingstonites were now working.

Despite the opposition to modifying the association, events spurred De Lanceyites to action. In late June word came that Parliament had at last authorized the colony to print paper money. And, on July 3, an express rider brought news that Boston remained as committed as Philadelphia to nonimportation. The committee of inspection consequently scheduled a meeting of the association's subscribers, for the following night, to reassess the situation.[47] But the radicals quickly gathered their supporters, and more people than expected attended the meeting. When the committee proposed polling the town again to determine how to proceed, the "general cry was no importation." The pro-boycott forces demanded, too, that the letters from Philadelphia and Boston be printed so that all might know the objections those cities had to the merchants' plan. Isaac Low, the De Lanceyite committee chair, initially agreed but reversed himself after one of the city's assemblymen admonished him that that would "overthrow their scheme." The meeting broke up in confusion.[48]

On Friday, July 6, three committee members met secretly with the antiboycott forces; together they decided to poll the city the next day to measure public opinion. Whatever the result, they were determined to end nonimportation, for they "agreed at all events to send their orders by the Packet to send them goods as usual."[49] On Saturday, "A Number of the Inhabitants" held a midday meeting to divulge what the merchants had decided clandestinely the night before. Not unexpectedly, the meeting voted "to use all lawful means" to uphold the association.[50] Sears "publicly declared" that "if any Merchant, or number of Merchants presumed to break through the non importation agreement till the several Provinces had agreed to do the same, he would lose his life in the attempt, or the goods imported should be burned as soon as landed."[51] That night almost sixty Liberty Boys paraded about town in support of the association. But they were ambushed and thrashed on Wall Street by an armed mob the merchants had organized. To add insult to injury, that same evening the committee of inspection endorsed the plan for a poll and set the date for Monday, July 9. In the event, the radicals suffered yet another defeat: 794 favored modifying the association; and only 465 were opposed.[52]

The odds had been against the radicals from the start. First, many residents either refused to take sides or had voted to end the boycott, for they were suffering terribly both from nonimportation and from the economic downturn. Alexander Colden said it best: "Many families must starve if an importation of goods from Great Britain did not soon take place." Why should New York endure so much suffering when the other cities had refused to meet in a general congress or to stop the cheating? Second, the incidents on Golden Hill, at Platt's home, and on Wall Street had left quite a few residents troubled about the violent turn of affairs. Perhaps now was the time to compromise before the situation got out of hand. Third, in a situation like this one, where a conflict drags on endlessly and its costs multiply, the radical leaders of the cause typically become more extreme, while their followers become less so. Not only have the leaders made a greater personal investment in the contest, but their status is also at stake. Sears had failed to discern people's emotional exhaustion, but the De Lanceys had been able to capitalize on it. Other than under exceptional circumstances, only a small segment of a population is ever genuinely radical. Hence, Sears's demand that the city ignore what looked like a British concession seemed to many people unwarranted and provocative. The De Lancey position, by contrast, appeared not only reasonable but better able to keep the city united.[53]

Though only a minority of residents had actually participated in the poll, the De Lanceyite Isaac Low, who chaired the committee of inspection, declared the boycott over and admonished traders not to import tea or any other item on which Parliament might levy a duty to raise revenue in America. The next day the merchants wrote to Philadelphia and Boston, justifying their decision. And on July 11 the *Earl of Halifax* sailed for Britain with orders for British goods.[54] The Liberty Boys tried in vain to reverse the decision. Meeting at Hampden Hall on July 25, they prepared "A Protest" condemning what had been done "upon this slender Voice" of 794 persons. About 225 people eventually signed the document, but they could not alter the course of events in New York, for the Liberty Boys had clearly misjudged public sentiment. When the merchandise arrived several months later, Sears never intervened to stop it from landing. By that time he had already sent his own order to Britain for goods.[55]

V

If the merchants had won the importation battle, the city had lost the respect it had earned throughout America in 1765 for its forthright defense of colonial rights. The unkindest cut of all came from Philadelphia, which scornfully demanded that New York take down its Liberty Pole, since the city had no further use for it. A Virginian lamented "that Men who have soar'd so high as to attract the Admiration and Esteem of all the virtuous Part of Mankind, should at once sink so low as to become the Contempt and Derision of every Individual!"[56]

The criticism was unfair. True, greed had led some individuals to abandon the boycott. One trader admitted that "it is for the interest of the city in particular, but not of the country in general, that we should import." But other cities bore responsibility, too, for they had not enforced their associations as well as they should have. Newport came into nonimportation late and sought to get out early. Philadelphia had almost abandoned the boycott before New York did, because of the struggle between its merchants and popular leaders for power. Moreover, the other cities soon put aside their righteousness and resumed importing British goods. Interestingly, despite the claims by historians that the behavior of the De Lanceys and the Livingstons was marked only by opportunism, New York and Philadelphia were the only cities that faithfully upheld the boycott against tea.[57]

Despite the criticism, perhaps because of it, the De Lanceys' popularity did not suffer. That became evident in October 1770 at the annual municipal elections, which the De Lancey and Livingston parties made a test of strength. The campaign was waged with such "great Heat" that 133 New Yorkers enrolled as freemen in September. Even the governor's Council entered the fray, when three De Lancey councillors violated tradition to cast ballots. Livingstonites pressured William Smith to vote for Abraham Lott, a Dutch Reformed merchant and a Livingstonite friend of Sears. Smith refused, arguing that it was wrong for councillors to meddle in local elections. Lott won anyway, and he was not the only Livingstonite to do so. But the De Lanceys nonetheless won control of the municipal government. Colden informed London that the Livingstons were "entirely defeated . . . in a violent struggle to turn out such of the elective Magistrates of the City as had distinguished themselves anyway in favour of Government." And James Rivington exulted, "Last Saturday a Struggle was made by the McDougall party to get the better in City Elections, of the Royalists, but the latter prevailed and Established an Everlasting and invincible Superiority."[58]

Events did not turn out as Rivington predicted. New York's new governor, Lord Dunmore, arrived on October 18 and took the oath of office the next day. After the ceremonies, the Council dined at a tavern at Colden's expense. It was an extravagance the old man quickly regretted, for Dunmore demanded straightaway that the lieutenant governor pay him one-half of all the "perquisites and Emoluments" of office from January 2 (the date of Dunmore's commission) until October 19 (the date he assumed power). A governor customarily had the right to that share of the spoils of office when out of the province. But Colden insisted that by "usage and Custom" a governor could claim those monies only after taking the oath of office, not before. Colden had the better argument, and Dunmore would leave office in 1771 without collecting what he believed his due.[59]

This quarrel between the two covetous placemen quickly became a political issue. On October 30 Dunmore asked William Smith for advice, and the latter soon became the former's confidant, tutoring him in the intricacies of local politics. That Smith was too good a mentor became evident in December. Smith had encouraged Robert R. Livingston to petition the governor concerning his right to an Assembly seat, and to ask Dunmore to remind the lawmakers that the king had disallowed their act barring judges from the Assembly. Dunmore's secretary wrote Colden for the necessary paperwork. When Colden's son David sent the material, he denied that his father had received one of the items requested, a Board of Trade report stating why the crown had rejected the law. Smith insisted that the document had been read in Council, but the other councillors either contradicted him or kept silent. Since three of them had earlier told Smith that they remembered it, he concluded that the De Lanceys had joined "the Plott to conceal from Ld Dunmore the Report." It quickly became clear, however, that Dunmore himself was participating in the cover-up when he declared that the important "Question is whether I shall lay the Refusal before the Assembly or not?" Only Smith thought that he should, and the governor decided not to do so. When someone asked whether minutes of the meeting should be kept, most said no, and Dunmore agreed. He was not going to provoke a political uproar in New York or risk damaging his reputation in London. Smith, however, soon warned the governor's secretary that if Dunmore did not act, the people would conclude "that the Govr was in their [the De Lanceys'] pocket."

Livingston would surely petition the king, and Dunmore "would be blamed there, especially if the Minority at home got in to the Administration." Dunmore, accordingly, spoke privately with each lawmaker, but when the matter again came before the House, it voted against Livingston. Dunmore could nonetheless write home that he had done his best to uphold the prerogative; dissolution was an alternative he had considered but rejected, because a new Assembly would act no differently.[60]

The De Lanceys struck at the Livingstons in other ways, too. The Assembly ordered McDougall to appear before it on December 13, 1770. When members grilled him about whether he had written *To the Betrayed Inhabitants*, he refused to answer on the grounds that doing so would put him in double jeopardy: he was still under grand jury indictment for authoring the broadside, which the House had branded a seditious libel. The House declared him in contempt and ordered his arrest. This time his confinement was met with indifference by a community weary of dissension. After writing two long epistles to the public, he fell silent. John Morin Scott tried to get him released by a writ of habeas corpus from the Supreme Court, but the Assembly made it clear it would ignore such an order. McDougall thus languished in jail until Dunmore prorogued the Assembly on March 4, 1771.[61]

De Lanceyites punished Sears, too. He had been appointed to the newly created post of inspector of pot and pearl ash for his work in the 1769 campaign, and within a year the Sears–De Lancey coalition had fallen apart. But the work of inspector had increased so much that Sears asked the Assembly in December 1770 for authority to appoint an assistant to serve when he was out of town. De Lanceyites used the occasion to besmirch him. Jauncey offered amendments to the bill that implied Sears was guilty of fraud and malfeasance. In March Sears again petitioned the House, this time denying any wrongdoing and demanding a full investigation. When the Assembly refused his request, he resigned. Despite Smith's objections, the Council then appointed Abraham De La Montayne, a Dutch Reformed De Lanceyite who knew little about pot or pearl ash, but whose politics were right. To add insult to injury, Joseph Allicocke, a former ally of Sears who had remained in the De Lancey camp, was named assistant inspector.[62]

Allicocke's career is worth exploring briefly because it demonstrates how complex were the choices people made in the small but polyglot society of New York City in 1770. Only a little is known of his background. Donald A. Grinde, Jr., has claimed that he was African American; the proof was a remark by Capt. John Montresor in his *Journal* that Allicocke was the "son of a mulatto woman." Was Montresor stating common knowledge, repeating a rumor, or inventing a falsehood? It is impossible to know. Allicocke told the Loyalist Commission after the war that he was a native of Ireland. William Franklin, the Governor of New Jersey at the start of the Revolution and a boyhood acquaintance of Allicocke, reported that Joseph's father was a resident of Antigua who had sent his son to Philadelphia for schooling. On January 31, 1760, in Trinity Church Parish, Allicocke married Martha Jardine, the daughter of Charles Jardine, a Staten Island "Gentleman" of Huguenot descent. Martha's sister Catherine had married John Lamb in 1755. Allicocke began his business career in 1762 as a clerk or (said William Smith) as "an under Agent to Watts & De Lancey in the Provision Contract" to supply the British forces stationed in New York. Sometime during the 1760s he made the transition to merchant; Pauline Maier thought he had done so by 1765. When he enrolled as a freeman in New York City on January 31, 1769, he styled himself a "Gentleman," though he became a member of the New York Chamber of Commerce only after the British occupied New York in 1776.[63]

His political career had begun during the Stamp Act crisis when he became a Liberty Boy leader and was often mentioned in connection with Sears and Lamb. At issue is why Allicocke sided with the De Lanceys in 1769, when that party broke with the Liberty Boys over the Quartering Act; then defended the Tea Act of 1773; and even defied the mob, in late 1775 and early 1776, by resupplying the naval vessels stationed at New York. He fled the city hastily in January 1776 but returned from Antigua in 1777 only to became a loyalist exile in England at war's end.

In the early 1760s Allicocke had clearly been a man on the make, one who had had the business savvy not only to land a job with influential patricians but to win their accolades for his work.[64] If he used his connections with John Watts and the De Lancey family to ease into the merchant class, did he use his ties with his in-laws to rise to a leadership role among the Liberty Boys? Did he rejoice at his good fortune that both Sears and James De Lancey became allies in December 1765? Did he keep De Lancey posted on what his radical friends were thinking and planning? When he broke with Sears in 1769, was it because James De Lancey had been his patron from the start? Had experience taught him how important the British army (and the money it brought) was, both to his own and to the city's economic welfare? Or had acceptance by the De Lanceys afforded this man (who perhaps had some African blood flowing in his veins) a social respectability the Liberty Boys could never give him? Though the extant records tell us almost nothing about his commitment to Anglicanism, might that faith, too, have been a force in his political life? Allicocke's history indicates how treacherous it can be to make generalizations about why people acted the way they did in New York between 1763 and 1776. Multiply Allicocke many times over, and it also becomes easier to grasp why it was so difficult for New Yorkers to hammer out a consensus on how best to resist British imperialism, and for historians to determine why they became such reluctant revolutionaries.

Whatever the reasons Allicocke traveled the path he did, the struggle between the De Lanceys and the Livingstons continued after William Tryon succeeded Dunmore in July 1771. Both parties again schemed to see who would win the new governor's ear, but Tryon, who as governor of North Carolina had just defeated the Regulator movement in that colony in the Battle of Alamance (May 1771), refused to become anyone's pawn. He informed Smith that "he was determined to be drawn into no dangerous Measures — That he meant to be independent." And he told his Council: "I wish to promote the Interest of the Province, and find it very disagreable to me to be crossed by your Parties. . . . I will take no sides myself, and desire that I may not be dealt with or crossed for Party Purposes." At times Tryon favored the De Lanceys; at other times, the Livingstons. He even consulted with Colden. He nearly resigned in 1772 out of frustration, but he succeeded in preserving his freedom of action while keeping the parties from harming his reputation in Britain.[65]

In hindsight, what was crucial about the political battles fought in the three years after the boycott's demise was not the details of how each party sought to wound the other. It was, instead, the ordinariness of what they were fighting about: tempers flared, but what was at stake was patronage and profit, not high principle. Lord North's tactic of sundering American unity by letting New York issue paper money and by rescinding all but one of the Townshend Duties had succeeded. He had defused the crisis, and New Yorkers had returned to squabbling over everyday issues. The economy remained weak, and Livingstonites had acquired popularity out of doors, but De Lanceyites retained control of the Council, the Assembly, and City Hall. The Liberty Boys had gained a storehouse of knowledge about organizing and operating extralegal committees and were increasingly influential in the Livingston camp, yet there was no broad support for the radical agenda. Political, religious, social, and economic tensions divided the city, but they were not driving it toward political instability or revolution. Indeed, the Assembly quietly voted money for the army every year until 1775. Nonetheless, if the ministry were to resume a hard-line imperialistic policy toward the colonies, the situation in New York would change rapidly.

New York's population, again, was heterogeneous. Because all the

groups that had been fighting the Townshend Duties had both conflicting and complementary relations with one other, it was impossible for
partisans to keep the imperial struggle separate from provincial politics.
Hence, the Anglo-American crisis exacerbated party conflict in New York,
and the latter did the same to the former. Because the long-term objectives and the costs of waging the struggle against Britain were different
for each group involved, the conflict's escalation and duration finally
undercut the unity that had initially determined the best mode of pursuing the conflict. That development allowed Britain to play one faction off
against the others. If New Yorkers had learned the perils of violence in
1765, they had discovered the pitfalls of disunity in 1770.[66]

The lesson for Britain should have been clear: a judicious use of compromise (even if only for tactical reasons) enhanced its power over the
colonies; confrontation dissolved the bonds of unity holding the empire
together. Still, even if Lord North had learned that much, he had not
won the war. The tea tax remained, but so too did New York's tea boycott.
The American opposition was divided, but Britain had not achieved the
long-term objectives for which it had waged the struggle in the first place.
So long as the ministry played divide and conquer, the imperial relationship was manageable, but if Britain were to challenge the status quo, there
was no telling what might happen. In sum, the second British-American
crisis had petered out, but questions remained. Was Britain prepared to
forgo exercising its alleged right to tax the colonies internally or to cease
exerting its sovereignty in ways that hackled Americans? Given all that
had happened, if another crisis emerged, could New Yorkers put aside
party animosity and unite in defense of American rights?

PART III

REVOLUTION AND INDEPENDENCE, 1773–1776

CHAPTER EIGHT

The Tea Act and
the Coercive Acts

Repealing the Townshend Duties and letting the province issue paper money calmed relations between Britain and New York, but the need to finance the huge debt incurred in the Seven Years' War finally embroiled the two sides in a third, decisive crisis. In its quest for revenue the ministry had reached an agreement in 1767 with the East India Company, whereby the latter would pay £400,000 a year to the Exchequer for two years, and in 1769 the arrangement was renewed for five more years. But war in India, fear of renewed war with France, famine in Bengal, the company's insistence on increasing the dividend it paid to stockholders, and the financial crash of 1772 nearly ruined the company. The government loaned it £1,400,000 and agreed to forgo the annual payments for several years.[1]

To regain financial health, however, the company needed to find a market for its surplus tea. The source of this predicament lay in the fact that duties on the beverage were so exorbitant that about half the tea consumed in Britain was smuggled into the country. The government had temporarily reduced the tax in 1767, but rates were to return to their previous levels in 1773, and the company once again faced a sharp drop in sales. One alternative was to dump the oversupply in Europe, but for exported tea to be competitive there, the government would have to give the company a rebate of all the duties collected on the beverage. But tea sold on the Continent without a duty could easily be smuggled back home. It was consequently decided that the product would be marketed in America. The Tea Act of May 1773 remitted all British duties on tea exported to the colonies and allowed the company to sell directly to consignees there, instead of at public auction in Britain. Company tea would thus be cheaper in America than smuggled tea. Company officials had asked that the law also abolish the Townshend tea tax; in return, they would agree to forgo a full drawback on duties paid in Britain. But Lord North would not forgo that symbol of parliamentary authority. The cabinet also gave scant thought to how colonists would react to a law that overturned long-established patterns of trade, ruined businesses by granting the East India Company a monopoly in America, and reopened the question of whether Parliament could tax the colonies.

The *New York Gazette* printed the Tea Act on September 6, 1773, and on Sunday, September 26, the *Lord Dunmore* brought word that the company was shipping six hundred chests of tea to the city; the firm's newly chosen agents were to pay the requisite duty upon the cargo's arrival. Isaac Sears and Alexander McDougall mobilized their forces at once. No longer neophytes, they could draw on their understanding of crowd psychology, their familiarity with local politics, their experiences (both successful and unsuccessful) over the past decade, and their network of like-minded partisans in other provinces.[2] Significantly, the strategy they devised to resist the Tea Act (and later the Coercive Acts) aimed not to overthrow an allegedly "unstable" old order in the province but to unite all New Yorkers, regardless of political affiliation, in a crusade against British imperialism.[3]

The radicals' first task was to explain why the Tea Act had to be resisted. Using the pseudonym "Hampden," McDougall began the propaganda barrage with five broadsides, entitled *The Alarm*. One asserted that

> The East India Company, obtained the monopoly . . . by bribery, and corruption. That the power thus obtained, they have prostituted to extortion, and other the most cruel and horrid purposes, the Sun ever beheld. That by the wealth obtained . . . they have poisoned the Constitution at home, into a system of corruption, which they are now endeavouring to extend to this country. That the Company, by the intended *importation* of Tea, will rob the colony, in a commercial view, of near twenty nine thousand pounds currency per annum.[4]

Others essayists followed suit; and the port was drenched in a deluge of words.[5] Three themes stood out. The first—that the law gave the East India Company an illegal monopoly—had wide appeal: smugglers knew that their illicit profits were jeopardized by cheap tea from England; reputable tea dealers, that their businesses had been arbitrarily assigned to company agents; traders in other products, that they might suffer a like fate; radicals, that economic opportunity had once again narrowed; and consumers, that the price of tea would increase.[6]

The second theme was that the act was a ruse to "trick" Americans into paying the Townshend tea tax.[7] As "Zeno" said, "If the *English Tea* is permitted to land here, before the *Tea-Act* is repealed; there is Nothing we possess, whether Lands, Houses, Cattle, Money, or any Thing else, which we can *then* call our own."[8] Another writer added that if residents paid the tax, "the Ministry, no longer under any restraint, will raise their exactions as high as they please." "Legion" feared "slavery."[9]

The third argument, though reflecting a view still not routinely held, was increasingly affecting how people saw the Tea Act and the empire. Vexed by a decade of crises, writers were not merely denying Parliament's power to tax them, they were disputing both its right to pass any legislation whatsoever for the colonies and its claim to sovereignty over them. Peter Van Schaack, a future tory, opined, "The benefits arising from our commerce is all Great Britain ought to expect. By grasping at more, they will probably lose all. The absurdity of uniting the idea of a right in the Americans to the liberties of Englishmen, with that of a subordination to the British Parliament, is every day growing more evident." In November 1773, "A Citizen" said that the issue was "whether we shall be governed by laws, made with our own consent, or by those to which neither we, nor our representatives, have contributed, or consented; whether we shall, in security, possess our lives and properties, or, that they shall be wholly dependent on the will of others." In December, "Americanus" would deny that Parliament could "make any laws binding upon us; because they neither are our representatives, nor have they our consent to make such laws." In September 1774, "A British American" would reject the Declaratory Act's claim that Parliament had "a Right to make Laws of sufficient Force to bind us *in all cases whatsoever.*" "All Men have a natural Right to Freedom" and "a Right to their Vote and Influence in every Restraint that can be laid upon it by human power; nor can these Restraints and Regulations, justly extend further than is necessary for the general Preservation and Security of Freedom and Property." The next month a writer would assert, "The Assemblies or Parliaments of the British Colonies in America, have an exclusive right, not only of taxation, but of legislation also; and that the British Parliament, so far from having a right to make laws binding upon those Colonies *in all cases whatsoever,* has really no just right to make any laws at all binding upon the Colonies."[10]

Not all New Yorkers endorsed this portentous line of reasoning. "Poplicola," for example, argued that a "patriot" put the "good of the *whole society*" first; "when men unite in civil society, a common interest of the whole is formed, and each member obliges himself to act jointly with the rest for the common interest." "A *sovereign* and *uncontrollable* authority" must govern every state. Though "*local* circumstances prevent our being completely *represented*" in Parliament, the general welfare required obedience. Hence, Americans must contest the "arbitrary incroachments of some men among us, who have assumed the legislative power of the colony, arrogated the privilege of decreeing what is right or wrong, and assumed the *judicial* and *executive* power of determining on the actions of any of the community."[11]

Radicals, of course, were not persuaded by such arguments. On October 14, 1773, a handbill warned company agents not to sell dutied tea. To consider doing so meant "you are lost, — lost to virtues, lost to your country. It is in vain to expect that AMERICANS can give a sanction *to your office*." A week later "Phileleutheros" argued that if the East India Company succeeded in establishing a monopoly, it would "be followed, by all the great manufacturing houses in England: So that they could not fail to engross, in a little time, the whole trade of this great and extensive continent." The writer cautioned the agents to brace themselves for "the gathering storm, before it . . . overwhelms you with a sudden, dreadful, and sure destruction." The same day "Brutus" (McDougall) reminded De Lanceyite "Friends of Liberty and Commerce" that they were obligated to continue the 1770 tea boycott.[12]

On October 15 a handbill had asked residents to convene that day to thank the sea captains who had refused to transport company tea to America. In the event, "most of the Merchants, and many other Inhabitants" assembled and warned all the captains that they would "incur" people's "just Indignation" if they imported company tea. The fact that merchants participated in the meeting at all demonstrates that they had joined the Liberty Boy–Livingston coalition in opposing the act. De Lanceyite importers were thus plainly in a quandary. If they accepted company tea, they would be conceding that the government could both create monopolies and tax them. They would also, by default, be ceding command of the protest movement to the radicals. Yet, resisting the law would lead inevitably to crowd action, nonimportation, and collaboration with the Liberty Boys. De Lanceyites apparently hoped to resolve their dilemma by pressuring captains not to bring tea into port, so that merchants could steer clear of both the radicals and the Tea Act.[13]

II

Clearly, Lord North had taken a fateful step in aiding the East India Company. If the repeal of the Townshend Duties had divided residents and defeated nonimportation, the Tea Act was reuniting them in defense of American rights. William Smith noted that the Liberty Boys and the tea smugglers had "set up the Cry of Liberty." He predicted that "Vertue and Vice being thus united, . . . we shall repeat all the Confusions of 1765 and 1766. — Time will shew the Event. Our Domestic Parties will probably die, and be swallowed up in the general Opposition to the Parliamentary Project of raising the Arm of Government by Revenue Laws."[14]

Radicals maintained the pressure on De Lanceyites. On November 5, "Cassius" reminded them that they had voted in 1770 to consider anyone who imported dutied items to be a public enemy. The writer consequently demanded that the Friends of Liberty and Commerce condemn William Kelly (who had returned to London) for telling the tea company that "there was no danger from the Resentment of the People of New York"; in 1765 "they had an old man (Mr. Colden) to deal with, but now they had Governor Tryon, (a Military Man) who . . . would cram the Tea down their Throats." The company had authorized Kelly to export tea to New York, and he had made Abraham Lott, the colony's treasurer, his agent. The night "Cassius's" article appeared, Kelly's effigy was carted about town and burned at the Coffee House before a crowd of thousands. If the spectacle intimidated importers, it also built group consciousness, afforded participants a feeling of power, and fostered the impression that victory was inevitable.[15]

The warnings soon became more "threatening." On November 10, "Legion" admonished the harbor pilots not to guide any ship with tea into port, or they would face "the vengeance of a free people."[16] "A number of our citizens," doubtless all radicals, chose a committee on November 24 to secure a pledge from the company's agents—Benjamin Booth and Henry White, who were Anglican, and Abraham Lott, who was Dutch Reformed—not to accept dutied tea. The next day the three (all of them future loyalists) declared that they had not yet received company appointments but vowed that they would not handle dutied goods.[17] On November 27, "the Mohawks" promised "an unwelcome visit" to anyone who landed the tea. Two days later, so "that no means might be neglected to insure a uniformity of conduct," radicals distributed copies of "The Association of the Sons of Liberty of New York" about town.[18] According to one of its authors, the association presented "the strongest terms of opposition, without actual violence, against the importation of that commodity . . ., leaving the use of force to prevent the mischief, to be resolved in some future time."[19]

How much support the Association had is unclear. Smith, a member of the governor's Council, wrote that as of December 7 few had signed their names to the document. Six days later McDougall conceded that a "secret opposition" existed but claimed that "a great number of the Principal Merchants, Lawyers, and other inhabitants" had subscribed to it. The tea agents had taken no chances, however. On December 1, upon receiving notice of their appointment, they had informed Tryon that they would not accept any company tea and had urged him to assume responsibility for it. The Council agreed the same day that the frigate *Swan* should guide into port the ship that was expected to arrive shortly with dutied tea, and that the tea should be warehoused in the fort. Smith thought the Council's handling of the crisis had calmed the city; and even McDougall seemed satisfied.[20]

What would have happened if the tea ship had appeared in December is unknown, but in fact it reached port only in April. Meanwhile, John and Samuel Broome (two Livingstonite, Presbyterian merchants), Philip Livingston, Alexander McDougall, Isaac Sears, and Isaac Low were notified on December 7 that a Boston town meeting had agreed that the tea that had just arrived there must be returned to London in the ship in which it had arrived. Why word was sent to the six is unknown. What is clear is that Livingstonites, De Lanceyites, and radicals were working together, another sign of how effective McDougall and Sears had been in broadening the base of opposition to the Tea Act.[21]

The six soon began urging the governor's councillors to persuade Tryon not to embroil himself in the controversy. The group's moderates worried about mob violence if the commodity were landed. The more radical feared that if the tea were stored, pressure would mount on Tryon to release it for sale. Isaac Low, a De Lanceyite, was spokesperson. He explained to each councillor that residents had not objected to storing the tea until the other royal governors had refused to accept responsibility for it. Smith told the group on December 10 that he would follow his own conscience in advising the governor. After the others gave like replies, the group warned Smith that there would be violence if the vessel failed to leave port promptly or attempted to unload its cargo. Smith answered that Tryon would soon visit England and "wished to be able to hold up his Head at Court." He could not do so unless he enforced his decision to land the tea. If the Low group did not relent, there would be rioting when the shipment arrived; if the army were insulted, bloodshed would follow. Low and Livingston wavered, but Sears remained adamant; and McDougall exclaimed, "What if we prevent the Landing, and kill Gov[erno]r and all the Council?"[22]

His belligerence bespoke frustration, not bloodthirstiness. The same day he wrote William Cooper in Boston that opinion against the Association remained strong, though opposition to landing the tea was building. He favored a "uniformity of conduct" in America and hoped New York would follow Boston's lead. But he could not predict the outcome of a meeting scheduled to pick a committee of correspondence. Nonetheless, McDougall's position was stronger than he realized, for events had underscored the logic of preventing the landing of the tea. And Low and Livingston were unlikely to disown the Association, especially since McDougall had mentioned murder. What was needed was a face-saving formula to spare Tryon embarrassment.[23]

On Wednesday, December 15, before a Council meeting, Smith briefed Tryon about Low's group and urged firmness. When the Council again voted to store the tea, Tryon found himself in an awkward spot. He did not want to appear weak, yet if he landed the tea, riots would ensue, as they had after the stamps had arrived in 1765. Nor was he the only one eager to avoid trouble. According to Smith, "the De Lanceys act and talk with us in Council, and yet give and take back — seem frigid, and I believe rather wonder at my Frankness for Storing the Téa." Tryon finally told his Council that he would land the tea but would not use armed force to do so. When someone objected, he said that he would risk the crowd's wrath and hoped the Council would support him. Smith urged the governor to publicize his plan and by so doing to divide the people, but Tryon wanted to handle matters quietly. The less he had to explain in London, the better.[24]

Tryon could not simply duck the issue, however. The next day "the committee of the Association" invited the townspeople to convene at City Hall on Friday. Despite inclement weather over two thousand attended the meeting, which John Lamb chaired. After letters from Philadelphia and Boston against importing company tea were read, a fifteen-member committee of correspondence was chosen, and "the Association of the Sons of Liberty of New York" was adopted. Smith later claimed that the De Lanceyites present had sided with the crowd "to save Interest."[25] Put differently, public opinion (and not the elite) was spearheading New York's resolute response to British imperialism.

The governor's Council, which was in session at the same time as the City Hall meeting, was bewildered. Was the public meeting legal? If not, how should the Council react? Smith suggested that if Tryon addressed the people, they would surely let the tea be warehoused. The Council finally decided that Mayor Whitehead Hicks and the city recorder should explain to those assembled that duty obliged Tryon to land the tea; but it would be unloaded in daylight without force and would not be distributed except on the king's direct order or with the Council's concurrence. After

Hicks spoke to the meeting, Lamb asked, "Is it then your Opinion, Gentlemen, that the Tea should be landed under this Circumstance?" The nays were nigh universal. Hicks's report to the Council was less than candid, however. He said that fewer than a thousand people were present and that they had appointed a committee of correspondence. "He had delivered No Message, but that the General Temper was agt. the Landing; That . . . the Question remained undecided, and that they adjourned to the Arrival of the Tea Ship." Only later would the Council learn the truth.[26]

On December 21 an express arrived with news of the Boston Tea Party. The next night radicals huddled in taverns, debating what to do when the tea reached New York. Henry White, a tea agent and councillor, told Smith he would urge Tryon to send the tea ship back to Britain without breaking cargo. White even asked if the agents themselves might order the ship home. When Smith said no, White insisted that he would not pay the duty but would get the collector of the customs to rule that the cargo could not be unloaded until the tax was paid. That way the cabinet could not rebuke Tryon for capitulating to the mob. White hinted that Smith should report their conversation to Sears and McDougall, but the councillor did not reply. Aware that the tea could not be landed without using force, Tryon welcomed White's advice, especially since he would not personally have to order the ship home. In the end, a three-way secret pact was worked out. Tryon agreed not to land the tea and to instruct the navy not to watch for the tea ship's arrival. The company's agents pledged that they would order the ship to sail without breaking cargo. And the Liberty Boys promised that if the ship's captain obeyed, he could resupply his vessel for the homeward voyage. Word of the bargain leaked, and when Tryon sailed for England on April 7, 1774, people gave him the biggest sendoff ever afforded a New York governor.[27]

On the night of April 18 the tea ship *Nancy* reached Sandy Hook. The pilots refused to guide it into port, and its captain, Benjamin Lockyer, was given the agents' letter that they would not accept his cargo or pay the duty on it and that he should not try to dock the vessel. The next morning the committee of correspondence announced that the ship would remain at Sandy Hook and that its captain would be allowed to buy provisions for his return voyage, which was scheduled for April 23. People were asked to assemble on that day to express "their detestation of the measures pursued by the Ministry and the India Company."[28]

There the affair should have ended. But the day the *Nancy* arrived, the committee learned that Capt. James Chambers had on board the *London* eighteen chests of tea. A committee of observation was promptly appointed to watch for his arrival. When the *London* reached port on April 22, Chambers assured the pilots and the committee of observation that he had no tea aboard. After he docked at Murray's Wharf, the committee of correspondence again asked about the tea. When at last he admitted the truth, the committee and the ship's owners interrogated him at the Queen's Head Tavern, where he confessed the tea was his own. Chambers had put everyone in a predicament. If a cargo's owner or consignee failed to pay the required duties within twenty days of a ship's arrival, customs officials could confiscate the vessel. But Chambers could not avoid that deadline by leaving port. To go he would need a permit from the governor, which was normally issued only upon clearance from customs. Thus, either Colden (acting in Tryon's absence) gave his approval for the ship to depart without paying the tea duty or the law would have to be broken and the commodity destroyed before twenty days had elapsed. That night the "Mohawks" began readying themselves to dump the tea into the harbor. But townspeople boarded the *London* first and did the job themselves. They did not otherwise injure the vessel or its cargo, though "it was not without some risk of his life" that Chambers escaped to the *Nancy* for his return to England.[29]

Thus, after a seven-month-long campaign, Sears and McDougall could at last savor victory. They had persuaded nearly everyone, from Tryon to the humblest resident, that landing the tea was not in New York's best interest. When an anonymous writer mocked how the city had treated Lockyer and Chambers, "Brutus" wrote a long letter in *Rivington's New York Gazetteer* (which James Rivington had been printing since 1773), reviewing the struggle that New York (and the radicals) had been waging— since passage of the Tea Act—for American liberty. At the end, he advised, "Beware" of those "who ever wear two faces; one to recommend them to ministerial favour, another to beguile the sons of liberty into bondage." He refused to name them, but everyone knew he meant the De Lanceys.[30] Though he was gloating, their dilemma was acute. Like other New Yorkers, they opposed the Tea Act. But the patricians among them worried about mob violence and the survival of elite rule. The merchants fretted over economic sanctions and their ability to trade within the empire. Anglicans feared that a challenge to their king might become a threat to their church. And all of them were uncomfortable because Sears was again center stage.

III

Three weeks later, on May 11, 1774, the *Concord* brought news that the House of Commons had passed a bill "for stoping up the Port of

Boston." The next day the *Samson* arrived both with word that Gen. Thomas Gage had been made governor of Massachusetts and with a copy of the Boston Port Act. The law forbade the loading or unloading of ships in that port, starting on June 1, unless it reimbursed the East India Company for the tea dumped into the harbor in December 1773.[31]

To the cabinet, the Boston Tea Party had not been the illicit destruction of private property by a group of lawbreakers; it had been a malicious assault upon parliamentary sovereignty by the city of Boston. General Gage, who was in England when word of the incident reached the cabinet, persuaded the king that force alone would make the colonies obey. North explained in Parliament, "We were now to consider only whether or not we have any authority there; that it is very clear we have none, if we suffer the property of our subjects to be destroyed."[32] Elsewhere he said, "We are not entering into a dispute between internal and external taxes, not between taxes laid for the purpose of revenues and taxes laid for the regulation of trade, not between representation and taxation, or legislation and taxation; but we are now to dispute the question whether we have, or have not any authority in that country."[33] By so defining the issue, he at once doomed compromise and justified an escalation in the modes being used to wage the conflict. Indeed, given the ministry's mistrust of America, built up over a decade of crises, there seemed to be no alternative. Earlier concessions had only emboldened the colonists. Another statement like the Declaratory Act would be worthless, for it had settled nothing in 1766. If a comparable act were passed now, everyone would think the government was backing down.[34] The conflict thus spiraled further out of control.

Parliament passed four bills, which Americans would term the Coercive or Intolerable Acts. All were punitive in intent, yet they were also meant to be remedial in effect. The Boston Port Act aimed not just to punish the city but to bring residents back to their senses. That law, however, was still not sufficient, the cabinet reasoned, for the executive power had already proved itself ineffectual. Company agents had requested help before the Tea Party, but civil officials had not acted, and the army had had to stand by as the tea was destroyed. The Government of Massachusetts Act thus tried to reinvigorate executive authority by altering the colony's charter. The governor's Council, which the lower house had hitherto elected, was replaced by one chosen by the crown. Towns could still meet yearly to select officials and to pass bylaws, but additional meetings could be held only with the governor's consent. Gage was made governor so as to give the executive ample power to summon military assistance whenever needed. "Your Authority as the first Magistrate, combined with your

Command over the King's Troops," explained Lord Dartmouth, the American secretary of state, "will enable you to meet every opposition, and fully to preserve the public peace, by employing those Troops with Effect, should the madness of the People . . . make it necessary." The general was to use "gentile persuasion" but was never to forget that parliamentary sovereignty demanded "a full and absolute submission."[35]

The Administration of Justice Act authorized the governor to move, either to another colony or to Britain, the trial of any crown official indicted for a capital offense for an act committed while quelling a riot or enforcing a revenue law. A new Quartering Act legalized the billeting of redcoats in barracks, taverns, "uninhabited houses, outhouses, barns, or other buildings" in the colonies. An American who lived in London and had excellent government contacts wrote that the cabinet was determined to take advantage of the present opportunity to secure the dependence of the colonies upon the mother country. If Bostonians resisted, Britain would use all of its power to punish them. Edmund Burke, whom the Assembly had appointed as New York's colonial agent in December 1770 following the death of Robert Charles, informed the House that the cabinet "defended" the four acts "on their absolute necessity, not only for the purpose of bringing that refractory Town and Province into proper Order, but for holding out an Example of Terrour to the other Colonies."[36]

The colonial reaction was more than the ministry expected, however. First, when a regime retaliates against an antigovernment group, it can generally only avoid escalating the conflict by limiting the sanctions to the guilty and by matching the punishment to the crime; overreacting (which the cabinet did by penalizing all Massachusetts for what a few lawbreakers had done) merely creates new grievances that protesters can use to justify coercive countermeasures. Second, when a party to conflict has "usually made concessions" in the past (as Britain had done in the Stamp and Townshend Act crises), its opponent "may expect more concessions" and be more enraged than it would otherwise have been by a harsh response (like the Coercive Acts). Third, most people unthinkingly accept a regime's legitimacy, a mindset that inhibits civil strife, but the use of coercion, especially when considered unjust, often engenders a sense of betrayal, and that can (and in the colonies did) palpably weaken the bonds tying a people to their rulers, rendering counterviolence acceptable.[37]

The Boston Port Act shocked New Yorkers, regardless of party. After eying the "General Consternation and Disgust," William Smith remarked, "We shall lose all that attachmt we once had to so great a Degree for the Parent Country." McDougall noted that the "intelligence was received with Great abhorrence and indignation by the Sons of Freedom." Oliver De Lancey avowed "that he would rather spend every shilling of his Fortune than that the Boston Port Bill be complied with." Someone opined that any Bostonian who submitted should be "Hanged and Quartered." Peter Van Schaack, a future loyalist, lamented that "the measures of government, so strongly indicating a determination to establish the supremacy of Parliament over these colonies, are truly alarming. . . . An appeal to the sword I am afraid is inevitable."[38]

As they had with the Tea Act, Sears and McDougall acted first to forge outrage into a weapon. On May 12 Sears began advocating nonimportation, while "Brutus" lauded the battle that residents had waged against the Tea Act. By May 14 both James Rivington (a future loyalist) and John Holt (a future whig) were selling copies of the Boston Port Act; McDougall felt that reading it would surely make people "warmer in their indignation." That same day the Liberty Boys and some dry-goods merchants agreed to consider an import boycott. And Sears began approaching other merchants, urging them to meet on May 16 at the Queen's Head Tavern to discuss nonimportation and to nominate "a Committee of Correspondence, to bring about a [general] Congress." Given the abortive efforts of 1770, Sears wanted a uniform agreement, so as to preclude cheating, and a congress was the best way to secure that objective.[39]

On May 15 the Liberty Boys parleyed again with some merchants, and together they agreed that Boston should be informed of New York's "readiness to come into a non-importation agreement of Goods from G B and non-exportation of Lumber to the" British West Indies. Extending the economic sanctions to the West Indies, it was believed, would be advantageous, because it would deprive British merchants of business and the imperial government of revenue. Sears and McDougall consequently wrote Boston's Committee of Correspondence, that same day, that they had "stimulated" the merchants to meet the next night to endorse "a Non-importation and Non-exportation Agreement" according to "such Regulations as may be agreed upon by Committees from the Principal towns on the Continent, to meet in a general Congress to be held here for that Purpose."[40]

The next morning McDougall posted a notice for the meeting that night at the Queen's Head Tavern. "Altho the advertisements were to the Merch[an]ts only," the De Lanceys "were at great Pains all the day to collect every tool who was under their influence as well those in Trade as out of it." Passions were running high, and James De Lancey had to hold together the coalition that had won the 1769 elections and had defeated nonimportation in 1770. The merchants were no problem. They knew the danger that economic sanctions posed to business; they remembered how Boston had cheated; and they feared the ministry might also close the port of New York.[41] Harder to manage, given the provocation, were the artisans and laborers who had, for years, supported De Lancey out of self-interest, dependence, or deference. He did not want raw emotions to excite them to demand steps, such as a ban on imports and exports, that might devastate the city economically or goad the cabinet to retaliate. While he was ready, now as before, to resist unconstitutional legislation, especially when it hurt the economy, he wanted above all to preserve the empire.

On a tactical level, De Lancey was plainly acting opportunistically, for Sears and McDougall were challenging elite rule and his party's economic interests. As a partisan leader De Lancey was maneuvering, as best he could, to safeguard his party's interests in a rapidly changing environment, one that every year allowed plebeians a greater political voice. Yet what seemed like opportunism was often ambivalence. De Lancey knew that Americans had legitimate grievances his party should address, but he feared that confronting those grievances would afford radicals political leverage and might even end in economic chaos or mob rule. It is no wonder, then, that his party was tacking to and fro across the political seascape in 1774. All the same, on a strategic level De Lancey remained true to the platform he had espoused since the Stamp Act crisis: elitism, Anglicanism, the empire, and commercial prosperity. Given these ultimate objectives and the revolutionary situation in which he found himself, it was no accident that he finally embraced loyalism and would forfeit his wealth, power, and status in New York.[42]

For the moment, however, De Lancey had to focus on the Queen's Head Tavern meeting. Party leaders had spent the day rounding up supporters. When three hundred people attended, the meeting had to be moved to larger accommodations at the Exchange. With Low acting as chair, De Lancey leaders circulated on the floor, arguing that if Boston simply paid for the tea, the crisis would end. They demanded that New York not adopt nonimportation until "the sense of the other Colonies" was known; the city should at least wait to "*see what Boston requires of us.*"[43] When a vote was taken to form a committee of correspondence, twenty De Lanceyites opposed the measure. Notwithstanding, the measure passed, and the key fights erupted over the committee's membership and size. The radicals wanted a small, efficient body of fifteen to twenty-one persons. McDougall felt that a majority did too, but that the De Lanceys deliberately confused matters by demanding a committee of fifty, with fifteen constituting a quorum. When a poll was taken, the proposal for a larger body won. De Lanceyites were equally effective in seeing that their own people were named to the new body; reportedly, they had come with a prepared list for the meeting to adopt. But Sears demanded that all nominations come from the floor. Philip Livingston, Sears, and McDougall were selected unanimously. But Low recognized De Lanceyites wishing to make a nomination more often than he did those wanting to name a friend of Sears. And when John Lamb and Francis Lewis, who both favored nonimportation, were proposed, the De Lanceys refused to accept either. Hence, only about fourteen members of the Liberty Boy–Livingston coalition were among the fifty.[44]

De Lanceyites later defended their nominees as "merchants — Men of property — Probity, and understanding, whose zeal for the public good can not be doubted; their own several private interests being so intimately connected with that of the whole community — And whose situations, connections" make them "proper persons to hold so important a trust." Colden reported that "the principal Inhabitants being now afraid that, these hot Headed Men might run the City into dangerous Measures, appeared in a considerable Body" and picked a committee that included "a number of the most prudent and considerate Persons." Several nominees had "not before join'd in the public Proceedings of the Opposition, and were induced to appear, in what they are sensible is an illegal Character, from a consideration that if they did not the Business would be left in the same rash hands as before."[45]

McDougall saw it differently: "The whole face of the Business" evinced "a design to get such a Com[mitte]e nominated as would be under their direction, with a view to gain credit with the people if any thing was done to advance the Liberty cause or to prevent any thing being done, in which case they would make a merit of it with administration, to procure places for themselves and their children." William Smith agreed: "The De Lanceys urged their Friends to attend and pushed them in to mix with the Liberty Boys, as well to drown the latter or to gain their Confidence."[46]

The battle had just begun, however, for townspeople had to approve the new committee. The next day a handbill asked residents to meet on May 19 to accept the fifty or to "appoint such other persons, as in their discretion and wisdom may seem meet." And Paul Revere arrived that night with news that a Boston town meeting had voted on May 13 to recommend "a non-importa and non-exportation of Goods to G Britain and the West Indies as the only effectual means to open their port and redress American Grievances." Now the De Lanceys could no longer insist that sanctions should be delayed till Boston had spoken. The next day,

May 18, New Yorkers were preoccupied debating strategy. De Lanceyites argued that the economy would suffer terribly if the radicals got their way. One De Lanceyite said that he opposed a boycott "from Interest"; another that it would "distress" the poor. By such arguments, McDougall claimed, "the Friends of Government and General Gage are industrious in their Endeavours to divide the People." That night the radicals called a "Mechanicks" meeting, which named a rival slate of twenty-five, all but two of whom came from the May 16 list and a majority of whom favored a boycott. Calling themselves Mechanics, not Liberty Boys, was significant. They were identifying themselves as an economic interest group that had as much right as the importers to decide how to help Boston.[47]

On election day, Low chaired the meeting and tried to start the proceedings early. Sears was desperate. McDougall was home sick, and there were not as many Liberty Boys present as Sears had hoped. The De Lanceys, however, had been much more successful in gathering their forces. Smith claimed, "The Merchants had stirred, dreading a Non Importa Agreent and appeared Numerous, as they had influenced the Cartmen and some Mechanics." Sears delayed the meeting till the appointed hour, but could not make Low read the Boston town meeting resolves. Instead, Low delivered an impassioned speech, urging election of the fifty candidates nominated on May 16: it was time to put aside "party distinctions, feuds and animosities" and to unite; "zeal in a good cause is most laudable, but when it transports beyond the bounds of reason it often leaves room for bitter reflection." Meanwhile, Sears began reading the Boston resolutions aloud, till Low made him stop. Sometime during the meeting, it is uncertain when, the radical Francis Lewis, a British-born Anglican merchant, was added to the fifty by unanimous vote.[48]

When Low asked those favoring the fifty-one to stay put and those for the twenty-five to draw off, Sears demanded the opposite. The chair agreed, but Sears said that his group would go to City Hall, where a subscription of signatures would decide which slate of candidates should serve. When a De Lanceyite insisted that only voters could sign the subscription, Sears argued convincingly that "every man whose Liberties were concerned should sign." His plan for an immediate subscription died, however, when many "Trades men who were for the 25" complained that they would have to return to work soon or lose a day's pay. Charges next began to fly that Low had spoken ill of the Mechanics. He called his accusers "damned Liars." But one said that he would put it in writing; another that the remarks had been made to him. Because the time for a vote had passed, it was agreed that representatives from both sides would, that night, draw up a list of people who would conduct a poll to determine which of the slates would be the committee of correspondence. When the representatives met, however, they "could not get any persons to go."[49]

Sears had won a tactical victory by blocking his opponents from electing their slate, but he had suffered a strategic defeat. New York needed a committee if it were to adopt economic sanctions or to participate in a general congress. The next day Smith began to nudge the radicals back within the consensus that New Yorkers had developed over how to counter British imperialism. He advised McDougall to forget his committee of twenty-five, to cease demanding nonimportation, and to forgo rioting. Smith was not asking the Liberty Boys to capitulate; rather, he was arguing that their best strategy was to work for a congress. Unity would be maintained in New York, and Britain would fear that the colonists might be planning to form an alliance with a foreign power. That night the Mechanics agreed to "try" the slate of fifty-one and to "prevent a division in this alarming Conjecture." Of course, "if they misbehaved," they "would be removed."[50]

The radicals tested the Committee of Fifty-one at once. When Paul Revere returned from Philadelphia on May 22, they persuaded him to stay the night, so that the committee could write Boston. At a committee meeting the next morning, several De Lanceyites proposed that the group adopt resolves akin to those approved in Philadelphia, where merchants now had the upper hand. Their resolutions called for a congress but barely mentioned economic sanctions and urged Boston to make restitution for destroying the tea. The meeting instead directed Isaac Sears, Isaac Low, James Duane, and John Jay to draft a letter to Boston and then adjourned until the evening. Both Duane and Jay were De Lanceyites who had married into the Livingston family. That night, before the subcommittee's report was even presented, several De Lanceyites vainly demanded that the letter not mention a congress. Once the proposed letter was read, they objected to the statement that Boston was suffering in the cause of liberty. But they were outvoted again, after Duane observed that if that were not true, then "we should cast them off and not write to them."[51]

The letter, which was approved with only a minor modification, was a compromise that showed that the public consensus on imperial affairs remained about where it had been after the Townshend Duties had been removed.[52] The letter declared that New Yorkers opposed the Boston Port Act, but because the issue concerned the whole continent, the remedy must be determined at "a Congress of Deputies from the Colonies in general." New York would not unilaterally adopt a nonimportation or nonexportation agreement. The radicals had thus wrung from the committee a commitment to participate in a congress if one were held. The De Lanceys could console themselves with the possibility that a congress might not take place; or if it did, that it might not adopt sanctions. When Revere departed, McDougall "urged upon him the expediency of their Com[mitte]es appointing time and place for the Congress as we did not do it [in] our Letter."[53] The radicals had done all they could. Boston needed to take the lead.

IV

The task ahead for the radicals was to ensure that the Committee of Fifty-one did not renege on its commitment to a congress, and that a suitable delegation was chosen once Boston had picked the time and place. And they soon had reason to suspect that De Lanceyites might try to "prevent any thing being done for the relief of Boston" in order to "make interest with Government." In late May a vexed John Watts tried to convince Francis Lewis that economic sanctions "would so distress the manufactures of G Britain that they would come over here and the national revenues would be so affected with non-exportation that it would be ruined." Tempers flared, and Lewis boasted that he would fight before seeing America enslaved. But his glib bellicosity only heightened De Lancey fears.[54]

Given the heterogeneity of the coalition opposing Britain, the parties to the alliance could not equally share the cost of waging the struggle. In such instances, those who expect to suffer the most generally strive to moderate the tactics used and the goals sought. Local merchants feared not only that the British army and navy might be used but that nonimportation would devastate the economy and cause political unrest. A New Yorker wrote that "many of the principal people" were "sorry for embarking in the cause so far" and "only want an opportunity to throw off the mask, to join with the friends of government." The writer wanted an end "put to all disputes between us and our mother country, that trade and commerce might flourish again, for whilst these contentions last, the merchants of your city must feel the effects of it as well as us."[55]

Anglican De Lanceyites had yet another reason for harboring doubts. "I am no friend to Presbyterians," said one. "I fix all the blame of those extraordinary American proceedings upon them." They "always do, and ever will act against government, from that restless and turbulent anti-monarchical spirit which has always distinguished them every where, whenever they had, or by any means could assume power, however illegally." Of course, most Anglicans, he said, did "from their own truly loyal principles" all "they could by writing and argument, and their influence, to stop the rapid progress of sedition, which would have gone much further lengths if it had not been for them."[56]

Though De Lanceyites had real misgivings, most of them continued jockeying for power on the Committee of Fifty-one. A fight developed, for example, over the May 15 letter Sears and McDougall had sent to Boston. On May 23 *The Boston Gazette, and Country Journal* printed excerpts from it, including the part that New York favored both nonimportation and nonexportation. Hoping to discredit the authors, the committee in New York tried futilely to uncover their identities. It also disavowed the letter, claiming that it did not reflect public opinion. On June 6, however, the committee received a letter from Boston's Committee of Correspondence. Ignoring the Committee of Fifty-one's May 23 communication, the Bostonians took the Sears-McDougall letter as their starting point. Arguing that it would take too long to organize a congress, they urged New York to adopt a nonimportation and nonexportation agreement. The Committee of Fifty-one replied that "you have made a mistake — for on revising our letter to you, so far from finding a word mentioned of a 'suspension of trade,' the idea is not even conceived." Sears could still take heart, for the committee reiterated New York's pledge to participate in a congress "at any time and place" Boston chose.[57]

Radicals soon began employing public theater (which the elite often used "to tie the worlds of patrician and plebeian closer together in moments of popular celebration") to pressure the committee. June 4 was the king's birthday. As customary, fireworks were set off that night, but candles illuminated only a "small number" of homes. "The Generality" refused to celebrate or to display "the least Appearance of public rejoicing, while it remains in Suspense whether we shall remain Freemen . . . or submit to be Slaves." On June 15, several thousand people carted a gallows to the Coffee House and burned the effigies of those imperial officials allegedly responsible for the present predicament: Lt. Gov. Thomas Hutchinson of Massachusetts, Lord North, and Solicitor General Alexander Wedderburn. Some patricians reacted by organizing an "Association" to keep order. But "A Freeman" warned them, "You endanger a Division, (which, at this interesting Crisis, may have the most fatal Consequences) and encourage a Swarm of Informers to ruin our Trade with Impunity." He claimed that the protest had been orderly, had broad public support, and had alarmed only the "*Few,* who are looking up to Government for Places of *Profit and Honour.*"[58]

On June 17 Massachusetts called for a congress to meet at Philadelphia in early September. At the Committee of Fifty-one's next meeting, on June 27, McDougall began a debate on "the most eligible mode of appointing Deputies." After arguing the whole evening about whether the De Lancey–controlled Assembly should name them, a decision was put off for two days. McDougall then moved that the committee nominate five persons to represent the city either "in a Convention of this Colony [which would then choose a slate of delegates to represent the whole province], or in the general Congress," if the city's nominees were acceptable to the entire province. He also wanted the five names "sent to the Committee of Mechanics for their concurrence; to be proposed on Tuesday next to the freeholders and freemen of this city." The challenge to the De Lanceys was palpable. McDougall wanted the committee to recognize the Mechanics Committee as coequal; to call a provincial convention (a precedent set by Philadelphia); and to give voters the final say over who represented them. "Debates arising," a decision was put off till July 4.[59]

By that date the De Lanceys knew how they wanted to proceed. The Committee of Fifty-one voted not to submit its nominees to the Mechanics for approval. Instead, the committee would nominate and the voters would accept or reject a slate of five congressional delegates. The committee also agreed to send a letter to the other counties, urging them to appoint delegates. De Lanceyites rejected McDougall's "Convention of this Colony," for it would supersede the Fifty-one in authority. After Sears vainly proposed that Isaac Low, James Duane, Alexander McDougall, John Morin Scott, and Philip Livingston be the nominees, the committee chose Livingston, Low, Duane, John Jay, and John Alsop. The replacement of Scott and McDougall, two politicians De Lanceyites despised, by Alsop and Jay was plainly a radical defeat. Alsop, a wealthy Anglican merchant, would become a loyalist. The conservative John Jay, however, might have been chosen to mollify the Livingstons. Though a De Lanceyite, he was a close friend and former law partner of Robert R. Livingston, Jr.; he had married a daughter of William Livingston in April 1774; and he would ultimately become a whig. Once the five had been selected, the committee set July 7 as the date for a public meeting at which the inhabitants would vote on the nominees.[60]

Refusing to concede defeat, Sears and McDougall appealed to public opinion. On July 5 the Mechanics selected a slate of candidates: Low, Jay, Livingston, McDougall, and Leonard Lispenard, a radical Dutch Reformed innkeeper. The next night, the radicals convened a meeting in the Fields, which approved a proposal "to stop all importation from, and exportation to Great Britain"; "directed" whomever was chosen on July 7 to work for both nonimportation and nonexportation; called for a provincial convention to elect deputies for "the general congress"; agreed to "obey" all "resolutions, determinations, and measures" adopted at Philadelphia; and instructed the Committee of Fifty-one "to use their utmost endeavours to carry these resolutions into execution."[61] But when residents gathered on July 7 they rejected both slates of candidates and moved to restore harmony. The two rival committees were each asked to appoint a subcommittee, and the next morning the two subcommittees were to select people from each ward to canvass voters to see whether the July 4 or the July 5 slate should go to Philadelphia.[62]

When the Committee of Fifty-one assembled on the night of July 7, it named nine members, including Sears and Lewis, to meet the next day with the Mechanics. The committee then vented its wrath upon the radicals for allegedly dividing the community. John Thurman, a De Lanceyite Anglican merchant and future loyalist, offered a motion rebuking the July 6 meeting as one "calculated to throw an odium on this Committee" and to cause "disunion among our fellow-citizens." No one, "especially a member of this Committee, had a right to call a meeting by an anonymous advertisement, much less to exhibit a set of resolves calculated for particular purposes, no motion ever having been made for resolves in this Committee, and that no resolves whatsoever should have been entered into, until when well digested by this Committee, and held up to the public for their consideration." In the name of moderation and unity, Thurman was claiming vast powers for the committee (and for any subsequent body that might win public support in a crisis).[63]

Given conflicting accounts, it is unclear what happened next. After a subcommittee was named to draft resolves against the Boston Port Bill, several people left, thinking the meeting was over. At that point, Charles McEvers (another De Lanceyite Anglican merchant and future loyalist) moved successfully that Thurman's resolution be published. The Sears-McDougall partisans still present became enraged, ordered their names removed from the Committee of Fifty-one's membership list, and ran outside yelling, "the Committee is dissolved; the Committee is dissolved." The next day Sears, McDougall, and nine others resigned from the body.[64] McDougall even refused to serve on the July 5 Mechanics' slate of delegates because the Fifty-one were insisting that voters must choose either the July 4 or the July 5 ticket, thereby depriving "the people of voting for any Five of the Seven nominated."[65]

The De Lanceys did not want to see the rump Committee of Fifty-one dissolved.[66] Thus, on July 13, the committee adopted a set of resolutions and ordered that both these resolves and the July 4 slate of delegates were to be presented for approval to a public meeting on July 19. Compared to the radical resolutions of July 6, those approved on July 13 were tepid, yet they articulated the De Lancey position. The first avowed New York's loyalty to George III but deplored "some late Acts" of Parliament, which "may be attended with the most fatal consequences." Another termed the Boston Port Act "arbitrary" and "oppressive." A third called the plan for a congress a "most prudent measure." Another stated that if a "nonimportation agreement" was adopted at Philadelphia, it "ought to be *very general* and *faithfully* adhered to," though it said nothing about nonexportation.[67]

If the committee thought that its resolutions mirrored public opinion, or that people supported the divisive tactics used by Thurman and McEvers, the July 19 meeting came as a rude shock. Evidently, the public mood was roiled both by news that Parliament was considering the Government of Massachusetts Act and by one of the committee's resolves, which some people construed as a criticism of the Boston Tea Party. The July 19 meeting, therefore, decisively rejected the July 13 resolutions. Instead of asking the Committee of Fifty-one to revise them, it appointed a Committee of Fifteen to draft new ones. It also added Lispenard and McDougall to the July 4 slate of delegates "to give satisfaction to all parties."[68]

The Committee of Fifty-one met that night to put the best possible face on its defeat. Since it could not repudiate a meeting it had sponsored, the logic of its argument was tortured. First, the committee declared that because only a few people had attended the meeting earlier in the day, "the sentiments of the majority still remain uncertain." The committee confessed that its own resolves could not "with certainty be said to correspond with the sentiments of the major part of the citizens"; yet it concluded that "in all probability they do." "To remove all doubts" it modestly revised its resolutions, ordered them printed, and agreed that at least two people from each ward should be chosen to poll freemen, freeholders, and taxpayers on two issues: who should represent them at Philadelphia and whether they approved the amended resolutions.[69]

The Committee of Fifty-one fought Sears with more than words. The next day, Alsop, Low, and Jay (mimicking a tactic that radicals had just used) announced that they would not go to Philadelphia unless public opinion was measured "with greater Precision." And Low, Jay, and two other De Lanceyites refused appointment to the Committee of Fifteen, since their "Election was too irregular" and "cast an invidious Reflection" on the Committee of Fifty-one. Thus, at a key moment, when unity was essential, the De Lanceys were threatening to withdraw if radicals demanded their own way. Each side invariably tried to put enough of its own partisans on a committee to control the outcome; yet both knew that the opposition had to be sufficiently represented so that the committee could legitimately be said to speak for the whole community. The De Lanceys needed Sears, for the July 19 meeting made it obvious they were out of step with public opinion. And Sears needed Jay, Low, and Alsop; without them the Committee of Fifteen and the city's delegation to Philadelphia lacked credibility.[70]

It took about a week to reach a compromise. On July 20 the Committee of Fifteen prepared thirteen resolves and called a meeting for July 25 to consider them. Though the resolutions represented the radical point of view, they never mentioned nonexportation. The omission was surely an effort to find common ground with the Committee of Fifty-one. Nonetheless, "nothing decisive was resolved upon" at the July 25 meeting, evidently because both sides were fast at work on a compromise.[71] The next day the Sears-McDougall group wrote the Committee of Fifty-one's five delegates, asking whether "you will engage to use your utmost endeavours at the proposed Congress, that an agreement [be adopted] not to import goods from Great Britain until the American grievances be redressed." When four of the five (Duane was away) agreed to do so, the Mechanics withdrew their slate, and John Holt reported that there was now "a Coalition of Parties" concerning the "Delegates" to be elected to, and the "Measures" to be pursued at, the "General Congress." That same day the Committee of Fifty-one's five nominees were duly elected. The next day letters were sent to the other counties in the province, urging them to adopt the five or to name their own representatives.[72]

Public opinion had thus forced both groups back within the popular consensus on how British imperialism should be resisted. Sears and McDougall, however, could be satisfied with what they had accomplished. The odds had been great: typically the more heterogeneous a conflict group, the more moderate its goals. Hence, it is no surprise that not one of the five delegates to Philadelphia was a radical and that the Committee of Fifty-one refused to call a provincial convention. No wonder, too, that Thomas Jones was able to remark, "With such a delegation, the New York Loyalists thought themselves safe." But the radical accomplishment was still substantial. Despite the reservations of people like William Smith concerning the course of events, the radical-Livingston alliance had held firm. Despite the misgivings of De Lanceyites like John Thurman, the radicals had succeeded, according to Jones, in persuading "*all parties, denominations and religions . . . that the Colonies laboured under grievances which wanted redressing.*"[73] A date and place had been set for a congress; and New York's delegation was committed to nonimportation. Sears and Mc-Dougall would never regret the compromises they had made to secure these victories. James De Lancey would.

Whigs and Tories

Sending delegates to the First Continental Congress was a strategic step in a bold campaign that Alexander McDougall, John Lamb, and Isaac Sears had waged to unite the city, the province, and the thirteen colonies against the Coercive Acts. The agenda was ambitious: the bonds the three had formed with radicals elsewhere had to be strengthened, public enthusiasm for Congress solidified, the measures it adopted enforced, and a provincial congress called to rally New Yorkers behind the cause. In short, a web of organizations, linking people within communities and throughout America, had to be forged, and New York's participation in the struggle was crucial.[1] In 1770 the De Lanceys had abandoned nonimportation, and the other American cities had followed suit. If that party now persuaded the city to repudiate the Continental Congress, the cause of liberty might collapse throughout America.

On August 20 the Massachusetts delegation visited New York en route to Philadelphia. McDougall became John Adams's unofficial host, introducing him to the city's vistas and its variegated political landscape. Adams judged him "a very sensible Man, and an open one" with "a thorough Knowledge of Politicks." Adams also met the city's leading politicians. John Morin Scott was "lazy" and "not very polite." William Smith "improves every Moment of his Time." Isaac Low "profess[ed] Attachment to the Cause of Liberty but his Sincerity is doubted." John Jay was a "hard Student and a good Speaker"; John Alsop, "unequal to the Trust in Point of Abilities"; and James Duane, "very sensible . . . and very artful." Philip Livingston was "a down right strait forward Man." "A great, rough, rappid Mortal," there was "no holding any Conversation with him; he blusters away. Says if England should turn us adrift we should instantly go to civil Wars among ourselves which Colony should govern all the rest." Overall, the visit was crucial. Now, whenever letters passed between the two cities, messages could be evaluated in light of the judgments that had been made about the people involved.[2]

Meanwhile, De Lanceyites were busy deriding the radicals and debunking Congress. "Mercator" berated John Holt and the *New York Journal:* When "a News-paper is wholly employed in prosecuting party designs, tending to inflame the minds of the people against government," the proprietor "justly renders himself abhorrent to all good men, and may well be considered as a pest to society." "Mercator" considered the writers in Holt's paper to be "of the lowest class," whose only aim was that of "enriching themselves by the spoils of their country." Mocking their ability to be "*a pilot to the state*," he criticized the "manifest defect in the circumstances of Grammar, propriety and elegance of stile; and for want of variety in the choice and disposition of words, we find them frequently repeated, . . . a certain proof that they are not the productions of men of parts and education."[3]

Eighteenth-century theatergoers relished seeing plebeians "strike the heroic poses of their betters," and "A Merchant of New York" exploited that tradition to eviscerate Sears: "We could not boast of more than one Sir *Francis Wronghead* in this city. . . . This *quidnunc* in politicks, who is for ever thrusting himself forward as a person of the *greatest consequence*, without sense to observe the ridiculous appearance he puts on, and without penetration enough to discover that he is the *butt* of every puny jester, and the *laughing-stock* of the whole town." He thinks himself "a leading man amongst us, without perceiving, that he is enlisted under a *party*, as a *tool* of the lowest order; — a *political cracker*, sent abroad to *alarm* and *terrify*, — sure to do mischief to the cause he means to support, and generally finishing his career in an *explosion*."[4]

De Lanceyites capitalized, too, on the antipathy that New Yorkers felt for New Englanders. The Committee of Fifty-one had appointed a subcommittee on July 19 to assist Bostonians suffering from the Coercive Acts. By August, money was being collected in every ward, when *Rivington's New York Gazetteer* accused Boston of using a donation from another colony to pave the streets, not to aid the poor. The radical Peter Curtenius wrote William Cooper, Boston's town clerk, that if unchecked the rumors would "put an entire stop to the subscription here" and shatter American unity. Boston had "many Enemies" in New York "who Improve on every report that is spread to your disadvantage." Cooper replied that the committee charged with dispensing the aid had held a public meeting to decide how to help the poor. Persuaded that jobs were better than handouts, the thrifty Bostonians had agreed that if the Overseers of the Streets would hire the unemployed to repair the roads, the committee would pay part of the cost of their labor. Thus, "a great Number of our most indigent Inhabitants [were] enabled to earn their Bread." The *New York Journal* printed Cooper's letter on September 29, and it evidently allayed the concerns many New Yorkers had. By January 1775, New York had donated more than one thousand pounds in food and supplies.[5]

A more explosive issue soon jolted New York. On September 6 a false report claimed that redcoats had killed six Bostonians.[6] Smith captured the outrage when he related that "instead of that Respect they formerly had for the King, you now hear the very lowest Orders call him *a Knave* or *a Fool.*" John Thurman, a De Lanceyite, warned a British correspondent that it would be easier to crush France than to conquer the colonies: "There is not a Man born in America that does not Understand the Use of Fire arms." Indeed, "it is Almost the First thing they Purchase and take to all the New Settlements and in the Cities you can scarcely find a Lad of 12 years old that does not go a Gunning."[7]

Radicals quickly initiated a campaign to block all aid from reaching the redcoats in Boston. A broadside dated September 9 thanked the "worthy citizens" who refused to lease vessels "for the base purpose of transporting troops, ammunition, etc., to oppress" Boston. A carpenter who had agreed to erect barracks there and another who had contracted to make chests to ship arms were dissuaded from doing so. These tactics worked, for Gen. Frederick Haldimand, the British commander in New York, wrote Gen. Thomas Gage on September 10 that the mob had thrown everything into confusion: government was in abeyance, and no one would rent him transports.[8]

On September 14, "the Free Citizens" warned the city's pilots not to assist any vessel commissioned to help the British army. On September 24, the Mechanics Committee learned that Gage planned to hire New York artisans to build fortifications in Boston. The committee pressured mechanics not to accept the work and again urged shipowners not to rent vessels "to transport the army and the horrid engines of war." When it became known that several local merchants were secretly dealing with British agents, a body of freeholders and freemen met on Tuesday, September 27, and appointed an ad hoc committee, one that included Sears, to demand a written answer from those guilty of not "sacrificing their private interest to the publick good." A mass meeting was scheduled for the next night to hear the committee's report and to consider appropriate measures. In the event, the report was read, some resolves adopted, and another meeting set for the following evening to finish the work.[9]

On Thursday the merchants retaliated. "Humanus" objected to denying the soldiers "Provisions and Clothing"; only the Continental Congress, "whose Determinations we have solemnly agreed to abide by," could do so. Besides, antagonizing the soldiers would "produce first Skirmishes, and then general Hostilities" at a time "when we should use every Means to conciliate their Friendship." On September 30 a broadside, signed by Joseph Totten, an Anglican De Lanceyite merchant, on behalf of a citizen's group, asked the rump Committee of Fifty-one to hold a public meeting that day to voice its "Sentiments" about those who had "disturb[ed] the Peace" by meeting "without any Notification from you, to whom the publick Voice gave the Care of the Community's Interest in all Affairs of a publick Nature." Totten condemned the radicals for having "censured and threatened several worthy and respectable Persons."[10]

Totten's meeting was interrupted by so much "Noise and Clamour" that it had to be moved from City Hall to the Coffee House, where merchants could better manage the proceedings. A majority then approved a motion censuring the "Persons who stile themselves a Committee, and have called upon several of our Fellow Citizens, to enquire into their private Business." The logic of the De Lancey argument that no one should be allowed pell-mell to form ad hoc committees or to make others obey their dictates struck a responsive cord among residents, especially since setting policy was to be the business of the Continental Congress. Though members of the September 27 committee later objected that their appointment was legal and that they had approached the offending merchants without "any Kind of Threat or Aggression," the community refused to support them. Lt. Gov. Cadwallader Colden reported on October 5 that "the Merchants go on completing their orders without farther Interruption."[11] On October 13, ships sailed for Boston with "a great number of Artificers, who have been engaged to work on the Barracks preparing for the accommodation of his Majesty's troops." On October 20 "Philo-Libertas" praised the merchants for "preserving your rights . . . against the unwarrantable and bold attempts of those persons who use the prostituted name of liberty, only to infringe that of others with success and impunity."[12]

The De Lancey victory was short-lived, however. On October 20, Congress adopted the Continental Association, which imposed the economic sanctions that city merchants opposed: the cessation of all British and Irish imports on December 1, 1774; nonconsumption of British and certain foreign products beginning March 1, 1775; and an embargo of all exports to Britain, Ireland, and the West Indies, effective September 10, 1775. Dutied tea could not be imported, purchased, or drunk after December 1, 1774; the same restrictions applied to all other tea on March 1, 1775. Congress directed, too, that committees be formed in every community to enforce the Continental Association. Non-Associators were to be boycotted and deemed enemies to American liberty.[13] Congress adjourned on October 26 but agreed to meet again in May if American grievances were not yet redressed.

De Lanceyites were incensed. Peter Van Schaack had initially supported Congress because he thought it would bring peace; now he feared it would provoke only war. Thomas Jones added, "The New York Loyalists being totally disappointed in the proceedings of the late Congress, and finding their delegates" transformed "into fixed republicans, came into a resolution . . . of opposing any future delegation." De Lanceyites were not the only people so troubled. Colden wrote Lord Dartmouth, the American secretary of state, on November 2 that "the measures of the Congress do not meet with rapid Applause Here." Farmers "will not bear the non Exportation"; and the merchants abhorred "non-importation" and were "endeavouring to sift out each others Sentiments. . . . A certain sign, I take it, that they wish to avoid it." John Adams, who revisited New York on October 30, reported that "the Sons of Liberty are in Horrors here. They think they have lost ground since We [first] passed thro this City."[14]

The inevitable test of strength arose over enforcing the Association. On November 7, in the still convening Committee of Fifty-one, Duane moved successfully that the voters in each ward should elect, on November 18, an eight-person committee of inspection to enforce the Association. It was a shrewd move. If there were seven ward committees instead of one citywide committee, the Committee of Fifty-one would continue to direct affairs. The Mechanics consequently assembled on Thursday, November 13, and called for a mass meeting the next day. What transpired at that meeting is unknown. But when it was over, Isaac Low, who chaired the Committee of Fifty-one, wrote his counterpart on the Mechanics Committee, Daniel Dunscomb, a prosperous cooper who worshiped at St. Paul's Episcopal Chapel, requesting a conference the next night. Upon meeting, the two sides agreed to "interchange one hundred names" out of which a committee of sixty would be nominated for enforcing the Association. The sixty names would then be submitted to the voters on November 22. The Committee of Fifty-one would disband once the new committee was elected and unity had thereby been restored.[15]

On November 17 a broadside listed the nominees the two committees had agreed upon. The next day the Mechanics assured the city's congressional delegation that they were "determined" to "assist in carrying the salutary measures of the General Congress into execution."[16] On election day only about two hundred voted, doubtless from a conviction that the outcome was predetermined, and they approved the sixty candidates. Though all viewpoints were present in the new body, radicals and Livingstonites were better represented than they had been on the Committee of Fifty-one. Smith reported that the new Committee of Sixty "consist[ed] of the Delegates and such a Sett as the most active Liberty Boys approve"; many of the conservative De Lanceyite merchants who had sat on the Committee of Fifty-one "have retired outwitted and disgusted and as they think betrayed."[17]

The radicals now became more assertive. On November 18 Dunscomb asked the artisans to meet on Monday evening, November 21, because Thomas Charles Williams, an Annapolis importer who had violated the Association, was in town. The day of the meeting "A Citizen" urged residents to ferret the culprit out "*without Violence*" and to send him home for his just reward. Williams was never apprehended, but the episode was a warning to local traders of what to expect if they defied the Association. Indeed, radicals reacted swiftly anytime anyone disobeyed Congress. When a British puppet show visited town, committeemen stopped it and made the managers agree never again to perform without the Committee of Sixty's approval. To make sure residents understood what was at issue, "Pro Patria" reminded them that the Association's eighth article forbade "*every species of extravagance and dissipation,* especially all horse racing, and all kinds of gaming, cock fighting, exhibitions of shews, PLAYS, and other expensive diversions."[18]

Not every initiative ended as radicals wanted, especially when violence threatened. In late December, acting upon a royal proclamation of October 19, 1774, the Customs House confiscated munitions shipped from London aboard the *Lady Gage* to a local merchant. When customs officials tried to store the cargo, angry citizens carted it away. Several other merchants, however, helped Andrew Elliot, collector of the customs, to recover the items, which were then put aboard a British warship. "The Mohawks and River Indians" then posted a notice at the Coffee House, warning Elliot to return the goods: "We would not have you to imagine that it is in the power of any set of men, either civil or military, to protect or shield you from our just revenge." When the collector objected, "Plain English" urged residents to "assemble together immediately, and go in a body to the Collector, insist upon the arms being relanded . . .; delays are dangerous." But the next morning a band of merchants and other inhabitants shielded Elliot from the group that had collected to intimidate him. If residents would not surrender to a tyrannical government, they would also not allow violence to jeopardize the conflict's peaceful resolution. Duane aptly described the public consensus: "It seems to be agreed here that every pacific and persuasive Expedient ought to be tried before a Recourse to Arms can be justified." McDougall agreed: "From the Knowledge I have of the State of this Colony, I am morally certain, they will not fly to Arms as a Colony; but by the Influence of one of these Contingencies, vizt. — The attack of the Troops on your People; Fear of the other Colonies, or stimulated by their Example, in taking up arms. Sure I am, we shall be the last of the Provinces to the Northward of Georgia, that will appeal to the Sword."[19]

Controversy moved indoors on November 28, when Duane proposed at the Committee of Sixty's first meeting that no tea whatsoever should be landed after December 1 and that all other goods arriving after that date should be sold "at *Public* auction." He was asking New York to adopt standards stricter than those specified in the Association, which provided that foreign teas could be bought and drunk until March 1, and that a merchant who imported goods between December 1 and February 1 was to have three options: return the items; store them until sanctions ended; or sell them under the committee's direction. If the goods were sold, the individual who had imported them was entitled to recover his costs; the profits, however, were to be donated to aid Boston's poor.[20] Radicals mistrusted Duane's motives: banning all tea would financially injure smugglers; forcing importers to sell at auction would raise the buyer's costs and thereby reduce the financial aid sent to Boston; and antagonizing the mercantile community would make enforcement more difficult. McDougall felt Duane's plan "would be construed a wanton exercise of Power, void of wisdom or justice, and the restless miscreants who are eagerly waiting to improve the least misconduct would not fail to lead the sufferers to charge the committees impolitic measures on the congress, and brand them all with Folly." The committee finally rejected the proposal and devoted its energies to enforcing the Association. Between December 1, 1774, and February 1, 1775, the committee sold the cargoes of twenty-one vessels and a trunk full of calicoes. It consequently donated almost three hundred fifty pounds to Boston. On January 30, the committee resolved that as of February 1 all British and Irish imports were to be reshipped at once in the vessels in which they had arrived; and it appointed a subcommittee to enforce the resolution. On March 1 Colden wrote Dartmouth that "the Non-importation Association of the Congress, is rigidly maintained even in this Place."[21]

Enforcement was not easy, especially in February. Events were moving so fast that partisans needed a face-off to test one another's strength and determination. On February 2 the *James*, commanded by a Captain Watson, arrived from Glasgow. The subcommittee ordered him to provision his ship and depart promptly. Goaded by some alleged "Ministerial tools" (or British sympathizers), Watson decided instead to defy the Continental Association. But when a large crowd gathered, he relented, and his vessel "fell down about four miles below the City," where it remained under the subcommittee's watchful eye. On February 8 Colden asked Capt. James Montagu of the *King Fisher*, a British naval vessel, to assist Watson.[22] The next night the *James* reentered the harbor, this time accompanied by a contingent from the *King Fisher*. Tempers flared, and Oliver De Lancey bellowed in the Coffee House: "What does that damn'd Rascal come up here again for? Why don't he quit the Port?" Residents seized the captain (who was lodged in town) and paraded him through the streets, before he escaped to the *King Fisher*. On February 11, when Watson tried to leave port, an overzealous naval lieutenant assigned to the *King Fisher* detained him. A crowd formed again; and Montagu overruled the officer and let the *James* depart.[23]

On February 16 the *Beulah*, a merchant ship out of London, anchored outside the harbor, and a subcommittee sloop moored nearby for surveillance. Colden reported that, unlike the "stupid" Watson, the ship's captain, William McBussell, was determined to land his cargo. The ship's Quaker owners, Robert and John Murray, of New York, soon asked the committee's permission to unload the freight and to reship it in another vessel for they felt that would save them money. A debate broke out, with those opposed arguing that that would breach the Association. After John De Lancey moved, in vain, that the committee reconsider its support for the Association, McBussell agreed to set sail on February 26 without breaking cargo. But the Murrays remained troubled about their financial situation. When the weather turned foul on the night of February 25 and the subcommittee's sloop fled to shore, the two hired men to transport part of the *Beulah's* cargo to New Jersey. When Sears learned of this, the two confessed, and the committee reshipped the merchandise to London. "A Son of Freedom" soon demanded that the Murrays be banished from the province; leniency would only encourage others to break the Association. Unnerved, the two merchants promised on March 18 to close their store and to let a citizens' committee guarantee that their doors would remain shut till the Association ended. On March 20 one of their wives wrote Sears and McDougall pleading for mercy. William Smith advised the two to deny leadership of the group demanding banishment, for they could later be prosecuted if the Murrays fled New York.[24]

The radicals proceeded cautiously. A public meeting on March 21 decided to allow the Murrays to stay but to have an oversight committee draw up a "line of Conduct" for them. "A Friend of Order" still objected: the Committee of Sixty was responsible for handling Association violators, and the Murrays had agreed to close their shop. Thus, on March 24, fearful that controversy would just erode mercantile support for the Association, the oversight committee concluded that "no such line [of conduct] ought to, or can, in our opinion, be drawn up by us." Though the radicals had relented, they had still won a great victory. Gage had written Colden on February 26 that he was waiting with "Impatience to hear the Fate of the Beulah. If she lands her Cargo it will be the means of inducing other Ports . . . to do the like." Instead, the Committee of Sixty was able to report to the New Haven Committee: "We have no Reason to apprehend a Defection of this Colony, whose Inhabitants are as sensible of the Blessings of Liberty as any People on the Continent." Even Colden conceded that the "violent Party" was in "great Spirits" over its triumph.[25]

In fact, what had emerged in New York was a whig or patriot party dedicated to the enforcement of the Continental Association and to the defense of American rights. The core of the party consisted of members of the Liberty Boy–Livingston coalition. Of course, not everyone who could be called a radical or a Livingstonite in 1773 identified with the new party. William Smith, for example, refused to sign the Association. Moreover, there were De Lanceyites like James Duane who understood the public consensus in New York and who were comfortable upholding it.[26]

II

As effective as the radicals had been, in and out of the Committee of Sixty, they were not unopposed. Because of the steps the First Continental Congress had taken, a loyalist or tory faction had also emerged in New York. As Thomas Jones explained, those who became tories had supported a congress because they had wanted "*a redress of grievances, and a firm union between Great Britain and America upon constitutional principles*"; what they felt they got was "a declaration of war." The loyalists constituted "perhaps 15 percent" of the population. An eclectic group, they came from all walks of life but were most prominent among crown officials, patricians, De Lanceyites, Anglicans, merchants, ideologues, and recent English immigrants. If they disagreed among themselves and with Britain over its right to tax the colonies, over the constitutionality of the Tea Act, and over the wisdom of the Coercive Acts, they were united by the realization that British America was moving inexorably toward independence. Some, like Cadwallader Colden, saw the handwriting on the wall straightaway; others, like Isaac Low, somewhat later; and yet others, like John Alsop, later still. Low—an ambitious, public-spirited man with a strong conscience and a merchant's respect for the empire—would abandon the patriot cause in November 1775 when the Provincial Congress named him to a committee to purchase gunpowder. Alsop remained in the Provincial Congress until July 16, 1776. His letter of resignation spoke for many loyalists: "As long as a door was left open for a reconciliation . . . I was willing and ready to render my country all the service in my power, and for which purpose I was appointed and sent to this Congress; but as you have . . . by that Declaration, closed the door of reconciliation, I must beg leave to resign my seat."[27]

Among the New York loyalists were the intellectual heirs of Viscount Bolingbroke, Baron de Montesquieu, Edmund Burke, and Sir William Blackstone. Genuinely conservative, they abhorred the whig preference for equality, individualism, and limited government. Other New Yorkers were persuaded instead by constitutional arguments supporting parliamentary supremacy; still others by animosity for those who became whigs. If what mattered to William Smith was his intellectual commitment to the empire, what concerned many De Lanceyite merchants were the economic links they had forged to the empire. Some residents sided with the king because of their commitment to elitist rule; others were loyal out of deference to political leaders whom they had followed for years. If the more famous loyalists tended to be wealthy, "A Poor Man" was nonetheless upset, in November 1775, because several of his impoverished neighbors still supported the ministry. Though many became loyalists because they feared anarchy, some worried that Parliament would punish the colony by razing the city. A number of loyalists, such as Cadwallader Colden and Robert Bayard, the latter a Judge of the Admiralty, had held appointive office or had fed at the royal trough for too long to abandon the crown; yet many more had never been placemen. Several, including Catherine Leach, a shopkeeper, James Deas, a Presbyterian hairdresser, and Myles Cooper, the president of King's College, had been born or educated in Britain; yet others had never lived outside New York. A few were Livingstonites who, when caught between their fears of royal tyranny and mobocracy, opted for the perils of the world they knew. More were De

Lanceyites who refused to abandon the empire. Though James Duane and John Jay could forsake their De Lancey roots and embrace the patriot cause, Low and Alsop could not.[28]

Cato Winslow, a slave, would flee New York City in mid-1775 and join Lord Dunmore in Virginia to fight for his freedom. He would not be the only black to become a loyalist. Of the approximately twenty-seven thousand African Americans who lived in either New York or New Jersey in 1770, 516 fugitive slaves, 92 freeborn blacks, and 50 manumitted slaves would depart New York City with the British in 1783 for Canada. According to Graham Russell Hodges, "blacks watched the unfolding conflict carefully, choosing sides according to their best interests, and were less pro-British than pro-black."[29]

For staunch Anglicans like Samuel Seabury, Myles Cooper, Thomas Bradbury Chandler, and Charles Inglis, who had been leaders in the movement to have an Anglican bishop sent to America, their loyalism reflected their church's theology and history: the conviction that society was hierarchic; that ordinary human beings were to be mistrusted; that faith required "obedience to God, king, lords and bishops — and in that order"; that predestinarianism undermined the political and social order; and that Presbyterianism invariably led, as it had in Oliver Cromwell's time, to revolution and republicanism. Persuaded that Episcopalians must obey the British government except when it would be sinful to do so, they could not have argued, as William Livingston did, that the "Voice of the People is the Voice of God." Bernard Semmel has aptly described what it was about evangelical Protestantism and Presbyterianism that so disturbed Anglicans: the "consciousness of election" seemed to "have endowed those who experienced it with a special confidence which made them ready to rent the political fabric, if necessary, to remove the godless from the seats of power, and install, in accordance with God's evident wishes, the Elect of the Lord."[30]

Anglicans were not the only loyalists, of course. They were joined by those members of the Dutch Reformed church, people such as Abraham Lott, the colony's Treasurer, who not only mistrusted the Presbyterians but who had also been Anglicized by contact with English culture and with the Society for the Propagation of the Gospel in Foreign Parts. A concern about evangelical Protestantism had also led John Wesley, the founder of Methodism, to reject predestination; to assert that Christians should concern themselves with their own salvation, not with politics; and to oppose the Revolution. Though a few American Methodists joined the whigs, most either became loyalists or remained neutral. The Lutherans, many of whom had reportedly been De Lanceyites in the 1760s, are more

difficult to trace, but of the five Lutheran merchants that Robert M. Dructor was able to find in New York at this time, three became loyalist and
two stayed neutral. Not one of the five served on a committee or played a
key role.[31]

The Society of Friends in New York, though often viewed as loyalist in
sympathy, actually strove for neutrality. Because the Bible requires Christians to love their enemies, Quakers were pacifists who could not bear
arms or wage war. Since God had instituted civil government, Friends
must obey it, unless its laws demanded that a Quaker act immorally. As a
result, between 1773 and 1776, especially as rebellion neared, the Society
of Friends would grow hostile toward the patriot cause. The New York
Meeting for Sufferings, for example, would pressure the two Quakers serving on the Committee of Sixty to resign. Nonetheless, there were some
Quakers who failed to see the difference between an opposition to the
whig cause that was rooted in pacifism and a contempt for the patriot
party that grew out of political beliefs or economic self-interest. These
people often sided with the British and sometimes even became loyalist
refugees.[32]

Perhaps because the decision to become a loyalist was so very personal,
the tories could not coalesce into a coherent, disciplined party capable of
thwarting the Revolution. Most had too much faith in the British army to
believe their own exertions vital to the outcome. Those who thought they
could play a role may have been perplexed, for to counter the enemy
they had to put aside constitutional scruples and become more like the
whigs in organization and tactics. Some royal officials, such as Cadwallader Colden, thought tories temperamentally unsuited for such a struggle. But that argument may well have been a phantasm to conceal the
painful truth that tories were often numerically too weak to make a stand.
Interestingly, in Queens County, Long Island, where loyalists outnum-
bered whigs two-to-one and where crown officials provided leadership,
the tories would effectively counter their enemies.[33]

Despite the odds, loyalists strove, especially in early 1775, to stem the
tide. Most evident was their propaganda campaign to dissuade New Yorkers from deserting the empire. Their best essayist, Samuel Seabury, an
Anglican minister who resided in Westchester, anonymously authored
four pamphlets between November 1774 and January 1775: *Free Thoughts
on the Proceedings of the Continental Congress, The Congress Canvassed, A View
of the Controversy between Great Britain and Her Colonies,* and *An Alarm to the
Legislature of New York.* In the first, he condemned Congress for rending
the bonds of civil society and implored his readers to repudiate the whigs.
"If I must be enslaved," he said, "let it be by a King at least, and not by a

parcel of upstart, lawless committee-men." In the second, he rebuked Congress for plotting to "contravene the authority of the British Parliament over the British dominions; on which authority the rights of Englishmen are . . . founded." In the third, he declared that "the right of the colonists to exercise a legislative power, is no natural right. They derive it not from nature, but from the indulgence or grant of the parent state." In the last, he asked the Assembly to settle the crisis quickly: "The *very next summer* will finish the dispute, either *peaceable*, or by *force of arms*."[34]

While writers like Seabury labored in prose and in verse to extol royal rule, others battled in the political arena. Paramount in their view was New York's strategic significance. After the Seven Years' War Gage had made the city his headquarters because of its excellent harbor; New York's central location, physically splitting the thirteen colonies in half; and the province's convenient overland route to Canada. If a rebellion ensued, British vessels from New York could land a military force at any key American city. Control of the Hudson would block the southern colonies from aiding New England. The city's hinterland would furnish the army with the matériel needed to retake America. And the many loyalists who allegedly lived there could bear arms for the crown.

Because these factors were evident to all, no one can claim sole credit for devising the strategy that crown officials and loyalists pursued at the time. Most were thinking along similar lines, and the endless repetition of these ideas bolstered confidence in them. Perhaps it is easiest to grasp the direction of events by focusing on Cadwallader Colden, the acting governor from April 1774 to June 1775. Central to his perspective was his belief that few New Yorkers were whigs. In dispatches to the cabinet he insisted that the patriot "frenzy" was confined to the city and had made little headway elsewhere in the province. It is impossible, however, to estimate precisely his influence on the ministry. British officials in America often grumbled about his temerity and his age (he was past eighty) and argued that only Gov. William Tryon's return could enhance British prospects in the colony. But Colden's optimism must have been balm to the cabinet, which seemed anxious to accept the most encouraging reports about the number of tories in America. Unhappily for the British, his estimates were far too sanguine. Though other officials shared his opinion, they realized that even friendly Americans were vexed by parliamentary pretensions. Tryon, for one, always insisted that New Yorkers would never accept taxation.[35]

For Colden, New York was the pivotal province, the ground where the crown had to make a stand. If New York were to remain loyal, it would cut the rebellion in half and hasten the return of peace. Yet he realized

the situation was volatile; the tories were moderates who abhorred violence and were easily intimidated by a mob. General Haldimand agreed
and wrote Lord Dartmouth that reasonable men did not "dare openly to
speak their minds and to oppose the torrent of licentiousness which now
prevails." To encourage these loyalists to support the crown actively, Colden urged the cabinet to stiffen their resolve by exhibitions of strength
that did not also provoke patriots to greater frenzy. Other observers cor-
roborated Colden's analysis. While visiting the province in late 1774,
North Carolina's Gov. Josiah Martin wrote Dartmouth that "the spirit of
loyalty runs higher here than in any other colony"; if "a body of troops"
were sent, it would bolster the morale of the "well-wishers to government" and "have a powerful effect on the rest of the continent." Gage
believed a tory victory in New York would surely lead to reconciliation
and make New Yorkers the saviors of the empire. In England, Gen. Henry
Clinton, the son of a New York governor and a future commander-in-
chief of the British army in America, saw the colony as a solid barrier that
would geographically divide the rebellion.[36]

Given New York's importance, rumors were rampant about how the
cabinet would entice it to remain loyal.[37] In late 1774 the talk in London
coffee houses was that eminent New Yorkers were being bribed to create
"a fatal disunion" in the whig camp. Another story said that "considerable immunities, and advantages" would be offered "to disunite [New
York] from the whole." In October 1774 James Duane wrote from Congress to John Tabor Kempe, New York's Attorney General: "A Report prevails that you have assured the Ministry that if they will furnish you with
£100000 you will undertake To buy off all the Patriots in our Province."[38]
In March 1775, *The Boston Gazette, and Country Journal* reported that the
cabinet planned "to bribe" New York's merchants. In April, *Dunlap's
Pennsylvania Packet* revealed that the ministry was confident of "the defection of New York." That same month, William Lee wrote from London
that the cabinet had sent Gage £125,000 to buy the loyalty of colonial
leaders, especially those in New York. And, in May, the *Pennsylvania Journal* reported that several New York lawmakers had been paid £1,000 each
for their votes in January 1775.[39]

Similar stories also appeared in New York. The "Citizens of New York"
had warned, in November 1774, that attempts would be "made to bribe
the printers of the public papers" and "that large sums have been issued
from the treasury . . . for secret services in America." Another writer said
that Gage had given North the names of several New Yorkers "of consequence" who would "sell their privileges" in exchange "for a Pension."
North had accordingly offered a local printer "£500 to promote Ministe-

rial Measures." The rumors resurfaced in February 1775 when John Holt printed a letter from London that "a good deal of public Money, has been put in the Hands of a Mr. —— one of the —— and some of your other great Men" to gain "their Influence." In March, Holt had "authentic accounts" that "a large sum of money" had been given "to the minister of State, *for secret service in America*." Another letter from Britain, dated May 5, 1775, said that Tryon would soon return to the province "to strengthen the ministerial party with you, and has the command of money to bribe."[40]

Though little hard evidence exists to substantiate these allegations, the cabinet believed that rewards to key people might pay handsome dividends. On April 5, 1775, John Pownall, the undersecretary for the American Department, had sent James Rivington a letter appointing him "His Ma[jes]tys Printer within the Province of N York"; the honor included an annual stipend of one hundred pounds. The same day Pownall awarded Myles Cooper and Thomas Bradbury Chandler a yearly stipend of two hundred pounds for their "merit and Services." Further, in a letter discussing the disputed claims that many New Yorkers had to land in what would become Vermont, Dartmouth had apprised Colden at the end of 1774: "Their Pretentions will meet with every Countenance and Support that can be shewn consistent with Justice; for . . . the Conduct of that Province . . . has been such as justly intitles its well disposed and peaceable Inhabitants to His Majesty's particular Favor." Between April 1775 and July 1776 Colden and Tryon approved land grants totaling almost 425,000 acres, over 64 percent of which went to prominent loyalists.[41] And a letter from London dated March 15, 1775, had reported that New York had not been named in the Restraining Act (which prohibited the colonies, after July 1, from trading anywhere but with Britain and the British West Indies) "in hopes of making that colony secede from the general American system of opposition." In May 1775 Dartmouth informed Tryon that New York City's Presbyterian Church might be granted a charter.[42]

The government's largess would be for naught, however, if the tories failed to keep the next Assembly from supporting Congress. Most observers assumed that the House would back the other colonies on taxation, but loyalists hoped it might adopt a more moderate stand on some other issue, thereby driving a wedge between New York and the patriot camp. On November 2, 1774, shortly after New York's congressional delegation had returned home, Colden wrote Dartmouth that he would delay calling the Assembly into session until he could determine whether it "will propose conciliatory Measures." But his hand was forced: if the House did not meet, patriots planned to call a provincial congress. He consequently set January 10 as the opening date for the legislative session.[43]

By the new year the air was thick with politics. The governor's Council met at eleven a.m. on January 5 to critique a draft of Colden's opening address to the Assembly. The meeting was out of the ordinary and violated established procedures: Smith was not summoned to attend until noon; and when he arrived, Colden was absent. Upon reading the proposed speech, Smith objected that it was so sharply worded it would force assemblymen to take sides and thereby hurt the crown. The Council finally concurred, and Colden agreed to revise his speech. Only later did Smith learn that before his arrival "the De Lanceys, Duane and Low" had persuaded Colden to write his "violent Speech." De Lancey leaders clearly feared that they lacked the votes to control the Assembly. A harsh speech would provoke an angry reply and give Colden an excuse to dissolve the House before it ratified the Association or appointed delegates to the next Continental Congress. And the public would not be able to blame the De Lanceys for what had happened. But Smith's argument thwarted the plan. Since minutes of the meeting would be sent to London, the De Lanceys did not want to risk being reproached in Britain if events proved Smith correct.[44]

Although Smith felt Colden's revised speech still stunned the Assembly, the governor had his own agenda, for he was getting advice from someone outside the Council, urging him to adopt a hard line. Smith suspected John Tabor Kempe or Myles Cooper. If it were the latter, he was only exhorting the governor to do what tory propagandists were already doing. Colden and these writers shared the view that if the people could be roused out of their apathy, that would reveal how small a minority the whigs really were. Colden had even informed the ministry of their strategy: "Several Pieces have been publish'd Here, exposing the extravagant and dangerous Proceedings of the Congress, and adviseing the People to rely on the Assembly, that they will take the most reasonable and constitutional Means of restoring Peace and Harmony between Great Britain and this Province." He felt the approach would persuade the House to adopt measures the cabinet found acceptable.[45]

When De Lanceyites met to plot strategy on January 9, they lacked Colden's optimism. Their estimate of how lawmakers already in town or living nearby would vote indicated that fourteen favored the Continental Congress and eleven opposed it. While debating whether to try to block the House from endorsing the measures Congress had approved, Hugh Wallace, a De Lanceyite councillor, urged that the De Lanceys push, as soon as the Assembly met, for an address to the king, as the first order of business. James De Lancey successfully opposed offering the motion straightaway. Either he thought it would deceive no one, or he did not want to act before he had the votes. There were thirty-one seats in the Assembly. Colden would write on February 1 that the nine lawmakers who had not yet arrived were all tories.[46]

Because it lacked a quorum, the Assembly did not open until January 13. By then the whigs were as confused as their opponents. "Finding a great Majority against them," the Livingstons successfully moved on January 17 "that the Consideration of the weighty Business which was before them should be put off" until February 7. And the Assembly "immediately sent out Orders for the absent Members to attend" by that date. But on January 26, after two more lawmakers, "who were known to be violent in the Opposition to Government," reached town, a Livingstonite moved that the House consider "the Proceedings of the Continental Congress." If he thought he had the votes, he erred, for the motion failed, eleven to ten.[47]

It is unclear how De Lanceyites on January 9 or Livingstonites on January 26 could have miscalculated the number of their supporters. The *Pennsylvania Journal* reported on May 17 that several New York lawmakers had been bribed a thousand pounds each for their votes in January 1775. No hard evidence exists to prove the allegation, and it is impossible to guess who the culprits might have been. It is just as easy to surmise that, given the stress of the moment, the De Lanceys had lost their nerve. The Livingstons, for their part, may have acted when they did because of the arrival of two allies. Almost all the lawmakers still absent were loyalist in sympathy. Moreover, Samuel Gale, an Orange County De Lanceyite, who was already in town, failed to vote on January 26 and may have been momentarily away. Even though the Livingstons could not win, the vote made them appear stronger than they actually were.[48]

While De Lancey strength grew as more members arrived, Livingstonites kept making motions that hurt their opponents out of doors and justified the need for maintaining extralegal bodies. On February 17 the House refused to thank New York's congressional delegation. On February 21, it voted against commending the merchants and inhabitants for upholding the Continental Association. And on February 23 it declined to appoint deputies to the Second Continental Congress. With each vote De Lanceyites in the Assembly moved farther away from public opinion and deeper into the loyalist camp. As Livingstonites surely understood, that was no accident: the De Lancey party's long-term commitment to the empire, Anglicanism, elitism, and commercial growth had by now made it impossible for many of its members to accept the Association or the path that patriots were taking.[49]

De Lanceyites presented their position on March 3, when the Assembly adopted a "State of Grievances" condemning unconstitutional taxation, the creation of admiralty courts that had concurrent jurisdiction with the common law courts, the New York Restraining Act, the Declaratory Act, the Coercive Acts, and the Currency Act of 1764. On March 8 the De Lancey–controlled House passed five resolutions: the first affirmed New York's allegiance to the crown; the second declared that all parliamentary laws not "inconsistent with the essential rights and liberties of Englishmen" and "for the general weal of the whole Empire" were binding on the colonies; the third that Americans had the right to tax themselves; the fourth that parliamentary taxation of the colonies and "extending the jurisdiction of the Courts of Admiralty beyond their ancient limits" were unconstitutional; and the last that "trial by a Jury" was "the birthright of Englishmen." The Assembly sent memorials to the King, Lords, and Commons, making the same argument.[50]

Crown officials were euphoric. Colden thought he could quell the rebellion by persuading New Yorkers to remain peaceable until Britain answered the petitions. Edmund Burke "congratulate[d]" James De Lancey and added that "the Ministry place their best hopes of dissolving the Union of the Colonies and breaking the present spirit of resistance, wholly in your Province." General Gage claimed the victory was already affecting Philadelphia. Governor Martin delayed calling North Carolina's Assembly, hoping that it might follow New York's lead. Lord Barrington, the secretary of war, felt the cabinet would not be able to reward the colony enough.[51]

Yet the kudos were overdone. The Assembly's petition to the king called for "such a system of government . . . as will sufficiently ascertain and limit the authority claimed by the British legislature."[52] The Assembly differed from Congress chiefly over the question of means. The De Lanceys wanted to petition for a redress of grievances; whigs, to enforce the Association through extralegal committees. Of course, De Lanceyite anxiety over methods sprang from their abhorrence of independence. Despite admitting that Britain was acting unconstitutionally, they would not approve steps that risked destroying the empire, and some already sensed how ineffectual that strategy was. James De Lancey left for Britain in May, never to return. He was a good seer, for Dartmouth informed Tryon at the end of May that the Assembly's addresses were unacceptable: they were "unfortunately blended with expressions containing claims which made it impossible for Parliament consistent with its justice and dignity to receive them."[53]

Before the ministry's answer crossed the Atlantic, however, crown officials in New York had sought to capitalize on their success in the Assembly by trying to divide the colonies in half. Colden wrote Vice Adm. Samuel Graves at Boston for naval support to protect New York's loyalists. The ships could also be used to block rebel troops and supplies from crossing the Hudson. The letter was first sent unsealed to Gage for his approval. The general and the admiral both endorsed the plan, but the former had no soldiers to spare. The cabinet was thinking along similar lines. On March 3 Lord Dartmouth wrote Gage that four regiments were being sent to Boston, but the general could order them to New York if he thought that best. In April the ministry decided that the regiments should go directly to New York. The reasons were Colden's: local loyalists would be encouraged, and rebel supply lines would be interdicted at the Hudson. But the troops never reached New York. Following the Battles of Lexington and Concord, Gage dispatched a frigate to order the regiments to Boston. The *Asia*, however, a naval vessel of sixty-four guns, reached New York on May 26, 1775.[54]

III

Meanwhile, whigs were working to ensure that New York did not abandon their cause. On February 9, 1775, McDougall had written to William Cooper in Boston that "we have not yet chosen Delegates to meet the next Congress, waiting till we know whether the Assembly will do it or not. If they don't, we shall be able with more Ease to bring about a Provincial Congress." Because residents staunchly supported participating in the next Continental Congress, radicals wanted to use the delegate-selection process to create a Provincial Congress that could supplant the De Lancey–controlled Assembly and transform what until now had been an urban movement into a colony-wide mass movement. To command legitimacy, New York's congressional delegation had to represent the whole province, not just the city.[55]

On February 27 and on March 1 the Committee of Sixty debated in vain how to choose delegates to the Continental Congress and finally decided to let residents settle the issue at a meeting on March 6. Tories quickly went on the offensive. On March 4, a group headed by John Thurman, an Anglican De Lanceyite, distributed a broadside, *To the Freemen and Freeholders of the City and County of New York*, which espoused prudence and emphasized the whigs' obligation to respect the right of residents to decide for themselves the best course of action. The Committee of Sixty should have polled residents about "*whether Delegates ought to be sent*" and should not simply have asked townspeople "to *deputize* others to *appoint* Delegates" for them. Thurman's group urged people to vote on March 6 to delay action until April 20, by which time they would surely have Britain's answer to the Assembly's petitions. Supporters of this plan were requested to march on March 6 "to the Exchange, and there to give your voices, for postponing the said Meeting, until Thursday 20th of April next." Left unsaid was that if nothing were done until that date, New York's delegation might well arrive at Philadelphia either too late to act in concert with the other colonies or after Congress had adjourned.[56]

Fearing a plot "to defeat the design of sending Delegates," the "Friends to Constitutional Liberty" held a rally on March 4 "to support" the Committee of Sixty's "virtue and patriotism." On March 6, the whigs assembled at the Liberty Pole and marched from there to the Exchange under a "Union Flag" in support of "the Liberties of America" and "the Measures of Congress." They reached the Exchange shortly before Thurman's group, which consisted mostly of placemen: "some Officers of the Army and Navy, several of His Majesty's Council, and those Members of the House of Representatives, who had refused taking into consideration the proceedings of the Congress, together with Officers of the Customs, and other dependents on the Court." A melee broke out at once between the two groups. William Cunningham, a member of Thurman's group who was in the employ of the city, had his clothes ripped off him and his money robbed from him before he was unceremoniously thrown into jail by the mob.[57]

Once calm had been restored and the meeting had been called to order, the chair asked two questions: whether delegates should be chosen for a Provincial Congress; and whether the committee should nominate eleven people to that end. The Thurman faction objected, demanding that the poll be restricted to legal voters. The meeting debated the two questions anyway, and John Holt claimed that they were carried in the affirmative by majorities "the most numerous and respectable ever known in this City." But "Impartial" protested that most of the participants were "the rabble, which may always be collected by the pagentry of a flag, and the sound of drum and fife." He thought it "the opinion of a very great majority of our fellow-citizens that no *new powers*" had "been vested in the Committee" and "that it was impossible from the nature of things, to determine on which side the majority was."[58]

On the night of March 6 the Committee of Sixty nominated eleven persons for the Provincial Congress, including the city's five delegates to the First Continental Congress. Of the other six, one became a loyalist and the rest remained radical in sentiment. On March 8 the committee voted unanimously to poll the freeholders and freemen on March 15 to determine whether they approved sending deputies to a Provincial Convention "for the *sole* Purpose of electing out of their Body, Delegates" to the Continental Congress and, if so, whether the March 6 nominees were acceptable. The propaganda battle grew more intense, but of the 988 people who voted on March 15, over 80 percent favored sending the eleven deputies to the convention. The committee accordingly set April 20 as the date for the convention to meet and asked the other counties in the province to select representatives.[59]

Meanwhile, the city's whigs and tories jousted for power. At a March 27 meeting of the Committee of Sixty, an artisan accused two hardware merchants—William Ustick (an Anglican, De Lanceyite, loyalist committeeman) and his brother James—of selling nails to General Gage. After a debate the committee condemned the exportation of nails, and on April 6, a mass meeting rebuked the Usticks and warned townspeople not to do business with the army. At the same meeting it was learned that Ralph Thurman and Robert Harding were loading a large ship with supplies for Gage. On April 11, Sears and Marinus Willett (an Anglican cabinetmaker and the son of a tavern owner) led their followers to Thurman's house to make him desist, but the Anglican De Lanceyite would not be cowed. Sears then called a meeting at the Liberty Pole for the evening of April 15, at which time Thurman and Harding were expected to explain why they were aiding the British.[60]

Thurman vented his outrage in a broadside: "Those Enemies to Peace and good Order shall not rule over me." "If the Civil Authority" could not "restrain the licentious Spirit of those arbitrary Sons of Discord, I am determined to do Justice to Liberty; I will die in her Cause. . . . He that will not defend his personal Safety, and that Liberty which the Laws of Society secure to him, is unworthy of her Blessings." After Thurman complained to the city government, Mayor Whitehead Hicks and Gen. James Robertson, the Barrack Master General for North America, asked the governor's Council on April 13 to investigate. Although the Council agreed to question those involved, Hicks issued warrants the next day, on his own authority, for the arrest of Sears and Willett. Not only had De Lancey councillors privately urged the mayor to make the arrests, so that they would not have to tackle the problem themselves, but the petty merchants had also demanded that the mayor act. Robertson had been complaining that he had already spent £260,000 in New York and would buy elsewhere if the city government failed to restrain the radicals.[61]

Willett put up bail, but Sears refused, and Hicks ordered William Cunningham to apprehend the radical on April 15. When Sears arrived at the jail, however, his followers set him free, gave Cunningham another drubbing, and paraded about town with their leader. That evening Sears addressed his supporters at the Liberty Pole. A crowd then proceeded to the homes of Thurman and Harding to demand that they request pardon. Again, the two refused. Harding's house was searched, but Sears and McDougall dissuaded the rioters from entering Thurman's abode. If De Lanceyites had strayed too far from public opinion by repudiating the Continental Congress, radicals did not want to sabotage their own cause by using excessive force. The two merchants thus got off lightly; and trade with the British in Boston continued for the moment. But a "Real Churchman" explained the import of what had happened: "From that time all the Civil Authority has been prostrate, and the Magistrates have not even the Shadow of power or Authority." Colden informed London that the events of April had "combined to depress legal authority — to increase the Terror of the Inhabitants, and which seemed to vanquish every thought of Resistance to popular Rage."[62] His strategy of defeating the rebellion by keeping New York loyal to the king had failed.

The Provincial Convention met on April 20, 1775. Eight counties besides New York sent delegates. Only Richmond refused outright to do so. Charlotte, Cumberland, Tryon, and Gloucester counties evidently took no action. Though it was not as solid a show of unity as radicals would have liked, it was a good start. The next day the Convention named twelve representatives to the Continental Congress. Of the city's five delegates to the First Continental Congress, only Low was not reappointed, for he had declared himself ineligible.[63] The Convention adjourned the next day.

Sears and McDougall had much to celebrate, for the outcome marked a resounding triumph for the strategy they had pursued since news of the Tea Act had reached New York. They had not only persuaded the city to establish the Committee of Fifty-one and then the Committee of Sixty, they had also been the first to propose a Continental Congress; they had convinced the city to send delegates to the Congress; and they had worked successfully for a Provincial Convention. They had even managed to bring some De Lanceyites like Jay and Duane into the whig fold. New York had thus advanced another cautious step down the road toward revolution.

Empire and Liberty

On Sunday, April 23, 1775, New Yorkers learned that four days earlier British troops had killed Americans at Lexington, Massachusetts. The incident was no accident, for on January 27, Lord Dartmouth, the secretary of state for America, had written Gen. Thomas Gage that events in New England "shew[ed] a Determination in the People to commit themselves at all Events in open Rebellion." Dartmouth directed the general "to arrest" the leaders of the Massachusetts Provincial Congress and to dismantle rebel fortifications in Connecticut and Rhode Island. "Any efforts of the People, unprepared to encounter with a regular force, cannot be very formidable"; it would "be better that the Conflict should be brought on, upon such ground, than in a riper state of Rebellion." Because most whig leaders had already fled Boston, and because Gage had only three thousand troops on hand, he decided that his best course of action would be to seize the matériel the patriots had stockpiled at Concord. That led directly to the Battles of Lexington and Concord.[1]

From the perspective of three thousand miles, the secretary's strategy was logical. The ministry considered New England to be the insurgency's center. If the army were to chastise the hotheads there, whigs elsewhere would be cowed, and the rebellion would crumble. But conflict theory suggests that other factors were at work, as well: "A good predictor of high levels of coercion and violence is earlier conflict behavior of a lesser magnitude." Britain and its American colonies had been at odds since the early 1760s; and the spiraling of the violence in 1775 was impelling both sides to act in ways that would have horrified them in 1760. Moreover, once a punitive course of action is undertaken, its initiator tends to persist, not to retreat, even if the action miscarries. Hence, even though the Coercive Acts had failed, the cabinet authorized still harsher measures. Further, a group usually escalates a conflict when either the reward for winning or the penalty for losing exceeds "the costs of raising the magnitude" of its "conflict behavior." In this case the cabinet believed war preferable to conceding American independence.[2]

Contrary to British expectations, but not to those of conflict theory, Lexington and Concord nudged New York closer to revolution. First, for military force to be effective in such circumstances it must be "threatened and applied precisely." But the rout of the redcoats in their retreat from Concord only emboldened whigs. A New Yorker exuded, "I know the value of British disciplined troops, but a thousand American gunmen, on their own intricate advantageous ground, 'tis likely at any time will defeat a large number of any European troops." Second, when an adversary's behavior (here, killing Americans) exceeds an opponent's "normative expectations," coercion is usually "counterproductive." The injured party becomes so outraged it feels free to escalate its own tactics. Finally, given the colonists' abiding ideological fear of standing armies, the ministry's resort to force confirmed their belief that Britain aimed to establish a tyranny and thus validated the whig argument that resistance was justified.[3]

The reaction was instantaneous. New Yorkers stood on street corners "inquisitive for news — Tales of all kinds invented believed, denied, discredited." "Reconciliation," wrote a resident, "is at a farther distance than we, of late, had rational ground to hope"; and "many persons of influence, who have been thought inimical to the cause, now come out boldly and declare their sentiments worthy of themselves."[4] Robert R. Livingston claimed "the Tories [here] turn Wigg so fast that they will soon be as much united as they are in Massachusetts Bay." Another New Yorker added that New Englanders "are held in the highest esteem for their bravery, and people here are determined to . . . march to their assistance when called for. The die is thrown, and every man of us, whether we are hearty in the cause or not, must abide by the cast."[5]

Again, it was the radicals who had blazed the path. Thomas Jones, a New York Supreme Court justice, caustically described how on Sunday, April 23, the streets became a public theater. Liberty Boys "paraded the town with drums beating and colours flying, (attended by a mob of negroes, boys, sailors, and pick-pockets) inviting all mankind to take up arms in defense of the 'injured rights and liberties of America.' The posts were stopped, the mails opened, and the letters read." A mob "seized upon a sloop loaded with provisions for [the army in] Boston . . . and cast the cargo into the dock." The Committee of Sixty gathered hastily before nightfall, scheduled a mass meeting for Monday, and sent envoys to Connecticut for help should New York be attacked. On Sunday night a crowd broke into an armory, distributed the weapons, and posted a guard to secure what remained. Demonstrators then threatened to attack the 106 redcoats barracked near the Fields. The soldiers' position was defenseless, and a mob assault would have ended in a slaughter. Colden was distraught. His plans to assemble a force to hold New York for the crown had failed, and now the mob held the army hostage. But as had typically happened in the years after 1765, cooler heads prevailed, and the troops were not harmed that night.[6]

Much as they had done after the 1765 riots, royal officials and tories described the following week as one of anarchy.[7] Reportedly, little business was transacted by day, and the taverns were jammed at night. Yet the radicals had achieved their objectives: they had negated the army's power in town, intercepted supplies intended for Gage, avoided indiscriminate violence, and had three to four hundred armed men patrolling the streets to keep order. Jasper Drake's Water Street tavern was the recruitment center; and Isaac Sears's home on Queen Street was military headquarters. Tories bewailed the chaos. But from a patriot standpoint that was good, for in their "Terror" the loyalists gave up "every thought of Resistance." "The Whig party gained a Compleat triumph."[8]

The town remained tense on Monday, for rumors of an impending assault upon the redcoats had resurfaced. When the governor's Council met that afternoon, Col. Leonard Lispenard, a radical Dutch Reformed innkeeper, reported that civil officials should expect "no aid from the Militia, for they were all Liberty Boys who would keep the Peace of the City in other Respects." Mayor Hicks added "that the Magistratic Authority was gone." Thomas Jones, who had been invited to the meeting, blustered "that the militia should be called out, the riot act read, and if the mob did not thereupon disperse, to apprehend and imprison the ringleaders." William Smith demurred, claiming the crisis would subside once grievances were redressed. In the end, all the Council could agree on was that it had "no power" and that "the best mode of proceeding . . . was to use Diswasion from Violence."[9]

The Committee of Sixty held its scheduled meeting in the Fields that afternoon, but by then the news from Massachusetts had made the people more militant than their leaders. After voting to form a new whig militia, the meeting pressed the committee to organize the city's defenses. Isaac Low, the committee chair, objected: "He wanted no new Powers and would not act upon any." Philip Livingston said he "did not think himself Qualified for a member of a committee of warr, which he understood was the Object of the New Powers." Their caution was understandable; they had been elected to enforce the Continental Association, not to wage war. The meeting ended without a vote on the matter, but on Wednesday, April 26, the committee called for the election that Friday of twenty delegates to a Provincial Congress to meet on May 22 and also of a Committee of One Hundred to direct affairs in town forthwith. The next day, Thursday, the Committee of Sixty published slates of candidates for these two proposed bodies.[10]

Sears was disgruntled: both sets of nominees included too many British sympathizers; merchants were still shipping matériel to the enemy in Boston; and a New Yorker had allegedly asked Gage for troops. Accordingly, the Sons of Liberty met on April 27 and formed a battalion of eight hundred men both to defend the city and to enhance radical power. The meeting next appointed a five-member ad hoc committee to visit the collector of the customs. About three hundred and sixty persons then escorted the five to Andrew Elliot's home, where they requested the keys to the Customs House and a pledge that he would no longer enter or clear any vessels according to the rules set down by Parliament. Elliot promptly sent a message to his deputy, who put the key in the Customs House door and fled.[11] Meanwhile, the meeting nominated its own candidates for the Provincial Congress and the Committee of One Hundred. Seventy-nine of the persons selected for the committee had been on the Committee of Sixty's list. The twenty-one whom the meeting replaced were mostly De Lanceyites, many of whom would become loyalists. Of those the meeting named for Congress, only six had been on the Committee of Sixty's slate of candidates, but the pattern was the same: Liberty Boy–Livingston coalition members were substituted for suspected tories. That done, the crowd marched to the Customs House, locked the door, and put a guard at the entrance. Smith reported that "the Merchants are amazed and yet so humbled as only to sigh or complain in whispers. They now dread Sears's Train of armed men."[12]

On Friday, April 28, the voting both for the Committee of One Hundred and for delegates to the Provincial Congress began as expected. But Sears "went with the Pride of a Dictator and forbid the Polls objecting to the List proposed by the Committee." In a broadside issued the same day the Committee of Sixty replied that unity could be preserved only if "every Member of Society will consent to be governed by the Sense of the Majority, and join in having that Sense fairly and candidly ascertained." To answer Sears's complaint that too many nominees were British sympathizers, the committee explained that the new committee "should consist of a large Number, in order that by interesting many of Weight and Consequence in all public Measures, they might meet with the more Advocates, receive less Opposition, and be attended with more certain Success." Maintaining a consensus was paramount: "Let us avoid Divisions; and instead of cherishing a Spirit of Animosity against one another, let us join in forwarding Reconciliation of all Parties, and thereby strengthen the general Cause." The Committee of Sixty reaffirmed its support for its slates of candidates and rescheduled the election for Monday, May 1.[13]

Meanwhile, alarmed by reports that Gage had ordered the army to seize the ordnance at Salem, Massachusetts, Sears and his men began carting the cannons from the Battery to Kings Bridge, fourteen miles up the Hudson. For the second time that day he was acting without authority, and on Friday night the committee adopted a General Association to reaffirm its authority and to restrain local militants. "Persuaded that the Salvation of the Rights and Liberties of America" required "the firm union of its inhabitants, in a vigorous prosecution of the Measures necessary for its Safety," the compact committed subscribers to obey "whatever measures may be recommended by the Continental Congress; or resolved upon by our Provincial Convention" and to "Follow the Advice of" the Committee of Sixty for "the Preservation of Peace and Good Order."[14]

But order was not promptly restored. The next afternoon the *Pennsylvania Journal* arrived with a letter from London claiming that Cadwallader Colden, John Watts, Myles Cooper, Henry White, and Oliver De Lancey—Anglicans all—had asked Britain for troops to assure New York's "defection and Submission." Even though the accused denied the story, several people became so enraged they "actually charged their pieces in order to shoot" the traitors.[15]

Harmony finally triumphed, however. On May 1 the Committee of Sixty issued a broadside with a revised slate of candidates. Of the twenty-one Committee of One Hundred nominees whom Sears opposed, four Anglican De Lanceyites were removed. One of the committee's replacements, John Imlay, had been nominated by the Liberty Boys on April 27. Two others, Samuel Broome and Eleazer Miller, were Presbyterian merchants. The last, Benjamin Helme, was a German Reformed attorney. Further, the Dutch Reformed James Beekman, who had helped the Sons of Liberty to buy Hampden Hall in 1770, replaced the Anglican John Thurman on the list of congressional nominees; and Jacobus Van Zandt, a Dutch Reformed Livingstonite merchant and confidant of Sears, was added as a twenty-first candidate for Congress. The elections thus went smoothly, and the revised slates of candidates were elected without opposition.[16]

Despite the tumultuous events of the preceding week, unity had been maintained, plans for a Provincial Congress had been set in motion, and the Committee of One Hundred had been accorded the legitimacy it needed to become the de facto authority in the city. The process had not always been orderly, but what revolution is? New York City's diverse population was entering uncharted territory and trying to do so by consensus, not by repudiating the colony's traditional political leadership. In fact, that was typical of what people were attempting elsewhere in the multiethnic Middle Colonies. In Pennsylvania, according to Joseph E. Illick, "the whole society" was "constantly aware of the importance of consensus" in resisting British imperialism. Though Sears had tested the limits of that consensus more than once, in the end he heeded the call for harmony and remained in the fold.[17]

II

In New York, the months after Lexington were marked by hesitancy, even confusion. How could it have been otherwise when so heterogeneous a group faced so daunting a challenge? Yet a broad-based understanding persisted, one to which the Provincial Congress and the Committee of One Hundred hewed throughout 1775. Robert R. Livingston said it best: "Every good man wishes that America may remain free: In this I join heartily; at the same time, I do not desire, we should be wholly independent of the mother country." In May the Committee of One Hundred declared that New Yorkers would resist till death the plan "to erect in this land of liberty a despotism scarcely to be paralleled in the pages of antiquity, or the volumes of modern times." But "when our unexampled grievances are redressed, our Prince will find his American subjects" exhibiting "the most unshaken fidelity to their Sovereign, and inviolable attachment to the welfare of his realm." Put succinctly, most New Yorkers wanted both empire and liberty.[18]

Public officials understood that fact. City magistrates avowed in an address to Gov. William Tryon on his return from Britain that New York "sigh[ed] with the utmost ardour for the re-establishment of the common tranquillity, upon that ancient system of Government and intercourse which has been such a fruitful source of general prosperity and opulence." Conversations with townspeople persuaded Tryon that these sentiments were genuine. On July 4 he warned the cabinet, "America will never receive Parliamentary taxation. I do not meet with any of the inhabitants who show the smallest inclination to draw the sword in support of that principle." The next month he added, "The friends of government in general consider themselves between Scylla and Carybdis, that is the dread of Parliamentary taxation and the tyranny of their present masters. Could the first principle be moved out of the way, His Majesty would probably see America put on a less determined complexion." William Smith agreed: "The Dread of being taxed by the Commons of Great Britain, is the Soul of the League, that bands the Provinces together. Give them a constitutional Security agt Arbitrary Levies; that is to say, covenant that they shall be Englishmen, and the Advocates for Independency, will be found such an inconsiderable Handful, even in the most suspected Colonies."[19]

There were powerful reasons, too, why New York was committed to empire and liberty. For one, the city was not, as Edward Countryman has argued, on the verge of internal revolution or political collapse in the 1770s. Sharp cleavages persisted, and these both antedated and outlasted the Revolution. They help to explain how the city reacted to the procession of imperial crises, but they were not sufficient to bring about a revolution in 1776. The impetus for change had come from Britain, not New York. Like people throughout the Middle Atlantic Colonies, most city residents wanted the ministry to rescind its policies; they did not want to quit the empire or to restructure New York society.[20] It was only when New Yorkers became convinced that Britain would not mend its ways that they reluctantly declared their independence. Even as late as June 1776 some whigs still felt that their side should eschew provocations that might push affairs to the breaking point.

New Yorkers were also reluctant because the city was composed of diverse ethnic, religious, and socioeconomic groups that found it difficult, throughout the eighteenth century, to reconcile their differences. Many feared revolution might end in chaos. Townspeople thus sought to use their formidable political skills to build a consensus over how best to resist British imperialism. Because the costs of opposing imperial initiatives varied from group to group, it took time to hammer out an understanding that most could support. Further, whenever a conflict group is in essence a coalition, the tendency is for it to embrace goals and tactics acceptable to the least militant and most conservative of its partners, for if the coalition is not to crumble, the group must adopt objectives all can approve. Thus, the restraints imposed by the city's heterogeneity abetted the emergence of leaders who were conciliatory in outlook.[21] Indicative of this reality is that although a disgusted Sears would leave the province in late 1775 and spend the war in New Haven and Boston, New Yorkers never repudiated their more cautious leaders in the Provincial Congress. Moreover, the fact that residents worked hard and often to forge a consensus in each of the imperial crises shows clearly that the key issue was not who should rule in New York but how best to defeat those British initiatives that residents considered both unconstitutional and ruinous to their well-being. Though real economic, ethnic, religious, and political divisions existed, New Yorkers considered unity essential and were prepared to pay a price for it.

It is in the context of pluralism, not political decay or instability, that New York politics must be evaluated. The Livingston and De Lancey parties were not simply bands of opportunistic aristocrats exploiting imperial crises for selfish advantage. They were coalitions of interest groups, and their leaders had to heed the myriad demands of their constituents. Nor did these leaders lack beliefs of their own.[22] James De Lancey had crafted a program after the 1765 riots that aimed to safeguard the empire, the Anglican Church, and elite rule, while revitalizing the city's economy. The plan failed, and he became a loyalist refugee. Yet his doing so was neither an accident nor the result of cynicism. It was a choice based on positions he had advocated throughout the period. If few joined him in his self-imposed exile, most remained receptive to the message he had preached for a decade: that the city's economic well-being was linked to its membership in the empire. Given the city's materialistic impulse, the De Lancey legacy contributed mightily to the citizenry's reluctance to declare independence. Anglican party members, of course, also had religious reasons for wanting to save the empire.[23]

The Livingstons, for their part, had stated their opposition to unconstitutional taxation as early as the 1750s, had reaffirmed it in the Stamp Act crisis, and had adhered to it in subsequent imperial crises. But the Real Whigs among them were torn between a fear of tyranny from above and a dread of anarchy from below. Party patricians worried that mob violence or independence would undermine elite rule. Party lawyers wanted Parliament to be resisted only by lawful methods. Nonetheless, the Livingstons had been allied with the radicals since 1769. Following the Tea Act, Isaac Sears, John Lamb, and Alexander McDougall typically held center stage, yet Livingstonites were present, too: supporting the cause in the Assembly and on extralegal committees, advising on strategy and tactics, and restraining the radicals when that seemed advisable. Though committed to upholding American rights, Livingstonites remained moderates who favored empire over independence, elitism over egalitarianism, and conciliation over confrontation. The need to find a common front that both radicals and moderates could accept propelled patriots toward the dual pillars of empire and liberty, delaying their embrace of independence.[24]

By cleaving to a platform of empire and liberty, Livingstonites could be content that they were safe from both autocracy and anarchy; Liberty Boys, that freedom would not be sacrificed for the sake of empire; and De Lanceyites, that the cry for liberty need not be a call for independence. Other factors were involved, too. De Lanceyites feared that if they quit the movement, the Liberty Boys would radicalize it. Colden, in fact, assured the cabinet that the best people served on whig committees only to restrain the hotheads. In Pennsylvania, when the old elite withdrew "from resistance activities," "radical leadership devolved" first to moderates and finally to "the laboring poor." That was exactly what De Lanceyites hoped to avoid in New York. Nevertheless, the city's radicals, who constituted the genuinely revolutionary force in the province, had much to gain by tempering their demands. In 1775 John Holt wrote that the lukewarm were elected to the committee and to Congress because they were often "men of weight and Fortune, who might contribute to the expense and give Credit to the proceedings." Another reason "was that they by Degrees might be drawn into a concurrence, and cooperation in the same publick Measures, with the rest of the colonies, and . . . for their own security [be] obliged to unite with, and Support them." Indeed, by placing Anglican conservatives like James Duane and John Jay in prominent roles, the whig party (unlike the Livingstons in the 1760s) made clear its ecumenical desire to unite all New Yorkers, Anglicans and dissenters alike, in the common defense. In explaining why the city voted for the least radical ticket in the April 1776 elections for the Third Provincial Congress, "A Sober Citizen" would say that with Britain ready to invade it was better to preserve unity, to keep conservatives tied to the cause, and not to risk their desertion to the enemy.[25]

Because of conflict over long-term objectives, quite a few opposed what the Committee of One Hundred and the Provincial Congress were doing in 1775 to advance the dual goals of empire and liberty. On one side were people like Isaac Low who prized the empire more than liberty; they disparaged the threat to freedom and the need for warlike preparations. Many such people had already or would become tories. On the other side were those like Sears who revered liberty more and spurred moderate whigs to act more boldly on behalf of American rights. Extremists in this group were nudging the city toward independence. Dissension thus led the committee and Congress to act cautiously, but critics were unfair to condemn them for timidity. Given the consensus' commitment to the empire, both bodies should be seen as resolute, not timid, in the steps they took to uphold liberty. Other colonies moved more swiftly or forcefully in 1775, but New York whigs were acting in an environment shaped by the city's history, ethnic and religious pluralism, economic divisions, political factionalism, and strategic significance. Better to proceed warily without stumbling than audaciously without success.

But neither the Committee of One Hundred nor the Provincial Congress confused prudence with submission, or patience with passivity. On the day the nominees for the two bodies were elected, the Committee of One Hundred began immediately to function as an extralegal government. Order was restored, and a night watch established. Once the port was reopened, the Continental Association was strictly enforced, and trade with Boston outlawed. Men were urged to begin military training; troops were raised; munitions were procured; and the export of critical matériel was prohibited. Residents were told to sign the Committee of Sixty's General Association of April 29 or be reported to the committee. On May 8 the Committee of One Hundred disarmed all tories within its jurisdiction; it wrote Colden that it had acted thus so as to strengthen "the hand of the civil Magistrate in every lawfull measure calculated to promote the Peace and just Rule of this Metropolis; and consistent with that jealous attention which above all things we are bound to pay to the violated Rights of America."[26]

Once the Provincial Congress convened on May 22, it assumed overall direction of the colony's affairs. It required its members to sign a General Association pledging allegiance to Congress and decreed that every New Yorker should do likewise. Though people were not persecuted for refusing, they were punished if they joined the British army, violated the Continental Association, or acted in some way "hostile to American liberty." Congress continued the work of defense that the committee had begun: provisions were collected; fortifications erected; a militia organized; and units raised for service in the Continental Army. Since money was scarce, individuals made contributions, and the provincial Treasurer and the Loan Office at Albany advanced funds. When that was not enough, Congress debated whether to tax residents. Though it decided against that, its vigor led Colden to lament, "You will be surprised . . . how entirely the legal authority of Governmt is now superceded in this Place, where only a few Months agoe the Prospect of public affairs gave so much satisfaction to the Friends of Government."[27]

Congress kept the door of conciliation ajar, however. Benjamin Kissam, a New York City Anglican attorney and future tory, declared in Congress on May 30 that a settlement based "on constitutional principles" was "essential to the well-being of both Countries" and would "prevent the horrours of a civil war." He asked that an ad hoc committee set down "the terms on which such reconciliation may be tendered to Great Britain,

consistent with the just liberties and freedom of the subject in America."
His motion passed on June 2. Although they opposed the idea, both John
Morin Scott and Alexander McDougall sat on the committee. On the basis
of the report the committee submitted on June 24 (a week after Bunker
Hill), Congress adopted a "Plan of Accommodation" on June 27. First,
Parliament should annul the acts that the Continental Congress had demanded be repealed in October 1774. Second, Britain could regulate
commerce, but revenues raised through tariffs should go directly into the
provincial treasuries. Third, elections for the colonial assemblies should
be held at least triennially. Fourth, if the crown approved, "a Continental
Congress" might "meet with a President appointed by the Crown, for the
purpose of raising and apportioning their general aids, upon application
made by the Crown, according to the advice of the British Parliament."
Fifth, Parliament should not interfere "in the religious and ecclesiastical
concerns of the Colonies." Sixth, the colonies should be guaranteed "a
free and exclusive power of legislation within themselves, respectively, in
all cases of internal polity whatsoever, subject only to the negative of their
Sovereign." For the sake of colonial unity, however, "no part" of the Plan
of Accommodation should "be deemed binding or obligatory upon the
Representatives of this Colony in Continental Congress." Though the
plan did not pass unanimously, most congressmen believed strongly that
compromise was a worthwhile stratagem. In contrast to Lord North, the
British prime minister, who saw the dispute as a struggle that only one
side could win, Congress wanted to "fractionate" the conflict into smaller
issues, so that compromise might be possible. If that were to succeed,
empire and liberty would still be compatible. The few, including Sears,
who voted against every motion favoring reconciliation constituted a distinct minority. Even McDougall refused to join them.[28]

On June 25, during Congress's debate on the "Plan of Accommodation," it happened that both Governor Tryon and General Washington
arrived in town. Congress tried to afford each the welcome his office demanded (see the Introduction). Whigs everywhere, however, were angered by the deference shown Tryon and feared the province might desert their cause. But if Congress's attachment to both empire and liberty
might to some have looked like waffling, patriots need not have worried.
Congress had directed that Tryon be greeted by uniformed soldiers from
among those it had raised for the colony's defense. Though these troops
were evidently elsewhere when Tryon landed, Congress's decision to use
them suggests that the welcome extended the governor was a calculated
show of autonomy, not a caitiff act of submission. On July 4, in fact, Congress directed the city magistrates not to wait upon Tryon with the formal

address customarily presented to a governor upon his return to the province. Tryon futilely asked Mayor Hicks to ignore the order, and a sympathetic Gage later wrote Tryon that New York's behavior was a sharp blow to the empire and that whig leaders throughout America had probably concocted the plan together.[29]

Notwithstanding New York's desire to remain in the empire, British military decisions created a dynamic that repeatedly forced whig leaders to reassess their policies. Several days after residents learned that the cabinet had ordered troops to the city, the Committee of One Hundred wrote the Second Continental Congress for guidance. That body promptly replied that any redcoats reaching port could join those in the barracks but should not be allowed to erect ramparts or to obstruct communications. Somewhat later, Congress directed that the city militia be held "in constant readiness" to thwart any attempt "to gain possession of the city and interrupt its intercourse with the country."[30]

Because the British army did not arrive in force in New York until 1776, the city's resolve was not abruptly tested. But the redcoats already in town were headaches enough. Their commander, Maj. Isaac Hamilton, had written Colden on May 26 that his troops were deserting, and that those who remained should be put aboard ship. Colden agreed, but the *Asia* was too small to accommodate Hamilton's men and their families, and the soldiers remained in the barracks. Meanwhile, rumors spread about town that the redcoats were to be withdrawn. On June 3, fearing trouble, the Provincial Congress urged residents to let the soldiers depart peaceably. After still more soldiers deserted, royal officials decided to move the redcoats to the *Asia* and their dependents to Governor's Island. When the troops left the barracks on the morning of June 6, Marinus Willett, a master cabinetmaker and Liberty Boy, was at Drake's tavern, a radical hangout. Upset by Congress's "timid disposition," Willett and some others decided to seize the arms the redcoats were carting from town. The conspirators raced across the city seeking help. When Willett reached Broad Street, he came upon the carts and a small guard of soldiers. Though alone, he impetuously halted "the whole line of march" and insisted that the committee had not given the troops permission to take "any other arms than those they carried about them." A Provincial Congressman objected, but Willett held his ground. And once Scott, a member of both the committee and Congress, backed him, a crowd confiscated the carts. The Provincial Congress warned residents not to take matters into their own hands and later ordered that the arms be turned over to the mayor. But the weapons remained hidden on property owned by Abraham Van Dyck, a Dutch tavern keeper and "a good Whig," until they were supplied to a regiment that McDougall raised for the Continental Army.[31]

If Willett had made the New York Congress appear timid, the *Asia* was a more intractable problem. On May 27 Abraham Lott, a navy contractor who had been pressured in 1773 not to accept appointment as a tea agent, had asked Congress whether he should fill a requisition from Capt. George Vandeput of the *Asia*. Since Congress had prohibited New York merchants from supplying British troops in Boston, could it let Lott provision the *Asia*, which was in New York to buttress royal authority? Because a negative reply might have triggered a violent response from Vandeput, Congress authorized Lott to furnish supplies to the *Asia* "*for her own use, while in this port.*"[32]

The *Asia* would remain a problem, especially after the Continental Congress stationed Connecticut soldiers, commanded by Capt. David Wooster, just outside the city. On July 13 two aldermen informed the Committee of Safety (an arm of the Provincial Congress that managed affairs when Congress was in recess) that Wooster's troops had seized a boat from the *Asia* and confiscated supplies from "His Majesty's Store" in town. When the committee investigated, Wooster explained that a Connecticut armed sloop had taken the boat, but he had ordered it released; the supplies were under guard in his camp and could be returned to the storehouse if the committee so directed. The crisis thus appeared resolved. But the two aldermen returned, right after Wooster left, with news that the boat had just been destroyed. An outraged Capt. Vandeput soon demanded "Satisfaction," or he would consider the incident "a direct Act of Hostility." City magistrates told Vandeput it was "the opinion of every one, that immediate Reparation should be made." They would not have said so unless they knew the Committee of Safety would go along. And quietly go along it did. But on July 18 the mayor informed the committee that he had tried to hire a carpenter to build the *Asia* a boat, but the artisan demanded "an order," to guarantee that "his fellow-citizens" would know "he is doing that work with the approbation of the Committee." The committee was thereby forced to record its approval in its minutes.[33] Construction of a new boat was begun, but a few days later someone sawed it into pieces. The committee investigated but could not discover who was responsible or find a carpenter willing to make another. Hence, on August 16, to the consternation of radicals, Congress ordered Henry Sheaf, a Presbyterian Livingstonite, to build the craft and Col. John Lasher (another Presbyterian) to guard it; anyone who obstructed Sheaf was "guilty of a dangerous attempt to destroy the authority of this Congress." The decision was understandable. In July, during a dispute over supplies, a British warship had bombarded Newport, and the Rhode Island General Assembly had responded to the incident by allowing the city to provision the ship.[34]

On August 22 the Provincial Congress authorized the clandestine removal of the cannon still on the Battery to a fort being built in the Highlands. Vandeput learned of the plan and ordered a barge to lie near the shore to keep him posted. About midnight, after the whigs, under the command of Sears and Lamb, began moving the artillery, an officer on the barge fired a musket to alert Vandeput. Assuming the shot was aimed at them, the Americans returned the fire with small arms. The *Asia* then answered with two of its cannons. After Vandeput learned that a sailor on the boat had been killed, the *Asia* then fired on the Battery again, killing one and wounding three. To protect those moving the cannons, Sears ordered a diversionary party to move a distance from the Battery and to begin making noise and firing small arms. The *Asia* replied with another broadside, but by sunrise Sears had removed twenty-one pieces of ordnance.[35]

In the morning Vandeput wrote the mayor that if residents persisted in such behavior, "the mischief that may arise must lye at their Doors." But when the magistrates replied the next day, it was clear how severely Vandeput had damaged his own cause. After accusing him of firing the first shot, they remarked: "As to the Taking away the Cannon we are to inform you, that the same were taken away by Permission of the provincial Congress," which "the People have thought proper to constitute to act for them in this critical Situation." Here were public officials, some tories, conceding the committee's right to take government property and to manage local affairs. Vandeput replied that it was his "duty to defend every Part of the King's Stores, wherever they may be." Yet he could not force residents to return the cannons. He could cannonade the city, but Congress would surely cut off his supplies, forcing him to leave port. The magistrates' letter should have warned him too that an attack would turn tories into patriots and make regaining the city's allegiance exceedingly difficult. Vandeput was learning, as had Sears, that New York's commitment to empire and liberty restricted his options.[36]

Meanwhile, families began fleeing town. Tryon learned of the gunfire exchange on August 24 and returned home from Long Island the next day. In the past he would have summoned his Council; this time he assembled his councillors, the city magistrates, and the members of the "Committees and Provincial Congress." To end the crisis he proposed a compromise: the purloined cannons would remain on the Commons; no more raids would be made on the "Kings Stores"; and the town would continue to provision the *Asia*; "but to prevent disorder the Boats from the city might carry the provision on Board."[37] That afternoon Congress "ordered, That no more Cannon or Stores be removed from the Battery." On August 29 it authorized Abraham Lott to continue supplying the *Asia*, but he was to leave the provisions on Governor's Island for the navy to pick up. On September 1, to make it harder for Vandeput to collect intelligence, Congress forbade all communications with the *Asia* undertaken without its permission.[38] Vandeput's superior, Vice Adm. Samuel Graves, directed him to destroy the homes of all known whig leaders in town and all the ships in the harbor if he were refused supplies. And Mayor Hicks alerted the Committee of Safety on September 19 that Lord Dartmouth had ordered British naval commanders "that in case any more Troops should be raised, or fortifications erected, or any of His Majesty's stores taken, that the commanders of the ships of war should consider such Cities or places in a state of rebellion."[39]

There the affair ended, however, for no one wanted to push matters to the breaking point. If Vandeput were to bombard the town, he would destroy loyalist property along with that belonging to whigs. And it would have been foolish to decimate a city the British army might someday want to occupy. Similar restraints were at work in the patriot camp. Though many observers, within and outside the province, bemoaned New York's timidity, members of the committee and Congress understandably feared the loss of lives and property and opposed doing anything that might cause the city's destruction. They also realized that razing the city might lead directly to civil war. Indeed, by September the *Asia* had come to symbolize residents' uneasy relationship with the empire. Provisioning the man-of-war served as a tangible link to a past they were not yet ready to abandon. And cutting off communications with the ship represented the new political world they were creating but would not yet embrace. Sears was unhappy, but between May and September Congress had mirrored the consensus of the city's residents and had thereby maintained the unity that was essential to the survival of the cause.[40]

III

Still, the Provincial Congress could not forever preserve both empire and liberty. The crisis had a momentum of its own that would not be denied. In August Tryon had informed Dartmouth that "Independency is shooting from the root of the present contest; it is confidently said if Great Britain does not within six months adopt some new plan of accommodation the colonies will be severed from her as to any system of solid and general union." William Smith wrote in October, "This Winter will decide the great Question, whether Great Britain and her Colonies, are to be happily reunited, or to prosecute their Animosities to an eternal Separation."[41] Their predictions were correct. Between September 1775 and April 1776 forces within and without the city pushed New York toward revolution. If the process was not complete by April, it was in any case irreversible.

The key to events was not the alleged "instability" of "society and politics" in New York but the cabinet's decision in the autumn of 1775 to abandon Boston and to make the province of New York the main theater of military operations.[42] The aim was the same one Colden had espoused in 1774: control of New York would geographically divide the colonies and strangle the rebellion. Lord George Germain, who was now the American secretary of state, believed Britain's setbacks in New England were "trifling" compared to those in New York: "As long as you maintained New Yorke the continent was divided." What had changed was the method to be used. Military control of New York City would give the navy a safe harbor from which to launch expeditions against New England, which supposedly was the rebellion's center, and the colonies to the south, where many tories were reportedly ready to fight for the crown. Aided by the navy, the army could advance up the Hudson, cut communications between north and south, and establish contact with British forces in Canada. The farmlands of Long Island, Westchester, and New Jersey would ease the military's dependence on Europe and thereby reduce the war's cost. Finally, despite the setbacks of 1775, the cabinet expected to enlist the support of the many British sympathizers reputedly living in the province.[43]

When word of Britain's plan reached town, it disturbed everyone, especially the tories, for it doomed reconciliation. Their anxiety, in turn, stirred them to action. Carl Becker has called what followed a "royalist reaction" that "was very nearly disastrous to the revolutionists," for the Provincial Congress "was barely able to hold together." Bernard Mason offered a different explanation: Becker had been correct in stating that five counties did not elect deputies to the Second Provincial Congress in November 1775; but he had been wrong in arguing that they failed to do so because the loyalists there had overpowered the whigs. That was true in Queens and Richmond, but in Cumberland, Charlotte, and Gloucester "communication difficulties, factionalism, and the Vermont controversy" with New Hampshire were the key reasons; and the three in any case eventually sent deputies. The extreme caution with which Congress managed affairs in this period resulted not from loyalism's numerical strength or influence but from "the powerful emotion of self-preservation." Vandeput's threats and the fear of a British invasion were what made whig leaders hesitate.[44]

Mason has effectively demonstrated that few New Yorkers were loyalists, but something serious was nonetheless afoot. Though it would be wrong to claim that New York lagged behind the other colonies because of the number of tories in the province, it is fair to say that its hesitancy resulted partly from the moderation of its leaders, some of whom would become loyalists. Moreover, too many partisans on both sides were talking about a loyalist threat for the threat to be ignored. In October, McDougall wrote Jay at Philadelphia "that the Tories are chearfal, and too many of the whigs make long Faces. Men of rank and Consideration refuse to accept of commissions as Field Officers of the Militia; so that these commissions have gone a beging for six or seven weeks." McDougall wrote Jay again in November and December, urging the Continental Congress to send troops to crush the Long Island tories. The situation was remarkably similar in New Jersey. According to Larry R. Gerlach, once independence became a genuine possibility, that colony experienced "a conservative backlash in some areas." It was not that New Jerseyans or New Yorkers were converting in droves to loyalism, but that they had not yet reconciled themselves to separation from Britain.[45]

Part of the stir flowed simply from the fact that nerves frayed as war neared. That was particularly true for the radicals, who wanted more done to ready the city for an invasion. Alarmed by the Provincial Congress's cautiousness, they began ascribing it to duplicity. The radical Hugh Hughes blamed Philip Livingston's "trimming" not on the fact that he was a moderate, committed to empire and liberty, but on a "connection" he allegedly had with Governor Tryon through "the medium of Hugh Wallace," a loyalist member of the provincial Council. Sears complained that most of New York's whig leaders were tories who would throw off their masks and declare their loyalism once the British arrived.[46]

Alexander McDougall was more sanguine than either Sears or Hughes, yet he was nonetheless exasperated. On November 14 McDougall protested to Maj. Gen. Philip Schuyler of the Continental Army that the Provincial Congress had "dissolved by the non-attendance of the members," who feared the navy might bombard the town and had fled "without appointing a Committee of Safety." McDougall worried about what loyalists might do if left unchecked. In a letter to Jay, urging that the tories in Queens County, Long Island, be disarmed, he explained that "altho a majority of the County are not against the Public measures, Yet a majority of those who are active are against them." If loyalists there were not punished, "Kings [County] will follow their example as Richmond [County] has done; and whenever a Considerable number of [British] Troops arrive, the Mal-Contents in Queens will join them."[47]

The belief that tories were a liability was no illusion, for they were working desperately in the vicinity of New York City to cripple the whig cause. In Queens a tory party headed by Cadwallader Colden and his son David blocked the election of delegates to the Second Provincial Congress, procured arms from Vandeput, formed a loyalist militia in the town of Hempstead, and issued a broadside declaring that they would resist all "Acts of violence" directed against them. In Dutchess County, there were enough armed loyalists to make a whig fret that "all are Tories, only a few excepted." After Tryon fled the city in October for the safety of a naval vessel, loyalists from Kings, Queens, Richmond, and New York City often visited him to provide intelligence and supplies. For example, Tryon enlisted James Leadbetter, a New York City brewer, to spy on the whigs and to purchase provisions. And David Matthews, who became New York City's mayor in February 1776, recruited David King, an African American slave and shoemaker, to carry messages to the governor. Tryon was also able to organize provisioning ships for Boston; to hire three local gunsmiths; to persuade Charles Inglis, an Anglican minister and a tory, to answer Thomas Paine's *Common Sense*; and to distribute counterfeit money to disrupt New York's economy. In December, persuaded that loyalists could make a difference, Tryon asked Gen. William Howe, who had replaced Gen. Thomas Gage as commander-in-chief, for "three thousand stand of arms." Howe declined; he would be in New York in the spring and wanted the tories to remain quiet to "lull the Rebels" into a false sense of security.[48]

Tory propaganda, too, was irksome to whigs. "An Occasional Remarker" was incensed: "Of late, I have observed in Mr. Rivington's and Mr. Gaine's newspapers, sundry publications that have the same pernicious tendency with those that used to abound in those papers some months ago." When he urged that they be "rooted out," he was perhaps justifying what was about to happen. On November 23 Sears and about eighty volunteers, mostly from Connecticut, stormed into James Rivington's shop in New York City, destroyed his printing press, packaged up his type, and raced away. Sears defended himself, claiming there were not "Spirited and leading men enough in N. York to undertake such a Business." His conduct was in any case disturbing. He had acted without authority and had raised the prickly issue of whether whigs from one colony could intervene in another without approval from the Continental Congress or the provincial congress in the colony under attack. On December 8 the Committee of One Hundred informed the Provincial Congress of the incident, and on December 12 Congress wrote Gov. Jonathan Trumbull of Connecticut, condemning the raid. By way of punishment the Continental Congress refused to appoint Sears to a naval post already promised him.[49]

Even more vexing to whigs was William Smith's scheme in December 1775 to revive royal government. McDougall called it "a Piece of Finesse difficult to obviate, considering the Temper of the Province." Distressed by the prospect of independence, Smith hoped to persuade the Provincial Congress to have its delegates in Philadelphia offer a new plan of reconciliation. If the Continental Congress then rejected it, he wanted the Provincial Congress to request a meeting of the New York General Assembly to consider Lord North's Conciliation Plan of February 1775. According to that proposal, Britain would recognize the Continental Congress and levy no taxes on America without the approval of the provincial assemblies; the colonies, for their part, would acknowledge parliamentary supremacy, and the Continental Congress would vote a revenue for the crown. The Continental Congress had rejected the plan in July 1775, for it required colonists to pay a tax; its only distinction was that they would be imposing the tax upon themselves. If the Assembly now approved North's proposal, as Smith hoped it would, that would most likely divide the colonies and end the threat of independence.[50]

On December 4, Smith persuaded Tryon to address the colony's inhabitants, asking them to deliberate "in a constitutional Manner" upon North's plan. And on December 8, Smith's brother Thomas introduced four resolutions in the Provincial Congress, accusing Gage of starting hostilities, affirming the colony's allegiance to the crown, inviting Tryon to return to town under a guarantee of safety, and declaring that the king deserved New York's answer to North's proposal. The Provincial Congress, however, decisively rejected Smith's four resolves. All but one county voted for Scott's resolution "that nothing of a salutary nature can be expected from the separate declaration" on North's plan. And every county approved McDougall's motion that the colony was "effectually represented in the Continental Congress" which had "fully and dispassionately expressed the sense of its inhabitants" on North's proposal.[51]

Still hopeful that New York residents supported a more conciliatory course, William Smith convinced Tryon to dissolve the Assembly on January 2, 1776, and to call elections for a new one that was to meet on February 14. Afraid of what tories might attempt, whigs began campaigning at once. "Philo-Demos" said the contest was between "the friends to America and the friends to the ministry"; voters should only choose men "whose principles are *well known*" and "meet with the approbation of the public." "Publicola" asked people to vote only for candidates who pledged to keep the Assembly's doors open while it was in session. And the Committee of Safety directed the members of the Second Provincial Congress to return by February 1, so that they might watch the Assembly. In the event, whig fears were unfounded. John Jay, John Alsop, Alexander McDougall, and Philip Livingston were nominated for New York City at a mass meeting of residents on January 17 and were elected without opposition on February 1. Of the twenty-nine candidates chosen throughout the province, twenty-four were whigs, and only four were tories. Thirteen of the patriots were also members of the Third Provincial Congress. The day the Assembly was to meet, Tryon prorogued it until March 14 and later until April 17. On that day the Assembly was dissolved, for Congress had cut all contact between the town and the warships in the harbor and Tryon was thus unable officially to prorogue the provincial legislature for a third time. The demise of the Assembly destroyed all hope for reviving royal government.[52]

Though Smith's plan was aborted, the chain of events set in motion by Britain's decision in the autumn of 1775 to occupy New York City persuaded the Continental Congress to monitor the province closely. For example, on the night of October 9 some Continental soldiers had stolen blankets and other items from a royal storehouse in town. After Tryon announced that Vandeput would "execute his orders" to bombard the city unless restitution was made, the Provincial Congress agreed unanimously to return the supplies. But the radicals were outraged, and the Continental Congress directed that the supplies be given to American troops.[53] The Provincial Congress objected, arguing that it was unwise to endanger the city for the sake of 150 blankets, or to risk infecting American troops "by sending the small-pox among them"; several blankets "had been used in the Hospital, and the rest were destroyed by the moth." There the matter ended, but it put New York whig leaders on notice that they would now have to pursue policies acceptable to a continental as well as a local audience. The Continental Congress was pushing New York toward revolution, and the province could do little about it without jeopardizing colonial unity.[54]

Even rumors of what the Continental Congress *might* do could cause a stir in New York. In October a motion had been made in that Congress to arrest Tryon. It failed to pass, but the governor learned of the motion and on October 13 warned city officials that if he were seized, Vandeput would "demand" his release and "enforce the demand" with the navy's "whole power." Mayor Hicks so informed the Committee of One Hundred, which the same day denied that the Provincial Congress had an "order" to seize the governor. The next day Tryon demanded "their assurances, either of protection while among them, or security to remove on board the King's ship." Though the committee again assured him he was welcome to stay, Tryon fled to a naval vessel stationed in the harbor.[55]

He was not the only one to panic. Before he left, tories had been boasting that they would "defend" him "at the Risk of their Lives." Their bravado persuaded already terrified residents that the navy was about to cannonade the town and that redcoats would soon be landing. People began to flee with their belongings. Some Provincial Congressmen even started moving furniture up the Hudson.[56] On November 4 a writer noted that "this great trading and flourishing city is now like an inland town, a vast number of its inhabitants moved away." Ten days later he reported that a meager two hundred people had voted at the election for delegates to the Provincial Congress.[57]

When the Continental Congress asked the Provincial Congress about Tryon's departure, the Provincial Congress forwarded the letters between Hicks and the Committee of One Hundred but declared that "no application relative to that affair was made to this Congress, nor have we taken any part therin." Sears was so frustrated with most whig leaders that in early November he left for Connecticut, conceding that he had lost his struggle with the moderates for control of the patriot cause in New York. What he could not accept was that the cause had developed an institutional life and momentum of its own. Though he had played a key role in erecting the whig infrastructure, he could not dominate it or bend it to his will. In part, he had become the victim of his own success. He had helped to mobilize so many diverse interest groups that leaders adept at mediation and organization were able to seize control from those skilled more in agitation. Moreover, the flight of so many residents had made public opinion and crowd action that much less influential in city politics, thereby affording moderates a freer hand to follow their own inclinations. But New York's reputation had suffered. Maj. Gen. Charles Lee of the Continental Army lamented to McDougall, "Let your City no longer hold the honest in suspense by their shilly shally mode of conduct[. Is] this a time when whole communities are laid waste by the Dogs of War to address or suffer addresses to the delegate of an infernal Despot?"[58]

In January Lee asked General Washington's permission to use troops from New Jersey and Connecticut to "effect the security of New York, and the expulsion or suppression of that dangerous banditti of Tories, who have appeared in Long Island." Washington was amenable. A British fleet was being fitted out at Boston, and he feared its destination was New York.

On January 8 he directed Lee to put the city "into the best Posture of Defence" and to disarm or to detain "all such persons on long Island and elsewhere . . . whose conduct, and declarations have rendered them justly suspected of Designes unfriendly to the Views of Congress." Washington also wrote New York's Committee of Safety about Lee's mission, but the letter was delayed in reaching its destination; and bad weather and the gout slowed Lee as well. Meantime, residents fretted that his arrival would provoke the navy to bombard them. On January 21, the committee wrote Lee, arguing that the city was short of gunpowder and that the season was too inclement for women and children to escape; the committee urged that fighting be delayed at least until March and that Lee keep his troops at the Connecticut border until he had informed the committee of his plans. Lee hastily wrote Washington, and a "violent debate" ensued in the Continental Congress. One side stressed the impropriety of ordering troops into a province without either permission from the local authorities or a direct order from Congress; to do so would set "the Military above the Civil." The other side "urged the absolute necessity of securing that province, the loss of which would cut off all communication between the Northern and Southern Colonies." By way of compromise, a delegation was sent to New York to confer with Lee and the Committee of Safety. The committee finally relented and let Lee's army enter the city.[59]

Lee's month-long stay in New York proved contentious. On February 4, the day he entered town, Gen. Henry Clinton, second in command to Gen. William Howe, arrived by ship for a conference with Tryon. Though the river was filled with ice and the weather frigid, people again began to flee. Lee announced that if the fleet bombarded the city, he would make the first building to burn a funeral pyre for one hundred tories. Whether or not the British heard his remark, they never fired their guns. Lee began calling the naval threat a "*brutum fulmen*" and ordered the remaining cannons removed from the Battery. Though the navy had orders to commence hostilities if that happened, the naval commander shot off a handbill instead, claiming he had held his fire because it had been New England troops that had caused the trouble. "The people here laugh," Lee said, "and begin to despise the menaces which formerly used to throw them into convulsions."[60]

Controversy continued to swirl after Lee tried but failed to get the Committee of Safety to cease resupplying the warships in the harbor and to cut off all contact with them. On February 16, because Tryon had persuaded some gunsmiths to leave town, Lee demanded that the Provincial Congress enjoin people from communicating with the warships. Congress refused, and Lee raised the issue again on February 18. This time Congress tightened its rules but would not be as bold as Lee had urged. After the British seized some sloops carrying foodstuffs, the general insisted again, and once more the answer was no. Lee, however, was not one to let civil authorities interfere with military necessity. On March 1 Elias Nixen, the Dutch Reformed port master, informed Congress that Lee's troops had fired on some warships and had arrested two of Tryon's servants who had come ashore. Lee had even instructed Nixen that no more provisions were to be provided Tryon, whose people had seized flour on February 23 from an American sloop. The Provincial Congress was displeased: the Hudson was frozen, and the navy might try to starve the city by intercepting supply ships from New Jersey and Connecticut. But when Lee remained adamant, Congress stopped issuing passes for people to visit British vessels. Lee's detractors would get their revenge shortly thereafter when the Continental Congress transferred him out of New York for mistreating some Long Island loyalists.[61]

Lee's replacement, William Alexander, who claimed to be the Earl of Stirling and who had been a member of the governor's Council in the 1760s, quickly agreed with the Provincial Congress on a new plan for supplying the British fleet. Tighter restrictions were put on the trade, which would now be allowed only on "condition that there be no obstruction given [by a warship] to any Boats or Vessels bringing Provisions" into the city. To avoid misunderstanding, Tryon was sent a copy. Tempers cooled, and the city became a beehive of activity, a veritable garrison town, as it prepared for a British onslaught.[62]

Upon arriving in April, Washington wrote the Committee of Safety that "the intercourse which has hitherto subsisted between the inhabitants . . . and the enemy on board the ships-of-war is injurious to the common cause." His logic was convincing: "We are to consider ourselves either in a state of peace or war with Great Britain. If the former, why are our ports shut up, our trade destroyed, our property seized, our towns burnt, and our worthy and valuable citizens led into captivity, and suffering the most cruel hardships? If the latter, my imagination is not fertile enough to suggest a reason in support of the intercourse." The next day the committee outlawed all contact with the navy. Denied provisions, the fleet soon dropped below the Narrows, and the city's symbolic link to the empire was severed.[63]

In sum, because Britain had decided to make New York its base of military operations, the whigs felt compelled to turn the city into a garrison town. The presence of the Continental Army, in turn, convinced the residents who remained to put aside their doubts and to march down the road to war. New York had thus joined the Revolution almost in spite of itself.

CHAPTER ELEVEN

Independence

As the imperial conflict grew more bellicose, New York whigs labored to justify their rebellious actions and to broaden the support for their cause. "Monitor," perhaps the most prolific apologist, inaugurated a series of articles in the *New York Journal* in November 1775 by avowing the colonists' right to wage civil war. It was "an evil" undertaken only "from motives of the most urgent necessity." Yet when one had "to defend the essential rights of humanity," it was "criminal" to refuse it. Though civil wars were "very sharp," they were short. But "once arbitrary government be introduced, people's miseries are endless; there is no prospect or hopes of redress." When tyranny threatened, "timidity and meanness . . . , falsely termed moderation and prudence," only "strengthen[ed] the hands of the common enemy."[1] "Monitor" also reviewed the troubled history of Anglo-American relations, from the Stamp Act to Lexington and Concord. Yet he believed the First Continental Congress could have resolved the conflict and safeguarded colonial rights if the New York Assembly had not, by itself, petitioned Britain. "Encouraged by the certain prospect . . . of a disunion," the cabinet "push[ed] matters to an extremity" and ordered troops to America. Though war was now inevitable, some New Yorkers were still pleading for a new peace overture. But "Monitor" warned residents not to delude themselves: Britain wanted "to bring them under the unlimited subjection to the Parliament." New Yorkers thus had "to strain every sinew in warlike preparations" and to "seize every opportunity of strengthening ourselves and materially weakening the enemy."[2]

Other writers joined "Monitor." "Philo Patriae," who first appeared in *The Constitutional Courant* in 1765, said that the "true patriot" was "more zealously concern'd for the public weal and prosperity, than for any private good of his own; and sedulously endeavours to promote it, by every medium within the compass of his power." The British were "strangers to this spirit; and not a few of the first rank and character endeavour to suppress" real patriotism "by cultivating a private selfish spirit." And "the same game they are now playing in America, by their agents, bribed into confederacy with that wicked ministry, by valuable sums in hand, the promise of pensions *in futuro*, or valuable tracts of land settled upon them, when America shall be subjugated to the iron yoke of their government." "An Occasional Remarker," who in November 1775 had forecast Sears's attack upon Rivington, declared, "I am ready to die" for liberty; and "I advise you to die, rather than to yield one tittle of your rights to the unjust, unconstitutional claims of a tyrannical Parliament and Ministry." "A Poor Man," who also had radical credentials, said that he "would rather die ten thousand deaths, than to see this country enslaved, and ruined by a venal, wicked, blundering parliament. Rouze then, Americans rouze, let no man sleep while the thief is at the door."[3]

Whig writers also undermined loyalty to George III. "Monitor" declared: "If we contemplate the character of the present B—t—sh Sovereign," it is "impossible to avoid the imputation of folly or tyranny."[4] "Philo Patriae" added that if the king were devoted to his "kingdom's safety and happiness, he would . . . encourage every sincere Patriot, banish from his presence every despotic tory minister, suppress all their arbitrary tools of cruelty, and give no heed to the deceitful sycophants and court flatterers."[5] Another whig wrote: "If the King gives his sanction to acts of Parliament, subversive of that grand charter by which he holds his crown, and endeavours to carry them into execution by force of arms, the people have a right to repel force by force."[6] "Lucius" (a twelfth-century pope who was forced from Rome after it became a city-republic) bluntly warned the king: "The man in your situation, who loses the common people, is either a tyrant or a lunatic." How had affairs reached such a state in America? It was because of the king's advisers: "Mischievous, as they affect the interests of the individuals. Wicked, as they tend to dismember the empire, arbitrary, as they violate the rights of Englishmen." Hence, "they make you one day ridiculous, the next day contemptible, and the third day ————."[7] "Obadiah" (a Hebrew prophet who prophesied Edom's destruction because of its treatment of the Israelites) spied a more vile ministerial plot: "It is more than probable, that whilst they are soothing King George's ambition and desire of absolute monarchy, they are insidiously paving the way to pluck the crown from his head. . . . For this purpose, they have ensnared the King, by inducing him to connive in persecuting the American people, because they insist upon their constitutional rights."[8]

Talk of independence inevitably followed. In December "Lycurgus" (a wise Athenian) berated the Pennsylvania Assembly for instructing its delegates at the Continental Congress to vote against independence. He urged people to keep an open mind: "Are they sure, that 'tis best America should not be independent as to government?" In January "Memento" declared that Americans would sacrifice their lives before surrendering their rights and that it was "not in the power of Great Britain, with the most vigorous exertion of her whole united strength, finally to take them from us." He favored separation over submission, yet hoped the empire could be preserved, bloodshed avoided, and "mutual faith and confidence" restored.[9] Later that month, Thomas Paine forthrightly advocated independence in *Common Sense*. "An Independent Whig" applauded Paine's conclusion: "We must be either independent, or be reduced to the most abject state of slavery; for an accommodation is utterly impracticable."[10]

Other whigs sought to allay people's fears of independence. "Candidus" argued that the city loses more than it gains by membership in the empire. When regulating trade and manufacturing, Britain always sought "rather to milk than to suckle" its colonies.[11] "Monitor" assured Anglicans that the "present commotion" was caused by "the intolerable oppression of the ministry" and was not "a plot to overturn the[ir] church" or "to reduce the whole continent under Presbyterian discipline and doctrine." If independence came, "a common interest would oblige us to avoid all discord and animosity, to form and cherish a well compacted government, capable of affording general security to all, and of preventing the ill effects of every kind of rivalship."[12] Another writer explained why reconciliation was impossible: "If the Colonies should be reunited to Great Britain, it must be to her as she is now at present, where the electors are bought, and the majority of the Commons are kept in pay by the Minister, and all places of honour and profit are conferred, not according to men's merit, by their wisdom and bravery, but as they vote, where the nation's money is expended by millions to pervert reason and support the Minister." That system had caused the crisis and would eventually provoke another, even should a compromise be reached this time.[13]

The fact that the newspapers were filled in March and April with essays advocating independence makes it clear that some people remained unconvinced. Yet there is compelling evidence that the public consensus in

favor of empire and liberty was breaking down, and that most New Yorkers were moving toward independence. In February the radical Hugh
Hughes wrote John and Samuel Adams that several prominent whigs had
pressured John Holt not to publish *Common Sense*. He did anyway, and
Hughes reported that the public reception was overwhelmingly positive:
"It is certain, there never was anything printed here within these thirty
years or since I been in this place that has been more universally approved
and admired."[14]

Hughes's radicalism may have colored his judgment. But on Monday,
March 18, the radical Mechanics Committee ordered Samuel Loudon,
printer of *The New York Packet* and a whig, to appear before it for advertis-
ing that he would soon have for sale *The Deceiver Unmasked; or Loyalty and
Interest United: In Answer to a Pamphlet Entitled Common Sense*. When he did
so, Christopher Duyckinck, an Anglican sailmaker who chaired the committee, demanded to know the author's identity. Loudon replied that it
had been given to him by a gentleman whose name he would not reveal.
When committee members threatened to burn the pamphlet, Loudon
asked how they could destroy something they had not read. Since the
Continental Congress had not declared independence, he argued, the
committee could not censure the work, and he asked that the matter be
referred to the Committee of Safety. The Mechanics instead went to his
shop, nailed shut in a box the sheets already printed, and locked the door
to a room where the rest were drying. On Tuesday night the Committee
of One Hundred warned Loudon, for his own safety, not to continue
printing the pamphlet. Though he accepted the advice, Duyckinck and
about forty others returned to Loudon's shop and burned the fifteen
hundred copies of *The Deceiver Unmasked* that had already been printed.
A loyalist lamented, "There is a great talk of independence, and the un-
thinking multitude are mad for it. . . . A pamphlet called Common Sense,
has carried off its thousands; an answer thereto has come out, but instantly seized in the printer's shop, and burnt in the street, as unfit to be
read at this time. I fear, from this line of conduct, the people . . . will
never be regained."[15]

Nor is it difficult to explain why the public consensus was moving
toward independence. On February 16 Robert R. Livingston, Jr., wrote
James Duane, "Another year of war and devastation will make me a republican though at present I wish to join hands with a nation which I have
been accustomed to respect, yet I am persuaded that the continuation of
the war will break my shackles." Though Livingston was slower than most
to embrace independence, his comment underscores how momentous
was Britain's decision to use force to crush the colonies. Not only did it

lead people to reassess their allegiance to the crown; but it provoked them to establish extralegal governments and committees and an army. Whig propagandists could thus argue that the colonies were already independent in all but name. That realization made it easier for New Yorkers, both intellectually and emotionally, to take the final step and to embrace independence rather than to travel an uncertain route backwards whereby to attempt to remake the empire into what it had been before 1763. In sum, at least for New York, Gage's pet solution to the recurring Anglo-American crises was a significant cause of the empire's undoing.[16]

II

What remained for those who favored the breakup of the empire was to convince the Third Provincial Congress, which was to convene on May 14, to declare independence. The effort began on the related question of whether to form a new government. Practical matters were involved. Gov. William Tryon had fled, and the Assembly had been dissolved. Congress and the Committee of One Hundred had filled the void, but only imperfectly. Whig leaders were at a loss over what to do about the court system, the criminal justice system, and the validity of contracts. Moreover, constitutional issues lurked beneath the surface: to create a new government, though expedient, was to declare de facto independence.

"Salus Populi" argued in February that the colonies were "in a state of absolute independence, without any settled form of Government," and were "obliged" to abolish their "present forms of government, and to create new ones." He thought a system like that in Connecticut, where people elected the governor, best suited to America: "The officer who is removeable by the people will serve the people with fidelity." "An Independent Whig" thought New York's colonial governmental structure acceptable, so long as the citizens elected the governor and the Assembly, and the latter chose the Council.[17] In April "A Free Citizen" addressed the Committee of Safety: "We daily see . . . citizens sent to the guards kept by the Continental army, there confined for crimes cognizable only at common law, and therefore must suffer perpetual imprisonment, or submit to a trial by Court Martial." In short, New York had no choice but to adopt "some regular form of government, which may be a protection to ourselves, and consistent with the interest of the other American colonies."[18]

The Continental Congress was concerned about the problem. In April

John Jay wrote that the time had come "to erect good and well ordered Governments in all the Colonies, and thereby exclude that Anarchy which already too much prevails." On May 9 William Floyd, another New York delegate, wrote, "It cannot be long before our Provincial Congress will think it necessary to take up some more stable form of Government than what is now exercised in that Province." The Provincial Congress would doubtless have ignored the advice had not the Continental Congress resolved on May 10 that the people of the several colonies should form their own new state governments. On May 17 Robert R. Livingston, Jr., wrote Jay, who had returned home for the Third Provincial Congress, "I hope they are satisfied of the necessity of assuming a new form of Government." The more conservative Duane, however, wrote Jay the next day that New York should not "be too precipitate in changing the present mode of Government." But Jay replied, "So great are the Inconveniences resulting from the present Mode of Government, that I believe our Convention will almost unanimously agree to institute a better."[19]

When the Provincial Congress debated the issue in late May, Gouverneur Morris proposed that a constitutional convention be called "to frame a Government." John Morin Scott countered that Congress already had the authority to proceed by itself. The conservative Morris sought a convention because that would delay a decision; the more militant Scott thought Congress competent to act, for he wanted action.[20] The Provincial Congress finally approved a series of resolutions that declared New York's colonial government "*ipso facto* dissolved" and the system of congresses and committees "subject to many defects." It was thus "absolutely necessary" to establish "a new and regular form of internal Government and Police."[21] Morris did not get his convention, for the idea was unwieldy: Would a convention and Congress meet concurrently? If not, who would oversee affairs while the former was in session? If so, could someone serve in both bodies? But he won a delay, for elections were to be held before a new constitution was to be written.

In the elections that followed, the Mechanics Committee objected that no provision had been made for the inhabitants "to accept or reject" the new frame of government. If the "supporters of oligarchy" in the next Congress were to draft one, and if it were not then ratified by the people, the new government "could be lawfully binding" only on "the legislators themselves." Put in an awkward spot, Congress neither recorded the protest in its *Journal* nor answered it. In calling for elections it had declared that it needed popular authorization to form a new government. Now the people, or at least some of them, were demanding the right to ratify the new constitution; and Congress was averse to hearing them. It doubtless hoped by its silence to bury the idea of a popular referendum. And so for the moment it did, but the next Congress would have to confront the issue.[22]

Independence became a more serious issue on June 3, when a newspaper printed the Virginia Convention's resolves directing its representatives in Philadelphia to press for independence. The next day Lewis Thibou, a saddler, and several other Mechanics petitioned the Provincial Congress "to instruct our most honourable Delegates in the Continental Congress to use their utmost endeavours" to persuade "these United Colonies to become independent."[23] Congress's response, given only after it had retreated behind closed doors to determine whether it should even accept the petition, plainly underscored its opposition to the proposal: only the Continental Congress could decide the issue, and the Provincial Congress would not issue "any declarations upon so general and momentous a concern; but are determined patiently to await and firmly abide by whatever a majority of that august body shall think needful." Two days later the New York Congress received a letter from the Virginia Convention, enclosing a copy of its resolutions and appealing for support. Congress evasively replied on June 6 that it would "pursue every measure which may tend to promote the union and secure the rights and happiness of the United Colonies." The next day Richard Henry Lee of Virginia asked the Continental Congress to declare independence. Robert R. Livingston, Jr., spoke for the measure, but the other New Yorkers were silent. In truth, they were in a quandary. Whatever their personal opinions, they lacked authority to speak for the province. According to their instructions they were in Philadelphia to work for the preservation of American liberty and the restoration of harmony in the empire.[24]

After New York's congressional delegation wrote home for instructions, the Provincial Congress unanimously passed two resolves on June 11. One said that the people had not authorized the Provincial or the Continental Congress "to declare" New York "independent." The other recommended that "by instructions or otherwise" the voters in the province should "inform their said Deputies of their sentiments relative to the great question of Independency" at the upcoming elections for the Fourth Provincial Congress. However, Congress also ordered that "the publishing of the aforegoing Resolves be postponed until after the election of Deputies with powers to establish a new form of Government." Apparently, the voters had to decide the issue, but Congress was not going to tell them so.[25]

Why were New York's whig leaders so averse to action, particularly when there seems to have been such strong support, especially in New York

City, for independence? First, the Provincial Congress was feeling harried, what with preparing for the anticipated invasion of a city that was already a shambles and dealing with the tories who were expected to aid the British upon their arrival. Vexed and perplexed by these matters, many congressmen were doubtless too preoccupied to reassess the issue of independence.[26] They therefore clung to the policy of empire and liberty, though it had been devised months earlier under different circumstances. Second, declaring independence meant risking their own lives. A few blanched at the prospect, and some even acted cowardly. In 1775 Philip and Peter Van Brugh Livingston had reportedly fled New York City and Congress for fear of the *Asia*. And Robert R. Livingston, Jr., was "mortified" that in June 1776, during the debates over independence, Gouverneur Morris had been able to persuade the Provincial Congress to adjourn to White Plains because the British were about to land on Staten Island. In October Livingston would object that "Gouverneur thro' what cause God alone knows has deserted in this hour of danger" and "retired to some obscure corner of the Jerseys . . . while his friends are struggling with every difficulty and danger and while they make those apologies for him which they do not themselves believe."[27] Third, whig leaders had other, very justifiable concerns. If Britain won, it would surely constrict their rights and confiscate their property. Even if America won, the battle for New York would likely devastate both the city and the province. The decision to embrace independence was consequently a difficult one to make. Moreover, a number of patricians held huge land grants, in what was to become the state of Vermont, that were disputed by New Englanders. If the empire were sundered, who would settle the competing claims, and how would it be done?[28] Still other New Yorkers, of course, made their living by trade within the empire. They worried about how the economy and their own finances would fare outside the empire.[29]

Most important, conservative and moderate whig leaders understood that independence meant republican government. The Mechanics Committee had made that clear on June 14, when it attacked the "selfish principles of corrupt oligarchy" and demanded that the new constitution be "freely ratified by the co-legislative power of the people — the sole lawful Legislature of this Colony."[30] In a series that appeared the same month in the *New York Journal*, "Spartanus" called for "a free popular government" that would vest power in the people who would annually elect representatives to a unicameral legislature. For the system to succeed, the people would have to reject "rich and aspiring" candidates who "will endeavour to corrupt, bribe and lead the populace." These "evil-designing men" speak fair but "will proceed from step to step, until you are under their foot." If "Spartanus" represented public opinion, independence would require New York's patricians to enter into a strange new world, one for which they had no map. Small wonder that they would resist the inevitable as long as possible and focus their attention on the expected British invasion.[31]

If the Provincial Congress was composed of such reluctant revolutionaries, could a New York City mob have nudged them onward? In truth, no, for the radical leadership had already dispersed. Exasperated at the slow pace of events, Isaac Sears had left for Connecticut in November 1775. Though he returned on occasion (to destroy Rivington's press, for example), he was no longer a force to be reckoned with in city affairs. John Lamb had been wounded and captured by the British at Quebec in December 1775. Alexander McDougall would retire from politics in April 1776 to concentrate on military affairs. And by February 1776 most of the population had fled what was soon to become a war zone.[32] The fewer the people in the city, the less able were the radicals to pressure Congress. Moreover, New York had become a garrison town, and Continental troops patrolled the streets to maintain order. Ironically, their presence enabled the Provincial Congress to hold out for reconciliation longer than it would otherwise have been able to do.

Still, however loath the Third Provincial Congress may have been to declare independence, it could not stay the course of events. On July 2, New York's Continental Congressmen again wrote the Provincial Congress, explaining that "the important Question of Independency was agitated yesterday in a Committee of the whole Congress, and this Day will be finally determined in the House." Aware that their instructions precluded them from voting for independence, the delegates wanted to know "what Part we are to act" once it was declared. The Provincial Congress never replied. Gen. William Howe landed on Staten Island the same day with ten thousand soldiers. In expectation of that event the Provincial Congress had on June 30 adjourned until July 2, when it was to meet at White Plains. But for lack of a quorum, it never met again. It was succeeded by the Fourth Provincial Congress, which met for the first time on July 9.[33]

III

As soon as it gathered on July 9, 1776, the Fourth Provincial Congress declared independence, and the next day changed its name to the Convention of the Representatives of the State of New York. Finally, on

April 20, 1777, the Convention approved a new state constitution. As the Mechanics Committee had feared, the document was not submitted to a popular referendum.[34]

The Constitution of 1777 established a bicameral legislature. Members of the lower house, or Assembly, were to be elected annually by county, each being allotted a number of representatives proportional to its overall population. Adult freemen possessing at least one of three qualifications could vote in Assembly elections: the right of freemanship in New York City or Albany; ownership of a freehold valued at twenty pounds or more; or a leasehold on which the annual rent was at least forty shillings. Members of the upper house, or Senate, were elected to a four-year term from one of four senatorial districts by adult freemen with property worth at least one hundred pounds. The governor, whose authority was rather circumscribed, was chosen for three years by persons eligible to vote in senatorial elections. A Council of Revision, which included the governor and the members of the Supreme Court, was empowered to veto legislative bills. A two-thirds majority in both houses was needed to override a veto. And a Council of Appointment, consisting of the governor and a senator from each district, was responsible for selecting people for major statewide offices. The court system remained much the same as it had been in the colonial period, except for a Court of Errors and Impeachment that exercised final appellate jurisdiction.

The state's first constitution was thus less democratic than radicals would have liked. William Duer, a conservative New Yorker in the Continental Congress, "congratulate[d]" Jay, who served on the committee that drafted the constitution: "I think it upon the maturest Reflection the best System which has as yet been adopted, and possibly as good as the Temper of the Times would admit of." How had that victory been possible? One reason was that, while many radical leaders were serving in uniform, enough conservatives and moderates were heeding William Smith's advice that men of property should go "rather to the Cabinet than the Fields." Equally important was the long experience patricians had had in provincial politics, which helped them to understand the tactics they would have to employ. Commenting on Pennsylvania's conservatives, after that state had adopted a much more radical constitution, Robert R. Livingston, Jr., extolled "the propriety of swimming with a stream, which it is impossible to stem." Indeed, he said, "I long ago advised them that they shd yield to the torrent if they hoped to direct its course—you know that nothing but well timed delays, indefatigable industry, and a minute attention to every favorable circumstance could have prevented our being in their situation."[35]

Though New York's Constitution of 1777 was a compromise that more closely resembled the government sought by the elite, radicals could nonetheless celebrate. Not only had a republican government been established, but the constitution permitted the secret ballot, prescribed annual elections for the Assembly, prohibited placemen from holding office in that body, and proclaimed the sovereignty of the people. Radicals would like to have achieved more, yet experience had taught them to balance their demands against the need for unity, and to recognize that New York's heterogeneous population was not yet ready to embrace their full agenda. Their pragmatism, in turn, was matched by the realism of the New York elite, who resisted change as long as possible, but who knew when it was time to accept the inevitable in order to forestall their own complete fall from power. In short, both sides understood, as they had in 1776 on the issues of revolution and independence, that the heterogeneity of New York's population required all sides to seek a consensus acceptable to the great majority of the people. They realized, too, that the Constitution of 1777 was but one battle in a struggle with a long history and a long future.

Given a political system that, supposedly, had already begun to decay by the early 1760s, New York's revolutionary leaders, despite their many differences and disagreements, had together accomplished a great deal in the tumultuous years that followed the Seven Years' War.[36] Moreover, in time, the political savvy and experience that colonial New Yorkers had acquired while learning to live in a mixed society would benefit the United States as its population grew more and more diverse.

The Demise of
Colonial New York City

The final ordeal of colonial New York City, however, had begun well before the state adopted its first constitution. On July 2, 1776, the British army occupied Staten Island. After pausing for reinforcements and trying to persuade the whigs to lay down their arms, Gen. William Howe landed fifteen thousand troops on Long Island on August 22. Five days later he defeated Washington's main army in the Battle of Long Island. Although the patriots suffered over fifteen hundred casualties, Washington deftly evacuated his forces to Manhattan Island on the night of August 29. An informal peace conference on Staten Island on September 6 failed when the Americans refused to revoke the Declaration of Independence as a preliminary step before formal negotiations could begin. On September 15 British troops took possession of New York City.[1]

New York's travails were not over, however. On September 21, sometime after midnight, a fire broke out at Whitehall Slip. The blaze spread "with inconceivable violence" and soon consumed all the buildings between Whitehall and Broad Street as far north as Beaver Street. At about two a.m. the wind shifted abruptly, driving the flames across Beaver toward Broadway. The situation was desperate. Few residents remained in town, and not that many redcoats had yet entered the city. Nor could a warning be sounded, for Washington had removed the bells from all the churches and public buildings. And to everyone's horror "the fire-engines and pumps were out of order." British soldiers and sailors were rushed ashore to fight the blaze, but the wind-whipped flames raced up both sides of New Street and crossed Broadway between Bowling Green

The New York Fire, 1776. (Collection of the New-York Historical Society)

and Trinity Church, which went up like "a vast pyramid of fire, exhibiting a most grand and awful spectacle." The blaze was not contained until about ten or eleven a.m., when it reached the yard that surrounded King's College.[2]

Many assumed that whigs had set the fire "to prevent the King's troops from having any benefit by the city."[3] Patriots had supposedly hidden in deserted buildings on September 15 and emerged six days later to burn the town to the ground. Reportedly, some arsonists were arrested during the fire, with incriminating evidence in their possession, and others were killed on the spot for shooting holes through water buckets or for impeding fire fighters. No hard evidence of arson exists, however. And when, before his departure, Washington had asked what he should do if forced to evacuate the town, the Continental Congress had ordered, on September 3, that "no damage be done to the said city by his troops, on their leaving it." A lone person or a small band acting on its own might have started the blaze, but no one could ever prove it. Gen. James Robertson, the city's commandant, in vain offered a reward on September 25 for information leading to the arrest of those guilty. And as late as 1783 Sir Guy Carleton, who was then commander-in-chief of the British Army in America, would set up an investigatory commission, but it could prove nothing.[4]

Whether or not whigs were guilty, the fire symbolized the death of colonial New York City. Over a thousand buildings, or about one-fourth of all the homes in town, had been destroyed. Gov. William Tryon wrote the cabinet of how "afflicting" it was "to view the wretched and miserable Inhabitants who have lost their all, and numbers of reputable Shopkeepers that are reduced to Beggary, and many in want for their families of the necessaries of life." Worse, Howe used the argument that whigs might set a new fire to justify keeping "the executive powers of civil government dormant" and leaving "everything to the direction of the military." For the next seven years "a military autocracy" governed the city. Its residents would thus not enjoy the fruits of independence until the British evacuated the city on November 25, 1783.[5]

Historiographical Essay

Historiographical Essay

The debate over why New Yorkers were reluctant to rebel has been a long, lively, and complicated one. My aim in offering this essay is neither to contradict other historians nor to quarrel with them. It is rather to place the present study in its proper historiographical context without distracting the general reader in the process.

As mentioned in the Introduction, two broad historiographical traditions have emerged: the Progressive and the Consensus (or neo-Conservative) Schools of American History. The first began operating in earnest in 1909 with Carl Becker's *History of Political Parties in the Province of New York, 1760–1776,* which minimized the role of ideas and emphasized class and economic issues. The Revolution resulted from "two general movements, the contest for home-rule and independence and the democratization of American politics and society." The struggle to determine "who should rule at home" was paramount and pitted the few against the many, the "landed and commercial aristocracy" that controlled the Assembly and Council against the politically impotent, which included "the mass of the freemen and freehold electors" and the "unfranchised" half of the adult male population. To resist British taxation the elite set up "extra-legal committees and congresses," which became an "open door through which the common freeholder and the unfranchised mechanic and artisan pushed their way into the political arena." The problem that aristocratic "conservatives" faced after 1765 was how to win home rule without losing power to the "radicals," especially the unfranchised, "whose poverty made them radical." After 1774 the extreme conservatives became loyalists, while their more moderate counterparts remained whig and vied successfully with radicals for power in the new state government.[1]

Critics have challenged Becker on several fronts. First, it is anachronistic to argue that "a conflict between property rights and human rights has been a persistent theme of American history from the beginning." Indeed, the Revolutionary generation coupled liberty and property. The slogan among New York's radical Liberty Boys in 1765 was "Liberty, Property, and No Stamps."[2] Second, Becker regularly associated loyalism with wealth, though people from all classes became tories. Third, New York aristocrats were not politically united; Livingston and De Lancey patricians bitterly opposed one another, and their parties had curried popular support well before 1765 to win political power. Fourth, probably from 50 to 80 percent of the colony's adult white males could vote. In the city almost any adult white male could do so by paying a small fee to become a freeman. Political participation was thus open to plebeians long before the Stamp Act crisis.[3]

Becker's interpretation also fails to show why New Yorkers hesitated to rebel. His key explanation was "the strong royalist reaction" that began in August 1775 "because of the failure of conciliation." This development proved "nearly disastrous" for the whigs in the November elections for the Second Provincial Congress and resulted the next April in the election of more loyalists to the Third Provincial Congress than had sat in the Second. But how was that possible? Most tories had supposedly come from the conservative party that had represented the "landed and commercial aristocracy" in the struggle of the few against the many. How could so few have provoked so massive a reaction? Both developments were possible if Becker the theoretician was wrong and Becker the researcher was correct. If the first argued that the struggle was between the few and the many, the second believed that conservatives had been the majority from the start. Becker said at one point that the "country population was strongly conservative" in 1765 and remained so after the Coercive Acts. According to the census of 1771, over 60 percent of the colony's adult white males over 16 (and that is who Becker was really discussing) lived in the "country." Moreover, radical "mob violence" in 1769 had "resulted in a closer union of property owners and conservative men of all classes." Thus, though he talked of a dual revolution, Becker adopted the argument that had been made in 1901 by Alexander Flick—that the colony was reluctant to rebel because most New Yorkers remained loyal to the king.[4]

Despite his critics, the tradition Becker established in New York historiography has its able contemporary proponents. Gary B. Nash, for example, has outlined the "popular ideology" he believed was shared "within the middle and lower strata of society" in eighteenth-century Boston, Philadelphia, and New York. That ideology abhorred the growing concentration of wealth and power in the upper classes of society and demanded a more equal distribution of wealth. "Although no social revolution occurred in America in the 1770s," Nash argued that the "Revolution could not have unfolded when or in the manner it did without the self-conscious action of urban laboring people." So why were New Yorkers reluctant to rebel? "Despite growing class hostility," Nash wrote, "a strong artisan bloc in politics" did not coalesce, for several reasons: viva voce voting, the frequency with which the resentment of the poor and the unemployed was deflected onto the redcoats stationed in town and not "channeled into efforts to restructure society internally," the economic leverage wealthy patricians had over artisans and laborers, the "sheer strength of conservative merchants and professionals to resist pressure from below," and even at times religious bigotry ("although too much . . . can be made of it."). The factors discussed by Nash were clearly at work in New York. What is also true, and what the present study attempts to show, is that ethnic and religious tensions often played a larger role, than did conflicts based on class, in shaping how New Yorkers acted in the imperial crises, and that shared economic interests frequently led to cooperation between the classes for mutual benefit.[5]

Support for the Progressive interpretation can be found, too, in Edward Countryman's *A People in Revolution*, which claimed that New York had a "real revolution," "a democratic revolution with a deep, though complicated, social content," that laid "the foundations of a liberal bourgeois society." A widening cleavage between wealthy "power wielders" and the people created "a situation in which both society and politics were highly unstable. That instability brought the collapse of existing political relationships and of many existing social ones during the independence crisis." Indeed, "three factors—social development, popular militancy, and political decay—" put "New Yorkers in a situation of readiness for a thoroughgoing revolution by 1773 or 1774." So why were whigs so reluctant to rebel? Countryman believed the hesitancy sprang from the fears " 'official' revolutionary leaders" had of "how volatile" the "people were." Yet if New York were so ready by 1774, because of internal reasons, "for a thoroughgoing revolution," why would it "not have broken out without the renewal then of the British issue"? If "the energy to oppose all three foes—Parliament, king, and their own rulers—came from 'the people,' " how could a small body of " 'official' revolutionary leaders" have delayed the outbreak of revolution? If the people were so "volatile," why could they not have handled their (unresponsive) leaders in the same way they had dealt with the Stamp Act?[6]

Countryman documented fifty-seven urban and rural riots between 1764 and 1775 and argued that together they "stretch[ed] the fabric of New York until it rent even while they helped to do the same thing to the British Empire."[7] But the assertion is debatable. First, he did not compare the number of riots in this period with their number in comparable time spans before or after to show how truly exceptional the rioting actually was. Second, there is no fixed or direct correlation between the degree of societal instability and the frequency of rioting. Opportunity ("the availability of persons, times, places, and occasions to assemble") is a better predictor of how often rioting will occur than is the magnitude of the grievance or the degree of societal stress.[8] Third, even if there was a direct relationship between the level of discontent and the extent of violence, Countryman would have to have explained why only three of the twenty-eight New York City riots took place between April 1768 and March 1775. Were residents loath to rebel because discontent was subsiding? Fourth, Countryman conceded that the "urban crowds were much more functional [than the rural] within the old order." If so, did these urban demonstrations against specific injustices not implicitly reaffirm the old order's legitimacy? Fifth, in analyzing these riots Countryman concluded that "leadership, precise make-up, and motivation varied rather than held constant" over time. Apparently, for Countryman, it was the violence itself that united these 57 disparate events and gave them meaning. Yet violence per se does not represent a challenge to a political order, and its mere presence is not necessarily the death rattle of that system. Rioting and demonstrations are usually associated with promoting or opposing specific government policies, not with overthrowing the regime.[9]

If Countryman's argument presents problems, questions can be raised, too, about the interpretation advanced by scholars writing in the other historiographical tradition of Revolutionary New York. Part of the Consensus or neo-Conservative School of American History, it deemphasized socioeconomic conflict between the classes and focused instead on dissensions and rivalries within the provincial elite in explaining the Revolution. In 1960 Roger J. Champagne rejected Becker's claim that economic divisions were salient, yet agreed that ideas and ideology were not crucial to explaining what happened. "New York politics was run by an aristocracy of landed and mercantile wealth, and any real political differences were between aristocrats, not between the have and have-nots." In the 1760s Livingston and De Lancey aristocrats "exploited popular agitation over imperial issues for local political purposes." By 1769 the De Lanceys "found it expedient to be on the side of the crown while Livingstonites had no choice but to associate" with the popular Sons of Liberty.[10] Though the Liberty Boys exploited the Tea Act and the Coercive Acts for partisan advantage, the Livingstons regained "complete domination of the revolutionary movement" and "frame[d] a new government" that continued "aristocratic control in the uncertain future of independence."[11]

New Yorkers were not in the vanguard opposing Britain after the Coercive Acts, Champagne wrote, because the Provincial Congress failed to "dominate" the colony. Causing the problem "were the steady growth of Loyalism and the presence within the [patriot] party of radicals who still insisted upon following a course of violence. Caught between the grinding action of these two extremes, the aristocratic Whig leadership barely survived." "Whig moderation" flowed too from a desire for reconciliation and from "a fear that British forces would retaliate if any move was made against royal officials or Loyalists." When Bernard Mason demonstrated in 1966 that loyalists were numerically too weak to have foiled the whigs, he also refined Champagne's explanation for why New Yorkers were reluctant to rebel. Mason ascribed their hesitancy to several factors, including royal influence in New York in 1774 and 1775, the dispersal of the radical leadership, and conservative whig leaders who dreaded the licentiousness of the lower classes and who were loath in 1776 to violate tradition by declaring independence. He especially emphasized "the powerful emotion of self-preservation" in the whig leadership. Given the "military threats hanging over the province," it was "understandable" that "New York was not in the van of the revolutionary movement." In sum, according to the Consensus School, the Livingstons' self-interested concern for their own lives, power, and property explains why New York was the last of the thirteen colonies to declare independence.[12]

Because a handful of opportunistic patricians supposedly held sway, neo-Conservative historians wrongly denied the Sons of Liberty their radicalism and made them tools of the rich. Whereas Arthur M. Schlesinger, Sr., a Progressive historian, had argued in 1918 that the Liberty Boys represented the "underprivileged classes" against the "large propertied interests," Champagne claimed they "did not have a program of political or economic reform to aid the 'unprivileged.' " Born under Livingston patronage, they "never really regarded themselves apart from the aristocratic parties which they frequently served." So what motivated the Liberty Boys? "They probably hoped to derive personal political benefit from the agitation of anti-British measures." But because they were driven by "psychological forces," "the records give only a fleeting glimpse" of their motives. In a 1968 dissertation on the Liberty Boy leader Isaac Sears, Robert Christen explained that the group opposed British policy mostly from economic self-interest, and that Sears's militancy mirrored his temperament: "It was not in Isaac Sears's nature to sit back while matters of vital concern to him were being decided." In 1980 Pauline Maier explained, "For Sears and the New Yorkers . . . there was no necessary conflict of public and private ends." Indeed, "the revolution promised to give far more than it asked, and its rewards would be of a material as well as a spiritual sort. Liberty was good business."[13]

Arguing that Maier had reduced Sears's "revolutionary radicalism" to little more than "a matter of vulgar self-interest," Bernard Friedman aptly described the Liberty Boys as antimercantilist entrepreneurs who believed that the "government should withdraw from the marketplace as it should also withdraw in matters of conscience." These genuine radicals were, in fact, the heralds of nineteenth-century "American liberalism." In an article published in 1965, Friedman had also refuted the idea that the Liberty Boys were "pawns" of the aristocracy. As a result, neither Christen's biography of Sears nor Champagne's study of McDougall linked Isaac Sears or John Lamb, two key Liberty Boy leaders, to the Livingston party. Christen even argued that after 1765 Sears was a forceful, independent actor in city politics.[14]

But no sooner had Sears been liberated from his supposed dependence on the Livingstons than Leopold Launitz-Schürer claimed that "circumstantial" evidence showed that James and Oliver De Lancey had been the offstage managers in the Stamp Act riots and had played a key role in organizing the Sons of Liberty. The evidence cited was a 1770 diary entry by William Smith, Jr., a Livingstonite, alleging that during the Stamp Act crisis the De Lanceys had "had Agents without Doors who mixed with the Rabble for the Purpose of acquiring their Confidence." But Smith did not date exactly when in 1765 the De Lancey party had begun to do so, and his remark must be weighed against what Sears said about De Lancey leaders: "None of them ever did publickly act in Opposition to the detestable Stamp-Act, or make their Appearance at our Associations, except once," when they "opposed all the Plans we were going upon, which affronted many so much." Indeed, at a meeting on November 26, 1765, James De Lancey and the Livingstons collaborated against the Liberty Boys. It was only in December after De Lancey had agreed to serve on a committee to persuade New York's lawyers to practice the law without stamps that Sears developed "a good opinion of him."[15]

Neo-Conservatives also minimized the role of idealism in shaping how partisans acted. Launitz-Schürer said it neatly: "If the accidents of political fortune led the De Lanceys to loyalism, so the same accidental working of events led to the Livingston triumph." According to Patricia Bonomi, no real "ideological distinction between the two parties" existed in the late 1760s, and their partisan battles carried over "to the Loyalist-Patriot division of the Revolution." "Many elements—principles, self-interest, patterns of life, and habits of mind—would influence the choices," but "it was politics itself—the very ongoing requirements, the very process of staking out separate political territory and then of explaining and defending the positions taken—that had more than a little to do with shaping and sharpening the final alternatives." The argument has merit. When the same people are involved, how they sided in earlier conflicts often determines how they will line up in later disputes.[16] Yet it is doubtful either party sided the way it did accidentally. Those Livingstonites who were Real Whigs rebelled on becoming convinced that British actions represented a deliberate assault of power upon liberty. Other Livingstonites identified primarily with the Presbyterian church; and colonists from that cultural background tended, according to Robert Kelley, to be "republicans by nature." Two key De Lancey groups had a vested interest in remaining in the empire: Anglicans who often equated fidelity to their church with loyalty to their king, and merchants who traded within the empire under the navy's protection. Launitz-Schürer conceded as much when he contradicted himself elsewhere in his book: "It has sometimes been argued that American loyalists became pro-British rather accidentally, through necessity rather than conviction. This may well have been true for many loyalists, but it is doubtful if this can be said of either New York's Anglican clergy or the De Lanceys."[17]

The argument that the Livingstons and the De Lanceys were inveterate opportunists following the Seven Years' War is also mistaken. True, William Smith often accused the De Lanceys of opportunism, and historians have applied his criticism to both parties. Like most colonists, Smith was anti-party and was dismayed that the De Lanceys were acting in ways modern political parties do. So too were the Livingstons, though he could not see that so clearly. Both parties were coalitions of disparate religious, ethnic, and economic interest groups, and no study of Revolutionary New York can ignore how the city's heterogeneity influenced the way townspeople responded to the imperial crises. As Colden explained, "From the different political and religious Principles of the Inhabitants, opposite Parties have at all Times, and will exist in this Province, which at different times have taken their denominations from some distinguished Person or Family who have appeared at their Head." Indeed, given New York's diversity, acting out of self-interest was becoming a legitimate form of political behavior. People like William Smith, who still believed that ruler and ruled alike should act only for the common good, tended to label self-interested behavior as opportunistic or worse.[18]

Caught in uncharted waters in a period of profound change, both parties at times acted expediently on a tactical level. Each had to hold together groups that had both complementary and conflicting interests. The task was not easy, as contemporary party leaders can attest. But in describing the difficulties that parties had surviving in a revolutionary environment, Consensus historians have generally upbraided the De Lanceys and Livingstons for acting opportunistically on a strategic level and have downplayed the role that ideas and beliefs played in shaping behavior. Mason claimed that neither party had a "platform" or any "proclaimed principles." Champagne saw the struggles before 1776 as a political rivalry between "ins" and "outs"; "such a pragmatic framework" spelled out "in ways not possible through an intellectualist's view of men and events, why some men chose rebellion and others did not."[19]

Not all historians agree, and that has especially been true of those who have adopted the interpretation advanced in Bernard Bailyn's *Ideological Origins of the American Revolution*. Bailyn argued that the colonists subscribed to the Real Whig theory of politics, which held that human nature was weak and unable to withstand the temptations of power; that power was aggressive and corrupting; and that "its natural prey . . . was liberty, or law, or right." British policies after 1763—"unconstitutional taxing, the invasion of placemen, the weakening of the judiciary, plural office-holding, Wilkes, standing armies"—convinced Americans that they faced "a deliberate assault of power upon liberty." Unwilling to accept enslavement, they rebelled. In "The King's College Controversy 1753–1756 and the Ideological Roots of Toryism in New York," Donald E. M. Gerardi found that the ideological cleavage between whigs and tories had already existed in the 1750s. "In the clash between the supporters of the college and its critics a bitter ideological conflict developed in which New York whigs were confronted with tory critics." The "polemics" of the latter proved that "there were tory ideologues in mid-eighteenth-century America" who offered "a foil for the 'Real Whig' political mentality that was to predominate twenty years later." Building upon Gerardi, Janice Potter argued in *The Liberty We Seek* that the ideological conflict between New York whigs and tories pitted Real Whigs against the followers of Viscount Bolingbroke, Edmund Burke, Baron de Montesquieu, and Sir William Blackstone.[20]

The problem with Bailyn's interpretation is that not all New York whigs were Real Whigs. The one organized group in which a significant number

shared that ideology was the Livingston party. Though most Livingstonites finally supported independence, they had labored between 1763 and
1776 to slow the revolutionary momentum in the province. The genuinely revolutionary force in New York sprang from Isaac Sears and the
Liberty Boys. Whether one accepts Friedman or Maier, Sears was quite
different from Samuel Adams, the archetypal Real Whig who acted on
the principle that people must sacrifice their own self-interest for the
common good.[21] One can question too whether New York loyalists shared
a common ideology that impelled them to resist the Revolution. Potter's
study was admittedly limited to the published writings of loyalists, but
more evidence is required to prove that the ideas advanced by this tiny
educated elite were shared by loyalist politicians and the rank and file.
The name De Lancey, in fact, never appears in the index to Potter's book.
Cadwallader Colden is listed once, and the reference to him is incidental
to her argument. Thomas Jones, one of the loyalists upon whom her study
was based, blamed the Revolution on the Livingstonite Whig "triumvirate" of William Livingston, John Morin Scott, and William Smith, Jr.,
whom Gerardi labeled Real Whigs.[22] Yet both Jones and Smith became
tories. And the "Dougliad" articles, which Potter offered as a forceful
statement of loyalist ideology, were authored anonymously by James
Duane, a De Lanceyite who ultimately became a whig.[23]

As the present study attempts to show, New York City's history between
1763 and 1776 is much richer and more variegated than either the Progressive or Consensus models allow. Ideas did count; New York's patrician
leaders were capable of more than cynicism; people can divide along lines
other than class; cooperation as well as conflict between the classes was
possible; and the Sons of Liberty played a key, independent role in the
years between 1763 and 1776. New Yorkers were reluctant revolutionaries
not because they were mostly loyalists or because a small group of aristocratic conservatives was able to withstand the forces of revolution. Instead,
the heterogeneity of the city's population made it very difficult for residents to hammer out a consensus, acceptable to the great majority of
people, over how to resist British imperialism. In the end, however, they
succeeded in doing so, and New Yorkers joined Americans elsewhere in
declaring their independence.

Notes

The following abbreviations are used in the notes.

AHR   *American Historical Review.*

CC   Cadwallader Colden.

C.O.   Colonial Office Papers, Public Record Office, London [Library of Congress microfilm].

DCHNY   O'Callaghan, Edmund B., ed. *Documents Relative to the Colonial History of the State of New York.* 15 vols. Albany, 1853–1887.

DHSNY   O'Callaghan, Edmund B., ed. *The Documentary History of the State of New York.* 4 vols. Albany, 1850.

Evans   Evans, Charles, ed. *American Bibliography: A Chronological Dictionary of All Books, Pamphlets, and Periodical Publications Printed in the United States of America . . . 1630 . . . to . . . 1820.* 12 vols. Chicago, 1903–1934.

JAH   *Journal of American History.*

NYAJ   *Journal of the Votes and Proceedings of the General Assembly of the Colony of New York.*

NYGWM   *New York Gazette and Weekly Mercury.*

NYH   *New York History.*

NYHS   New-York Historical Society, New York City.

NYHSQ   *New-York Historical Society Quarterly.*

NYJ   *New York Journal.*

NYPL   Rare Books and Manuscripts Division, New York Public Library, Astor, Lenox, and Tilden Foundations, New York City.

RRL   Robert R. Livingston.

WMQ   *William and Mary Quarterly,* 3rd Series.

WPB   *New York Gazette, or, The Weekly Post Boy.*

Introduction

1. CC to Gen. Thomas Gage, July 8, 1765, *The Colden Letter Books*, 2 vols. (NYHS, *Collections*, vols. 9–10 [New York, 1877–1878]), 2:23, herein cited as *CC Letter Books*; Paul A. Gilje, *The Road to Mobocracy: Popular Disorder in New York City, 1763–1834* (Chapel Hill, N.C., 1987), 5, 12. The quote is from RRL to Robert Monckton, Nov. 8, 1765, Thomas Aspinwall, ed., *Aspinwall Papers*, 2 vols. (Massachusetts Historical Society, *Collections*, 4th ser., vols. 9–10 [Boston, 1871]), 10:565, herein cited as *Aspinwall Papers*. For contemporary descriptions of the rioting, see "G" to Printer, *WPB*, Nov. 7, 1765; "No Stamped Paper to be Had," [*New York Mercury*, herein cited as *Mercury*], Nov. 4, 1765; RRL to [Robert Livingston], Nov. 2, 1765, Livingston Family Papers, NYPL; RRL to Monckton, Nov. 8, 1765, *Aspinwall Papers* 10:559–567; E. Carther to Unk., Nov. 2, 1765, New York Mercantile Library Association, *New York City during the American Revolution, Being a Collection of Original Papers from the Manuscripts in the Possession of the Mercantile Library Association* (New York, 1861), 42–49, herein cited as *New York in the Revolution*; Gage to Henry Seymour Conway, Nov. 4, 1765, Clarence Edwin Carter, ed., *The Correspondence of General Thomas Gage . . .*, 2 vols. (New Haven, 1931–1933), 1:70–71, herein cited as *Gage Correspondence*; *The Journals of Captain John Montresor*, ed. G. D. Scull (NYHS, *Collections*, 14 [New York, 1882]), 336–337, herein cited as *Montresor Journals*; and CC to Board of Trade, Dec. 6, 1765, *CC Letter Books* 2:78–82.

2. *WPB*, Nov. 7, 1765; *Montresor Journals*, 336.

3. C[olden] to John Cruger, Oct. 31, 1764, [CC to George Grenville, Oct. 22, 1768], *CC Letter Books* 2:53, 177; the quote is from Maj. Thomas James to CC, [Dec. 1765?], *The Letters and Papers of Cadwallader Colden*, 8 vols. (NYHS, *Collections*, vols. 50–56, 67 [New York, 1917–1923, 1937]), 7:99, herein cited as *CC Papers*.

4. RRL to [R. Livingston], Nov. 2, 1765, Livingston Family Papers, NYPL; Notice Served on Governor Colden concerning the Stamp Act, [Nov. 1, 1765], *CC Papers* 8:84–85.

5. "Amicus Publico" to Printer, *WPB*, Nov. 7, 1765.

6. "No Stamped Paper to be Had," [*Mercury*], Nov. 4, 1765; Gilje, *Road to Mobocracy*, 28–29, 44–45. Also see Peter Shaw, *American Patriots and the Rituals of Revolution* (Cambridge, Mass., 1981), 179, 216–217.

7. *WPB*, Apr. 17, 1769; *NYGWM*, July 3, 1769; *NYJ*, Oct. 5, 1769; Carther to Unk., Nov. 2, 1765, *New York in the Revolution*, 46–47. The first quote is from RRL to Monckton, Nov. 8, 1765, *Aspinwall Papers* 10:561; the second from CC to Conway, Nov. 5, 1765, *CC Letter Books* 2:55.

8. CC to Conway, Nov. 5, 1775, *CC Letter Books* 2:55. Massachusetts also held a funeral ceremony on Nov. 1; Dirk Hoerder, *Crowd Action in Revolutionary Massachusetts, 1765–1780* (New York, 1977), 122.

9. The first and third quotes are from "G" to Printer, *WPB*, Nov. 7, 1765; the second from RRL to Monckton, Nov. 8, 1765, *Aspinwall Papers* 10:562.

10. Peter Force, ed., *American Archives . . . A Documentary History of . . . the North American Colonies*, 4th ser., 6 vols. (Washington, D.C., 1837–1846), 2:1314, 1318, herein cited as *American Archives*.

11. The quotes are from Thomas Jones, *History of New York during the Revolutionary War, and of the Leading Events in the Other Colonies at That Period*, ed. Edward Floyd De Lancey, 2 vols. (New York, 1879), 1:55–57, herein cited as Jones, *History*. Also see William Smith, *Historical Memoirs of William Smith, Historian of the Province of New York,*

Member of the Governor's Council . . ., ed. William H. W. Sabine, 2 vols. (New York, 1956–1958), 1:228c–228d, herein cited as Smith, *Memoirs*; Cruger to Peter Van Schaack, June 26, 1775, Misc. Mss., NYHS; and *Pennsylvania Journal*, June 28, 1775.

12. Joseph Reed to Josiah Quincy, Nov. 6, 1774, *American Archives*, 4th ser., 1:1964; John Adams to William Tudor, June 24, 1776, Robert J. Taylor et al., eds., *Papers of John Adams*, 8 vols. (Cambridge, Mass., 1977–), 4:335.

13. Larry R. Gerlach, *Prologue to Independence: New Jersey in the Coming of the American Revolution* (New Brunswick, N.J., 1976), 129.

14. George W. Edwards, *New York as an Eighteenth Century Municipality, 1731–1776* (New York, 1917); Oscar Theodore Barck, Jr., *New York City during the War for Independence* (New York, 1931); Wilbur C. Abbott, *New York in the American Revolution* (New York, 1929); Thomas Jefferson Wertenbaker, *Father Knickerbocker Rebels: New York City during the Revolution* (New York, 1948); Malcolm Decker, *Brink of Revolution: New York in Crisis, 1765–1776* (New York, 1964).

15. Alexander Clarence Flick, *Loyalism in New York during the American Revolution* (New York, 1901), 180–182; the quotes are from pp. 180, 181. Wallace Brown, *The King's Friends: The Composition and Motives of the American Loyalist Claimants* (Providence, 1965), 77. Also see William H. Nelson, *The American Tory* (Oxford, 1961), 92; Esmond Wright, "The New York Loyalists: A Cross-section of Colonial Society," in Robert A. East and Jacob Judd, eds., *The Loyalist Americans: A Focus on Greater New York* (Tarrytown, N.Y., 1975), 78–79; and Janice Potter, *The Liberty We Seek: Loyalist Ideology in Colonial New York and Massachusetts* (Cambridge, Mass., 1983), 1.

16. Bernard Mason, *The Road to Independence: The Revolutionary Movement in New York, 1773–1777* (Lexington, Ky., 1966), 64; Philip Ranlet, *The New York Loyalists* (Knoxville, 1986), 186. A writer at the time estimated that only 2,000 of the 40,000 men able to bear arms were tories; Extract of a Letter, dated New York, Jan. 6, 1776, John Almon, ed., *The Remembrancer or Impartial Repository of Public Events*, 17 vols. (London, 1775–1784), 2:238.

17. For a detailed analysis of both these schools of thought, please consult the Historiographical Essay at the end of this study. I have organized the discussion in this manner so that I could address the historiographical issues at length without distracting the general reader.

18. Carl Lotus Becker, *The History of Political Parties in the Province of New York, 1760–1776* (Madison, Wisc., 1909), 5–22; the quote is from p. 5. Jack P. Greene, "Changing Interpretations of Early American Politics," in Ray Allen Billington, ed., *The Reinterpretation of Early American History: Essays in Honor of John Edwin Pomfret* (San Marino, Calif., 1966), 156.

19. Edward Countryman, *A People in Revolution: The American Revolution and Political Society in New York, 1760–1790* (Baltimore, 1981), 4.

20. The first quote is from Louis Kriesberg, *Social Conflicts*, 2d ed. (Englewood Cliffs, N.J., 1982), 66. Walter Laqueur, "Revolution," in *International Encyclopedia of the Social Sciences* ([New York], 1968), 13:501; Theda Skocpol, *States and Social Revolutions: A Comparative Analysis of France, Russia, and China* (Cambridge, Mass., 1979), 3–43. Also see Skocpol, "Explaining Revolutions: In Quest of a Social-Structural Approach," in Lewis A. Coser and Otto N. Larsen, eds., *Uses of Controversy in Sociology* (New York, 1976), 156.

21. The aim of the present study, however, is not to revisit the Imperial School of historiography that flourished before World War II. As far as New York is concerned,

this study disagrees with several key arguments associated with that school. First, before the Seven Years' War, New Yorkers were not especially unhappy with how mercantilism or the empire operated. Second, if the removal of the French from Canada after the French and Indian War made New Yorkers readier to question British authority, it also induced Britain to be much more inflexible in its handling of Anglo-American affairs. Third, though the confidence colonists had in their ability to govern themselves was growing during the 1750s and 1760s, the explanation for what happened in 1776 was not "the social and political tendencies" they had developed "toward independence." Fourth, responsibility for causing the Revolution in New York does not rest primarily on its residents, who remained on the defensive for over a decade before reluctantly concluding that their only alternative was rebellion. For the Imperial School, see Herbert Levi Osgood, "The American Revolution," *Political Science Quarterly* 13 (1898): 41–59; George Lewis Beer, *British Colonial Policy, 1754–1765* (New York, 1907); Charles M. Andrews, *The Colonial Background of the American Revolution* (New Haven, 1924); Andrews, "The American Revolution: An Interpretation," *AHR* 31 (1926): 218–232; Lawrence H. Gipson, *The British Empire before the American Revolution*, 15 vols. (New York, 1936–1970); and Gipson, "The American Revolution as an Aftermath of the Great War for the Empire," *Political Science Quarterly* 65 (1950): 86–104.

22. Skocpol, *States and Social Revolutions*, 24–33; the quotes in this paragraph are from pp. 28, 29, 32.

23. In describing British attitudes at the end of the Seven Years' War, Robert Middlekauff, *The Glorious Cause: The American Revolution, 1763–1789* (New York, 1982), 11, wrote, "English energies were formidable and bent on finding expression in war, trade, and domination. In the capacity to grow, to concentrate power and energy, to bring force to bear in the service of an expansionist policy, no nation in 1760 could match England."

24. See Colin Bonwick, "The American Revolution as a Social Movement Revisited," *Journal of American Studies* 20 (1986): 355–373.

25. Jeff Goodwin and Theda Skocpol, "Explaining Revolutions in the Contemporary Third World," *Politics and Society* 17 (1989): 497. The quote is from Lord Dartmouth to Gage, Apr. 9, 1774, *Gage Correspondence* 2:158–162.

26. For a longer-term perspective on the politico-economic changes taking place in Britain and how warfare led to government centralization, see James H. Hutson, "Country, Court, and Constitution: Antifederalism and the Historians," *WMQ* 38 (1981): 337–368; E. James Ferguson, "Political Economy, Public Liberty, and the Formation of the Constitution," *WMQ* 40 (1983): 389–412; and John Brewer, *The Sinews of Power: War, Money, and the English State, 1688–1783* (New York, 1989), esp. pp. xiii–xxi.

27. Shaw, *American Patriots*, chap. 9; Gilje, *Road to Mobocracy*, chap. 2.

28. Kriesberg, *Social Conflicts*, 317–327, provides a succinct overview of his model.

29. Milton M. Klein, "The Cultural Tyros of Colonial New York," *South Atlantic Quarterly* 66 (1967): 218–232; Klein, "Shaping the American Tradition: The Microcosm of Colonial New York," *NYH* 59 (1978): 173–197; Patricia U. Bonomi, *A Factious People: Politics and Society in Colonial New York* (New York, 1971), esp. pp. 10–14; Michael Kammen, *Colonial New York: A History* (New York, 1975), 216–241.

30. For example, John M. Head realized that the colony's heterogeneity was crucial to understanding New York, but he did not grasp how or why pluralism affected the final outcome. In particular, he did not appreciate the role political parties played in

managing the "explosive mixture of cultural groups" and instead thought the fact that New York "had plenty of room" was the key. In the 1760s and 1770s, he said, the Livingston–De Lancey "rivalry continued only out of habit, but it was a habit with a meaning, for control of the government of New York could be the means of preferment and wealth." John M. Head, *A Time to Rend: An Essay on the Decision for American Independence* (Madison, Wisc., 1968), 14–33; the quotes are from pp. 19, 28. Kammen, *Colonial New York*, 348, emphasized that "an excess of pluralism and materialism combined with a lack of coherent community . . . to make rebellion in New York a fairly distinctive phenomenon." Also see Robert McCluer Calhoon, *The Loyalists in Revolutionary America, 1760–1781* (New York, 1973), 371; and Robert Kelley, *The Cultural Patterns of American Politics: The First Century* (New York, 1979), chap. 2.

31. H. James Henderson, *Party Politics in the Continental Congress* (New York, 1974), 78.

32. Kriesberg, *Social Conflicts*, 323–324.

1. New York City on the Eve of the First Crisis

1. William Smith, Jr., *The History of the Province of New York*, ed. Michael Kammen, 2 vols. (Cambridge, Mass., 1972), 1:202, herein cited as Smith, *History*.

2. William Livingston and Others, *The Independent Reflector*, ed. Milton M. Klein (Cambridge, Mass., 1963), 104, herein cited as *Independent Reflector*.

3. "Journal of a French Traveler in the Colonies, 1765," *AHR* 27 (1921): 82; Thomas Pownall, *A Topographical Description of the Dominions of the United States of America. . .*, ed. Lois Mulkearn (Pittsburgh, 1949), 45; "Report of Governor Tryon on the State of the Province of New York, 1774," *DHSNY* 1:510.

4. *Independent Reflector*, 434; the quote is from p. 105. "Journal of a French Traveler," *AHR* 27 (1921): 82; Larry R. Gerlach, *Prologue to Independence: New Jersey in the Coming of the American Revolution* (New Brunswick, N.J., 1976), 29; Smith, *History* 1:201.

5. *DHSNY* 1:471–474; Pownall, *Topographical Description*, 44; Esther Singleton, *Social New York under the Georges, 1714–1776* (New York, 1902), 4; Sidney Pomerantz, *New York: An American City, 1783–1803* (New York, 1932), 227; Bruce M. Wilkenfeld, "The New York City Shipowning Community, 1715–1764," *American Neptune* 37 (1977): 61; Smith, *History* 1:210n.

6. Peter Kalm, *The America of 1750: Peter Kalm's Travels in North America, The English Version of 1770*, ed. Adolph B. Benson, 2 vols. (New York, 1937), 1:131–132, herein cited as *Kalm's Travels*.

7. Quoted in Carl Bridenbaugh, *Cities in Revolt: Urban Life in America, 1743–1776* (New York, 1955), 42.

8. Robert Honyman, *Colonial Panorama 1775: Dr. Robert Honyman's Journal for March and April*, ed. Philip Padelford (San Marino, Ca., 1939), 27, herein cited as Honyman, *Colonial Panorama*.

9. "Report of Governor Tryon on the Province of New York," *DHSNY* 1:513–514; Wilkenfeld, "New York Shipowning Community," *Amer. Neptune* 37 (1977): 61; Virginia D. Harrington, *The New York Merchant on the Eve of the Revolution* (New York, 1935), 189–190; Smith, *History* 1:229; *Kalm's Travels* 1:134–136; Edward Countryman, *A People in Revolution: The American Revolution and Political Society in New York, 1760–1790* (Baltimore, 1981), 8.

10. Smith, *History* 1:230; "Report of Governor Tryon on the Province of New York," *DHSNY* 1:513–514.

11. The description of New York's neighborhoods presented here is based on Carl Abbott, "The Neighborhoods of New York, 1760–1775," *NYH* 55 (1974): 35–54; and Wilkenfeld, "Revolutionary New York, 1776," in Milton M. Klein, ed., *New York: The Centennial Years, 1677–1976* (Port Washington, N.Y., 1976), 43–70.

12. Andrew Burnaby, *Travels through the Middle Settlements of North America, 1759–1760* (New York, 1904), 112. For Trinity Church Yard, see Graham Russell Hodges, *New York City Cartmen, 1667–1850* (New York, 1986), 46–48, 55–57. For King's College in this period, see David C. Humphrey, *From King's College to Columbia, 1746–1800* (New York, 1976), 3–100.

13. New York Mercantile Library Association, *New York City during the American Revolution, Being a Collection of Original Papers from the Manuscripts in the Possession of the Mercantile Library Association* (New York, 1861), 14–15, herein cited as *New York in the Revolution*; Harrington, *New York Merchant*, 22; *Abstract of Wills on File in the Surrogate's Office, City of New York*, 17 vols. (NYHS, *Collections*, vols. 25–41 [New York, 1893–1913]), 5:241.

14. Honyman, *Colonial Panorama*, 28–30; Smith, *History* 1:204–205.

15. Countryman, *People in Revolution*, 10.

16. Honyman, *Colonial Panorama*, 30.

17. Harrington, *New York Merchant*, 22, 31; Abbott, "Neighborhoods of New York," *NYH* 55 (1974): 43; *New York in the Revolution*, 17, 19; Smith, *History* 1:208–209. For the development of printing in New York, see Lawrence C. Wroth, *The Colonial Printer*, 2d ed. (Portland, Mass., 1938); and Clarence S. Brigham, *History and Bibliography of American Newspapers, 1690–1820*, 2 vols. (Westport, Conn., 1975).

18. Abbott, "Neighborhoods of New York," *NYH* 55 (1974): 46.

19. *New York in the Revolution*, 20, 22, 24; the quote is from p. 20.

20. The quote comes from the title of Patricia U. Bonomi, *A Factious People: Politics and Society in Colonial New York* (New York, 1971). For the impact of population growth on the American colonies, see James A. Henretta, *The Evolution of American Society, 1700–1815: An Interdisciplinary Analysis* (Lexington, Mass., 1973), esp. chap. 1; and Bernard Bailyn, *Voyages to the West: A Passage in the Peopling of America on the Eve of the Revolution* (New York, 1986).

21. Smith, *History* 1:204; the quotes are on pp. 234, 235. George W. Edwards, *New York as an Eighteenth Century Municipality, 1731–1776* (New York, 1917), 54; Honyman, *Colonial Panorama*, 30; Thomas Jones, *History of New York during the Revolutionary War, and of the Leading Events in the Other Colonies at That Period*, ed. Edward Floyd De Lancey, 2 vols. (New York, 1879), 1:2, herein cited as Jones, *History*; *Colonial Laws of the State of New York from the Year 1664 to the Revolution*, 5 vols. (New York, 1894), 1:328–331.

22. Edwards, *New York*, 55; Michael Kammen, *Colonial New York: A History* (New York, 1975), 238; Leonard J. Trinterud, *The Forming of an American Tradition: A Re-Examination of Colonial Presbyterianism* (Philadelphia, 1949), 122–134; Jones, *History* 1:2. For the Whig "triumvirate," see Dorothy R. Dillon, *The New York Triumvirate: A Study of the Legal and Political Careers of William Livingston, John Morin Scott, and William Smith, Jr.* (New York, 1949).

23. For the fight over the Ministry Act, see John Webb Pratt, *Religion, Politics, and Diversity: The Church-State Theme in New York History* (Ithaca, N.Y., 1967), 76. The law was repealed in 1784; *Laws of the State of New York Passed at the Sessions of the Legislature*, 7th Session, Apr. 20, 1784, Chapter 38.

24. See Donald E. M. Gerardi, "The King's College Controversy 1753–1756 and

the Ideological Roots of Toryism in New York," *Perspectives in American History* 11 (1977–1978): 147–198; Pratt, *Religion, Politics, and Diversity*, 68–69; Kammen, *Colonial New York*, 250–252; Humphrey, *From King's College to Columbia*, 18–100; *Independent Reflector*, 171–214; Jones, *History* 1:10–17.

25. Carl Bridenbaugh, *Mitre and Sceptre: Transatlantic Faiths, Ideas, Personalities, and Politics, 1689–1775* (New York, 1962), 260–261, 288–314; Pratt, *Religion, Politics, and Diversity*, 74; Trinterud, *Forming of an American Tradition*, 230–231; Gerardi, "King's College Controversy," *Perspectives in Amer. Hist.* 11 (1977–1978): 148–149; "The American Whig," *NYGWM*, Mar. 14 – July 24, 1769; William Smith, *Historical Memoirs of William Smith, Historian of the Province of New York, Member of the Governor's Council . . .*, ed. William H. W. Sabine, 2 vols. (New York, 1956–1958), 1:42–43, herein cited as Smith, *Memoirs*.

26. Jones, *History* 1:2; Arthur J. Wall, "The Controversy in the Dutch Church in New York concerning Preaching in English, 1754–1768," *NYHSQ* 12 (1928): 39–58; John W. Beardslee, "The Dutch Reformed Church and the American Revolution," *Journal of Presbyterian History* 54 (1976): 165–181; Nelson R. Burr, "The Episcopal Church and the Dutch in Colonial New York and New Jersey: 1664–1784," *Historical Magazine of the Protestant Episcopal Church* 19 (1950): 90–111; Kammen, *Colonial New York*, 221, 237, 251.

27. Randall Balmer, *A Perfect Babel of Confusion: Dutch Religion and English Culture in the Middle Colonies* (New York, 1989), esp. pp. viii–ix, 38–39, 106–108, 141–156; the quote is from p. ix. Signed Petition of 87 Members of the Reformed Dutch Church Favoring Preaching in English in One of the Reformed Dutch Churches. New York, Feb. 1754; NYC Churches, Box 30 (II), NYHS.

28. CC to Lord Hillsborough, Feb. 21, 1770, *The Colden Letter Books*, 2 vols. (NYHS, *Collections*, vols. 9–10 [New York, 1877–1878]), 2:211, herein cited as *CC Letter Books*. Arthur J. Mekeel, *The Relation of the Quakers to the American Revolution* (Washington, D.C., 1979), 330, n. 4; the quotes are from pp. 7, 6.

29. Klein, "Shaping the American Tradition," *NYH* 69 (1978): 173–197; the quote is from p. 196. Klein, "The Cultural Tyros of Colonial New York," *South Atlantic Quarterly*, 66 (1967): 218–232.

30. Unlike a modern party, however, no colonial party was able to institutionalize itself as a political organization for an extended period of time. Benjamin H. Newcomb, *Political Partisanship in the American Middle Colonies, 1700–1776* (Baton Rouge, 1995), 4–9; the quote is from p. 7.

31. For the opposing view, see Countryman, *People in Revolution*, 72–98; the quote is from p. ix.

32. *The Charter of the City of New York. . .* (New York, 1765), Evans, 10100; Edwards, *New York*, 22–41; Smith, *History* 1:245–272.

33. Countryman, *People in Revolution*, 36–47; Edwards, *New York*, 126–127. For a full discussion of this issue, see Douglas Greenberg, *Crime and Law Enforcement in the Colony of New York, 1691–1776* (Ithaca, N.Y., 1976).

34. For the activities of the Common Council, see *Minutes of the Common Council of the City of New York, 1675–1776*, 8 vols. (New York, 1905).

35. Wilkenfeld, "The New York City Common Council, 1689–1800," *NYH* 52 (1971): 262–266; Beverly McAnear, "The Place of the Freeman in Old New York," *NYH* 21 (1940): 418–430. The quote is from Klein, "Democracy and Politics in Colonial New York," *NYH* 60 (1959): 235.

36. Jessica Kross, " 'Patronage Most Ardently Sought': The New York Council, 1665–1775," in Bruce C. Daniels, ed., *Power and Status: Officeholding in Colonial America* (Middletown, Conn., 1986), 222.

37. See Gov. Henry Moore to Hillsborough, Mar. 30, 1769, *DCHNY* 8:157.

38. Smith, *History* 1:245–254; the quotes are from pp. 247, 248, 249.

39. "Report of Governor Tryon on the Province of New York, 1774," *DHSNY* 1:511.

40. Smith, *Memoirs* 1:118; the quotes are from p. 254. Kross, " 'Patronage Most Ardently Sought,' " 205–231.

41. Smith, *Memoirs* 1:256; Peter R. Livingston to Philip Schuyler, Feb. 6, 27, 1769, Philip Schuyler Papers, NYPL; Klein, "Democracy and Politics," *NYH* 60 (1959): 228–232; *DHSNY* 1:474; Edwards, *New York*, 36. For criticism of the way the Assembly was allegedly augmenting its power at the expense of the royal prerogative and the other branches of government, see [Archibald Kennedy], *An Essay on the Government of the Colonies* . . . [New York, 1752], Evans, 40619.

42. Smith, *History* 1:256–258; [Kennedy], *Essay on Government*, 14–15.

43. *Kalm's Travels* 1:137. Because New York was one of the four colonies where the governor's salary was appropriated annually, a directive was sent to the customs officials in America to pay Lord Dunmore, who became New York's governor in 1770, £2,000 per year out of the duties on tea; Leonard Woods Labaree, *Royal Government in America: A Study of the British Colonial System before 1783* (New Haven, 1930), 340.

44. Smith, *Memoirs* 1:181; Carl Lotus Becker, *The History of Political Parties in the Province of New York, 1760–1776* (Madison, Wisc., 1909), 12; [Kennedy], *Essay on Government*, 32–35; Gov. William Tryon to Dartmouth, Sept. 5, 1775, *DCHNY* 8:633.

45. *DHSNY* 1:511; Bailyn, *The Origins of American Politics* (New York, 1967), 24–25; Smith, *Memoirs* 1:181.

46. Tryon to Dartmouth, Sept. 5, 1775, *DCHNY* 8:633.

47. *WPB*, Jan. 16, 1766; *NYJ*, Nov. 4, 1773.

48. Louis Kriesberg, *Social Conflicts*, 2d ed. (Englewood Cliffs, N.J., 1982), 105, 150.

49. For De Lancey's rise to prominence, see Stanley Nider Katz, "Between Scylla and Charybdis: James De Lancey and Anglo-American Politics in Early Eighteenth-Century New York," in Alison G. Olson and Richard M. Brown, eds., *Anglo-American Political Relations, 1675–1775* (New Brunswick, N.J., 1970), 92–108; and Bonomi, *Factious People*, 143–149.

50. Quoted in Katz, "Between Scylla and Charybdis," 92.

51. Marc Egnal, *A Mighty Empire: The Origins of the American Revolution* (Ithaca, N.Y., 1988), 61–62; Bonomi, *Factious People*, 150–151.

52. Robert McCluer Calhoon, *The Loyalists in Revolutionary America, 1760–1781* (New York, 1973), 43; Oliver De Lancey to Susannah Warren, July 30, 1760, Oliver De Lancey Papers, NYHS; Lord Halifax to Peter Collinson, Oct. 12, 1760, Cadwallader Colden Papers, NYPL.

53. *New York Mercury*, Feb. 2, 23, 1761; Bonomi, *Factious People*, 235.

54. Smith, *Memoirs* 1:33, 47–49, 60, 72; the quote is from pp. 175–176.

55. Cynthia Anne Kierner, *Traders and Gentlefolk: The Livingstons of Colonial New York, 1675–1790* (Ithaca, N.Y., 1992), 173–178; Smith, *Memoirs* 1:172, 176; Bonomi, *Factious People*, 150–151; Egnal, *Mighty Empire*, 61–66; *Independent Reflector*, 219. The quote is from "The Sentinel, No. VII," *WPB*, Apr. 11, 1765.

56. Bonomi, *Factious People*, 232, 239, 279–286, not only questions whether a Livingston party really existed in the early 1760s, but also doubts that the ideological

differences between the De Lanceys and the Livingstons were as sharp as those described in this chapter.

57. William Warren Sweet, *Religion in Colonial America* (New York, 1942), 8–10; Smith, *History* 2:237; Kierner, *Traders and Gentlefolk*, 165; P. R. Livingston to Robert Livingston, Apr. 20, 1770, Livingston Family Papers, Johnson Redmond Collection, Reel 6, NYHS (microfilm). For the importance of family, see P. R. Livingston to Oliver Wendell, Jan. 19, 1769, Livingston Papers, Museum of the City of New York. Though some Livingstons were Anglican and thus disturbed by the religious bigotry of the 1760s, they stayed in the party for familial, ideological, and economic reasons; see Robert Livingston, Jr., to James Duane, Mar. 9, Apr. 6, 1772, James Duane Papers, 1680–1853, NYHS.

58. My argument in this and the next paragraph is based on Bernard Friedman, "The Shaping of the Radical Consciousness in Provincial New York," *JAH* 56 (1970): 781–801; and Joyce Appleby, "The Social Origins of American Revolutionary Ideology," *JAH* 64 (1978): 935–958.

59. Smith, *History* 2:252–253; Jones, *History* 1:17; *Independent Reflector*, 319–327, 328–335; "The Sentinel, No. XXI," *WPB*, July 18, 1765. The first quote is from Friedman, "Shaping the Radical Consciousness," *JAH* 56 (1970): 786; the second from *Independent Reflector*, 288.

60. *Independent Reflector*, 111–117, 215–220, 278–284, 286–291; the quotes are from pp. 280, 218, 286.

61. "The Sentinel, No. X," *WPB*, Apr. 25, 1765.

62. RRL to Hy Beekman, July 11, 1764, Livingston Family Papers, NYPL; Worthington C. Ford et al., eds., *Journals of the Continental Congress, 1774–1789*, 34 vols. (Washington, D.C., 1904–1937), 1:82–90; John Jay to Susanna Philipse Robinson, Mar. 21, Jay to RRL and Gouverneur Morris, April 29, 1777, Richard B. Morris, ed., *John Jay, The Making of a Revolutionary: Unpublished Papers, 1745–1780* (New York, 1975), 136, 353, 401, 402, n. 4; Thelma Wills Foote, "Black Life in Colonial Manhattan, 1664–1786" (Ph.D. diss., Harvard University, 1991), 359; *Journals of the Provincial Congress, Provincial Convention, Committee of Safety, and Council of Safety of the State of New York*, 2 vols. (Albany, 1842), 1:887, 889, herein cited as *Journals of the Provincial Congress*.

63. *Independent Reflector*, 143–150; the quotes are from pp. 143, 148, 145. See *The American Chronicle*, Apr. 19, 1762, for a citizen's right to resist arbitrary government.

64. Smith to Monckton, Nov. 8, 1765; Smith, *Memoirs* 1:30.

65. [William Livingston], "A Review of Military Operations in North America . . .," Massachusetts Historical Society, *Collections*, 1st ser., vols. 7–8 (Boston, 1801–1856), 1:85; Leopold S. Launitz-Schürer, *Loyal Whigs and Revolutionaries: The Making of the Revolution in New York* (New York, 1980), 14; *Independent Reflector*, 25.

66. Friedman, "Shaping the Radical Consciousness," *JAH* 56 (1970): 785; Smith, *Memoirs* 1:95. The quotes are from *Independent Reflector*, 145, 287.

67. "State of the Province of New York," Dec. 6, 1765, *CC Letter Books* 2:68. Individuals suffering from status inconsistency often become resentful of the status quo and nurse a sense of grievance. That is especially true in a small group or community where face-to-face interactions are frequent and where there is an opportunity to develop and to reinforce shared beliefs. Besides, the fact that the Liberty Boys had demonstrated their talents in the Seven Years' War and that they had an ideology (political and economic individualism) justifying a higher status for themselves (as an aristocracy of talent) only bolstered their confidence that they deserved to be better ranked in New

York society. Kriesberg, *Social Conflicts*, 79. For the qualifications that an individual needed in order to be considered a gentleman, see Gordon S. Wood, *The Radicalism of the American Revolution* (New York, 1992), 24–42.

68. Roger J. Champagne, "The Sons of Liberty and the Aristocracy in New York Politics, 1765–1790" (Ph.D. diss., University of Wisconsin, 1960), 11–13; Isaac Q. Leake, *Memoir of the Life and Times of General John Lamb* (Albany, 1857), 9–10. For the symbolic significance of the term "King Sears," see Peter Shaw, *American Patriots and the Rituals of Revolution* (Cambridge, Mass., 1981), 188.

69. Friedman, "Shaping the Radical Consciousness," *JAH* 56 (1970): 781–801; Friedman, "Hugh Hughes, A Study in Revolutionary Idealism," *NYH* 64 (1983): 229–259; Appleby, "Social Origins of American Revolutionary Ideology," *JAH* 64 (1978): 935–958; Eric Foner, *Tom Paine and Revolutionary America* (New York, 1976); Robert J. Christen, *King Sears: Politician and Patriot in a Decade of Revolution* (New York, 1982), 30–31; Isaac Sears, *An Advertisement*, Jan. 24, 1769 [New York, 1769], Evans, 11458; *NYJ*, Nov. 4, 1773. The final quote is from Pauline Maier, *The Old Revolutionaries: Political Lives in the Age of Samuel Adams* (New York, 1980), 99, n. 70.

70. Friedman, "Shaping the Radical Consciousness," *JAH* 56 (1970): 793.

71. An important article that describes how the American Revolution challenged elite attitudes is Colin Bonwick, "The American Revolution as a Social Movement Revisited," *Journal of American Studies* 20 (1986): 355–373.

72. Appleby, "Social Origins of American Revolutionary Ideology," *JAH* 64 (1978): 941. Concerning the significance of the emergence of interest-group politics, see Wood, *Radicalism of the Revolution*, 243–270.

73. Wood, *Radicalism of the Revolution*, 232.

74. Smith, *Memoirs* 1:148; Bonomi, *Factious People*, 241. Perhaps the best statement of De Lancey political beliefs is in the "State of Grievances" that the De Lancey-controlled Assembly passed on Mar. 3, 1775, and in the five resolutions it approved on Mar. 8, 1775. See *NYAJ*, Mar. 3, 8, 1775.

75. Robert Kelley, "Ideology and Political Culture from Jefferson to Nixon," *AHR* 82 (1977): 533–534, 538.

2. The Onset of Conflict

1. *WPB*, July 21, 1763.

2. For the war's economic benefits, see Virginia D. Harrington, *The New York Merchant on the Eve of the Revolution* (New York, 1935), 289–315; and Gary B. Nash, *The Urban Crucible: Social Change, Political Consciousness, and the Origins of the American Revolution* (Cambridge, Mass., 1979), 233-246. John Watts to Isaac Barré, Feb. 28, 1762, *Letter Book of John Watts, Merchant and Councillor of New York, January 1, 1762 – December 22, 1765* (NYHS, *Collections*, 41 [New York, 1928]), 26, herein cited as *Watts Letter Book*.

3. Harrington, *New York Merchant*, 304; L. Jesse Lemisch, "Jack Tar vs. John Bull: The Role of New York's Seamen in Precipitating the Revolution" (Ph.D. diss., Yale University, 1962), 25–26; Roger J. Champagne, *Alexander McDougall and the American Revolution* (Syracuse, 1975), 8; Robert J. Christen, *King Sears: Politician and Patriot in a Decade of Revolution* (New York, 1982), 21.

4. Nash, *Urban Crucible*, 233–246.

5. New York's postwar economic problems are detailed in William S. Sachs, "The Business Outlook in the Northern Colonies, 1750–1775" (Ph.D. diss., Columbia University, 1957), 109–126. For a merchant's description of the economy, see Gentleman

in Town to a Friend in the Country, *WPB*, June 7, 1764; *New York Mercury*, Mar. 12, 1762, herein cited as *Mercury*; A General State of the Public Funds in the Province of New York, 1767," *DHSNY* 1:480.

6. Sachs, "Business Outlook," 132–133; Nash, "Social Change and the Growth of Prerevolutionary Radicalism," in Alfred F. Young, ed., *The American Revolution: Explorations in the History of American Radicalism* (De Kalb, Ill., 1976), 9; Raymond H. Mohl, "Poverty in Early America, A Reappraisal: The Case of Eighteenth-Century New York City," *NYH* 50 (1969): 14–16; Nash, *Urban Crucible*, 402; Carl Bridenbaugh, *Cities in Revolt: Urban Life in America, 1743–1776* (New York, 1955), 233; *Mercury*, Feb. 9, 1761.

7. *WPB*, Aug. 26, 1762.

8. Edward Countryman, *A People in Revolution: The American Revolution and Political Society in New York, 1760–1790* (Baltimore, 1981), 60; Paul A. Gilje, *The Road to Mobocracy: Popular Disorder in New York City, 1763–1834* (Chapel Hill, N.C., 1987), 9–10, 12.

9. *Weyman's New York Gazette*, Apr. 2, Dec. 3, 1764, herein cited as *Weyman's*; "State of the Province of New York," Dec. 6, 1765, *The Colden Letter Books*, 2 vols. (NYHS, *Collections*, vols. 9–10 [New York, 1877-1878]), 2:77–78, herein cited as *CC Letter Books*; Gov. Henry Moore to Board of Trade, Jan. 12, 1767, *DCHNY* 7:888-889.

10. "G" to Printer, *WPB*, Nov. 7, 1765. Bridenbaugh, *Cities in Revolt*, chap. 6; and Cynthia Anne Kierner, *Traders and Gentlefolk: The Livingstons of Colonial New York, 1675–1790* (Ithaca, N.Y., 1992), chap. 4, provide the best descriptions of the elaborate lifestyle of the urban elites.

11. Isaac N. Phelps Stokes, *The Iconography of Manhattan Island, 1498–1905*, 6 vols. (New York, 1915), 4:801; "The Sentinel, No. XI," *WPB*, May 9, 1765; *WPB*, Aug. 20, 1767. Also see Extract of a letter from England, July 17, 1764, *Weyman's*, Oct. 1, 1764.

12. James L. Huston, "The American Revolutionaries, the Political Economy of Aristocracy, and the American Concept of the Distribution of Wealth, 1765–1900," *AHR* 98 (1993): 1080; "A.B.C." to Printer, *WPB*, July 11, 1765; "Friend to the Distressed" to Mr. Hugh Gaine, *Mercury*, Jan. 27, 1766.

13. Lemisch, "Jack Tar," 29–30, 35–36; *Mercury*, Sept. 12, 1761; CC to Board of Trade, Aug. 30, 1760, *CC Letter Books* 1:14–17; *WPB*, July 12, 1764. In 1771 the adult white males in New York totaled 5,363, and seamen numbered 3,300; *DHSNY* 1:696-697; and *DCHNY* 8:434–457.

14. RRL to Robert Monckton, Nov. 7, 1765, Thomas Aspinwall, ed., *Aspinwall Papers*, 2 vols. (Massachusetts Historical Society, *Collections*, 4th ser., vols. 9–10 [Boston, 1871]), 10:566–567, herein cited as *Aspinwall Papers*; Gouverneur Morris to Mr. [?John] Penn, May 20, 1774, Peter Force, ed., *American Archives . . . A Documentary History of . . . the North American Colonies*, 4th ser., 6 vols. (Washington, D.C., 1837–1846), 1:342-343. Also see Richard B. Morris, "Class Struggle and the American Revolution," *WMQ* 19 (1962): 3–29.

15. Charles Tilly, *From Mobilization to Revolution* (Reading, Mass., 1978), 141-142; Huston, "American Revolutionaries," *AHR* 98 (1993): 1080; Gordon S. Wood, *The Radicalism of the American Revolution* (New York, 1992), 60–61.

16. Class consciousness is more typical among people of high status than among those of low status; Louis Kriesberg, *Social Conflicts*, 2d ed. (Englewood Cliffs, N.J., 1982), 71; Gilje, *Road to Mobocracy*, 30–32.

17. There have been a number of recent works on African Americans in the eighteenth century, but these have said very little about the role that blacks played in the coming of the Revolution during the years from 1763 to 1776, primarily because of a

lack of evidence. Thomas Joseph Davis, "Slavery in Colonial New York City" (Ph.D. diss., Columbia University, 1974); Richard Shannon Moss, "Slavery on Long Island: Its Rise and Decline during the Seventeenth through Nineteenth Centuries" (Ph.D. diss., St. John's University, 1985); Vivienne L. Kruger, "Born to Run: The Slave Family in Early New York, 1627–1827" (Ph.D. diss., Columbia University, 1985); Thelma Wills Foote, "Black Life in Colonial Manhattan, 1664–1786" (Ph.D. diss., Harvard University, 1991); Shane White, *Somewhat More Independent: The End of Slavery in New York City, 1770–1810* (Athens, Ga., 1991).

18. Gilje, *Road to Mobocracy,* 16–17.

19. Christen, *King Sears,* 225–227, 196–197; the quote is from p. 196. Deference can be voluntary or coerced, and individuals can have both shared and conflicting interests. In any given situation it is often difficult to determine why someone sided with the De Lanceys: Did he do so voluntarily? Was he being subtly or brazenly manipulated? Did he believe that in this particular instance he shared a common interest with the De Lanceys? Was he moved by some combination of the three? Or had deference, whether voluntary or coerced, overcome interest? See Richard R. Beeman, "Deference, Republicanism, and the Emergence of Popular Politics in Eighteenth-Century America," *WMQ* 49 (1992): 401–430, for a discussion of the issues involved.

20. "The pretensions of the elite notwithstanding, it is clear that its leadership rested firmly on the support of the common people, to whose views the leaders were obliged to refer"; Leopold S. Launitz-Schürer, *Loyal Whigs and Revolutionaries: The Making of the Revolution in New York* (New York, 1980), 5.

21. R. S. Neale, *Class in English History, 1680–1850* (Totowa, N.J., 1981), 41; Huston, "American Revolutionaries," *AHR* 98 (1993): 1080. Bernard Friedman, "The Shaping of the Radical Consciousness in Provincial New York," *JAH* 56 (1970): 781–801; the quotes are from pp. 795, 796, 800.

22. James C. Davies, "The J-Curve of Rising and Declining Satisfactions as a Cause of Some Great Revolutions and a Contained Revolution," in Hugh Davis Graham and Ted Robert Gurr, eds., *The History of Violence in America* (New York, 1969), 690–730; the quote is from p. 690. Also see his "Toward a Theory of Revolution," *American Sociological Review* 27 (1962): 5–19.

23. Peter A. Lupsha, "Explanation of Political Violence: Some Psychological Theories versus Indignation," *Politics and Society* 2 (1972): 96; Theda Skocpol, *States and Social Revolutions: A Comparative Analysis of France, Russia, and China* (Cambridge, 1979), xii; Tilly, *From Mobilization to Revolution,* 141–142. It is usually the richer, higher-status groups, not the most deprived, who develop the greatest sense of grievance or group consciousness; hence, it is not those who suffer the most who ordinarily rebel. Kriesberg, *Social Conflicts,* 74–75.

24. Thomas Gage to Viscount Barrington, July 1, 1772, Clarence Edwin Carter, ed., *The Correspondence of General Thomas Gage . . .,* 2 vols. (New Haven, 1931–1933), 2:611. For CC's political career, see Alice M. Keys, *Cadwallader Colden: A Representative Eighteenth Century Official* (New York, 1906); Allan R. Raymond, "The Political Career of Cadwallader Colden" (Ph.D. diss., Ohio State University, 1970); Carole Shammas, "Cadwallader Colden and the Role of the King's Prerogative," *NYHSQ* 53 (1969): 103–126; Robert McCluer Calhoon, *The Loyalists in Revolutionary America, 1760–1781* (New York, 1973), 42–49; and Alfred R. Hoermann, "A Savant in the Wilderness: Cadwallader Colden of New York," *NYHSQ* 62 (1978): 271–288.

25. *DCHNY* 6:674; CC to William Shirley, July 25, 1749, "Observations on the Bal-

ance of Power within Government," [1744–1745?], *The Letters and Papers of Cadwallader Colden*, 8 vols. (NYHS, *Collections*, vols. 50-56, 67 [New York, 1917–1923, 1937]), 4:124–125, 9:257, herein cited as *CC Papers*; CC to Lord Halifax, Feb. 22, 1765, *CC Letter Books* 1:470.

26. See his "Address to the Freeholders and Freemen of the Cities and Counties of the Province of New York," "Colden's Observations on the Balance of Power in Government," and "History of Gov. Cosby's Administration and of Lt. Gov. George Clark's Administration through 1737," *CC Papers* 3:327–328, 9:255, 257, 354-355; and his "State of the Province of New York," Dec. 6, 1765, *CC Letter Books* 2:68-69.

27. William Pencak, "Warfare and Political Change in Mid-Eighteenth-Century Massachusetts," in Peter Marshall and Glyn Williams, eds., *The British-Atlantic Empire before the American Revolution* (London, 1980), 51–73; Watts to Monckton, Feb. 22, 1766, *Aspinwall Papers* 10:590.

28. The quote is from Calhoon, *Loyalists in America*, 48.

29. CC to Board of Trade, Aug. 7, Nov. 11, CC to Halifax, Aug. 11, CC to John Pownall, Aug. 22, 1760, *CC Letter Books* 1:5-6, 32-34, 9-11, 13-14.

30. For CC's battles with the De Lanceys, see CC to Gen. Jeffrey Amherst, Aug. 11, Sept. 22, Nov. 8, 1760, CC to Pownall, Nov. 11, 1760, May 16, 1761, CC to Peter Collinson, Jan. 10, 1761, *CC Letter Books* 1:7, 22, 32, 38, 85, 56; Ross J. S. Hoffman, *Edmund Burke: New York Agent with His Letters to the New York Assembly and Intimate Correspondence with Charles O'Hara, 1761–1776* (Philadelphia, 1956), 15–17; and Nicholas Varga, "Robert Charles: New York Agent, 1748–1770," *WMQ* 18 (1961): 211-235.

31. Kierner, *Traders and Gentlefolk*, 169–172; Milton M. Klein, *The American Whig: William Livingston of New York* (New York, 1990), 397–401; W[illiam] Smith to Horatio Gates, Nov. 22, 1763, Horatio Gates Papers, 1726–1828, Reel 1, NYHS (microfilm); CC to William Pitt, Dec. 27, 1760, *CC Letter Books* 1:49-53.

32. Klein, "Prelude to Revolution in New York: Jury Trials and Judicial Tenure," *WMQ* 17 (1960): 446–453; Report of the Lords of Trade on the Commissions of Judges in New York, Nov. 18, Order of the King in Council on a Report of the Lords of Trade, Nov. 23, Board of Trade to CC, Dec. 11, 1761, *DHSNY* 7:471–476, 480; *CC Letter Books* 1:35, 48–49, 54–55, 58, 79–80, 88–89, 104, 106, 122, 126, 113–114, 148–150, 171, 174–176, 2:78–79, 88–90; New York (Colony), *Minutes of the Executive Council*, ed. V. H. Palsits (Albany, 1910), July 15, 1761. For Benjamin Pratt's legal career, see L. Kinvin Wroth and Hiller B. Zobel, eds., *Legal Papers of John Adams*, 3 vols. (Cambridge, Mass., 1965), 1:cvi; and Clifford K. Shipton, *Biographical Sketches of Those Who Attended Harvard College* (Cambridge, Mass., 1933–1975), 10:229.

33. CC to Pownall, Nov. 26, 1761, CC to Board of Trade, Nov. 25, 1761, Feb. 11, 1762, Pratt to Speaker of the General Assembly, Mar. 15, 1762, Speaker of the Assembly to Pratt, Mar. 16, 1762, *CC Letter Books* 1:135–137, 137–138, 159–161, 174–176; Board of Trade to CC, Jan. 20, June 11, 1762, *DHSNY* 7:485, 503–504; Robert Livingston, Jr., to Abraham Yates, Dec. 8, 1761, Abraham Yates, Jr., Papers, NYPL; New York Council to Monckton, June 26, Watts, William Walton, and Oliver De Lancey to Monckton, June 26, 1763, Chalmers Collection, NYPL; *American Chronicle*, Mar. 20, 1762.

34. CC to Monckton, Mar. 30, CC to Board of Trade, Apr. 7, 1762, *CC Letter Books* 1:183–184, 190; William Smith, *Historical Memoirs of William Smith, Historian of the Province of New York, Member of the Governor's Council, and Late Chief Justice of That Province under the Crown, Chief Justice of Quebec*, ed. William H. W. Sabine, 2 vols. (New York, 1956–1958), 1:17-22, herein cited as Smith, *Memoirs*; Klein, *American Whig*, 411; Mor-

ton Deutsch, *The Resolution of Conflict, Constructive and Destructive Processes* (New Haven, 1973), 351–359.

35. *WPB*, Aug. 25, Sept. 1, 1763; Greg, Cunningham, and Co. to W[addel] Cunningham, Oct. 26, 27, 1764, "Greg, Cunningham, and Company Letter Book, Sept. 22, 1764 – Sept. 24, 1765," BV Greg, Cunningham, NYHS; Herbert A. Johnson, "George Harison's Protest: New Light on Forsey versus Cunningham," *NYH* 50 (1969): 61–83; Klein, "Prelude to Revolution," *WMQ* 17 (1960): 439–462. Cunningham later settled in Belfast, Ireland; R. J. Dickson, *Ulster Emigration to Colonial America* (London, 1966), 74, 210.

36. An appeal, however, took cognizance of everything between the crime and the fixing of its penalty, points of fact and law alike. Smith, *Memoirs* 1:24.

37. *CC Letter Books* 1:407–414; the quotes are from pp. 410, 411.

38. CC to Sir William Johnson, Dec. 10, CC to Halifax, Dec. 13, 1764, CC to Amherst, May 3, 1765, *CC Letter Books* 1:420, 429, 2:1–2.

39. "The Sentinel, No. XXVI," *WPB*, Aug. 15, 1765; Watts to Monckton, Nov. 6, 1764, Chalmers Collection; RRL to Monckton, Feb. 23, 1765, *Aspinwall Papers* 10:557–558. Cunningham's business associates believed the ministry would force a judge appointed "during pleasure" to issue the necessary papers, so that the appeal could go to the governor in Council and, if necessary, to the Privy Council; Greg, Cunningham, and Co. to [William Shie and Co.], Nov. 5, 1764, "Greg, Cunningham Letter Book."

40. Greg, Cunningham, and Co. to [Walter Shie and Sons], Nov. 5, Greg, Cunningham, and Co. to Thomas Greg, Nov. 10, 1764, "Greg, Cunningham Letter Book"; Watts to Monckton, Dec. 10, 1764, *Watts Letter Book*, 313; Smith to Monckton, Jan. 25, 1765, *Aspinwall Papers* 10:552–553. CC stated publicly that "trials before the Council were much to be preferred" to jury trials and that "the King . . . might institute what Courts he thought proper"; RRL to Monckton, Jan. 26, 1765, *Aspinwall Papers* 10:556; Larry R. Gerlach, *Prologue to Independence: New Jersey in the Coming of the American Revolution* (New Brunswick, N.J., 1976), 31.

41. CC to Board of Trade, Nov. 7, Dec. 13, CC to Halifax, Dec. 13, 1764, *CC Letter Books* 1:394–398, 421–425, 427–435; the quote is from p. 397.

42. Smith to Monckton, Jan. 25, 1765, *Aspinwall Papers* 10:553; Smith to Monckton, Dec. 3, 1764, Chalmers Collection; *WPB*, Feb. 28, Mar. 7, 14, 1765.

43. CC to Halifax, May 31, "State of the Province of New York," Dec. 6, 1765, *CC Letter Books* 2:5, 74; Watts to Monckton, Feb. 22, 1766, *Aspinwall Papers* 10:590; Smith to Monckton, Nov. 8, 1765, Smith, *Memoirs* 1:31; Johnson to CC, Jan. 9, 1766, Alexander C. Flick and James Sullivan, eds., *The Papers of Sir William Johnson*, 14 vols. (New York, 1921–1965), 5:6–7.

44. Skocpol, *States and Social Revolution*, 3–43. The quote is from Kriesberg, *Social Conflicts*, 100.

45. Quoted in Bernhard Knollenberg, *Origins of the American Revolution, 1759–1766* (New York, 1960), 23.

46. Quoted in Hoffman, *Edmund Burke*, 131. Also see *The Speech of Th-m-s P-wn-ll, Esq., Late G-v-rn-r of This Province in the House of Commons in Favor of America* (Boston, 1768), 1–9, 16.

47. My argument in this and the following paragraph is based on Jack P. Greene, "An Uneasy Connection: An Analysis of the Preconditions of the American Revolution," in Stephen G. Kurtz and James H. Hutson, eds., *Essays on the Revolution* (Chapel Hill, N.C., 1973), 66–80. To place this particular period in the context of the history

of British imperialism in Colonial America, see Stephen Saunders Webb, "Army and Empire: English Garrison Government in Britain and America, 1569 to 1763," *WMQ* 34 (1977): 1–31. For British fears that America would seek independence, see J. M. Bumsted, " 'Things in the Womb of Time': Ideas of American Independence, 1633–1763," *WMQ* 31 (1974): 533–564.

48. Greene, "The Seven Years' War," in Marshall and Williams, eds., *British-Atlantic Empire*, 98; Greene believed America contributed far more than Britain realized. Lawrence H. Gipson, *Triumphant Empire: Thunder-Clouds Gather in the West*, vol. 10 of his *The British Empire before the American Revolution*, 15 vols. (New York, 1936–1970), 182; Jack M. Sosin, *Agents and Merchants: British Colonial Policy and the Origins of the American Revolution, 1763–1775* (Lincoln, Nebr., 1965), 37. For the tax burden New Yorkers shouldered, see Jessica Kross, "Taxation and the Seven Years' War: A New York Test Case," *The Canadian Review of American Studies* 18 (1987): 351–366.

49. Thomas C. Barrow, "A Project for Imperial Reform: 'Hints Respecting the Settlement for our American Provinces,' 1763," *WMQ* 24 (1967): 108–126; John L. Bullion, " 'The Ten Thousand in America': More Light on the Decision on the American Army, 1762–1763," *WMQ* 43 (1986): 646–657; John Shy, *Toward Lexington: The Role of the British Army in the Coming of the American Revolution* (Princeton, N.J., 1965), 52–68; Sosin, *Agents and Merchants*, 33; Greene, "Seven Years' War," 93–94.

50. See Barrow, "Background to the Grenville Program, 1757–1763," *WMQ* 22 (1965): 93–104; Sosin, *Agents and Merchants*, 90; and Gipson, *Triumphant Empire: Thunder-Clouds in the West*, 218. For a good description of the illegal trade New Yorkers were conducting and the acting governor's inability to get his Council even to acknowledge its existence, see Colden to Pitt, Dec. 27, 1760, *CC Letter Books* 1:49–53.

51. CC to Pitt, Dec. 27, 1760, *CC Letter Books* 1:49–53; Watts to Barré, Feb. 28, 1762, *Watts Letter Book*, 24–27; Christen, *King Sears*, 23–24. The trade situation was more complex than New Yorkers realized; British defense expenditures, which exceeded sixteen million pounds sterling between 1740 and 1775, "went a very long way to balance the continent's deficit in commodity trade with" Britain. Julian Gwyn, "British Government Spending and the North American Colonies, 1740–1775," in Marshall and Williams, eds., *The British-Atlantic Empire*, 74–83; the quote is from p. 81.

52. Petition of George Spencer to CC, Nov. 25, 1761, *CC Papers* 6:89–99; Petition of Spencer to Monckton, Aug. 2, 1763, Chalmers Collection; Gipson, *Triumphant Empire: Thunder-Clouds in the West*, 209–210; Klein, "The Rise of the New York Bar: The Legal Career of William Livingston," *WMQ* 15 (1958): 348–349.

53. Watts to Barré, Feb. 28, 1762, *Watts Letter Book*, 27; Memorial of Sundry Merchants to CC, May 29, 1762, Chalmers Collection; Sachs, "Business Outlook," 109. See John Tabor Kempe to Monckton, Nov. 3, 1762, *Aspinwall Papers* 9:469–473, for the effort in New York to stop the smuggling.

54. Kriesberg, *Social Conflicts*, 94.

55. Alan Rogers, *Empire and Liberty: American Resistance to British Authority, 1755–1763* (Berkeley, 1974), 133.

56. Gipson, *Triumphant Empire: Thunder-Clouds in the West*, chap. 1. Also see Greene, "Seven Years' War," 85-86; Max Savelle, "The Appearance of an American Attitude toward External Affairs, 1750–1775," *AHR* 52 (1947): 655-666; and Savelle, "Nationalism and Other Loyalties in the American Revolution," *AHR* 67 (1963): 901–923.

57. "The Account between Britain and Her Colonies Candidly Stated," *NYGWM*, June 6, 1774; Greene, "Uneasy Connection," 61; Wood, *Radicalism of the Revolution*, 145–168.

58. Greene, "Seven Years' War," 90, 94; Gipson, *Triumphant Empire: Thunder-Clouds in the West*, 202–207.

59. Lord Egremont to Governor of New York, July 9, 1763, *CC Papers* 6:223; Rear Adm. Lord Colvil to CC, Oct. 14, 1763, Cadwallader Colden Papers, NYPL; Knollenberg, *Origins of the Revolution*, 134–135; and Sosin, *Agents and Merchants*, 39.

60. Gipson, *Triumphant Empire: Thunder-Clouds in the West*, 226–228; Edmund S. Morgan and Helen M. Morgan, *The Stamp Act Crisis: Prologue to Revolution*, rev. ed. (New York, 1963), 78–79; Oliver M. Dickerson, *The Navigation Acts and the American Revolution* (Philadelphia, 1951), 172-175, 179–184. The quote is from Christen, *King Sears*, 31.

61. Gipson, *Triumphant Empire: Thunder-Clouds in the West*, 228–231; Knollenberg, *Origins of the Revolution*, 166–168.

62. Greene and Richard M. Jellison, "The Currency Act of 1764 in Imperial Colonial Relations, 1764–1776," *WMQ* 18 (1961): 485–518; the quote is from p. 518. Also see Sosin, "Imperial Regulation of Colonial Paper Money, 1764–1773," *Pennsylvania Magazine of History and Biography* 88 (1964): 174–198.

63. For the constitutional issues at stake, see John Phillip Reid, "'In Our Contracted Sphere': The Constitutional Contract, the Stamp Act Crisis, and the Coming of the American Revolution," *Columbia Law Review*, 76 (1976), 21–47; Reid, *Constitutional History of the American Revolution: The Authority to Legislate* (Madison, Wisc., 1991), esp. chaps. 4, 5, and 6; and Greene, *Peripheries and Center: Constitutional Development in the Extended Polities of the British Empire and the United States, 1607–1788* (Athens, Ga., 1986), esp. pp. 144–150.

3. The Stamp Act

1. The quotes are from Edward Countryman, *A People in Revolution: The American Revolution and Political Society in New York, 1760–1790* (Baltimore, 1981), xiii, 4.

2. To the Printer, *WPB*, Jan. 19, 1764. Also see John Watts to Gedney Clarke, Dec. 2, 1763, Watts to Scott, Pringle, Cheap, and Co., Feb. 5, 1764, *Letter Book of John Watts, Merchant and Councillor of New York, January 1, 1762 – December 22, 1765* (NYHS, *Collections*, 41 [New York, 1928]), 205, 228, herein cited as *Watts Letter Book*; and "State of the Province of New York," Dec. 6, 1765, *The Colden Letter Books*, 2 vols. (NYHS, *Collections*, vols. 9–10 [New York, 1877–1878]), 2:68, herein cited as *CC Letter Books*.

3. *WPB*, Jan. 30, Feb. 2, 1764; Arthur M. Schlesinger, *The Colonial Merchants and the American Revolution, 1763–1776* (New York, 1918), 61; Watts to Robert Monckton, Mar. 11, 1764, Chalmers Collection, NYPL; CC to Board of Trade, Mar. 9, 1764, *CC Letter Books* 2:312–313; *Weyman's New York Gazette*, May 7, 1764.

4. *The Memorial of the Merchants of the City of New York, in the Colony of New York, in America; To the Honourable The Knights, Citizens, and Burgesses, in Parliament Assembled. Read in the General Assembly of Said Colony, the 20th of April, 1764* [New York, 1764], Evans, 10101.

5. *WPB*, May 10, 1764; CC to Robert Charles, June 8, 1764, *CC Letter Books* 1:331. Also see Watts to Monckton, Apr. 14, 1764, *Watts Letter Book*, 242; and "S.F.V." to Printer, *New York Mercury*, Apr. 23, 1764, herein cited as *Mercury*.

6. *WPB*, May 3, 24, 1764.

7. Watts to Monckton, May 16, 1764, *Watts Letter Book*, 255; Lawrence Henry Gipson, "The American Revolution as an Aftermath of the Great War for the Empire," *Political Science Quarterly* 65 (1950): 86–104.

8. To Printer, *WPB*, Oct. 17, 1765.

9. Watts to Moses Franks, June 9, 1764, *Watts Letter Book*, 261–262; *Mercury*, Nov. 7, 1763; RRL to Robert Livingston, [June 15, 1764], Apr. 10, 1765, Robert R. Livingston Papers, Reel 1, NYHS (microfilm), herein cited as RRL Papers; William Smith, *Historical Memoirs of William Smith, Historian of the Province of New York, Member of the Governor's Council . . .*, ed. William H. W. Sabine, 2 vols. (New York, 1956–1958), 1:30, herein cited as Smith, *Memoirs*. For the Livingston family's long-term opposition to land taxes, see Robert A. Becker, *Revolution, Reform, and the Politics of American Taxation, 1763–1783* (Baton Rouge, 1980), chap. 2.

10. CC to Board of Trade, Sept. 20, 1764, *CC Letter Books* 1:361–364; Smith to Monckton, Apr. 13, 1764, Chalmers Collection. Also see [Goldsbrow Banyar] to [George Clarke], Sept. 21, 1764, Goldsbrow Banyar Papers, 1746–1820, NYHS; and RRL to R. Livingston, Apr. 10, 1765, RRL Papers, Reel 1.

11. William Livingston and Others, *The Independent Reflector*, ed. Milton M. Klein (Cambridge, Mass., 1963), 62; "A.B." to Printer, *WPB*, May 24, 1764. Also see the Assembly's Petition to the House of Lords, Oct. 18, 1764; *NYAJ*, Oct. 18, 1764.

12. The quote is from *Boston Evening Post*, Feb. 17, 1766. Roger J. Champagne, "The Sons of Liberty and the Aristocracy in New York Politics, 1765–1790" (Ph.D. diss., University of Wisconsin, 1960), 28; "Remarks on the Sundry Articles of News, and Prices relating to the British American Colonies, Publish'd in the Late English Papers," *WPB*, May 2, 1765. See To Printer, *Mercury*, Aug. 29, 1765; and "Sic Precanties Americante," *WPB*, Aug. 29, 1765, for a defense of New York's right to petition for a redress of grievances.

13. Edmund S. Morgan and Helen M. Morgan, *The Stamp Act Crisis: Prologue to Revolution*, rev. ed. (New York, 1963), 243; RRL to Monckton, Nov. 7, 1765, Thomas Aspinwall, ed., *Aspinwall Papers*, 2 vols. (Massachusetts Historical Society, *Collections*, 4th ser., vols. 9–10 [Boston, 1871]), 10:566–567, herein cited as *Aspinwall Papers*; RRL to John Sergant, Dec. 20, 1765, Livingston Family Papers, NYPL. For several reasons radicals had the advantage over moderates in all three crises. First, the mere existence of a method of coercion often becomes a compelling reason for its use, especially when a specific group will benefit from it. Second, a tactic like a demonstration or riot frequently spreads among groups and populations as if by contagion. When that happens, those opposed are usually powerless to stop it. Third, because groups generally follow historical precedent, the colonial tradition of crowd action, which Paul A. Gilje has ably documented for New York, justified rioting in 1765 and beyond. Louis Kriesberg, *Social Conflicts*, 2d ed. (Englewood Cliffs, N.J., 1982), 133, 148, 149; Paul A. Gilje, *The Road to Mobocracy: Popular Disorder in New York City, 1763–1834* (Chapel Hill, N.C., 1987), esp. pp. 3–68.

14. James McEvers to CC, [Aug. 1765], *The Letters and Papers of Cadwallader Colden*, 8 vols. (NYHS, *Collections*, vols. 50–56, 67 [New York, 1917–1923, 1937]), 7:56, herein cited as *CC Papers*; Champagne, "Sons of Liberty," 29; Peter Shaw, *American Patriots and the Rituals of Revolution* (Cambridge, Mass., 1981), 182.

15. CC to Sir William Johnson, Sept. 3, 1764, *CC Letter Books* 1:357.

16. *NYAJ*, Sept. 11, 1764; CC to Board of Trade, Sept. 20, 1764, *CC Letter Books* 1:361–364; Watts to Monckton, Sept. 22, 1764, *Watts Letter Book*, 290–292.

17. *NYAJ*, Oct. 18, 1764; Smith, *Memoirs*, 24; Bernhard Knollenberg, *Origins of the American Revolution, 1759–1766* (New York, 1960), 205.

18. William S. Sachs, "The Business Outlook in the Northern Colonies, 1750–

1775" (Ph.D. diss., Columbia University, 1957), 133; Virginia D. Harrington, *The New York Merchant on the Eve of the Revolution* (New York, 1935), 322–323; *Mercury*, Feb. 4, 1765; [Banyar] to Clarke, Aug. 10, 1765, Banyar Papers; Pomeroys and Hodgkins to John Keteltas, June 29, 1765, Keteltas Family Papers, 1694–1915, NYHS; Thomas Harris to James Beekman, Jan. 9, 1766, Philip L. White, ed., *The Beekman Mercantile Papers, 1746–1799*, 3 vols. (New York, 1956), 2:766–767; Francis Lewis to Horatio Gates, Dec. 10, 1764, Horatio Gates Papers, 1726–1828, Reel 1, NYHS (microfilm). The quote is from Harrington, *The New York Merchant*, 323.

19. *WPB*, Apr. 11, 1765; Peter D. G. Thomas, *British Politics and the Stamp Act Crisis: The First Phase of the American Revolution, 1763–1767* (Oxford, 1975), 86; Morgan and Morgan, *Stamp Act Crisis*, 96–98; "S.F.V." to Printer, *Mercury*, Apr. 23, 1764.

20. *Mercury*, Sept. 16, 1765.

21. Schlesinger, *Prelude to Independence: The Newspaper War on Britain, 1764–1776* (New York, 1958), 68. The fears about freedom of the press were well founded; in 1776 the ministry would try to silence its British critics by a stamp tax; Solomon Lutnick, *The American Revolution and the British Press, 1775–1783* (Columbia, Mo., 1967), 4.

22. To Printer, *WPB*, May 16, 1765.

23. *WPB*, June 13, July 11, 1765.

24. *WPB*, Apr. 11, 1765.

25. "G" to Printer, *WPB*, Nov. 7, 1765; Smith to Monckton, May 30, 1765, *Aspinwall Papers* 10:571. Charles refused to present the Assembly's petition to Parliament because it was "too warm assuming and tedious"; see Watts to Monckton, Apr. 15, 1765, *Watts Letter Book*, 346; Nicholas Varga, "Robert Charles: New York Agent, 1748–1770," *WMQ* 18 (1961): 231–232.

26. Champagne, "Sons of Liberty," 44; Watts to Monckton, Oct. 12, 1765, *Aspinwall Papers* 10:579.

27. First, a group's preference for a specific mode of conflict is related to the cost of using it. Since rioting might have ended not only in British retaliation but in property destruction, patricians wanted to keep a lid on the situation. Second, the greater the contact between partisans of two opposing camps and the greater the extent to which they have reciprocal relations relative to conflicting ones, the less chance there is that they will advocate violence as a tactic for pursuing conflict. Third, the higher a man's status, income, and education, the less disposed he generally is to the use of violence as a means to an end, for he has more options open to him to attain his objective. Kriesberg, *Social Conflicts*, 134–135, 137, 126–127.

28. "The Sentinel, VI, XXI," *WPB*, Apr. 4, July 18, 1765. The situation had become so volatile by the end of August that Livingston discontinued "The Sentinel" series, though he was criticized for doing so; *WPB*, Oct. 10, 30, 1765.

29. *WPB*, Oct. 10, 1765.

30. Milton M. Klein, *The American Whig: William Livingston of New York* (New York, 1990), 442–443; Champagne, "Sons of Liberty," 56–60.

31. *WPB*, Sept. 5, Oct. 5, 10, 1765. When "Publicus" argued that under the law "bonds, etc. not stamped, are still valid" and that readers should do business without stamps, Holt disputed that interpretation of the law; *WPB*, Oct. 17, 1765.

32. *WPB*, Aug. 1, Sept. 12, Nov. 7, 1765; *Mercury*, Oct. 28, Nov. 7, 1765; Dirk Hoerder, *Crowd Action in Revolutionary Massachusetts, 1765–1780* (New York, 1977), 122. Support for a boycott can also be found in *Mercury*, Aug. 29, 1765.

33. *WPB*, June 6, 13, 1765. "Freeman," too, had difficulty getting Holt to publish his letters; Watts to Monckton, June 8, 1765, *Watts Letter Book*, 357–358. A defense of crowd action, supposedly written by a New Yorker, appeared in the *The Boston Gazette, and Country Journal*, Dec. 2, 1765.

34. *WPB*, Aug. 22, Sept. 12, 1765; CC to Johnson, Aug. 31, CC to McEvers, Sept. 3, 1765, *CC Letter Books* 2:27–28; Klein, *American Whig*, 443–444; Hiller B. Zobel, *The Boston Massacre* (New York, 1970), 29–40. Leaders who have few ongoing contacts with an opponent tend to be more willing to use violence than those who interact frequently with the opposite side; Kriesberg, *Social Conflicts*, 132.

35. *The Constitutional Courant*, Sept. 21, 1765.

36. CC to Henry Conway, Oct. 12, 1765, *CC Letter Books* 2:45; Oliver De Lancey to Susan Warren, Jan. 10, 1766, Oliver De Lancey Papers, NYHS; Ward L. Miner, *William Goddard, Newspaperman* (Durham, N.C., 1962), 48–52. Also see Champagne, "Sons of Liberty," 55.

37. Robert J. Christen, *King Sears: Politician and Patriot in a Decade of Revolution* (New York, 1982), 49–50. Also see Carl Lotus Becker, *The History of Political Parties in the Province of New York, 1760–1776* (Madison, Wisc., 1909), 43, n. 80; and Herbert M. Morais, "The Sons of Liberty in New York," in Richard B. Morris, ed., *The Era of the American Revolution: Studies Inscribed to Evarts Boutell Greene* (New York, 1939), 269–289. Bernard Friedman suggested that "some sort of formal leadership was evidently at work prior to the rioting of November 1": Friedman, "The New York Assembly Elections of 1768 and 1769," *NYH* 46 (1965): 21, n. 14. The fact that the Liberty Boys had directed the opposition to the Stamp Act is clear from Sears to Holt, *NYJ*, May 10, 1770.

38. *WPB*, Dec. 27, 1765; *NYGWM*, Nov. 2, 1769; *Mercury*, Jan. 16, 1769; *NYJ*, Dec. 31, 1767, Oct. 21, 1773, Nov. 2, 1775; John Cruger, James De Lancey, Jacob Walton, and James Jauncey, *Whereas a Paper, Signed Philo Patriae, Appeared . . .* [New York, 1769], Evans, 11230.

39. *WPB*, Oct. 17, 31, 1765. A copy of "Vox Populi's" broadside can be found in CC to Conway, Oct. 26, 1765, CO 5/1098.

40. CC to Thomas Gage, July 8, 1765, *CC Letter Books* 2:23–24; Gage to CC, July 8, 1765, *CC Papers* 7:46. Also see F. L. Engleman, "Cadwallader Colden and the New York Stamp Act Riots," *WMQ* 10 (1953): 560–578.

41. Philip Livingston to William Nicoll, Aug. 26, 1765, Livingston Family Papers, NYPL; McEvers to CC, [Aug. 1765], *CC Papers* 7:56–57; CC to Capt. Archibald Kennedy, Sept. 23, CC to Johnson, Aug. 31, 1765, *CC Letter Books* 2:29, 27.

42. Gage to CC, Aug. 31, 1765, *CC Papers* 7:57–58, 59–62.

43. CC to Conway, Sept. 23, David Colden to Commissioners of the Stamp Office, Oct. 26, 1765, *CC Letter Books* 2:35, 51.

44. *WPB*, Oct. 24, 1765; *The Journals of Captain John Montresor*, ed. G. D. Scull (NYHS, *Collections*, 14 [New York, 1882]), 335–336, herein cited as *Montresor Journals*; CC to Conway, Oct. 26, 1765, *CC Letter Books* 2:48; Meeting of the Council, Oct. 24, 1765, *CC Papers* 7:63; RRL to Monckton, Nov. 8, 1765, *Aspinwall Papers* 10:559–560; Champagne, "Sons of Liberty," 60–61.

45. A Copy of "Vox Populi's" message was included in CC to Conway, Oct. 26, 1765, C.O. 5/1098; "Americanus" to Printer, *WPB*, Sept. 19, 1765; Watts to Monckton, Sept. 24, 1765, *Aspinwall Papers* 10:576.

46. Minutes of a Council Meeting, Oct. 31, 1765, *CC Papers* 7:64; RRL to Monckton, Nov. 8, 1765, *Aspinwall Papers* 10:559–567; *Montresor Journals*, 336.

47. Minutes of a Council Meeting, Nov. 2, A.M., Engineers Report on Means of Strengthening Fort George, Nov. 2, 1765, *CC Papers* 7:64–65, 87–88; William Gordon, *History of the Rise, Progress, and Establishment of Independence in the United States of America*, 4 vols. (London, 1788), 1:186.

48. This and the next paragraph are based on RRL to Monckton, Nov. 8, 1765, *Aspinwall Papers* 10:559–567.

49. *The Lieutenant Governor declares that he will do nothing in Relation to the Stamps . . .* [New York, 1765], Evans, 10096; Conway to CC, Dec. 15, 1765, *DCHNY* 7:97; Christen, *King Sears*, 45–47.

50. "Benevolus" to CC, [Nov. 3, 1765], *CC Papers* 7:88; RRL to Monckton, Nov. 8, 1765, *Aspinwall Papers* 10:559–567.

51. CC to the Marquis of Granby, Nov. 5, 1765, *CC Letter Books* 2:54.

52. CC to Conway, Nov. 5, 1765, *CC Letter Books* 2:55; Gage to Conway, Nov. 4, 1765, *Gage Correspondence* 1:70–71; *Montresor Journals*, 338.

53. CC to Board of Trade, Dec. 6, 1765, *CC Letter Books* 2:80–81; Neil R. Stout, "Captain Kennedy and the Stamp Act," *NYH* 45 (1964): 44–58.

54. Minutes of a Council Meeting, Nov. 5, 1765, *CC Papers* 7:67–68; CC to Maj. Thomas James, Nov. 6, 1765, *CC Letter Books* 2:58–59.

55. Gage to Conway, Nov. 8, 1765, Clarence Edwin Carter, ed., *The Correspondence of General Thomas Gage . . .*, 2 vols. (New Haven, 1931–1933), 1:72–73, herein cited as *Gage Correspondence*; CC to Gage, Nov. 5, 1765, *CC Letter Books* 2:56; Gage to CC, CC to the Mayor and Gentlemen of the Corporation, Nov. 5, 1765, *CC Papers* 7:69–71; Champagne, "Sons of Liberty," 76.

56. *Montresor Journals*, 339.

57. Watts to Monckton, Nov. 22, 1765, *Watts Letter Book*, 404.

58. *WPB*, Nov. 21, 1765; CC to Conway, Dec. 13, 1765, *CC Letter Books* 2:66–67; Sir Henry Moore to Conway, Nov. 21, 1765, *DCHNY* 7:789–799.

59. Moore to Conway, Dec. 21, 1765, *DCHNY* 7:802; Gage to Conway, Nov. 8, 1765, *Gage Correspondence* 1:73.

60. *WPB*, Oct. 17, 1765.

61. *WPB*, Nov. 28, 1765; *Mercury*, Dec. 10, 1765.

62. *WPB*, Dec. 27, 1765.

63. *WPB*, Nov. 28, 1765; Gordon, *History* 1:195; Christen, *King Sears*, 55; Morgan and Morgan, *Stamp Act Crisis*, 194.

64. *Mercury*, Dec. 7, 1765; RRL to R. Livingston, Nov. 20, 1765, Livingston Papers, 1755–1843, NYPL. Criminal cases were tried, since they did not require the use of stamps; Klein, "New York Lawyers and the Coming of the American Revolution," *NYH* 55 (1974): 399.

65. *NYJ*, May 10, 1770; *Mercury*, Dec. 9, 23, 1765; [Banyar] to Clarke, Dec. 21, 1765, Banyar Papers; "Philolutherus" to Holt, *WPB*, Dec. 27, 1765; David Clarkson to John Bennett, Dec. 28, 1765, "David Clarkson Letter Book, 1765–1786," NYHS (microfilm); Gage to Conway, Dec. 21, 1765, *Gage Correspondence* 1:78–79. Philadelphia's lawyers reopened that city's civil courts in December without stamps; Theodore Thayer, *Pennsylvania Politics and the Growth of Democracy, 1740–1776* (Harrisburg, 1953), 124. Boston's radicals were also more successful than those in New York; Zobel, *Boston Massacre*, 42–45; Hoerder, *Crowd Action in Massachusetts*, 126–128.

66. *NYJ*, May 10, 1770; Gilje, *Road to Mobocracy*, 5, 10; Patricia U. Bonomi, *A Factious People: Politics and Society in Colonial New York* (New York, 1971), 235–236; O. De Lancey to Susan Warren, Jan. 10, 1766, O. De Lancey Papers.

67. "Freeman," "An Address to the Inhabitants of New York," *WPB*, Dec. 19, 1765; RRL to R. Livingston, Nov. 20, 1765, Livingston Papers, 1755–1843, NYPL; [Banyar] to Clarke, Dec. 21, 1765, Banyar Papers.

68. Peter R. Livingston to Oliver Wendell, Dec. 2, 1765, Livingston Papers, Museum of the City of New York; [Banyar] to Clarke, Dec. 21, 1765, Banyar Papers; *Montresor Journals*, 342; Gage to Conway, Dec. 21, 1765, *Gage Correspondence* 1:78; *Mercury*, Dec. 23, 1765; Merrill Jensen, *The Founding of a Nation: A History of the American Revolution* (New York, 1969), 136. The port of Boston was opened without stamps on Dec. 17, 1765; Hoerder, *Crowd Action in Massachusetts*, 125.

69. *WPB*, Dec. 19, 27, 1765.

70. *Montresor Journals*, 343.

71. Gage to Conway, Dec. 21, 1765, *Gage Correspondence* 1:78; *Montresor Journals*, 343–344; Countryman, *People in Revolution*, 72–98.

4. The Aftermath

1. Philip Ranlet, *The New York Loyalists* (Knoxville, 1986), 10–12; the quote is from p. 12.

2. John Watts to Robert Monckton, Dec. 30, 1765, Thomas Aspinwall, ed., *Aspinwall Papers*, 2 vols. (Massachusetts Historical Society, *Collections*, 4th ser., vols. 9–10 [Boston, 1871]), 10:587, herein cited as *Aspinwall Papers*; *The Journals of Captain John Montresor*, ed. G. D. Scull (NYHS, *Collections*, 14 [New York, 1882]), 346, herein cited as *Montresor Journals*. Also see [Goldsbrow Banyar] to Gedney Clarke, Feb. 22, 1766, Goldsbrow Banyar Papers, 1746–1820, NYHS; and Roger J. Champagne, *Alexander McDougall and the American Revolution* (Syracuse, 1975), 13. Concerning the symbolic significance of Montresor's depiction of these demonstrators, see Peter Shaw, *American Patriots and the Rituals of Revolution* (Cambridge, Mass., 1981), chap. 8, esp. p. 191.

3. *DHSNY* 3:299–300; *New York Mercury*, Dec. 16, 1765, herein cited as *Mercury*.

4. Watts to William Barker, Nov. 22, 1765, *Letter Book of John Watts, Merchant and Councillor of New York, January 1, 1762 – December 22, 1765* (NYHS, *Collections*, 41 [New York, 1928]), 403, herein cited as *Watts Letter Book*; *WPB*, Nov. 28, Dec. 5, 1765; *Weyman's New York Gazette*, Dec. 2, 1765, herein cited as *Weyman's*; *Mercury*, Dec. 2, 9, 1765; Champagne, "The Sons of Liberty and the Aristocracy in New York Politics, 1765–1790" (Ph.D. diss., University of Wisconsin, 1960), 96. *Montresor Journals*, 340; the quote is from p. 342.

5. *Mercury*, Jan. 13, 1766; Gov. Henry Moore to Lord Dartmouth, Jan. 16, 1766, *DCHNY* 7:807; *Montresor Journals*, 345–346, 348.

6. *Montresor Journals*, 347–350; the quote is from p. 349. *Mercury*, Feb. 17, 1766; *WPB*, Feb. 20, 1766; Edmund S. Morgan and Helen M. Morgan, *The Stamp Act Crisis: Prologue to Revolution*, rev. ed. (New York, 1963), 250–251; Ranlet, *New York Loyalists*, 22–23. For Allicocke's career, see Donald A. Grinde, Jr., "Joseph Allicocke: African-American Leader of the Sons of Liberty," *Afro-Americans in New York History and Life* 14 (1990): 61–69.

7. *Montresor Journals*, 350–353; the quote is from p. 352. *Mercury*, Mar. 10, 1766; David Clarkson to friend, Mar. 15, 1766, "David Clarkson Letter Book, 1765–1786," NYHS (microfilm).

8. *Montresor Journals*, 353–355; *Weyman's*, Mar. 30, 1766; *Mercury*, Mar. 24, 1766; *WPB*, Mar. 20, 1766; Champagne, "Sons of Liberty," 106. The quote is from a Deposi-

tion by Sears before John Bogart, Mar. 20, 1766, John Lamb Papers, 1735–1800, NYHS.

9. *Montresor Journals,* 356, 357.

10. *Montresor Journals,* 360; *Mercury,* Apr. 28, 1766.

11. Champagne, "Sons of Liberty," 106–107; *Mercury,* Mar. 10, 17, 1766; Gen. Thomas Gage to Henry Conway, Feb. 22, 1766, Clarence Edwin Carter, ed., *The Correspondence of General Thomas Gage . . .,* 2 vols. (New Haven, 1931–1933), 1:84, herein cited as *Gage Correspondence;* Moore to Dartmouth, Moore to Conway, Nov. 21, 1765, Moore to Dartmouth, Jan. 16, 1766, *DCHNY* 7:789, 807; Watts to James Napier, Nov. 7, 1765, *Watts Letter Book,* 398; RRL to Robert Livingston, [Feb. 18, 1766], Robert R. Livingston Papers, Reel 1, NYHS (microfilm); R R. Livingston to R. Livingston, Nov. 20, 1765, R. Livingston to RRL, Jan. 11, 1766, Livingston Family Papers, NYPL.

12. Oliver De Lancey to Susan Warren, Jan. 10, 1766, Oliver De Lancey Papers, NYHS; RRL to Monckton, Nov. 8, 1765, *Aspinwall Papers* 10:566. Alexander Colden to CC, n.d., *The Letters and Papers of Cadwallader Colden,* 8 vols. (NYHS, *Collections,* vols. 50–56, 67 [New York, 1917–1923, 1937]), 7:94; for the dating of this letter, see Ranlet, *New York Loyalists,* 200–201, n. 13.

13. See Louis Kriesberg, *Social Conflicts,* 2d ed. (Englewood Cliffs, N.J., 1982), 237, 306, 309.

14. CC to Board of Trade, Dec. 6, 1765, *The Colden Letter Books,* 2 vols. (NYHS, *Collections,* vols. 9–10 [New York, 1877–1878]), 2:79, herein cited as *CC Letter Books;* Moore to Conway, Feb. 20, 1766, *DCHNY* 7:810.

15. Gage to Conway, Jan. 16, Feb. 22, Gage to Lord Barrington, Jan. 16, May 7, 1766, *Gage Correspondence* 1:81–82, 84, 2:334, 351; Moore to Conway, Feb. 20, 1766, *DCHNY* 7:810.

16. *Montresor Journals,* 346, 354, 378, 374; Frederick Haldimand to Gage, Oct. 4, 1773, Sir Frederick Haldimand Papers, Additional Manuscripts, No. 21665, British Museum, London.

17. CC to Conway, Nov. 9, Dec. 13, 1765, *CC Letter Books* 2:61, 66.

18. John Shy, *Toward Lexington: The Role of the British Army in the Coming of the American Revolution* (Princeton, N.J., 1965), 213, 215–216; Kriesberg, *Social Conflicts,* 125. The quote is from Paul A. Gilje, *The Road to Mobocracy: Popular Disorder in New York City, 1763–1834* (Chapel Hill, N.C., 1987), vii.

19. Moore to Lord Hillsborough, May 9, 1768, *DCHNY* 8:67–68. The first quote is from "The Conduct of Cadwallader Colden, Esquire, Late Lieutenant-Governor of New York: Relating to The Judges Commissions, Appeals to the King, and the Stamp-Duty," *CC Letter Books* 2:465. The second and third are from Clarkson to friend, Nov. 23, 1765, Clarkson to Sir John Biddle, Nov. 11, 1766, "Clarkson Letter Book," MS, NYHS.

20. *Weyman's,* Dec. 2, 1765; *Montresor Journals,* 349.

21. CC to Conway, Dec. 13, 1765, *CC Letter Books* 2:66–67; *Montresor Journals,* 344; Moore to Board of Trade, July 15, 1766, Treasury 1/452, Public Record Office, London.

22. *Mercury,* Dec. 2, 1765. The resolves are available in Edmund S. Morgan, ed., *Prologue to Revolution: Sources and Documents on the Stamp Act Crisis, 1764–1766* (Chapel Hill, N.C., 1959), 60–62.

23. Jack M. Sosin, *Agents and Merchants: British Colonial Policy and the Origins of the American Revolution, 1763–1775* (Lincoln, Nebr., 1965), 34–36. Shy, *Toward Lexington,* 178–190; the quote is from p. 188.

24. The Assembly offered £400 to buy firewood and candles for the troops garrisoned at Fort George. Gage to Moore, Dec. 1, 1765, *Gage Correspondence* 1:16–77; *NYAJ*, Dec. 3, 13, 1765; *Mercury*, Dec. 9, 1765; *Weyman's*, Dec. 12, 1765; Gage to Conway, Dec. 21, 1765, Gage to Barrington, Feb. 21, 1766, *Gage Correspondence* 1:76–77, 2:328–329; Lee E. Olm, "The Mutiny Act for America: New York's Noncompliance," *NYHSQ* 57 (1974): 197.

25. For historians who belong to the first group, see Irving Mark, *Agrarian Conflicts in Colonial New York, 1711–1775* (New York, 1940), 65–66, 72, 195; Staughton Lynd, *Anti-Federalism in Dutchess County, New York: A Study of Democracy and Class Conflict in the Revolutionary Era* (Chicago, 1962), 37–54; and Edward Countryman, *A People in Revolution: The American Revolution and Political Society in New York, 1760–1790* (Baltimore, 1981), 47–55. For historians in the second group, see Patricia U. Bonomi, *A Factious People: Politics and Society in Colonial New York* (New York, 1971), 218–224; and Sung Bok Kim, *Landlord and Tenant in Colonial New York: Manorial Society, 1664–1775* (Chapel Hill, N.C., 1977), 346–415.

26. Moore to Conway, Apr. 30, 1766, *DCHNY* 7:825; *Montresor Journals*, 363; "A Son of Liberty," *To the Public* [New York, 1766], Evans, 41592.

27. Thomas Jones, *History of New York during the Revolutionary War, and of the Leading Events in the Other Colonies at That Period*, ed. Edward Floyd De Lancey, 2 vols. (New York, 1879), 2:340–343, 1:24–26. Concerning Lamb's father, see Carl and Jessica Bridenbaugh, *Rebels and Gentlemen: Philadelphia in the Age of Franklin* (New York, 1942), 38.

28. See "Freeman," "Liberty, Property, and No Stamps," *Mercury*, Dec. 23, 1765, and "A Son of Liberty," *WPB*, Dec. 26, 1765, for two anonymous pleas for unity.

29. See Joseph S. Tiedemann, "A Revolution Foiled: Queens County, New York, 1775–1776," *JAH* 75 (1988): 420.

30. See "Freeman," *WPB*, June 6, 13, 1765; and *The Constitutional Courant*, Sept. 21, 1765.

31. Revealing hints about the organization the Liberty Boys formed can be found in Joseph Allicocke to [John Lamb], Nov. 21, 1765, Lamb Papers.

32. The standard account of this meeting and what followed is Champagne, "The Military Association of the Sons of Liberty," *NYHSQ* 41 (1957): 338–350. Champagne believed the meeting took place on December 25. "Philolutherus" to John Holt, *WPB*, Dec. 27, 1765; *Mercury*, Dec. 16, 1765. William Gordon, *History of the Rise, Progress, and Establishment of Independence in the United States of America*, 4 vols. (London, 1788), 1:195–199; the quote is from p. 197. Francis Bernard to Conway, Jan. 19, 1766, *The Fitch Papers* (Connecticut Historical Society, *Collections*, 18 [Hartford, 1920]), 384–386.

33. Morgan and Morgan, *Stamp Act Crisis*, 258. Kriesberg, *Social Conflicts*, 292–294, 125; for the factors causing a conflict's escalation, see pp. 166–174.

34. *WPB*, Jan. 9, 1766.

35. "Americanus" to Holt, *NYJ*, June 14, 1770; O. De Lancey to S. Warren, Jan. 10, 1766, O. De Lancey Papers.

36. *WPB*, Feb. 6, 1766; Gordon, *History* 1:186–187; Robert J. Christen, *King Sears: Politician and Patriot in a Decade of Revolution* (New York, 1982), 74–75, 90, n. 26; Carl Bridenbaugh, *Cities in Revolt: Urban Life in America, 1743–1776* (New York, 1955), 188, 202–203.

37. *WPB*, Feb. 20, 1766; Sons of Liberty in New York to Sons of Liberty [in Lyme,

Connecticut], Feb. 20, 1766, Lamb Papers; Champagne, "Military Association of the Sons of Liberty," *NYHSQ* 41 (1957): 344–348.

38. New York Sons of Liberty to Boston Sons of Liberty, Apr. 2, 1766, Lamb Papers; Morgan and Morgan, *Stamp Act Crisis*, 260.

39. Conway to Gage, Oct. 24, 1765, Gage to Barrington, Jan. 16, 1766, *Gage Correspondence* 2:28, 334–335; Kriesberg, *Social Conflicts*, 241.

40. Memorandum by the King, [Feb. 11, 1766], John W. Fortescue, ed., *The Correspondence of King George the Third . . .*, 6 vols. (London, 1927–1928) 1:269; [Narrative by Lord Barrington], May 10, 1766, England and America, George Bancroft Collection, NYHS; Conway to Gage, May 20, 1766, *Gage Correspondence* 2:37; Sosin, *Agents and Merchants*, 67, 78, 80.

41. *Montresor Journals*, 362, 367, 368, 369; the quote is from p. 368. *Mercury*, May 26, 1766; Champagne, "Sons of Liberty," 110. For a different viewpoint, see Countryman, *People in Revolution*, 72–98.

42. See New York Sons of Liberty to Albany Sons of Liberty, May 31, 1766, [New York, 1766], Broadside Collection, NYHS.

43. Gage to Monckton, Sept. 28, 1765, *Gage Correspondence* 2:304; Watts to Monckton, Nov. 9, 1765, *Watts Letter Book*, 400; Clarkson to friend, June 28, 1766, "Clarkson Letter Book," MS.; "Cethegus" to Printer, *WPB*, Oct. 8, 1770.

44. Kriesberg, *Social Conflicts*, 213–217; the quote is from p. 213.

45. Merrill Jensen, ed., *American Colonial Documents to 1776* (London, 1955), 695–696; Peter D. G. Thomas, *British Politics and the Stamp Act Crisis: The First Phase of the American Revolution, 1763–1767* (Oxford, 1975), 184, 238–240; Edmund S. Morgan, "Colonial Ideas of Parliamentary Power, 1764–1766," *WMQ* 5 (1948): 311–341. The quote of the attorney general is from Morgan and Morgan, *Stamp Act Crisis*, 347–348.

46. Alison G. Olson, "The Board of Trade and London-American Interest Groups in the Eighteenth Century," in Peter Marshall and Glyn Williams, eds., *The British-Atlantic Empire before the American Revolution* (London, 1980), 45. Also see Jensen, *The Founding of a Nation: A History of the American Revolution* (New York, 1969), 317–322.

47. Robert M. Calhoon, "William Smith, Jr.'s Alternative to the American Revolution," *WMQ* 22 (1965): 105–118; the quotes are on pp. 113, 112, 114, 115. Smith was not the only New Yorker to recommend an American Parliament; see "Americanus," *WPB*, Aug. 15, 1765; and Watts to Monckton, Nov. 9, 1765, *Watts Letter Book*, 400–401.

48. Kriesberg, *Social Conflicts*, 68, 87, 94, 100.

5. Conflict Anew

1. Henry Conway to Governors in America, Mar. 31, 1766, *DCHNY* 7:823–824; Duke of Richmond to Gov. Henry Moore, June 12, 1766, Additional Manuscripts, No. 12440, British Museum, London; Merrill Jensen, ed., *American Colonial Documents to 1776* (London, 1955), 696–698.

2. Jack M. Sosin, *Agents and Merchants: British Colonial Policy and the Origins of the American Revolution, 1763–1775* (Lincoln, Nebr., 1965), 81–86; Peter D. G. Thomas, *British Politics and the Stamp Act Crisis: The First Phase of the American Revolution, 1763–1767* (Oxford, 1975), 257–273.

3. Moore to Board of Trade, Mar. 28, "Representation of Lords of Trade on the Circulation of Bills of Credit," May 16, 1766, *DCHNY* 7:820–821, 827–828; Great Britain, Commissioners for Trade and Plantations, *Journal of the Commissioners for Trade and Plantation*, 14 vols. (London, 1920–1938), 12:280, 292; Charles Z. Lincoln, ed.,

Messages from the Governors, Comprising Executive Communications to the Legislature and Other Papers Relating to Legislation . . ., 11 vols. (Albany, 1909), 1:715–716; Joseph Albert Ernst, "The Currency Act Repeal Movement: A Study of Imperial Politics and the Revolutionary Crises, 1764–1767," *WMQ* 25 (1968): 177–211.

4. *WPB*, June 19, 23, 1766; Jensen, *The Founding of a Nation: A History of the American Revolution* (New York, 1969), 220; Lawrence Henry Gipson, *The Coming of the Revolution* (New York, 1954), 170; Sir Lewis Namier and John Brooke, *Charles Townshend* (London, 1964), 37–41, 172-179; Sosin, *Agents and Merchants*, 101, n. 21. Robert J. Chaffin, "The Townshend Acts of 1767," *WMQ* 27 (1970): 90–121; the quote is from p. 94.

5. *WPB*, May 8, 15, 1766.

6. "Petition of the Merchants of the City of New York, Addressed to the House of Commons," [Nov. 28, 1766], *New York Mercury*, Apr. 27, 1767, May 26, 1766, herein cited as *Mercury*; Robert J. Christen, *King Sears: Politician and Patriot in a Decade of Revolution* (New York, 1982), 105–106.

7. Earl of Chatham to Lord Shelburne, Feb. 3, 1767, W. S. Taylor and J. H. Pringle, eds., *Correspondence of William Pitt, Earl of Chatham*, 4 vols. (London, 1838–1840), 3:188–89; Shelburne to Moore, Feb. 20, 1767, C.O. 5/1098; Louis Kriesberg, *Social Conflicts*, 2d ed. (Englewood Cliffs, N.J., 1982), 66, 166.

8. John and Henry Cruger to Moses Franks, Apr. 22, 1767, "John and Henry Cruger Letter Book, June 1766 – August 1767," BV Cruger, NYHS; John Watts to Robert Monckton, Apr. 30, 1767, Chalmers Collection, NYPL; Christen, *King Sears*, 107.

9. Thomas, *British Politics*, 342–344; Sosin, *Agents and Merchants*, 100; Chaffin, "Townshend Acts," *WMQ* 27 (1970): 91–93; Shelburne to Gen. Thomas Gage, Dec. 11, 1766, Clarence Edwin Carter, ed., *The Correspondence of General Thomas Gage* . . ., 2 vols. (New Haven, 1931-1933), 2:47–51, herein cited as *Gage Correspondence*; Shelburne to Chatham, Feb. 1, 1766, Taylor and Pringle, eds., *Correspondence of Chatham* 3:182–188. The quotes are from William Samuel Johnson to William Pitkin, May 16, 1767, *Jonathan Trumbull Papers* (Massachusetts Historical Society, *Collections*, 5th ser., 9 [Boston, 1885]), 229, 230.

10. Thomas C. Barrow, *Trade and Empire: The British Customs Service in Colonial America, 1660-1775* (Cambridge, Mass., 1967), 226; Robert Middlekauff, *The Glorious Cause: The American Revolution, 1763–1789* (New York, 1982), 146–152.

11. Quoted in Jack P. Greene, "The Seven Years' War," in Peter Marshall and Glyn Williams, eds., *The British-Atlantic Empire before the American Revolution* (London, 1980), 94. For civil-military violence in another city, see Hiller B. Zobel, *The Boston Massacre* (New York, 1970); and Dirk Hoerder, *Crowd Action in Revolutionary Massachusetts, 1765–1780* (New York, 1977), chap. 8.

12. Kriesberg, *Social Conflicts*, 94, 95, 100.

13. Gage to Conway, Feb. 22, Mar. 28, Gage to Lord Barrington, May 7, 1766, *Gage Correspondence* 1:84, 87, 351; the quote is from p. 351.

14. Alan Rogers, *Empire and Liberty: American Resistance to British Authority, 1755–1763* (Berkeley, 1974), ix, 62; Kriesberg, *Social Conflicts*, 143.

15. Isaac N. Phelps Stokes, *The Iconography of Manhattan Island, 1498–1905*, 6 vols. (New York, 1915), 4:767; Moore to Richmond, Aug. 23, 1766, *DCHNY* 7:867; *The Journals of Captain John Montresor*, ed. G. D. Scull (NYHS, *Collections*, 14 [New York, 1882]), 378, herein cited as *Montresor Journals*; *WPB*, July 17, 1766.

16. *NYJ*, Nov. 6, 13, 1766. For examples, see *Mercury*, Oct. 27, 1766; *Weyman's New*

York Gazette, Nov. 17, 1766; *NYJ,* Nov. 13, 1766, Apr. 9, Sept. 3, 1767, Feb. 4, 1768, Aug. 31, 1769; and *WPB,* June 25, 1767.

17. Moore to Richmond, Aug. 23, 1766, *DCHNY* 7:867; *Montresor Journals,* 382; *WPB,* Aug. 14, 1766; *Mercury,* Aug. 25, 1766; Paul A. Gilje, *The Road to Mobocracy: Popular Disorder in New York City, 1763–1834* (Chapel Hill, N.C., 1987), 52–58; Roger J. Champagne, "The Sons of Liberty and the Aristocracy in New York Politics, 1765–1790" (Ph.D. diss., University of Wisconsin, 1960), 121–122.

18. *WPB,* Aug. 14, 1766; see *Mercury,* Apr. 13, 1767, for the fears New Yorkers had that the army was being used to keep them in line.

19. *Montresor Journals,* 382, 383.

20. *Mercury,* Aug. 25, 1766; Gage to Richmond, Aug. 26, 1766, *Gage Correspondence* 1:103.

21. *Montresor Journals,* 383–384; Gage to Richmond, Aug. 26, 1766, Gage to Shelburne, Jan. 17, 1767, *Gage Correspondence* 1:103–104, 118; Moore to Richmond, Aug. 23, 1766, *DCHNY* 7:867.

22. Moore to Richmond, Aug. 23, 1766, *DCHNY* 7:868; *WPB,* Sept. 25, 1766. The same economic calculations influenced communities in New Jersey and Massachusetts in their dealings with the military; Larry R. Gerlach, *Prologue to Independence: New Jersey in the Coming of the American Revolution* (New Brunswick, N.J., 1976), 74–75; Hoerder, *Crowd Action in Massachusetts,* 183, 194.

23. *WPB,* Mar. 19, 26, 1767; *Mercury,* Mar. 30, 1766, Mar. 9, 1767; Christen, *King Sears,* 117–118.

24. *WPB,* Aug. 20, 1767; RRL to Robert Livingston, Sept. 18, 1767, Robert R. Livingston Papers, Reel 1, NYHS (microfilm); *NYJ,* Oct. 6, 1768; Thomas Whately to George Grenville, Oct. 28, 1768, William James Smith, ed., *The Grenville Papers: Being the Correspondence of Richard Grenville, Earl Temple, K.G., and the Right Honorable George Grenville, Their Friends and Contemporaries* (London, 1853), 4:391.

25. Moore to Shelburne, Mar. 5, 1768, *DCHNY* 8:15–19. Gage to Amherst, Mar. 19, Gage to Barrington, Mar. 28, 1768, *Gage Correspondence* 2:455–458; the quote is from p. 457.

26. *Montresor Journals,* 370–371; Gage to Barrington, Sept. 10, 1768, *Gage Correspondence* 2:487; John Maunsell to Horatio Gates, May 15, 1767, Gates Papers, 1726–1828, Reel 1, NYHS (microfilm). Moore to Lord Hillsborough, Aug. 19, 1768, *DCHNY* 8:97–99; the quote is from p. 98. For the 1760 Order in Council, see "British Headquarters Orderly Book, New York City, 1766–1768," MS, Feb. 22, 1768, NYHS.

27. Moore to Shelburne, Mar. 5, 1768, *DCHNY* 8:16.

28. Moore to Shelburne, Mar. 5, 1768, *DCHNY* 8:15–19; Gage to Barrington, Sept. 10, 1768, *Gage Correspondence* 2:487; *Montresor Journals,* 351, 352, 353, 365, 369.

29. Gage to Richmond, Aug. 26, 1766, *Gage Correspondence* 1:104; *Montresor Journals,* 346, 351, 354, 369.

30. Hillsborough to Moore, May 14, 1768, *DCHNY* 8:73; Hillsborough to Gage, Aug. 4, 1770, Gage to Barrington, Feb. 4, July 1, 1772, *Gage Correspondence* 2:111–113, 599, 611; New York, June 6, 1768, *Pennsylvania Journal,* June 9, 1768; Tryon to Lord Dartmouth, Mar. 29, Sept. 7, 1775, C.O. 5/1106; Paul David Nelson, *William Tryon and the Course of Empire: A Life in British Imperial Service* (Chapel Hill, N.C., 1990), 99–100.

31. Worthington C. Ford et al., eds., *Journals of the Continental Congress, 1774–1789,* 34 vols. (Washington, D.C., 1904–1937), 1:116.

32. John Shy, *Toward Lexington: The Role of the British Army in the Coming of the Ameri-*

can Revolution (Princeton, N.J., 1965), 422. Also see Clarence E. Carter, "The Significance of the Military Office in America, 1763-1775," *AHR* 38 (1923): 487; and Gage to Shelburne, Apr. 3, 1767, *Gage Correspondence* 1:126–127.

33. Watts to William Baker, Mar. 30, Watts to Monckton, Apr. 16, 1765, *Letter Book of John Watts, Merchant and Councillor of New York, January 1, 1762 – December 22, 1765* (NYHS, *Collections*, 41 [New York, 1928]), 341, 346; Moore to Board of Trade, Mar. 28, "Representation of Lords of Trade on the Circulation of Bills of Credit," May 16, Board of Trade to Moore, July 11, 1766, *DCHNY* 7:820–821, 827–828, 844; Great Britain, Commissioners for Trade and Plantations, *Journal* 12:280, 292; Lincoln, ed., *Messages from the Governors* 1:715–716; Nicholas Varga, "Robert Charles: New York Agent, 1748–1770," *WMQ* 18 (1961): 231-232. For the role of the Currency Act in colonial politics, see Ernst, *Money and Politics in America, 1755-1775: A Study in the Currency Act of 1764 and the Political Economy of Revolution* (Chapel Hill, N.C., 1973).

34. *NYAJ*, Nov. 13, 1766; James Duane to Colo [R.] Livingston, Nov. 15, Peter R. Livingston to R. Livingston, Nov. 24, 1766, Livingston Family Papers, Johnson Redmond Collection, Reel 6, NYHS (microfilm); *Mercury*, July 14, 1766; Petition of the General Assembly to the House of Commons, Dec. 11, 1766, C.O. 5/1098.

35. *NYJ*, Nov. 19, Dec. 17, 1767.

36. James Beekman to Samuel and Thomas Fludyer, Nov. 26, 1766, Beekman to Pomeroys and Hodgkin, Sept. 24, 1767, Philip L. White, ed., *The Beekman Mercantile Papers, 1746–1799*, 3 vols. (New York, 1956), 2:708, 913.

37. *NYJ*, Dec. 17, 1767. Also see "Philaretes," *Mercury*, Dec. 7, 1767.

38. "To the Printer," *NYJ*, Feb. 4, 1768; *NYGWM*, Feb. 22, 1768.

39. *NYJ*, Dec. 24, 31, 1767, Jan. 14, Feb. 4, 1768; *NYGWM*, Jan. 4, 25, Feb. 1, 1768.

40. *WPB*, Sept. 24, 1767. For an account of this affair and its implications, see Ernst, *Money and Politics*, 258. Also see Watts to Monckton, Jan. 23, 1768, Thomas Aspinwall, ed., *Aspinwall Papers*, 2 vols. (Massachusetts Historical Society, *Collections*, 4th ser., vols. 9–10 [Boston, 1871]), 10:599, herein cited as *Aspinwall Papers*; and David Clarkson to Thomas Streatfield, Feb. 6, 1768, "David Clarkson Letter Book, 1765–1786," NYHS (microfilm).

41. Moore to Shelburne, Jan. 3, Hillsborough to Moore, Feb. 25, July 9, Oct. 12, Moore to Hillsborough, May 14, Aug. 18, 1768, *DCHNY* 8:1, 13, 82, 72, 96, 101; Ernst, *Money and Politics*, 250, 254.

42. Edward Countryman, *A People in Revolution: The American Revolution and Political Society in New York, 1760–1790* (Baltimore, 1981), 78; Patricia U. Bonomi, *A Factious People: Politics and Society in Colonial New York* (New York, 1971), 230.

43. *NYAJ*, Dec. 3, 5, 13, 1765; Gage to Conway, May 6, Gage to Richmond, Aug. 25, 1766, *Gage Correspondence* 1:89, 101. For the role of the Quartering Act in New York politics, see Lee E. Olm, "The Mutiny Act for America: New York's Noncompliance," *NYHSQ* 57 (1974): 188-214.

44. Gage to Conway, June 24, 1766, *Gage Correspondence* 1:95; William Smith, *Historical Memoirs of William Smith, Historian of the Province of New York . . .*, ed. William H. W. Sabine, 2 vols. (New York, 1956–1958), 1:33, herein cited as Smith, *Memoirs*.

45. *NYAJ*, June 13, 19, 1766. Moore to Conway, June 20, 1766, *DCHNY* 7:831; the quote is from *Montresor Journals*, 373.

46. *NYAJ*, June 19, 1766.

47. Smith, *Memoirs* 1:33; Gage to Richmond, Aug. 25, 1766, *Gage Correspondence* 1:101; *NYAJ*, June 20, 23, 1766; Moore to Conway, June 20, 1766, *DCHNY* 7:831.

48. Shelburne to Moore, Aug. 9, Moore to Shelburne, Dec. 19, 1766, *DCHNY* 7:848, 884; *NYAJ*, Nov. 17, 18, 1766; Petition of the New York General Assembly to Governor Moore, Dec. 15, 1766, C.O. 5/1098.

49. *NYAJ*, Dec. 19, 1766.

50. Moore to Shelburne, Aug. 21, 1767, *DCHNY* 7:948–949; Gage to Shelburne, Aug. 31, 1767, *Gage Correspondence* 1:150; *Mercury*, Apr. 13, 20, 1767; *NYJ*, Apr. 16, 1767; *WPB*, Apr. 16, 1767; Gipson, *Coming of the Revolution*, 133; Champagne, "Sons of Liberty," 144.

51. Gage to Barrington, Gage to Shelburne, Jan. 17, 1767, *Gage Correspondence* 2:406, 1:118–119; Shelburne to Moore, Feb. 20, 1767, *DCHNY* 7:900-905; William L. Grant and James Munro, eds., *Acts of the Privy Council of England: Colonial Series, 1766–1783* (London, 1912), 444. Townshend probably proposed that the New York Assembly be suspended; see Jensen, *Founding of a Nation*, 225, n. 28; and Namier and Brooke, *Townshend*, 176–177. Thomas, *British Politics*, 308–309, 322–323.

52. Jensen, *Founding of a Nation*, 227; William Cobbett and Thomas C. Hansard, eds., *The Parliamentary History of England from the Earliest Period to the Year 1803*, 36 vols. (London, 1806–1820), 16:336. Also see Varga, "The New York Restraining Act: Its Passage and Some Effects, 1766-1768," *NYH* 37 (1956): 233–258.

53. *NYAJ*, Dec. 9, 1766. CC to Peter Collinson, Nov. 10, CC to William Nichol, Dec. 1, CC to Shelburne, Dec. 21, 1766, CC to Amherst, n.d., *The Colden Letter Books*, 2 vols. (NYHS, *Collections*, vols. 9–10 [New York, 1877–1878]), 2:119-121, 121–122, 122–124, 124–126; for the pamphlet, see pp. 429–467. Champagne, "Sons of Liberty," 129; Moore to Dartmouth, Apr. 30, Shelburne to Moore, Dec. 11, 1766, Moore to Shelburne, Feb. 20, Dec. 29, 1767, *DCHNY* 7:826-827, 880, 900, 1006.

54. Moore to Shelburne, Aug. 21, Oct. 5, Dec. 29, 1767, *DCHNY* 7:949, 980, 1006.

55. "To the Freeholders and Freemen and Inhabitants of the City and Province of New York," *NYJ*, Supplement, Mar. 8, 1770. The article also provides a history of New York's efforts to evade the Quartering Act. Moore to Shelburne, Dec. 29, 1767, *DCHNY* 7:1006. For a historian who stresses opportunism, see Roger J. Champagne, "Family Politics versus Constitutional Principles: The New York Assembly Elections of 1768 and 1769," *WMQ* 20 (1963): 59.

56. Jensen, *Founding of a Nation*, 245; *NYJ*, Sept. 10, Oct. 2, 29, Nov. 5, 12, 19, 26, 1767. The first quote is from Watts to Monckton, Jan. 23, 1768, *Aspinwall Papers* 10:600; and the rest are from "Sui Imperator" to Edes and Gill and "A. F." to Edes and Gill, *NYJ*, Sept. 10, 1767.

57. See "Britano Americus," *NYJ*, Oct. 27, 1767, for a defense of American rights.

6. Urban Politics and the Imperial Crisis

1. *NYJ*, May 10, 1770; William Smith, *Historical Memoirs of William Smith, Historian of the Province of New York, Member of the Governor's Council . . .*, ed. William H. W. Sabine, 2 vols. (New York, 1956–1958), 1:33, herein cited as Smith, *Memoirs*; John Watts to Robert Monckton, Jan. 23, 1768, Thomas Aspinwall, ed., *Aspinwall Papers*, 2 vols. (Massachusetts Historical Society, *Collections*, 4th ser., vols. 9–10 [Boston, 1871]), 10:559.

2. *NYGWM*, Feb. 15, 1768; *NYJ*, Feb. 18, 1768. For the 1768 election, see Patricia U. Bonomi, "Political Patterns in Colonial New York City: The General Assembly Election of 1768," *Political Science Quarterly* 81 (1966): 432–447; Bernard Friedman, "The New York Assembly Elections of 1768 and 1769," *NYH* 46 (1965): 3–24. William Bayard, a wealthy, elderly merchant who had been in the Assembly since 1761, and

Amos Dodge, a carpenter, also ran, but neither candidate was taken seriously or gained many votes.

3. For the De Lancey argument, see *A Card*, Feb. 20, 1768 [New York, 1768], Evans, 10848; "To the Freemen and Freeholders of the City and County of New York," *NYJ*, Supplement, Feb. 20, 1768; *A Card* [New York, 1768], Evans, 10849; "John A Noyes, Versus Tom A Stiles," No. III, *NYJ*, Supplement, Mar. 4, 1768; *The Voter's New Cathecism* [New York, 1768], Evans, 11108; *A Portrait, and a Dialogue between Two Respectable Personages* [New York, 1768], Evans, 11048; *Merchants' Hall* [New York, 1768], Evans, 10974. The quote is from "Philanthropos," "To the Freeholders and Freemen of the City and County of New York," *NYJ*, Supplement, Feb. 25, 1768.

4. *To the Freemen and Freeholders of the City and County of New York* [New York, 1768], Evans, 11088; "To the Freemen and Freeholders of the City and County of New York; John A Nokes versus Tom A Stiles," *NYJ*, Feb. 25, 1768. For the Livingston defense, see "From Parker's *New-York Gazette*" [New York, 1768], Evans, 10908; "A Freeman," "To the Freeholders and Freemen of the City of New York," *NYJ*, Supplement, Feb. 20, 1768; and *To the Freeholders and Freemen of the City and County of New York* [New York, 1768], Evans, 41892.

5. "Philanthropos," "To the Freeholders and Freemen of the City and County of New York," *NYJ*, Supplement, Feb. 25, 1768; *The Voter's New Cathecism* [New York, 1768], Evans, 11108; *A Word of Advice* [New York, 1768], Evans, 11125; *To the Freemen and Freeholders of the City and County of New York* [New York, 1768], Evans, 11088. For Scott's defense, see "A Freeman," "To the Freeholders and Freemen of the City of New York," *NYJ*, Feb. 20, 1768; and *A Political Creed for the Day* [New York, 1768], Evans, 11047.

6. "An Old Whig," "To the Freemen and Freeholders of the City and County of New York," *NYJ*, Mar. 3, 1768; "A Citizen" to Hugh Gaine, *NYGWM*, Feb. 29, 1768.

7. William Livingston, *A Letter to the Right Reverend Father in God, John, Lord Bishop of Landaff . . .* [New York, 1768], Evans, 10948. Also see *Reason for the Present Glorious Combination of the Dissenters in This City, against the Farther Encroachments and the Stratagems of the Episcopalians . . .* [New York, 1769], Evans, 11436.

8. Thomas B. Chandler, *An Appeal to the Public in Behalf of the Church of England in America* (New York, 1767); *To the Worthy Freeholders and Freemen of New York*, Mar. 8, 1768 [New York, 1768], Evans, 11091; *A Better Creed than the Last* [New York, 1768], Evans, 10832. For the dispute over bishops and its impact on the Revolution, see Milton M. Klein, *The American Whig: William Livingston of New York* (New York, 1990), 471–504; Arthur Lyon Cross, *The American Episcopate and the American Colonies* (Cambridge, Mass., 1924), chaps. 8 and 9; Carl Bridenbaugh, *Mitre and Sceptre: Transatlantic Faiths, Ideas, Personalities, and Politics, 1689–1775* (New York, 1962), chap. 10; Frederick V. Mills, Sr., *Bishops by Ballot: An Eighteenth-Century Ecclesiastical Revolution* (New York, 1978), chap. 2; and Bonomi, *Under the Cope of Heaven: Religion, Society, and Politics in Colonial America* (New York, 1986), 199–209.

9. *A Word of Advice* [New York, 1768], Evans, 11126; *Plain Truths in Few Words* [New York, 1768], Evans, 11046; *Whereas on the Late Examination before the Honourable House of Assembly, It Appeared That Mr. Jauncey . . .*, Jan. 16, 1769 [New York, 1769], Evans, 11529; *A Member of the Church of England to the Freeholders and Freemen of the City and County of New York* [New York, 1769], Evans, 11394; "A Believer in Politicks," *A Political Creed for the Day* [New York, 1768], Evans, 11047; *To the Worthy Freeholders and Freemen*, Mar. 8, 1768 [New York, 1768], Evans, 11091; Edward P. Alexander, *A Revolutionary Conservative, James Duane of New York* (New York, 1938), 46.

10. "The Watchman," No. II, *NYJ*, Apr. 12, 1770; *NYGWM*, Mar. 14, 1768; Roger J. Champagne, "The Sons of Liberty and the Aristocracy in New York Politics, 1765–1790" (Ph.D. diss., University of Wisconsin, 1960), 166; Don R. Gerlach, *Philip Schuyler and the American Revolution in New York, 1733–1777* (Lincoln, Nebr., 1964), 142; Bonomi, *A Factious People: Politics and Society in Colonial New York* (New York, 1971), 245.

11. *NYJ*, Jan. 14, 28, Feb. 4, 1768; *The Committee Appointed by the Inhabitants of the City of New York* . . . [New York, 1768], Evans, 11008. The emphasis on economy and frugality followed John Dickinson's *Letters from a Farmer in Pennsylvania*, which first appeared in the *Pennsylvania Chronicle and Universal Advertiser*, Dec. 2, 1767.

12. *NYJ*, Mar. 31, Apr. 14, 21, 1768; *WPB*, Apr. 4, 1768; Smith, *Memoirs* 1:44–45; Gov. Henry Moore to Lord Hillsborough, May 12, 1768, *DCHNY* 8:68–69; Gen. Thomas Gage to Lord Barrington, May 13, 1768, Clarence Edwin Carter, ed., *The Correspondence of General Thomas Gage* . . ., 2 vols. (New Haven, 1931–1933), 2:468; Arthur M. Schlesinger, *The Colonial Merchants and the American Revolution, 1763–1776* (New York, 1918), 119; Dirk Hoerder, *Crowd Action in Revolutionary Massachusetts, 1765–1780* (New York, 1977), 152–153; Thomas M. Doerflinger, *A Vigorous Spirit of Enterprise: Merchants and Economic Development in Revolutionary Philadelphia* (Chapel Hill, N.C., 1986), 167–180. Marc Egnal and Joseph Albert Ernst, "An Economic Interpretation of the American Revolution," *WMQ* 29 (1972): 21, argued that the desire of merchants to clear out inventories was a more important reason for backing the boycott than was the wish to make Parliament repeal the Townshend Duties.

13. *NYJ*, Sept. 8, 15, 1768; Isaac N. Phelps Stokes, *The Iconography of Manhattan Island, 1498–1905*, 6 vols. (New York, 1915), 4:792; Champagne, "Sons of Liberty," 174–175.

14. *DCHNY* 8:58–59; *NYJ*, Sept. 29, Oct. 20, 1768.

15. *NYAJ*, Oct. 31, Nov. 8, 1768; Champagne, "Sons of Liberty," 177; *An Answer to the Foolish Reason That Is Given for Re-choosing the Old Members* . . . [New York, 1769], Evans, 11160. Britain rejected the petitions, for they denied Parliament's right to tax the colonies; Hillsborough to Moore, Mar. 24, 1769, *DCHNY* 8:155–156. Joseph Galloway introduced the letter from the Virginia House of Burgesses in the Pennsylvania Assembly on September 13; the Assembly answered the letter but made no reply to the Massachusetts Circular Letter; Richard Alan Ryerson, *The Revolution Is Now Begun: The Radical Committees of Philadelphia, 1765–1776* (Philadelphia, 1978), 21. For a De Lanceyite view on how the Livingstons reacted to the Massachusetts Circular Letter, see *As A Scandalous Paper Has Appeared, Stiled, An Answer to the Foolish Reason for Re-Choosing the Old Members* [New York, 1769], Evans, 11163.

16. *As A Scandalous Paper Has Appeared, Stiled, An Answer to the Foolish Reason for Re-Choosing the Old Members* [New York, 1769], Evans, 11163; Champagne, "Sons of Liberty," 178–179; *NYJ*, Nov. 17, 24, 1768; *NYGWM*, Nov. 21, 28, 1768; *NYAJ*, Nov. 22, 24, 1768. The first quote is from Moore to Hillsborough, Jan. 4, 1769, *DCHNY* 8:143; the second from Smith, *Memoirs* 1:46.

17. *NYJ*, Nov. 17, Dec. 1, 1768; Isaac Corsa to Robert Murray, *NYGWM*, Feb. 20, 1769; Smith, *Memoirs* 1:46; Robert J. Christen, *King Sears: Politician and Patriot in a Decade of Revolution* (New York, 1982), 127; Merrill Jensen, *The Founding of a Nation: A History of the American Revolution* (New York, 1969), 263; Anne M. Ousterhout, *A State Divided: Opposition in Pennsylvania to the American Revolution* (New York, 1987), 24, 41.

18. RRL to Robert Livingston, Dec. 12, 1768, Livingston Family Papers, NYPL; *NYAJ*, Dec. 31, 1768; *NYJ*, Feb. 9, 1769; Champagne, "Sons of Liberty," 181. The quote is from Smith, *Memoirs* 1:48–49.

19. Moore to Hillsborough, Jan. 4, 1769, *DCHNY* 8:143. Champagne, "Family Politics versus Constitutional Principles: The New York Assembly Elections of 1768 and 1769," *WMQ* 20 (1963): 57–59, believed the De Lanceys voted for a dissolution; but Moore to Hillsborough, Jan. 21, 1769, *DCHNY* 8:148, makes it clear that they voted against one. Friedman, "New York Assembly Elections of 1768 and 1769," *NYH* 46 (1965): 3–24, thought the De Lanceys feared new elections. Christen, *King Sears*, 142, n. 41, believed their support for the Assembly was the key issue. The two reasons are not mutually exclusive, however. For British criticism of Hillsborough, see Edmund Burke to Charles O'Hara, Sept. 1 [1768], Thomas W. Copeland et al., eds., *The Correspondence of Edmund Burke*, 9 vols. (Cambridge, U.K., 1958–1970), 2:14.

20. For alternate interpretations, see Champagne, "Family Politics versus Constitutional Principles," *WMQ* 20 (1963): 69–73; and Leopold S. Launitz-Schürer, *Loyal Whigs and Revolutionaries: The Making of the Revolution in New York* (New York, 1980), 59–63.

21. *An Answer to the Foolish Reason That Is Given for Re-choosing the Old Members . . .* [New York, 1769], Evans, 11160; Smith, *Memoirs* 1:48.

22. William Smith to RRL, Jan. 5, 1769, Robert R. Livingston Papers, Reel 1, NYHS (microfilm), herein cited as RRL Papers. For the 1769 election, also see Lawrence H. Leder, "The New York Elections of 1769: An Assault on Privilige," *Mississippi Valley Historical Review* 49 (1963): 675–682.

23. James Duane to R. Livingston, June 3, 1769, Livingston Family Papers, Johnson Redmond Collection, Reel 6, NYHS (microfilm), herein cited as Livingston-Redmond Papers; John Stevens to Lord Stirling, Jan. 28, 1769, William Alexander Papers, 1753–1835, NYPL; Smith to RRL, Jan. 5, 1769, RRL Papers, Reel 1; *To the Freeholders and Freemen of the City and County of New York* [New York, 1769], Evans, 11496; Philip Livingston, Peter Van Brugh Livingston, John Morin Scott, and Theodorus Van Wyck, *Election Ticket, 1769* [New York, 1769], Evans, 41984; Philip Livingston, *To the Freeholders and Freemen of the City and County of New York* [New York, 1769], Evans, 11311; Philip Livingston, T. Van Wyck, P. V. B. Livingston, and Scott, *To the Freeholders and Freemen of the City and County of New York* [New York, 1769], Evans, 11312; John Jay to RRL, [Jan.] 1769, Richard B. Morris, ed., *John Jay, The Making of a Revolutionary: Unpublished Papers, 1745–1780* (New York, 1975), 96.

24. Peter R. Livingston to Philip Schuyler, Jan. 16, 23, 1769, Philip Schuyler Revolutionary Papers, NYPL; P. R. Livingston to Oliver Wendell, Jan. 19, 1769, Livingston Papers, Museum of the City of New York.

25. *Reasons for the Present Glorious Combination of the Dissenters in This City, against the Farther Encroachments and Stratagems of the Episcopalians . . .* [New York, 1769], Evans, 11436; *As a Scandalous Paper Appeared Stiled An Answer to the Foolish Reasons for the Re-Choosing the Old Members* [New York, 1769], Evans, 11163. For the De Lancey campaign literature on the issue, see "Philanthropos" to Public, and "The Examiner," No. I, *NYJ*, Jan. 12, 1769. For the Livingston response, see *An Answer to the Foolish Reason That Is Given for Re-choosing the Old Members . . .* [New York, 1769], Evans, 11160; and *The Freeholders and Freemen of the City of New York* [New York, 1769], Evans, 11264.

26. *The Examiner*, No. II [New York, 1769], Evans, 11253; David Colden to his brother, Jan. 31, 1769, Cadwallader Colden Papers, NYPL.

27. *Impartial to the Dissenting Electors of All Denominations* [New York, 1769], Evans, 11494; Klein, *American Whig*, 487–498; Janice Potter, *The Liberty We Seek: Loyalist Ideology in Colonial New York and Massachusetts* (Cambridge, Mass., 1983), 74–77.

28. *All the Real Friends of Liberty.* . . (New York, 1770), Evans, 11779; Gary B. Nash, *The Urban Crucible: Social Change, Political Consciousness, and the Origins of the American Revolution* (Cambridge, Mass., 1979), 367.

29. John Cruger, James De Lancey, Jacob Walton, and James Jauncey, *Whereas a Paper, Signed Philo Patriae, Appeared* . . . [New York, 1769], Evans, 11230. The Dutch Reformed church was divided at the time, and Livingstonites hoped to win votes among the Coetus party that wanted to ordain ministers in America and to use English in church services; *Reason for the Present Glorious Combination of the Dissenters in This City, against the Farther Encroachments and Stratagems of the Episcopalians* . . . [New York, 1769], Evans, 11436. For the De Lancey reply, see "The Freeholder," *Answers to the Reasons Lately Published by the Independents, in Support of Their Malicious Combination* [New York, 1769], Nos. I, II, III, Evans, 11260, 11261, 11262.

30. "Honestus," *An Anecdote of a Candidate, for the Ensuing Election* [New York, 1769], Broadside Collection, NYHS; *An Anecdote, Recommended to the Friends* [New York, 1769], Evans, 11155; "To the Freeholders and Freemen of the City and County of New York," *NYGWM*, Jan. 23, 1769; "The Querist," *To the Freeholders and Freemen of the City and County of New York* [New York, 1769], Nos. I, II, Evans, 11431, 11432; *The Examiner*, No. III [New York, 1769], Evans, 11254.

31. Klein, "Democracy and Politics in Colonial New York," *NYH* 40 (1959): 221, estimated that 53.6% of the adult white males voted in 1768 but only 40.6% in 1769.

32. Duane to R. Livingston, June 3, 1769, Livingston-Redmond Papers, Reel 6; Champagne, "Family Politics versus Constitutional Principles," *WMQ* 20 (1963): 59; Friedman, "New York Assembly Elections of 1768 and 1769," *NYH* 46 (1965): 6–7; Nash, *Urban Crucible*, 366–368. Criticism of Nash's statistics can be found in Benjamin H. Newcomb, *Political Partisanship in the American Middle Colonies, 1700–1776* (Baton Rouge, 1995), 176–177. Bonomi, *Factious People*, 253, 254, concluded that "the soundness of the" Livingston "defeat resulted at least partially from the poisonous effects of their anti-Church propaganda. The religious issue was in any case much more important than family names." But "the very frequency with which the 'Common people' were now being referred to, and the growing prominence of the Sons of Liberty, give more than a little reason to doubt that either church or family was the decisive issue." See Peter Van Schaack to Henry Van Schaack, Jan. 27, 1769, Henry Cruger Van Schaack, *The Life of Peter Van Schaack, L.L.D., Embracing Selections from His Correspondence and Other Writings* . . . (New York, 1842), 10–12; and John Wetherhead to Sir William Johnson, [Jan. 23, 1769], Alexander C. Flick and James Sullivan, eds., *The Papers of Sir William Johnson*, 14 vols. (New York, 1921–1965), 6:606, for contemporary criticism of how the Livingstons exploited religion in the campaign.

33. Concerning deference and dependence, see Gordon S. Wood, *The Radicalism of the American Revolution* (New York, 1992), 63–65, 88; and Richard R. Beeman, "Deference, Republicanism, and the Emergence of Popular Politics in Eighteenth-Century America," *WMQ* 49 (1992): 401–430. In January and February of 1769 more artisans and shopkeepers than usual registered to become freemen. Bernard Friedman claimed that that development signaled the growing politicization and radicalization of the lower and middling classes. If Nash is correct that economic dependence played a crucial role in the election, would these registrants have bothered to register for the vote following the election, knowing that all they were probably gaining was the right to vote as directed? Friedman, "New York Assembly Elections of 1768 and 1769," *NYH* 46 (1965): 10; *The Burghers of New Amsterdam and the Freemen of New York* (NYHS, *Collections*, 18 [New York, 1886]), 216–226, herein cited as *Burghers and Freemen of New York*.

34. Graham Russell Hodges, *New York City Cartmen, 1667–1850* (New York, 1986), 55–57.

35. P. R. Livingston to Schuyler, Feb. 6, 27, 1769, Philip Schuyler Papers, NYPL. For New York's efforts to evade compliance with the Quartering Act, see Alexander McDougall, "To the Freeholders and Freemen and Inhabitants of the City and Province of New York," *NYJ*, Supplement, Mar. 8, 1770.

36. *NYGWM*, July 24, 1769; *NYJ*, Sept. 14, 1769; Smith, *Memoirs* 1:51; P. R. Livingston to R. Livingston, June 15, 1769, Livingston-Redmond Papers, Reel 6; CC to Hillsborough, Feb. 21, 1770, *The Colden Letter Books*, 2 vols. (NYHS, *Collections*, vols. 9–10 [New York, 1877–1878]), 2:211, herein cited as *CC Letter Books*; Cynthia Anne Kierner, *Traders and Gentlefolk: The Livingstons of Colonial New York, 1675–1790* (Ithaca, N.Y., 1992), 188–189, 199; Louis Kriesberg, *Social Conflicts*, 2d ed. (Englewood Cliffs, N.J., 1982), 166–167; *Burghers and Freemen of New York*, 217–226.

37. P. R. Livingston to Schuyler, Feb. 27, 1769, Schuyler Papers; "A Countryman" to Printer, *NYJ*, Mar. 16, 1769.

38. *NYAJ*, Apr. 4, 1769; Smith, *Memoirs* 1:60; "T" to Printer, *NYJ*, Mar. 19, 1767; P. R. Livingston to R. Livingston, May 6, 1769, Livingston-Redmond Papers, Reel 6. For the legislative session, see Champagne, "Sons of Liberty," 190–194.

39. *NYAJ*, Apr. 6, 7, 8, 10, 12, 1769; Smith, *Memoirs* 1:65.

40. *NYAJ*, Apr. 20, May 12, 1769. Principle was not involved, for the Assembly decided on April 26 that nonresident freeholders could vote; Smith, *Memoirs* 1:64.

41. P. R. Livingston to his father, May 15, 1769, Livingston-Redmond Papers, Reel 6; Smith, *Memoirs* 1:66; *NYAJ*, May 17, 1769.

42. *NYAJ*, Dec. 21, 1769, Jan. 25, 1771, Feb. 26, 1774; *The Address of Mr. Justice Livingston to the House of Assembly of New York, in Support of His Right to a Seat* [New York 1769], Evans, 11314; *The Case of the Manor of Livingston, and the Conduct of the Honourable House of Assembly, towards It, Considered* [New York, 1769], Evans, 11201.

43. Hillsborough to Moore, Nov. 15, 1768, June 7, 1769, *DCHNY* 8:108, 171–172; *NYAJ*, Apr. 4, 8, 14, May 20, 1769; Smith, *Memoirs* 1:62.

44. Smith, *Memoirs* 1:66; "The Paper Signed A Son of Liberty contains the following Assertions," Alexander McDougall Papers, NYHS; *NYJ*, May 3, 1770; Ernst, *Money and Politics in America, 1755–1775: A Study in the Currency Act of 1764 and the Political Economy of Revolution* (Chapel Hill, N.C., 1973), 266; Champagne, "Sons of Liberty," 204; Moore to Hillsborough, May 29, 1769, *DCHNY* 8:170.

45. Moore to Hillsborough, May 29, July 11, 1769, *DCHNY* 8:169–170, 175–176; Address of the New York Assembly to Governor Moore, May 20, 1769, C.O. 5/1100; *NYAJ*, Apr. 11, 14, May 6, 1769. The De Lancey plan was not reckless; that same year Gov. William Franklin of New Jersey staked his political reputation on gaining cabinet approval of a law to ease New Jersey's paper money shortage; Robert McCluer Calhoon, *The Loyalists in Revolutionary America, 1760–1781* (New York, 1973), 25.

46. Philip Livingston, Jr., to Hillsborough, Sept. 11, 1769, *DCHNY* 8:188.

47. CC to Hillsborough, Oct. 4, 1769, *CC Letter Books* 2:188–189.

48. CC to [Peter Collinson], David Colden to [Collinson], Dec. 16, 17, 1765, New Netherlands Historical Letters and Manuscripts, NYHS; D. Colden to CC, Jr., May 17, 1768, Cadwallader Colden Papers; Henry Conway to CC, Dec. 15, 1766, CC to Lord Grenville, Jan. 6, 1769, *CC Letter Books* 2:94–96, 180–183; CC to Hillsborough, Jan. 7, 1769, *DCHNY* 8:146–147.

49. CC to Hillsborough, Oct. 4, CC to Grenville, Oct. 5, 1769, *CC Letter Books*

2:188–190; the quote is from p. 190. "New York," Isaac Sears to John Holt, *NYJ*, Nov. 2, 1769, May 10, 1770; P. R. Livingston to R. Livingston, Dec. 2, 1769, Livingston-Redmond Papers, Reel 6.

50. Smith, *Memoirs* 1:67; Hillsborough to Moore, July 15, 1769, *DCHNY* 8:177; Hillsborough to CC, Nov. 4, 1769, *The Letters and Papers of Cadwallader Colden*, 8 vols. (NYHS, *Collections*, vols. 50–56, 67 [New York, 1917–1923, 1937]), 7:162; CC to Hillsborough, Dec. 4, 1769, *CC Letter Books* 2:193–194.

51. CC to Hillsborough, Dec. 4, 1769, *CC Letter Books* 2:194.

52. CC to Hillsborough, Dec. 16, 1769, *CC Letter Books* 2:195; *NYAJ*, Dec. 15, 1769. For the maneuvering in the Assembly the day the measure passed, see Alex[ander] McDougall, "To the Freeholders, Freeman, and Inhabitants of the Colony of New York; and to all Friends of Liberty in North America," *NYJ*, Feb. 15, 1770.

53. CC to Hillsborough, Jan. 6, 1770, *CC Letter Books* 2:200–201.

54. "New York," Sears to Holt, *NYJ*, Nov. 2, 1769, May 10, 1770; "To the Printer," *NYJ*, June 21, 1770; Christen, *King Sears*, 127, 162.

55. Kriesberg, *Social Conflicts*, 175–176, 168.

56. "A Son of Liberty," *To the Betrayed Inhabitants of the City and Colony of New York*, Dec. 16, 1769 [New York, 1769], Evans, 11319; Smith, *Memoirs* 1:67. For the authorship of this broadside, see Roger J. Champagne, *Alexander McDougall and the American Revolution* (Syracuse, 1975), 29–30.

57. "A Son of Liberty," *Union, Activity, and Freedom, or Division, Supineness, and Slavery* [New York, 1769], Evans, 11508.

58. *A Citizen's Address to the Public*, Dec. 18, 1769 [New York, 1769], Evans, 11209.

59. *NYGWM*, Dec. 25, 1769.

60. Christen, *King Sears*, 136, 152–154; *NYJ*, Mar. 16, 1769, May 10, 1770; "At this alarming Crisis . . .," July 7, 1769 [New York, 1769], Evans, 11379. The quote is from "Semper Idem" to Holt, *NYJ*, Mar. 1, 1770.

61. *New York Mercury*, Dec. 25, 1765; *NYAJ*, Dec. 20, 30, 1769; "On the Nature of Representation; and the Right of Instructing our Representatives," *WPB*, Jan. 8, 1770.

62. CC, *A Proclamation*, Dec. 20, 1769, [New York, 1769], Evans, 11362; *NYGWM*, Dec. 25, 1769; P. R. Livingston to R. Livingston, Dec. 23, 1769, Livingston-Redmond Papers, Reel 6.

63. For the dynamics in such situations, see Kriesberg, *Social Conflicts*, 170–171. *NYAJ*, Dec. 20, 1769; *NYJ*, May 3, 10, 1770; P. R. Livingston to R. Livingston, Dec. 23, 1769, Livingston-Redmond Papers, Reel 6. For Stephen Sayre, see John R. Alden, *Stephen Sayre: American Revolutionary Adventurer* (Baton Rouge, 1983).

64. *To the Freeholders and Freemen of the City and Province of New York* [New York, 1769], Evans, 11497; "A Freeholder" to Printer, *NYJ*, Dec. 7, 1769; *NYAJ*, Dec. 22, 1769; P. R. Livingston to R. Livingston, Dec. 25, 1769, Livingston-Redmond Papers, Reel 6; *NYJ*, Jan. 4, 1770; Champagne, "Sons of Liberty," 222–225. For the De Lancey counterattack, see "J. W. a Squinter on the Public Affairs," *The Mode of Elections Considered*, Dec. 29, 1769 [New York, 1769], Evans, 11517.

65. *To the Independent Freeholders and Freemen of this City and County* [New York, 1770], Evans, 11677. For a Livingston rebuttal, see *To the Freeholders and Freemen of the City and County of New York* [New York, 1770], Evans, 11883.

66. *NYGWM*, Jan. 1, 8, 22, 29, 1770; *NYJ*, Jan. 4, 11, 1770; *NYAJ*, Jan. 9, 1770; P. R. Livingston to R. Livingston, Feb. 5, 1770, Livingston-Redmond Papers, Reel 6.

67. Interestingly, the indexes to Bonomi's *Factious People* and Edward Countryman's

A People in Revolution: The American Revolution and Political Society in New York, 1760–1790 (Baltimore, 1981) do not list the term "nonimportation." Yet a careful appraisal of how Livingstonites and De Lanceyites handled the boycott is essential to any evaluation of whether or not they were opportunists. Launitz-Schürer, *Loyal Whigs*, 74, mentioned that New Yorkers upheld nonimportation but assigned no particular significance to the fact.

68. "A. B." to Printer, *NYJ*, Jan. 18, 1770; "To the Printer," *WPB*, Feb. 5, 1770; "Brutus," *To the Public* [New York, 1770], Evans, 11589; *NYJ*, Jan. 25, 1770; "Resolutions of the Inhabitants of the City of New York in Regard to the Cruel Treatment by the Troops Stationed in the City, with List of Names," New York City, Misc. Mss., NYHS.

69. What was emerging among the soldiers was a sense of group solidarity and of being part of something important; the exhilaration that accompanied this new outlook restored their self-confidence and overcame the frustration they felt about affairs since Nov. 1765. Kriesberg, *Social Conflicts*, 185.

70. 16th Regiment of Foot, *God and a Soldier All Men Doth Adore . . .* [New York, 1770], Broadside Collection, NYHS; "To the Public," *WPB*, Feb. 5, 1770; *To the Inhabitants of This City*, Jan. 22, 1770 [New York, 1770], Evans, 11776; Stokes, *Iconography* 4:804; Lee R. Boyer, "Lobster Backs, Liberty Boys, and Laborers in the Streets: New York's Golden Hill and Nassau Street Riots," *NYHSQ* 57 (1973): 281–308.

71. Hiller B. Zobel, *The Boston Massacre* (New York, 1970), 181. Colden thought that radicals in both places were acting "in Concert"; CC to Hillsborough, Apr. 25, 1770, *CC Letter Books* 2:217. For the meeting, see Smith, *Memoirs* 1:72–73.

72. Christen, *King Sears*, 189–190; *NYJ*, Feb. 8, 1770. The minutes of the City Council Meeting were printed in *NYGWM*, Feb. 5, 1770. Redcoats again tried on Mar. 24 to destroy the Liberty Pole but failed; *WPB*, Apr. 2, 1770.

7. "Liberty and Trade"

1. Alexander McDougall, "To the Freeholders, Freemen, and Inhabitants of New York; and to All the Friends of Liberty in North America," *NYJ*, Feb. 15, 1770; *WPB*, Mar. 19, 1770; William Smith, *Historical Memoirs of William Smith, Historian of the Province of New York, Member of the Governor's Council . . .*, ed. William H. W. Sabine, 2 vols. (New York, 1956–1958), 1:73–74, 76, herein cited as Smith, *Memoirs*; Thomas Jones, *History of New York during the Revolutionary War, and of the Leading Events in the Other Colonies at That Period*, ed. Edward Floyd De Lancey, 2 vols. (New York, 1879), 1:23–24, 26–27, herein cited as Jones, *History*; *Outlines*, Feb. 9, 1770 [New York, 1770], Evans, 11795; Dorothy Rita Dillon, *The New York Triumvirate* (New York, 1949), 107–108; Roger J. Champagne, *Alexander McDougall and the American Revolution* (Syracuse, 1975), 27–40.

2. Louis Kriesberg, *Social Conflicts*, 2d ed. (Englewood Cliffs, N.J., 1982), 171; *NYJ*, Mar. 29, 1770; Extract of a Letter from New York, *Pennsylvania Gazette*, Postscript Extraordinary, Mar. 22, 1770. For the significance that John Wilkes had for Americans, see Peter Shaw, *American Patriots and the Rituals of Revolution* (Cambridge, Mass., 1981), chap. 3.

3. *NYGWM*, Feb. 5, Mar. 26, 1770; *NYJ*, Feb. 8, Mar. 8, 22, 1770; Robert J. Christen, *King Sears: Politician and Patriot in a Decade of Revolution* (New York, 1982), 194.

4. James Duane to Robert Livingston, Feb. 19, 1770, Livingston Family Papers, Johnson Redmond Collection, Reel 6, NYHS (microfilm); *The Watchman*, No. I [New

York, 1770], Evans, 11916; "The Watchman," Nos. II, III, *NYJ*, Apr. 12, 19, 1770. The twelve "Dougliad" articles appeared in *NYGWM*, Apr. 9 – June 25, 1770.

5. *NYJ*, Mar. 1, 22, 29, May 3, 1770.

6. The first Isaac Sears quote is from *NYJ*, May 10, 1770; the second from *NYJ*, Feb. 22, 1770.

7. "To the Printer," *NYJ*, Feb. 22, 1770; Jones, *History* 1:28–29; Christen, *King Sears*, 191; *WPB*, Apr. 16, 1770; James Rivington to Sir William Johnson, Apr. 23, 1770, Alexander C. Flick and James Sullivan, eds., *The Papers of Sir William Johnson*, 14 vols. (New York, 1921–1965), 7:579.

8. *NYJ*, Feb. 22, Mar. 1, 8, 15, 1770; *WPB*, Feb. 19, Mar. 5, 12, 19, Apr. 2, 16, 1770; *NYGWM*, Apr. 9, 1770; Jones, *History* 1:29.

9. Jones, *History* 1:30; Dillon, *New York Triumvirate*, 113; *NYGWM*, Apr. 30, 1770.

10. For the political developments in Britain that led the ministry to change its policy, see Merrill Jensen, *The Founding of a Nation: A History of the American Revolution* (New York, 1969), 314–322.

11. John Shy, *Toward Lexington: The Role of the British Army in the Coming of the American Revolution* (Princeton, N.J., 1965), 292–294, 301–302; Jack M. Sosin, *Agents and Merchants: British Colonial Policy and the Origins of the American Revolution, 1763–1775* (Lincoln, Nebr., 1965), 115–117. Lord Hillsborough to George III, Feb. 15, 1769, "Measures Proposed by Lord Hillsborough to the Cabinet," and a "Memorandum by George III," [Feb. 1769], John W. Fortescue, ed., *The Correspondence of King George the Third . . .*, 6 vols. (London, 1927–1928), 2:81–84; the quote is from p. 83.

12. Hillsborough to Governors in America, May 13, 1769, *DCHNY* 8:164–165; Robert W. Tucker and David C. Hendrickson, *The Fall of the First British Empire: Origins of the War of American Independence* (Baltimore, 1982), 274; Thomas C. Barrow, *Trade and Empire: The British Customs Service in Colonial America, 1660–1775* (Cambridge, Mass., 1967), 243; Sosin, *Agents and Merchants*, 132–134.

13. William L. Grant and James Munro, eds., *Acts of the Privy Council of England: Colonial Series, 1766–1783* (London, 1912), 215–216; Sosin, *Agents and Merchants*, 137.

14. Kriesberg, *Social Conflicts*, 141, 114–119.

15. Gen. Thomas Gage to Henry Conway, May 6, 1766, Clarence Edwin Carter, ed., *The Correspondence of General Thomas Gage . . .*, 2 vols. (New Haven, 1931–1933), 1:91, herein cited as *Gage Correspondence*; CC to [Hillsborough], July 7, 1770, *The Colden Letter Books*, 2 vols. (NYHS, *Collections*, vols. 9–10 [New York, 1877–1878]), 2:223, herein cited as *CC Letter Books*. The more people have to lose, the more likely they are to favor compromise over violence. New York patricians had to worry about both property destruction and the price Britain might make them pay if a riot took place. Kriesberg, *Social Conflicts*, 134–135.

16. *New York Chronicle*, May 8, 15, June 22, 1769; Edward Countryman, *A People in Revolution: The American Revolution and Political Society in New York, 1760–1790* (Baltimore, 1981), 37–45. Also see "To the Printer," "The New York Preacher," No. II, *WPB*, May 1, 15, 1769; "A. Z." to John Holt, *NYJ*, Nov. 16, 1769.

17. "Aureng Zebe" to Printer, *NYJ*, July 27, 1769.

18. Lyman H. Butterfield et al., eds., *Diary and Autobiography of John Adams*, 4 vols. (Boston, 1961), 2:148–149; *NYGWM*, Mar. 6, 20, 1769. As in the first imperial crisis, conflict led to innovations in the methods used to wage the struggle; Kriesberg, *Social Conflicts*, 292. Gage to Lord Barrington, Dec. 2, 1769, *Gage Correspondence* 2:530.

19. *Advertisement, of the Greatest Importance to the Public*, July 20, 1769 [New York,

1769], Evans, 11380; *NYJ*, July 27, 1769; Champagne, "The Sons of Liberty and the Aristocracy in New York Politics, 1765–1790" (Ph.D. diss., University of Wisconsin, 1960), 252–253.

20. Gage to Barrington, July 22, 1769, *Gage Correspondence* 2:518.

21. *NYJ*, Sept. 28, 1769; *A Pill for the Committees of Non-Importation*, Oct. 1, 1769 [New York, 1769], Evans, 11395; *NYGWM*, Feb. 26, 1770.

22. *Advertisement*, Sept. 18, 1769 [New York, 1769], Evans, 11381; *NYJ*, Sept. 21, 1769; Champagne, "Sons of Liberty," 253.

23. *NYJ*, May 4, Oct. 12, 1769; *NYGWM*, May 15, 1769; "Paracelsus," *A Pill for the Committees of Non-Importation*, Oct. 1, 1769 [New York, 1769], Evans, 11395; "Paracelsus," *A Draught to Wash the Pill Down* [New York, 1769], Evans, 11395.

24. *NYJ*, Nov. 23, 1769; Gage to Barrington, May 14, 1769, *Gage Correspondence* 2:510; John Wetherhead to Johnson, Sept. 15, 1769, Flick and Sullivan, eds., *Papers of Johnson* 7:172–173.

25. Countryman, *People in Revolution*, xiii, 72–98; Value of Colonial Exports to and Imports from England, 1762–1775, Jensen, ed., *American Colonial Documents to 1776* (London, 1955), 392; *NYGWM*, May 8, June 19, 1769; *NYJ*, May 11, June 22, 29, 1769; *Advertisement of Great Importance to the Public* [New York, 1769], Evans, 11137; Christen, *King Sears*, 150–151. The Robertson quote is from Alexander Robertson to Public, *NYJ*, June 29, 1769.

26. *Advertisement of Great Importance to the Public* [New York, 1769], Evans, 11137; Kriesberg, *Social Conflicts*, 93; Timothy M. Barnes and Robert M. Calhoon, "Moral Allegiance: John Witherspoon and Loyalist Recantation," *American Presbyterians: The Journal of Presbyterian History* 63 (1985): 273–284.

27. Kriesberg, *Social Conflicts*, 177.

28. Isaac Sears et al. to "Friends of Just Liberty in Philadelphia," Mar. 10, 1770, New York City, Misc. Mss., NYHS; *WPB*, Mar. 26, 1770; *NYJ*, Mar. 22, 1770.

29. Smith, *Memoirs* 1:80–81. Exports to Britain were down in 1769; Jensen, ed., *American Colonial Documents*, 392; *NYJ*, May 4, June 22, 1769, Jan. 4, 1770; *The Boston Gazette, and Country Journal*, Dec. 16, 1769, Jan. 15, 1770, herein cited as *Boston Gazette*; Gage to Hillsborough, Dec. 4, 1769, *Gage Correspondence* 1:242; Hiller B. Zobel, *The Boston Massacre* (New York, 1970), 146, 152–179.

30. "A. Z." to Holt, *NYJ*, Nov. 16, 1769; Kriesberg, *Social Conflicts*, 101, 142. According to Sosin, *Agents and Merchants*, 109, "the nonimportation movement between 1768 and 1770 was not the major cause for the repeal of the Townshend duties."

31. The De Lancey reaction to the change in British policy was not atypical or extreme. Albany amended its nonimportation agreement on May 10 to apply only to tea; *WPB*, May 14, 1770.

32. *WPB*, May 14, 1770; *NYJ*, May 17, Aug. 30, 1770; *The Dying Speech of the Effigy of a Wretched Importer* [New York, 1770], Evans, 11639; "Diary of political activities of Alexander McDougall covering the period from May 1 to July 17, 1770" (hereafter cited as Diary), Alexander McDougall Papers, NYHS. For the use of effigies and for how the victim can substitute for a leader, like the king or James De Lancey, see Shaw, *American Patriot*, 216–221.

33. CC to [Hillsborough], July 7, Aug. 18, 1770, *CC Letter Books* 2:222–223, 225–228; Isaac N. Phelps Stokes, *The Iconography of Manhattan Island, 1498–1905*, 6 vols. (New York, 1915), 4:811; *WPB*, May 14, Aug. 6, 1770; *NYJ*, May 17, 24, June 28, 1770; *NYGWM*, Aug. 13, 1770; *Advertisement* [New York, 1770], Evans, 11780; Samuel

Stringer to Johnson, May 19, 1770, Flick and Sullivan, eds., *Papers of Johnson* 7:685–686.

34. "Brutus," *To the Free and Loyal Inhabitants of the City and Colony of New York* [New York, 1770], Evans, 13180; "The Salvation of American Liberty," *WPB*, May 21, 1770.

35. *NYGWM*, June 4, 1770. Also see *NYJ*, May 24, 31, 1770.

36. Champagne, "Sons of Liberty," 262; *Advertisement*, May 30, 1770 [New York, 1770], Evans, 11781; "New York," May 30, 1770, *NYJ*, June 7, 1770.

37. *Advertisement*, May 31, 1770 [New York, 1770], Evans, 11782; *WPB*, June 4, 1770; Diary, McDougall Papers; *NYGWM*, Aug. 6, 1770.

38. Diary, McDougall Papers; *Pennsylvania Gazette*, May 24, 1770; *Boston Gazette*, May 28, 1770; *NYJ*, Aug. 9, 1770; Carl Lotus Becker, *The History of Political Parties in the Province of New York, 1760–1776* (Madison, Wisc., 1909), 91; Gibson, *Coming of Revolution*, 204; Arthur M. Schlesinger, *The Colonial Merchants and the American Revolution, 1763–1776* (New York, 1918), 221–222; Jensen, *Founding of a Nation*, 365; Christen, *King Sears*, 216.

39. CC to Hillsborough, Oct. 5, 1770, *CC Letter Books* 2:229; Schlesinger, *Colonial Merchants*, 221, 222, 224–25; Christen, *King Sears*, 217; "Brutus," *To the Free and Loyal Inhabitants of the City and Colony of New York* [New York, 1770], Evans, 13180; *WPB*, June 18, 1770.

40. Diary, McDougall Papers; *NYGWM*, June 25, 1770; *Whereas a Number of People . . .*, June 12, 1770 [New York, 1770], Evans, 11783; *NYJ*, July 12, 1770.

41. "New York," *Boston Evening Post*, June 25, 1770.

42. *NYJ*, June 21, 1770; Diary, McDougall Papers; Champagne, "Sons of Liberty," 265.

43. *NYGWM*, June 25, 1770.

44. *NYJ*, June 21, 31, July 12, 1770; *NYGWM*, June 25, July 2, 1770; Philadelphia Committee of Merchants to New York Committee of Merchants, June 18, 1770, *NYJ*, Aug. 9, 1770.

45. "A Card," No. II, *WPB*, June 25, 1770; Christen, *King Sears*, 221–222.

46. *NYJ*, July 5, 1770.

47. Isaac Low, *The Subscribers to the Nonimportation Agreement*, July 3, 1770 [New York, 1770], Broadside Collection, NYHS; Boston Committeee of Merchants to New York Committee of Merchants, June 24, 1770, *NYJ*, Aug. 9, 1770.

48. Extract of a Letter from New York, dated July 9, 1770, *Boston Evening Post*, July 16, 1770; Champagne, "Sons of Liberty," 269–270.

49. See the accounts of the meeting in the letters from New York printed in the *Boston Gazette*, July 16, 1770, and the *Boston Evening Post*, July 16, 1770. Alexander Colden to Anthony Todd, July 11, 1770, *DCHNY* 8:219.

50. *Advertisement*, July 7, 1770 [New York, 1770], Evans, 11785; *Boston Gazette*, July 16, 1770; *Boston Evening Post*, July 16, 23, 1770.

51. A. Colden to Todd, July 11, 1770, *DCHNY* 8:220.

52. *Boston Evening Post*, July 16, 1770; *WPB*, July 16, 23, 30, 1770; *Massachusetts Gazette and Boston Weekly News-Letter*, July 19, 1770; *NYJ*, Sept. 27, 1770; Diary, McDougall Papers.

53. A. Colden to Todd, July 11, 1770, *DCHNY* 8:220; Gary B. Nash, *The Urban Crucible: Social Change, Political Consciousness, and the Origins of the American Revolution* (Cambridge, Mass., 1979), 367; Kriesberg, *Social Conflicts*, 132, 94. Interestingly, "the evidence for Boston" shows a "decreasing militancy among mechanics after the

nonimportation period": Dirk Hoerder, *Crowd Action in Revolutionary Massachusetts, 1765–1780* (New York, 1977), xi.

54. Low, *Advertisement to the Public* [New York, July 9, 1770], Broadside Collection, NYHS.

55. "A Protest," McDougall Papers; "A Protest," *NYJ*, Aug. 2, 1770; A. Colden to Todd, July 11, 1770, *DCHNY* 8:219; Christen, *King Sears*, 233.

56. *Pennsylvania Gazette*, July 19, 1770; *NYGWM*, July 16, 1770. For the reaction elsewhere, see *NYJ*, July 19, 26, Aug. 2, 9, 23, 30, Sept. 27, Oct. 11, 1770.

57. Egbert Benson to Peter Van Schaack, June 21, 1770, Henry Cruger Van Schaack, *The Life of Peter Van Schaack, L.L.D., Embracing Selections from His Correspondence and Other Writings* . . . (New York, 1842), 12–13; Schlesinger, *Colonial Merchants*, 218–227, 246–247; Jensen, *Founding of a Nation*, 312; Countryman, *People in Revolution*, 78.

58. Smith, *Memoirs* 1:82; *Minutes of the Common Council of the City of New York, 1675–1776*, 8 vols. (New York, 1905), 7:132, 184, 232, 233; CC to Hillsborough, Oct. 4, 1770, *CC Letter Books* 2:229; Rivington to Johnson, Oct. 2, 1770, Flick and Sullivan, eds., *Papers of Johnson* 7:924; *The Burghers of New Amsterdam and the Freemen of New York* (NYHS, *Collections*, 18 [New York, 1886]), 230–235, herein cited as *Burghers and Freemen of New York*.

59. Hillsborough to Lord Dunmore, July 16, 1770, *DCHNY* 8:223; CC to Hillsborough, Nov. 10, 1770, *CC Letter Books* 2:233.

60. Smith, *Memoirs* 1:83, 84, 91–92, 205; Dunmore to Hillsborough, Mar. 9, 1771, C.O. 5/1102. The issue was refought after William Tryon became governor; see Paul David Nelson, *William Tryon and the Course of Empire: A Life in British Imperial Service* (Chapel Hill, N.C., 1990), 114–115.

61. *NYGWM*, Dec. 24, 1770; Champagne, *Alexander McDougall*, 43.

62. Christen, *King Sears*, 259–260.

63. For the material on Allicocke in this and the next paragraph, see Donald A. Grinde, Jr., "Joseph Allicocke: African-American Leader of the Sons of Liberty," *Afro-Americans in New York History and Life* 14 (1990): 61–69; *The Journals of Captain John Montresor*, ed. G. D. Scull (NYHS, *Collections*, 14 [New York, 1882]), 368; Petition of Joseph Allicocke, April 23, 1783, Audit Office 12/24, Public Record Office, London (Library of Congress microfilm); Testimonial by George Vandeput, January 6, 1776, Testimonial by William Franklin, May 31, 1785, Audit Office 13/63, 64, 56; *Abstract of Wills on File in the Surrogate's Office, City of New York*, 17 vols. (NYHS, *Collections*, vols. 25–41 [New York, 1893–1913]), 9:101–102, 12:349–350; *Burghers and Freemen of New York*, 217; Robert M. Dructor, "The New York Commercial Community: The Revolutionary Experience" (Ph.D. diss., University of Pittsburgh, 1975), 269, 325, 345, 478; "Records of Trinity Church Parish," *New York Genealogical and Biographical Record*, 69 (1938), 375; Smith, *Memoirs* 1:103; Pauline Maier, *From Resistance to Revolution: Colonial Radicals and the Development of American Opposition to Britain, 1765–1776* (New York, 1974), 303.

64. *Letter Book of John Watts, Merchant and Councillor of New York, January 1, 1762–December 22, 1765* (NYHS, *Collections*, 41 [New York, 1928]), 279–280, 286–288, 301.

65. Smith, *Memoirs* 1:118, 128, 143–144, 153. For Tryon's career as New York's governor, see Nelson, *William Tryon*, chap. 6.

66. Kriesberg, *Social Conflicts*, 189–190, 193.

8. The Tea Act and the Coercive Acts

1. See Ian R. Christie, *Wars and Revolution: Britain, 1760–1815* (Cambridge, Mass., 1982), 85–86; Jack M. Sosin, *Agents and Merchants: British Colonial Policy and the Origins*

of the American Revolution, 1763–1775 (Lincoln, Nebr., 1965), 164–165; Thomas C. Barrow, *Trade and Empire: The British Customs Service in Colonial America, 1660–1775* (Cambridge, Mass., 1967), 249; Robert W. Tucker and David C. Hendrickson, *The Fall of the First British Empire: Origins of the War of American Independence* (Baltimore, 1982), 312–313; and Benjamin W. Labaree, *The Boston Tea Party* (New York, 1964), 89–97.

2. William Smith, *Historical Memoirs of William Smith, Historian of the Province of New York, Member of the Governor's Council . . .*, ed. William H. W. Sabine, 2 vols. (New York, 1956–1958), 1:156, herein cited as Smith, *Memoirs*; William Gordon, *History of the Rise, Progress, and Establishment of Independence in the United States of America*, 4 vols. (London, 1788), 1:332; Roger J. Champagne, "The Sons of Liberty and the Aristocracy in New York Politics, 1765–1790" (Ph.D. diss., University of Wisconsin, 1960), 295; Jeff Goodwin and Theda Skocpol, "Explaining Revolutions in the Contemporary Third World," *Politics and Society* 17 (1989): 497.

3. Edward Countryman, *A People in Revolution: The American Revolution and Political Society in New York, 1760–1790* (Baltimore, 1981), xiii.

4. "Hampden," *The Alarm*, Oct. 6, 9, 15, 19, 27, 1773 [New York, 1773], Evans, 12799–12803; the quote is from *The Alarm*, No. V. Bernard Mason, *The Road to Independence: The Revolutionary Movement in New York, 1773–1777* (Lexington, Ky., 1966), 4, estimated that the Tea Act would have cost the colonies between £12,500 and £18,750 per year in taxes for tea. "Hampden" calculated that the duty would amount to £4,537 sterling per annum in New York; *Alarm*, No. IV, Oct. 19, 1774 [New York, 1773], Evans, 12802.

5. See "Scaevola," *To the Commissioners Appointed by the East India Company, for the Sale of Tea in America* [New York, 1773], Evans, 42521; "A Citizen" to Printer, *NYJ*, Nov. 4, 1773; "A Tradesman," "To the Freeholders and Freemen of the City and County of New York," *Rivington's New York Gazetteer; or the Connecticut, New Jersey, Hudson's River, and Quebec Weekly Advertiser*, Nov. 18, 1773, herein cited as *Rivington*; "A Student of Law," *Fellow Citizens, Friends of Liberty and Equal Commerce*, Nov. 19, 1773 [New York, 1773], Evans, 12765; "Z," "To the People of New York"; "Queries"; "A Constitutional Catechism"; "Americanus," "To the Public"; "Zeno," "A Demonstration"; *NYJ*, Nov. 25, Dec. 9, 16, 23, 1773; "A Mechanic," *To the Worthy Inhabitants of New York* [New York, 1773], Evans, 13042.

6. See Gov. William Tryon to Lord Dartmouth, Nov. 3, 1773, *DCHNY* 8:400–401, concerning the radical appeal to smugglers. See Isaac Sears et al. to the Boston Committee of Correspondence, Feb. 28, 1774, Draughts of Letters from the Boston Committee to the Other Towns in and out of Massachusetts, 1772–1775, George Bancroft Collection, NYPL (herein cited as Boston Committee of Correspondence, George Bancroft Collection) for the fear that Britain might use the Tea Act as a precedent to create other monopolies. The quote is from "New York," *NYJ*, Oct. 7, 1773.

7. "New York," *NYJ*, Oct. 7, 1773.

8. *NYJ*, Dec. 23, 1773.

9. "To the Printer," *NYJ*, Oct. 14, 1773. For "Legion," see *Rivington*, Nov. 18, 1773.

10. Peter Van Schaack to John Vardill, Feb. 19, 1774, Henry Cruger Van Schaack, *Memoir of Henry Van Schaack, Embracing Selections of His Correspondence and Other Writings* (Chicago, 1892), 23–24; *NYJ*, Nov. 4, Dec. 16, 1773, Sept. 1, Oct. 13, 1774.

11. *Rivington*, Nov. 18, Dec. 2, 1773. For a refutation, see "A Tradesman," "To the Freeholders and Freemen of the City and County of New York," *Rivington*, Nov. 18, 1773.

12. "Scaevola," *To the Commissioners Appointed by the East India Company, for the Sale of Tea in America* [New York, 1773], Evans, 42521; Smith, *Memoirs* 1:156. "Phileleutheros" and "Brutus" appeared in *NYJ*, Oct. 21, 1773.

13. *NYJ*, Oct. 21, 1773. See Smith, *Memoirs* 1:156–157, for his view of the problems the Tea Act caused the De Lanceys.

14. Smith, *Memoirs* 1:156–157.

15. *NYJ*, Nov. 18, 1773; Smith, *Memoirs* 1:156; Robert J. Christen, *King Sears: Politician and Patriot in a Decade of Revolution* (New York, 1982), 280–281; Louis Kriesberg, *Social Conflicts*, 2d ed. (Englewood Cliffs, N.J., 1982), 66–67, 92–93.

16. Gordon, *History* 1:333; *Rivington*, Nov. 18, 1773.

17. Peter Force, ed., *American Archives . . . A Documentary History of . . . the North American Colonies*, 4th ser., 6 vols. (Washington, D.C., 1837–1846), 1:253n, herein cited as *American Archives*; *NYJ*, Dec. 2, 1773.

18. *Rivington*, Dec. 2, 1773; *Proceedings at a Numerous Meeting of the Citizens of New York* [New York, 1773], Evans, 12894.

19. *American Archives*, 4th ser., 1:254n.

20. Smith, *Memoirs* 1:157; Alexander McDougall to William Cooper, Dec. 13, 1773, Boston Committee of Correspondence, George Bancroft Collection; *NYJ*, Dec. 2, 1773; Memorial of Henry White, Abraham Lott, and Benjamin Booth to Tryon, Dec. 1, Tryon to Dartmouth, Dec. 1, 1773, C.O. 5/1105; Champagne, *Alexander McDougall and the American Revolution* (Syracuse, 1975), 46.

21. Smith, *Memoirs* 1:157.

22. Smith, *Memoirs* 1:158.

23. McDougall to Cooper, Dec. 13, 1773, Boston Committee of Correspondence, George Bancroft Collection.

24. Smith, *Memoirs* 1:158–159.

25. Mason, *Road to Independence*, 15, n. 29; *Proceedings at a Numerous Meeting of the Citizens of New York* [New York, 1773], Evans, 12894; *American Archives*, 4th ser., 1:254n; Smith, *Memoirs* 1:162.

26. Smith, *Memoirs* 1:159–161, 164; *Proceedings at a Numerous Meeting of the Citizens of New York* [New York, 1773], Evans, 12894.

27. Smith, *Memoirs* 1:163-166, 173; *American Archives*, 4th ser., 1:255n; *NYJ*, Dec. 22, 1773; Tryon to Dartmouth, Jan. 3, 1774, *DCHNY* 8:1774; Mason, *Road to Independence*, 17–18.

28. For the affair, see *American Archives*, 4th ser., 1:249–251, 255; *To the Public* [New York, 1774], Evans, 13671; Gordon, *History* 1:334; and Christen, *King Sears*, 302. The quote is from *To the Public* [New York, 1774], Evans, 13672.

29. Christen, *King Sears*, 302; *American Archives*, 4th ser., 1:249–251, 255. The quote is from "New York," *NYJ*, Apr. 28, 1774.

30. "Brutus" to Printer, *Rivington*, May 12, 1774.

31. The quote is from Alexander McDougall, "Political Memorandums Relative to the Conduct of the Citizens on the Boston Port Bill," May 11, 1774, Alexander McDougall Papers, NYHS. Extract of a Letter from New York, May 14, 1774, *Boston Evening Post*, May 23, 1774.

32. William Cobbett and Thomas C. Hansard, eds., *The Parliamentary History of England from the Earliest Period to the Year 1803*, 36 vols. (London, 1806-1820), 17:1167. Also see Labaree, *Boston Tea Party*, chap. 9; Sosin, *Agents and Merchants*, chap. 7; Christie, *Wars and Revolutions*, 100–105; John Shy, *Toward Lexington: The Role of the British*

Army in the Coming of the American Revolution (Princeton, N.J., 1965), 406–410; and Robert Middlekauff, *The Glorious Cause: The American Revolution, 1763–1789* (New York, 1982), 227–231.

33. Quoted in Bernard Donoughue, *British Politics and the American Revolution: The Path to War, 1773–1775* (London, 1964), 77.

34. The more critical the issue in dispute, the greater the chance of escalation; Kriesberg, *Social Conflicts*, 37, 199.

35. For these acts, see Merrill Jensen, ed., *American Colonial Documents to 1776* (London, 1955), 779-785; Dartmouth to Gen. Thomas Gage, Apr. 9, 1774, Clarence Edwin Carter, ed., *The Correspondence of General Thomas Gage . . .*, 2 vols. (New Haven, 1931–1933), 2:158-162. Colonists viewed the Quebec Act as an Intolerable Act, but it was not part of Parliament's response to the Boston Tea Party.

36. Jensen, ed., *American Colonial Documents*, 785; Vardill to Van Schaack, Apr. 5, 1774, Spec. Ms. Coll., Van Schaack Family, Columbia University, New York City; Edmund Burke to Committee of the New York Assembly, Aug. 2, 1774, Thomas W. Copeland et al., eds., *The Correspondence of Edmund Burke*, 9 vols. (Cambridge, U.K., 1958–1970), 3:14.

37. Kriesberg, *Social Conflicts*, 193–195, 198, 203; the quotes are from p. 198.

38. Kriesberg, *Social Conflicts*, 140; Smith, *Memoirs* 1:186; McDougall, "Political Memorandums," May 12, 13, 1774, McDougall Papers; Van Schaack to Vardill, May 13, 1774, Van Schaack, *Memoir of Henry Van Schaack*, 28.

39. *The Mechanics of This City . . .*, May 11, 1774 [New York, 1774], Evans, 13490; *Rivington*, May 12, 1774; Champagne, *Alexander McDougall*, 54. The quotes are from McDougall, "Political Memorandums," May 14, 1774, McDougall Papers. The previous committee, which had been appointed to keep the tea from landing, considered its work done once the tea ships had left New York. "Americanus" had broached the idea of an *"annual congress"* in *NYJ*, Feb. 24, 1774. Christen, *King Sears*, 314, considered the call by Sears and McDougall for a congress to be the first following the Boston Port Act.

40. McDougall, "Political Memorandums," May 15, 1774, McDougall Papers. Sears and McDougall to Boston Committee of Correspondence, May 15, 1774, Boston Committee of Correspondence, George Bancroft Collection. Though New York was unaware, a Boston town meeting had voted on May 13 for nonimportation and nonexportation against both Britain and the West Indies; Arthur M. Schlesinger, *The Colonial Merchants and the American Revolution, 1763–1776* (New York, 1918), 313. Boycotting the West Indies would force "wet goods" merchants who traded with those islands to share the economic burdens that nonimportation imposed on the "dry goods" merchants who traded chiefly with Britain; Charles S. Olton, *Artisans for Independence: Philadelphia Merchants and the American Revolution* (Syracuse, 1975), 41.

41. Van Schaack to Peter Silvester, May 21, 1774, Van Schaack, *Memoir of Henry Van Schaack*, 16–17. The quote is from McDougall, "Political Memorandums," May 16, 1774, McDougall Papers. John A. Neuenschwander, *The Middle Colonies and the Coming of the American Revolution* (Port Washington, N.Y., 1973), 38, believed politics was less contentious in New Jersey and Delaware than in Pennsylvania and New York because fewer merchants resided in the first two colonies.

42. For what the De Lanceys thought were legitimate American grievances, see the Assembly's March 1775 "State of Grievances"; *American Archives*, 4th ser., 1:1297–1304. For the charge of opportunism, see "The Monitor," No. VIII, *NYJ*, Dec. 28,

1775; Smith, *Memoirs* 1:186; Christian, *King Sears*, 275; and Champagne, "New York Politics and Independence, 1776," *NYHSQ* 46 (1962): 282.

43. The best account of the meeting and the events preceding it is in McDougall, "Political Memorandums," McDougall Papers; the quote was dated May 16, 1774.

44. Gordon, *History* 1:362. For the list of those selected, see *At a Meeting at the Exchange, May 16 . . .* [New York, 1774], Evans, 13125. Also see Leopold S. Launitz-Schürer, *Loyal Whigs and Revolutionaries: The Making of the Revolution in New York* (New York, 1980), 110; and Mason, *Road to Independence*, 26, n. 63, 27, n. 64.

45. *Rivington*, May 19, 1774; CC to Dartmouth, June 1, 1774, *The Colden Letter Books*, 2 vols. (NYHS, *Collections*, vols. 9–10 [New York, 1877–1878]), 2:340, herein cited as *CC Letter Books*.

46. McDougall, "Political Memorandums," May 16, 1774, McDougall Papers; Smith, *Memoirs* 1:186.

47. *American Archives*, 4th ser., 1:294; McDougall, "Political Memorandums," May 17, 18, 1774, McDougall Papers; *Rivington*, May 19, 1774; Christen, *King Sears*, 321; Champagne, *Alexander McDougall*, 55. A list of those selected can be found in *A Committee of Twenty-Five* [New York, 1774], Evans, 13474. For a somewhat different viewpoint, see Launitz-Schürer, *Loyal Whigs*, 111; and Mason, *Road to Independence*, 27, n. 66.

48. McDougall, "Political Memorandums," May 19, 1774, McDougall Papers; Smith, *Memoirs* 1:187. For Low's speech, see *American Archives*, 4th ser., 1:294–295.

49. McDougall, "Political Memorandums," May 19, 1774, McDougall Papers; Christen, *King Sears*, 322–323.

50. Smith, *Memoirs* 1:187, 186; McDougall, "Political Memorandums," May 20, 1774, McDougall Papers.

51. McDougall, "Political Memorandums," May 23, 1774, McDougall Papers; Labaree, *Boston Tea Party*, 231; and *American Archives*, 4th ser., 1:296.

52. Carl Lotus Becker, *The History of Political Parties in the Province of New York, 1760–1776* (Madison, Wisc., 1909), 118, called the letter a conservative triumph; Launitz-Schürer, *Loyal Whigs*, 114, saw it as a sign of "the growing radicalism of the population as a whole."

53. *American Archives*, 4th ser., 1:297–298; McDougall, "Political Memorandums," May 24, 1774, McDougall Papers. The merchants may have known nonimportation was inevitable but were delaying it as long as possible so that they could stock up on British manufactures; Gov. William Franklin to Dartmouth, May 31, 1774, Kenneth G. Davies, ed., *Documents of the American Revolution, 1770–1783*, 21 vols. (Kill-o'-the-Grange, Ireland, 1972–1981), 8:118.

54. McDougall, "Political Memorandums," May 25, 1774, McDougall Papers.

55. Kriesberg, *Social Conflicts*, 189; Extract of a Letter from New York, May 30, 1774, *NYJ*, Oct. 13, 1774; Christen, *King Sears*, 330. Also see Boston Committee of Correspondence to Daniel Dunscomb, June 10, 1774, Boston Committee of Correspondence, George Bancroft Collection.

56. Extract of a Letter to a Gentleman in London, May 31, 1774, *NYJ*, Aug. 25, 1774.

57. Smith, *Memoirs* 1:188; David Colden to Tryon, June 1, 1774, *CC Letter Books* 2:343; *Rivington*, June 2, 1774; Champagne, "Sons of Liberty," 330. The quote is from *American Archives*, 4th ser., 1:303.

58. *NYJ*, June 9, 16, 23, 1774; "A Citizen," *To the People of New York* [New York, 1774], Evans, 13665; "A Freeman," *To the Public*, June 20, 1774 [New York, 1774],

Evans, 13670. For the first quote and the significance of illuminating widows, see Paul A. Gilje, *The Road to Mobocracy: Popular Disorder in New York City, 1763–1834* (Chapel Hill, N.C., 1987), 17. For the use of effigies in demonstrations, see Peter Shaw, *American Patriots and the Rituals of Revolution* (Cambridge, Mass., 1981), 216–221.

59. *American Archives*, 4th ser., 1:307, 309–311; Richard Alan Ryerson, *The Revolution Is Now Begun: The Radical Committees of Philadelphia, 1765–1776* (Philadelphia, 1978), 47–48; Champagne, "Sons of Liberty," 330–331. For the debates on this issue, see *NYJ*, June 30, 1774; *Rivington*, June 30, 1774; and "An American," *To the Inhabitants of the City and Colony of New York*, July 5, 1774 [New York, 1774], Evans, 42652.

60. American Archives, 4th ser., 1:307–309; Herbert A. Johnson, *John Jay: Colonial Lawyer* (New York, 1989), 149–153.

61. *Advertisement*, July 6, 1774 [New York, 1774], Evans, 13093; Sears and McDougall to Samuel Adams, July 25, 1774, Samuel Adams Papers, 1635-1827, NYPL. For the July 6 meeting, see *NYJ*, July 7, 1774.

62. "Another Citizen," *To the Inhabitants of the City and County of New York*, June [sic] 5, 1774 [New York, 1774], Evans, 13661; *American Archives*, 4th ser., 1:309–310; To the Inhabitants of the City and County of New York, July 7, 1774 [New York, 1774], Evans, 42713; Sears and McDougall to Samuel Adams, July 25, 1774, S. Adams Papers.

63. *American Archives*, 4th ser., 1:311; Champagne, "Sons of Liberty," 336–337.

64. Aside from the fact that 9 of the 11 were merchants, the group was diverse: 4 were Anglican, 4 Presbyterian, and 3 Dutch Reformed; 7 had voted with the Livingstons in 1768–1769 (including the 4 Presbyterians), and 4 had voted with the De Lanceys (including 3 of the 4 Anglicans).

65. *Rivington*, July 14, 1774; *American Archives*, 4th ser., 1:312–314; "One of the Committee," *To the Worthy Inhabitants of the City and County of New-York*, July 9, 1774 [New York, 1774], Evans, 13683; *Extract of the Proceedings of the Committee of Correspondence of the City* [New York, 1774]. Evans, 13476; Alexander McDougall, *To the Freeholders, Freemen, and Inhabitants of the City and County of New York*, July 9, 1774 [New York, 1774], Evans, 13384.

66. "One of the Committee," *To the Worthy Inhabitants of the City and County of New-York*, July 9, 1774 [New York, 1774], Evans, 13683.

67. *American Archives*, 4th ser., 1:315; *Proceedings of the Committee of Correspondence in New York*, July 13, 1774 [New York, 1774], Evans, 13477.

68. *Rivington*, July 14, 1774; *NYGWM*, July 25, 1774. The quote is from Sears and McDougall to Samuel Adams, July 25, 1774, S. Adams Papers.

69. A key difference was that the revisions stated explicitly that British taxation of America was "unjust and unconstitutional"; *American Archives*, 4th ser., 1:315–317. De Lanceyites also employed satire against their enemies: *Debates at the Robin-Hood Society, in the City of New York, on Monday Night 19th July, 1774* [New York, 1774], Evans, 13486; "Agricola," *Advertisement*, July 15, 1774; *To the Public*, July 20, 1774 [New York, 1774], Evans, 13097; "A Citizen," *To John M. S——, Esq.*, July 23, 1774 [New York, 1774], Evans, 13653; and "Ebenezer Snuffle, Secretary," *At a Meeting of the True Sons of Liberty, in the City of New York, July 27, 1774, Properly Convened* [New York, 1774], Evans, 13126.

70. John Alsop, Isaac Low, and John Jay, *To the Respectable Public*, July 20, 1774 [New York, 1774], Evans, 13680; Isaac Low et al., *To the Respectable Public*, July 20, 1774 [New York, 1774], Evans, 13681.

71. *NYGWM*, July 25, 1774; *To the Inhabitants of the City and County of New York*, July 23, 1774 [New York, 1774], Evans, 13662; "New York," *Rivington*, July 28, 1774; Champagne, "Sons of Liberty," 340; Mason, *Road to Independence*, 35.

72. *American Archives*, 4th ser., 1:319–320, 322; *NYJ*, July 28, 1774.

73. Kriesberg, *Social Conflicts*, 71; CC to Dartmouth, Oct. 5, 1774, *CC Letter Books* 2:366; Thomas Jones, *History of New York during the Revolutionary War, and of the Leading Events in the Other Colonies at That Period*, ed. Edward Floyd De Lancey, 2 vols. (New York, 1879), 1:35, 34.

9. Whigs and Tories

1. "The longer a conflict relationship persists, the more organized the conflict groups become," and the greater their need to mobilize people and develop an effective communications network; Louis Kriesberg, *Social Conflicts*, 2d ed. (Englewood Cliffs, N.J., 1982), 11–12, 69–70, 91.

2. Lyman H. Butterfield et al., eds., *Diary and Autobiography of John Adams*, 4 vols. (Boston, 1961), 2:102–111; the quotes are from pp. 103, 105, 106–107. Roger J. Champagne, *Alexander McDougall and the American Revolution* (Syracuse, 1975), 67–68.

3. *Rivington's New York Gazetteer; or the Connecticut, New Jersey, Hudson's River, and Quebec Weekly Advertiser*, Aug. 11, 1774, herein cited as *Rivington*. For the whig reply, see *NYJ*, Aug. 18, 1774.

4. Gordon S. Wood, *The Radicalism of the American Revolution* (New York, 1992), 29; *Rivington*, Aug. 18, 1774.

5. *Proceedings of the Committee of Correspondence*, July 19, 1774 [New York, 1774], Evans, 13479; *Rivington*, Aug. 18, 25, 1774; Dirk Hoerder, *Crowd Action in Revolutionary Massachusetts, 1765–1780* (New York, 1977), 279. The first quote is from Isaac N. Phelps Stokes, *The Iconography of Manhattan Island, 1498–1905*, 6 vols. (New York, 1915), 4:864; the second from Peter Force, ed., *American Archives . . . A Documentary History of . . . the North American Colonies*, 4th ser., 6 vols. (Washington, D.C., 1837–1846), 1:1106–1107, herein cited as *American Archives*.

6. *Rivington*, Sept. 8, 1774; Merrill Jensen, *The Founding of a Nation: A History of the American Revolution* (New York, 1969), 535–536; Hoerder, *Crowd Action in Massachusetts*, 294–295.

7. William Smith, *Historical Memoirs of William Smith, Historian of the Province of New York, Member of the Governor's Council . . .*, ed. William H. W. Sabine, 2 vols. (New York, 1956–1958), 1:192, herein cited as Smith, *Memoirs*; Stokes, *Iconography* 4:866.

8. *A Card*, Sept. 9, 1774 [New York, 1774], Evans, 13184; Frederick Haldimand to Thomas Gage, Sept. 10, 1774, Haldimand Papers, Additional Manuscripts, No. 21665, British Museum, London.

9. "The Free Citizens," *To the Public*, Sept. 14, 1774 [New York, 1774], Evans, 13668; *NYGWM*, Sept. 26, 1774; *American Archives*, 4th ser., 1:803–804, 809.

10. "Humanus," *To the Inhabitants of New-York*, Sept. 29, 1774 [New York, 1774], Evans, 13342; *To the Respectable Body of Gentlemen Nominated by the Public Voice as a Committee* [New York, 1774], Evans, 13483.

11. *NYGWM*, Oct. 3, 1774; Isaac Sears et al., *To the Public*, Oct. 1, 1774 [New York, 1774], Evans, 13484; Robert J. Christen, *King Sears: Politician and Patriot in a Decade of Revolution* (New York, 1982), 351. For the anti-radical propaganda, see *To the Freeholders, Freemen, and Inhabitants of the City of New York; and particularly to Our Steady Friends and Associates, the Children and Negroes of the Said City* [New York, 1774], Evans, 13656.

12. CC to Lord Dartmouth, Oct. 5, 1774, *The Colden Letter Books*, 2 vols. (NYHS, *Collections*, vols. 9–10 [New York, 1877–1878]), 2:368, herein cited as *CC Letter Books*; "New York," *Boston Evening Post*, Oct. 17, 1774; *Rivington*, Oct. 20, 1774.

13. Jensen, ed., *American Colonial Documents to 1776* (London, 1955), 813–816.

14. Peter Van Schaack to John Vardill, Jan. 3, 1775, Peter Van Schaack Papers, Columbia University, New York City; Thomas Jones, *History of New York during the Revolutionary War, and of the Leading Events in the Other Colonies at That Period*, ed. Edward Floyd De Lancey, 2 vols. (New York, 1879), 1:37, herein cited as Jones, *History*; CC to Dartmouth, Nov. 2, 1774, *CC Letter Books* 2:369, 370; Butterfield et al., eds., *Diary of John Adams* 2:157.

15. *American Archives*, 4th ser., 1:328–330, 967; Carl Lotus Becker, *The History of Political Parties in the Province of New York, 1760–1776* (Madison, Wisc., 1909), 165; Smith, *Memoirs* 1:203; *Rivington*, Nov. 17, 1774.

16. *The Following Are the Names of Persons Proposed to be Elected as a Committee*, Nov. 17, 1774 [New York, 1774], Evans, 13485; *American Archives*, 4th ser., 1:987.

17. *NYGWM*, Nov. 28, 1774; Smith, *Memoirs* 1:203. Analyses of the committee's membership can be found in Becker, *History of Political Parties*, 167–168; and Bernard Mason, *The Road to Independence: The Revolutionary Movement in New York, 1773–1777* (Lexington, Ky., 1966), 38–41.

18. Daniel Dunscomb, *The Mechanics of This City . . .*, Nov. 18, 1774 [New York, 1774], Evans, 42653; "A Citizen," *To the Public. Stop Him! Stop Him! Stop Him!*, Nov. 21, 1774 [New York, 1774], Evans, 13676; *NYJ*, Dec. 15, 1774.

19. Dartmouth to the Governors in America, Oct. 19, 1774, *DCHNY* 8:509; CC to Dartmouth, Jan. 4, 1775, *CC Letter Books* 2:377–379; *To the Public*, Dec. 30, 1774 [New York, 1774], Evans, 13666; *American Archives*, 4th ser., 1:1070–1072, the first quote is from p. 1070; "Plain English," *To the Inhabitants of New-York* [New York, 1774], Evans, 13658; "A Number of Citizens," *To the Public*, Dec. 30, 1774 [New York, 1774], Evans, 13666; James Duane to Thomas Jefferson, Dec. 29, 1774, Paul H. Smith et al., eds. *Letters of Delegates to Congress, 1774–1789*, 14 vols. (Washington, D.C., 1976–), 1:281; Alexander McDougall to William Cooper, Feb. 9, 1775, Alexander McDougall Papers, NYHS.

20. Hugh Hughes to John Lamb, Nov. 23, 1774, John Lamb Papers, 1735–1800, NYHS; Jensen, ed., *American Colonial Documents*, 815. The quote is from "Marcus Brutus" [Alexander McDougall] to Samuel Adams, Jan. 29, 1774, McDougall Papers.

21. CC to Dartmouth, Dec. 7, 1774, Mar. 1, 1775, *CC Letter Books* 2:372–375, 389; Roger J. Champagne, "The Sons of Liberty and the Aristocracy in New York Politics, 1765–1790" (Ph.D. diss., University of Wisconsin, 1960), 371; "Marcus Brutus" [McDougall] to S. Adams, Jan. 29, 1774, McDougall Papers; *NYGWM*, Dec. 12, 1774; *American Archives*, 4th ser., 1:1203, 2:342–343; "A Freeholder," *To the Freeholders, Freemen, and Inhabitants of the City and County of New York*, Feb. 6, 1775 [New York, 1775], Evans, 14497.

22. Kriesberg, *Social Conflicts*, 13. CC to Capt. James Montagu, Feb. 8, CC to Gage, Feb. 20, 1775, *CC Letter Books* 2:384–385, 386–387; Smith, *Memoirs* 1:210. The quote is from *American Archives*, 4th ser., 1:1243–1244.

23. Smith, *Memoirs* 1:210; Christen, *King Sears*, 358–359.

24. *American Archives*, 4th ser., 1:1257, 2:145, 283–284; Alexander McDougall, "Minutes of the Committee of Sixty," Feb. 20, 1775, McDougall to Thaddeus Burr, Feb. 26, 1775, McDougall Papers; Peter R. Livingston to Robert Livingston, Feb. 19, 1775, Livingston Family Papers, Johnson Redmond Collection, Reel 6, NYHS (microfilm); CC to Gage, Feb. 20, 1775, *CC Letter Books* 2:386–387; *To the Freeholders, Freemen, and Inhabitants of the City and County of New-York*, Feb. 25, 1775 [New York, 1775],

Evans, 14496; "A Son of Freedom," *The Following Letter Was Some Nights Ago Thrown in among the Sons of Liberty*, Mar. 17, 1775 [New York, 1775], Evans, 14031; *To the Public*, Mar. 18, 21, 1775 [New York, 1775], Evans, 14266, 14267; *The Following Is a Copy of a Letter Wrote by a Lady of This City to Capt. S—s and Capt. McD—l*, Mar. 20, 1775 [New York, 1775], Evans, 14032; *NYJ*, Mar. 23, 1775; Robert Honyman, *Colonial Panorama 1775: Dr. Robert Honyman's Journal for March and April*, ed. Philip Padelford (San Marino, Ca., 1939), 31, herein cited as Honyman, *Colonial Panorama*. Smith, *Memoirs* 1:214; Champagne, "Sons of Liberty," 372–373.

25. Jacobus Van Zandt et al., *To the Public*, Mar. 24, 1775 [New York, 1775], Evans, 14514; "A Friend of Order," *To the Public*, Mar. 22, 1775 [New York, 1775], Evans, 14513; Gage to CC, Feb. 26, 1775, *The Letters and Papers of Cadwallader Colden*, 8 vols. (NYHS, *Collections*, vols. 50–56, 67 [New York, 1917–1923, 1937]), 7:267; Committee of Sixty to the New Haven Committee, Apr. 17, 1775, Richard B. Morris, ed., *John Jay, The Making of a Revolutionary: Unpublished Papers, 1745–1780* (New York, 1975), 143; CC to Dartmouth, Mar. 1, 1775, *CC Letter Books* 2:389.

26. Jones, *History* 1:45.

27. In order, the quotes are from Jones, *History* 1:35–36; Philip Ranlet, *The New York Loyalists* (Knoxville, 1986), 186; Rick J. Ashton, "The Loyalist Congressmen of New York," *NYHSQ* 60 (1976): 104–105. Robert Ernst, "Isaac Low and the American Revolution," *NYH* 74 (1993): 133–158. Compare P. Van Schaack to Vardill, May 13, 1774, Henry Cruger Van Schaack, *Memoir of Henry Van Schaack, Embracing Selections of His Correspondence and Other Writings* (Chicago, 1892), 27–29, with "Phileleutherus Caesarienses" to Hugh Gaine, *NYGWM*, Oct. 3, 1774.

28. Janice Potter, *The Liberty We Seek: Loyalist Ideology in Colonial New York and Massachusetts* (Cambridge, Mass., 1983), 60, 84–106; Hilda Neatby, "Chief Justice William Smith: An Eighteenth Century Whig Imperialist," *Canadian Historical Review* 28 (1949): 44–67; William A. Benton, *Whig-Loyalism: An Aspect of Political Ideology in the American Revolutionary Era* (Rutherford, N.J., 1968), 174–175; Memorial of Catherine Leach, June 1789, Audit Office 13/65, 34, Public Record Office, London [Library of Congress microfilm], herein cited as A.O.; Memorial of Myles Cooper, Nov. 13, 1782, A.O. 13/64, 125; Memorial of Robert Bayard, n.d., Memorial of James Deas, n.d., A.O. 13/113, 104, 225; "To the Inhabitants of New-York," Oct. 20, 1774, *American Archives*, 4th ser., 1:886–888; "A New-York Freeholder," "To the Inhabitants of North America," *NYGWM*, Oct. 3, 1774; "A Poor Man" to the Printer, *Constitutional Gazette*, Nov. 25, 1775.

29. By way of comparison, from 5,000 to 8,000 African Americans, probably most from the North, fought in the Continental Army; in 1770 there were approximately 50,000 blacks in the North and 460,000 in what was to become the United States. Graham Russell Hodges, "Black Revolt in New York City and the Neutral Zone: 1775–83" in Paul A. Gilje and William Pencak, eds., *New York in the Age of the Constitution, 1775–1800* (Rutherford, N.J., 1992), 20–21, 25, 28–30; the quote is from p. 23. Philip S. Foner, *Blacks in the American Revolution* (Westport, Conn., 1976), 67; *The Statistical History of the United States from Colonial Times to the Present* (Stamford, Conn., 1965), 756.

30. Extract of a Letter from New York, *NYJ*, Aug. 25, 1774; David C. Humphrey, *From King's College to Columbia, 1746–1800* (New York, 1976), 22, 28, 51; Bruce E. Steiner, *Samuel Seabury, 1729–1796: A Study in the High Church Tradition* (Oberlin, Ohio 1971), 99–101, 128–129; Jeremy Gregory, "Anglicanism and the Arts: Religion, Culture and Politics in the Eighteenth Century" in Jeremy Black and Jeremy Gregory,

eds., *Culture, Politics, and Society in Britain* (Manchester, 1991), 82, 102. John Frederick Woolverton, *Colonial Anglicanism in North America* (Detroit, 1984), 185–186; the first quote is from p. 185. Bernard Semmel, *The Methodist Revolution* (New York, 1977), 14–15, 56–71; the second quote is from pp. 25–26.

31. Randall Balmer, *A Perfect Babel of Confusion: Dutch Religion and English Culture in the Middle Colonies* (New York, 1989), viii–xix; Mark Noll, *Christians in the American Revolution* (Washington, D.C., 1977), 115–116. According to Dructor's study, 83.5% of the Anglican (96 of 115), 27.5% of the Dutch Reformed (19 of 69), 34.1% of the Presbyterian (15 of 44), 26.1% of the Jewish (4 of 15), 100% of the Quaker (11 of 11), 60% of the Lutheran (3 of 5), and 100% of the Baptist merchants (1 of 1) became loyalists; Robert M. Dructor, "The New York Commercial Community: The Revolutionary Experience" (Ph.D. diss., University of Pittsburgh, 1975), 47.

32. Joseph S. Tiedemann, "Queens County, New York Quakers in the American Revolution: Loyalists or Neutrals?" *Historical Magazine of the Protestant Episcopal Church* 52 (1983): 215–228; Arthur J. Mekeel, *The Relation of the Quakers to the American Revolution* (Washington, D.C., 1979), 101–102.

33. For articles that show how personal the decision was, see Carl L. Becker, "John Jay and Peter Van Schaack," *NYH* 1 (1919): 1–12; and Michael Kammen, "The American Revolution as a *Crise de Conscience*: The Case of New York," in Richard M. Jellison, ed., *Society, Freedom, and Conscience: The American Revolution in Virginia, Masachusetts, and New York* (New York, 1976), 125–189. CC to Dartmouth, Dec. 7, 1774, *CC Letter Books* 2:372–375; Haldimand to Dartmouth, May 4, 1774, Kenneth G. Davies, ed., *Documents of the American Revolution, 1770–1783*, 21 vols. (Kill-o'-the-Grange, Ireland, 1972–1981), 8:107–108, herein cited as *Documents of the Revolution*; Tiedemann, "A Revolution Foiled: Queens County, New York, 1775–1776," *JAH* 75 (1988): 417–444; Potter, *Liberty We Seek*, 147–148.

34. Samuel Seabury, *Letters of a Westchester Farmer*, ed. Clarence H. Vance (White Plains, N.Y., 1930), 43–48; the quotes are from pp. 61, 73, 111, 133, and 157. Philip Davidson, *Propaganda and the American Revolution, 1763–1783* (Chapel Hill, N.C., 1941), 249–251. For criticism of the whig leadership, see *Rivington*, Aug. 11, Sept. 22, 29, Oct. 20, Dec. 8, 15, 1774; "Ebenezer Snuffle, Secretary," *At a Meeting of the True Sons of Liberty, in the City of New York* . . . [New York, 1774], Evans, 13126; *Debates at the Robin-Hood Society, in the City of New York, on Monday Night 19th of July 1774* [New York, 1774], Evans, 13486; "Agricola," *To the Inhabitants of the City and County of New York*, July 12, 1774 [New York, 1774], Evans, 13097.

35. CC to Dartmouth, July 6, Aug. 2, Dec. 7, 1774, *CC Letter Books* 2:346–347, 349–351, 372–375; Mason, *Road to Independence*, 64; Ranlet, *New York Loyalists*, 8, 186; Gov. William Tryon to Dartmouth, July 4, 1775, C.O. 5/1106; Tryon to Dartmouth, July 7, 1775, Historical Manuscripts Commission, *The Manuscripts of the Earl of Dartmouth*, vol. 2 (*Fourteenth Report, Appendix, Pt. 10* [London, 1895]), 328.

36. CC to Gage, June 5, 1774, Gage to CC, May 23, 1775, Military Papers of Gen. Thomas Gage, William L. Clements Library, Ann Arbor, herein cited as Gage Papers; Haldimand to Dartmouth, May 4, 1774, *Documents of the Revolution* 8:107; CC to Dartmouth, Dec. 7, 1774, *CC Letter Books* 2:372–375; Josiah Martin to Dartmouth, Nov. 4, 1774, *Documents of the Revolution* 8:225–228; "Plan Made in England," [1775], Sir Henry Clinton Papers, 1750–1812, Clements Library.

37. For the efforts by the British government to influence events in New York, see Mason, *Road to Independence*, 42–63.

38. Josiah Quincy to Joseph Reed, Dec. 17, 1774, Dennis DeBirdt to Reed, Jan. 6, 1775, Joseph Reed Papers, NYHS; Duane to John Tabor Kempe, Oct. 11, 1774, Smith, ed., *Letters of Delegates to Congress* 1:174. Also see William Lee to Richard Henry Lee, Sept. 19, 1774, Jan. 10, Feb. 25, 1775, Worthington C. Ford, ed., *Letters of William Lee, 1766–1783* (New York, 1891), 90, 96, 119–120, 127–129; William Hooper to Duane, Dec. 22, 1774, James Duane Papers, 1680–1853, NYHS; and "New York," *Dunlap's Pennsylvania Packet*, Oct. 31, 1774.

39. *The Boston Gazette, and Country Journal*, Mar. 27, 1775. *Dunlap's Pennsylvania Packet*, Apr. 19, 1775; the person referred to was John Jay; Arthur Lee to Richard Henry Lee, Feb. 25, 1775, Ford, ed., *Letters of William Lee*, 127; Lee to Samuel Adams, Apr. 10, 1775, Samuel Adams Papers, 1635–1827, NYPL; *Pennsylvania Journal*, May 17, 1775.

40. "Citizens of New York," *To the Public*, Nov. 16, 1774 [New York, 1774], Evans, 13677; *Extract of a Letter from London, July 25, 1774* [New York, 1774], Evans, 13493; *NYJ*, Feb. 9, Mar. 2, 1775; *American Archives*, 4th ser., 2:508. Also see *To the Inhabitants of the City and County of New-York*, Mar. 4, 1775 [New York, 1775], Evans, 14162; *To the Inhabitants of the City, County and Province of New York*, Mar. 11, 1775 [New York, 1775], Evans, 14506; and *No Placemen, Pensioners, Ministerial Hirelings, Popery, nor Arbitrary Power!*, Mar. 13, 1775 [New York, 1775], Evans, 14399.

41. Dartmouth to CC, Dec. 10, 1774, John Pownall to James Rivington, Apr. 5, Pownall to Myles Cooper and Thomas Bradbury Chandler, Apr. 5, 1775, *DCHNY* 8:514, 568, 569; Mason, *Road to Independence*, 48.

42. *The Plot Discovered* [New York, 1775], Evans, 14408; *DCHNY* 8:573.

43. CC to Dartmouth, Nov. 2, Dec. 7, 1774, Jan. 4, 1775, *CC Letter Books* 2:370, 374–375, 378.

44. Smith, *Memoirs* 1:206–209; the quote is from p. 207. Champagne, "Sons of Liberty," 375. For a somewhat different interpretation, see Leopold S. Launitz-Schürer, *Loyal Whigs and Revolutionaries: The Making of the Revolution in New York* (New York, 1980), 131.

45. Smith, *Memoirs* 1:209, 208; CC to Dartmouth, Dec. 7, 1774, *CC Letter Books* 2:375.

46. Smith, *Memoirs* 1:208. CC to Dartmouth, Feb. 1, 1775, *CC Letter Books* 2:383. Colden was not far from the mark. Of the 9 individuals to whom he was evidently referring, 4 voted loyalist on the key votes for which they were present; three never attended; only 1 voted whig on all the key votes; and 1 voted loyalist on 3 out of 4 votes.

47. CC to Dartmouth, Feb. 1, 1775, *CC Letter Books* 2:382–383; *American Archives*, 4th ser., 1:1286–1287. The move was prearranged, for a notice in John Holt's paper advised residents to attend the session; *NYJ*, Jan. 26, 1775.

48. For a discussion of whether these bribery charges were true, see Mason, *Road to Independence*, 50–53. Only one individual who arrived after January 26, John Thomas of Westchester, voted pro-American on all the key votes that followed. William Nicoll, however, who voted with the whigs on January 26, voted with the loyalists for the remainder of the session.

49. *American Archives*, 4th ser., 1:1289–1290. For a different view, see Champagne, "New York Politics and Independence, 1776," *NYHSQ* 46 (1962): 282.

50. *American Archives*, 4th ser., 1:1313–1321; the quote is from p. 1302.

51. See CC to Dartmouth, Feb. 1, Mar. 1, Apr. 5, 1775, *CC Letter Books* 2:382–384, 388–391, 395–398; CC to Gage, Jan. 29, Gage to Dartmouth, Feb. 17, Barrington to

Gage, Apr. 4, 1775, Gage Papers; Burke to James De Lancey, Mar. 14, 1775, Ross J. S. Hoffman, *Edmund Burke: New York Agent with His Letters to the New York Assembly and Intimate Correspondence with Charles O'Hara, 1761–1776* (Philadelphia, 1956), 262–263; Josiah Martin to Dartmouth, Jan. 26, 1775, *Documents of the Revolution* 9:36–37.

52. *American Archives*, 4 ser., 1:1315.

53. Jones, *History* 2:270; Lorenzo Sabine, *Biographical Sketches of Loyalists of the American Revolution, with an Historical Essay*, 2 vols. (Boston, 1864), 1:368, 2:404. Dartmouth to Tryon, May 23, 1775, C.O. 5/1106.

54. CC to Dartmouth, July 6, 1774, CC to Graves, Feb. 20, CC to Gage, Feb. 20, Apr. 13, CC to Capt. George Vandeput, May 27, 1775, *CC Letter Books* 2:346–347, 387–389, 386–387, 410–412, 413; Gage to CC, Feb. 26, Samuel Graves to Gage, Mar. 22, Gage to Graves, Mar. 23, 1775, Gage Papers; Gage to Dartmouth, May 13, 1775, Clarence Edwin Carter, ed., *The Correspondence of General Thomas Gage . . .*, 2 vols. (New Haven, 1931–1933), 1:397–398; Graves to Philip Stevens, Mar. 4, 1775, Admiralty Papers 1/485, Public Record Office, London [Library of Congress microfilm]; Dartmouth to Gage, Mar. 3, Apr. 15, Gage to Dartmouth, June 12, 1775, C.O. 5/92; Smith, *Memoirs* 1:228c; *American Archives*, 4th ser., 2:106; Peter Keteltas to John Alsop, May 27, 1775, Misc. Mss., NYHS.

55. McDougall to Cooper, Feb. 9, 1775, McDougall Papers. John Dickinson had proposed the same idea in Pennsylvania in June 1774; Richard Alan Ryerson, *The Revolution Is Now Begun: The Radical Committees of Philadelphia, 1765–1776* (Philadelphia, 1978), 47.

56. *The Following Extracts from the Proceedings of the Committee of Observation . . .* [New York, 1775], Evans, 14318; John Thurman, Chairman, *To the Freemen and Freeholders of the City and County of New York*, Mar. 4, 1774 [sic] [New York, 1775], Evans, 14500. Also see *Rivington*, Mar. 2, 1775; "A Citizen of New-York," *NYGWM*, Mar. 6, 1775. For the whig reply, see *American Archives*, 4th ser., 2:50; "A Citizen," *To the Inhabitants of the City and County of New-York*, Mar. 4, 1775 [New York, 1775], Evans, 14162; and "Americanus," *To the Freeholders and Freemen of the City of New-York*, Mar. 4, 1775 [New York, 1775], Evans, 13809.

57. *American Archives*, 4th ser., 2:48–49; Champagne, *Alexander McDougall*, 79; Memorial of William Cunningham, Mar. 17, 1784, A.O. 13/64, 183. Also see "Phileleutheros," *No Placemen, Pensioners, Ministerial Hirelings, Popery, nor Arbitrary Power!*, Mar. 13, 1775 [New York, 1775], Evans, 14399.

58. *NYJ*, Mar. 9, 1775; "Impartial," *Rivington*, Mar. 9, 1775; *American Archives*, 4th ser., 2:48–50; Jones, *History* 1:38; William Gordon, *History of the Rise, Progress, and Establishment of Independence in the United States of America*, 4 vols. (London, 1788), 1:472. Smith, *Memoirs* 1:211, believed the margin in favor of the motions was between three-to-one and ten-to-one.

59. *The Following Extracts from the Proceedings of the Committee of Observation . . .* [New York, 1775], Evans, 14318; *American Archives*, 4th ser., 2:137–139. Writers before and after April 15 referred to the Provincial Convention of April 1775 as a Provincial Congress, but since the decision was made at this time that the agenda would be limited to electing delegates to the Second Continental Congress, I will henceforth, except in direct quotations, refer to the body as the Provincial Convention. For the tory propaganda, see "A Freeman," *To the Freeholders and Freemen of the City and County of New York* [New York, 1775], Broadside Collection, NYHS. On the patriot side, see "A Whig," *To the Inhabitants of the City, County and Province of New York*, Mar. 11, 1775

[New York, 1775], Evans, 14506; *To the Freeholders, and Freemen, of the City of New York,* Mar. 14, 1775 [New York, 1775], Evans, 14495; and "A Tincker," *To the Free and Respectable Mechanicks, and the Other Inhabitants of the City and County of New-York,* Mar. 13, 1775 [New York, 1775], Evans, 14491. For the political maneuvering, see *Election Proxy* [New York, 1775], Evans, 42902; Isaac Low, *To the Respectful Public,* Mar. 15, 1775 [New York, 1775], Evans, 14167; *To Mr. Isaac Low,* Mar. 16, 1775 [New York, 1775], Evans, 42945; and Smith, *Memoirs* 1:212–213.

60. McDougall, "Minutes of the Committee of Sixty," Mar. 27, 1775, McDougall Papers; *NYGWM,* Apr. 3, 1775; *NYJ,* Apr. 13, 1775; "Anti-Licentiousness," *Rivington,* Apr. 20, 1775; Smith, *Memoirs* 1:219; *To the Inhabitants of the City and County of New York,* Apr. 3, 1775 [New York, 1775], Evans, 14505. The quote is from Honyman, *Colonial Panorama,* 68. Also see Ranlet, *New York Loyalists,* 57; and Christen, *King Sears,* 368, 370.

61. Ralph Thurman, *To the Inhabitants of the City and County of New-York,* Apr. 15, 1775 [New York, 1775], Evans, 14484; Smith, *Memoirs* 1:212–213, 220; Warrant for Sears's Arrest, Apr. 14, 1775, McDougall Papers.

62. "A Real Churchman" to Vardill, May 2, 1775, Egerton Manuscripts, British Museum; CC to Dartmouth, May 3, 1775, *CC Letter Books* 2:401–402; "Anti-Licentiousness," *Rivington,* Apr. 20, 1775; Smith, *Memoirs* 1:220–221.

63. Force, ed. *American Archives,* 4th ser., 2:357.

10. Empire and Liberty

1. *The Provincial Congress at Their Meeting . . .,* Apr. 22, 1775 [New York, 1775], Evans, 14416; William Smith, *Historical Memoirs of William Smith, Historian of the Province of New York, Member of the Governor's Council . . .,* ed. William H. W. Sabine, 2 vols. (New York, 1956–1958), 1:221–222, herein cited as Smith, *Memoirs; The Following Interesting Advices, Were This Day Received . . .,* Apr. 23, 1775 [New York, 1775], Evans, 14337; Lord Dartmouth to Gen. Thomas Gage, Jan. 27, 1775, Clarence Edwin Carter, ed., *The Correspondence of General Thomas Gage . . .,* 2 vols. (New Haven, 1931–1933), 2:179–183; the quotes are on pp. 180, 181.

2. John Shy, "The Military Conflict as a Revolutionary War," in Stephen G. Kurtz and James H. Hutson, eds., *Essays on the Revolution* (Chapel Hill, N.C., 1973), 131. Louis Kriesberg, *Social Conflicts,* 2d ed. (Englewood Cliffs, N.J., 1982), 164–167; the quotes are on pp. 164, 165.

3. Kriesberg, *Social Conflicts,* 195, 186, 198, 187, 87; "S. Sp. Skinner," "To the Right Honourable Lord ———," *Rivington's New York Gazetteer; or the Connecticut, New Jersey, Hudson's River, and Quebec Weekly Advertiser,* July 6, 1775.

4. Smith, *Memoirs* 1:222; Peter Force, ed., *American Archives . . . A Documentary History of . . . the North American Colonies,* 4th ser., 6 vols. (Washington, D.C., 1837–1846), 2:364, herein cited as *American Archives.* Philadelphia's experience was very similar; see George Atkinson Ward, ed., *Journal and Letters of the Late Samuel Curwen* (New York, 1845), 26.

5. RRL to Unk., Apr. 27, 1775, Livingston Family Papers, NYPL; *American Archives,* 4th ser., 2:449.

6. Thomas Jones, *History of New York during the Revolutionary War, and of the Leading Events in the Other Colonies at That Period,* ed. Edward Floyd De Lancey, 2 vols. (New York, 1879), 1:39–40, herein cited as Jones, *History;* the quote is from p. 39. Alexander McDougall, "Minutes of the Committee of Sixty," Apr. 24, 1775, Alexander McDou-

gall Papers, NYHS; Merrill Jensen, *The Founding of a Nation: A History of the American Revolution* (New York, 1969), 594; Smith, *Memoirs* 1:222; New York Mercantile Library Association, *New York City during the American Revolution, Being a Collection of Original Papers from the Manuscripts in the Possession of the Mercantile Library Association* (New York, 1861), 54–56, herein cited as *New York in the Revolution*.

7. CC to Dartmouth, May 3, 1775, *The Colden Letter Books*, 2 vols. (NYHS, *Collections*, vols. 9–10 [New York, 1877–1878]), 2:400–403, herein cited as *CC Letter Books*; Extract of a Letter from Guy Johnson to Henry Van Schaack, Apr. 25, 1775, Alexander C. Flick and James Sullivan, eds., *The Papers of Sir William Johnson*, 14 vols. (New York, 1921–1965), 7:450; Capt. James Montagu to Vice Adm. Samuel Graves, Apr. 26, 1775, William Bell Clark et al., eds., *Naval Documents of the American Revolution*, 9 vols. (Washington, D.C., 1964–), 1:228; Peter Van Schaack to Col. John Maunsell, May 7, 1775, Henry Cruger Van Schaack, *Memoir of Henry Van Schaack, Embracing Selections of His Correspondence and Other Writings* (Chicago, 1892), 37.

8. Smith, *Memoirs* 1:222; Montagu to Graves, Apr. 26, 1775, Clark et al., eds., *Naval Documents* 1:228; Robert J. Christen, *King Sears: Politician and Patriot in a Decade of Revolution* (New York, 1982), 383. The first quote is from CC to Dartmouth, May 3, 1775, *CC Letter Books* 2:402; the second from Letter by a Real Churchman, May 2, 1775, Egerton Manuscripts, British Museum, London.

9. Smith, *Memoirs* 1:221; Jones, *History* 1:41.

10. *Calendar of Historical Manuscripts Relating to the War of the Revolution, in the Office of the Secretary of State*, ed. Edmund B. O'Callaghan, 2 vols. (Albany, 1868), 1:3–4, herein cited as *Calendar of Historical Manuscripts*. On Apr. 28, the committee asked the counties to appoint delegates; Isaac Low, *Committee-Chamber, New York, Apr. 28, 1775* [New York, 1775], Evans, 14323; *The Following Persons Are Recommended to the Public*, Apr. 27, 1775 [New York, 1775], Evans, 14034. The quotes are from McDougall, "Minutes of the Committee of Sixty," Apr. 24, 1775, McDougall Papers.

11. Draft of letter by the Committee of Sixty, Apr. 27, 1775, Robert R. Livingston Papers, Reel 18, NYHS (microfilm); "Military Association," New York City, Misc. Mss., NYHS; Ralph Thurman, *To the Inhabitants of the City and Colony of New-York*, Apr. 15, 1775 [New York, 1775], Evans, 14484; Christen, *King Sears*, 390–391; Roger J. Champagne, "New York's Radicals and the Coming of Independence," *JAH* 51 (1964): 23, n. 4; Robert Ernst, "Andrew Elliot, Forgotten Loyalist of Occupied New York," *NYH* 57 (1976): 285–320; "A Short Detail of the Conduct of the Collector of New York from December 1774 to March 1776," Andrew Elliot Papers, 1747–1777, New York State Library, Albany.

12. Both slates were published the next day; *The Following Persons Are Nominated by the Sons of Liberty . . .*, Apr. 28, 1775 [New York, 1775], Evans, 14033; Smith, *Memoirs* 1:222; Champagne, "New York's Radicals and Independence," *JAH* 51 (1964): 23; Christen, *King Sears*, 395.

13. Smith, *Memoirs* 1:222; *To the Freeholders and Freemen of the City and County of New-York*, Apr. 28, 1775 [New York, 1775], Evans, 42898.

14. *American Archives*, 4th ser., 2:448–449; Smith, *Memoirs* 1:222, 223; RRL to his wife, May 3, 1775, Livingston Family Papers, NYPL; Jones, *History* 1:42; *A General Association, Agreed to, and Subscribed by the Freeholders, Freemen, and Inhabitants of the City and County of New York*, Apr. and May 1775 [New York, 1775], Evans, 14339. Christen, *King Sears*, 397–398, offers a different view of the Association's significance.

15. *Extracts from Bradford's Pennsylvania Journal of Apr. 26, 1775* [New York, 1775],

Evans, 14028; Jones, *History* 1:41–44. The quotes are from *American Archives*, 4th ser., 2:449; and RRL to his wife, May 3, 1775, Livingston Family Papers, NYPL. Henry White, *To the Public* [New York, 1775], Evans, 14624. White had asked that troops not be withdrawn; Mr. W[hite] to [William Tryon], Dec. 7, 1774, Historical Manuscripts Commission, *The Manuscripts of the Earl of Dartmouth*, vol. 2 (*Fourteenth Report, Appendix, Pt. 10* [London, 1895]), 237.

16. *General Committee*, May 1, 1775 [New York, 1775], Evans, 14325; *American Archives*, 4th ser., 2:468; Christen, *King Sears*, 194, 218, 393–398; Jones, *History* 1:41–44.

17. Joseph E. Illick, *Colonial Pennsylvania: A History* (New York, 1976), 310.

18. Champagne, "The Sons of Liberty and the Aristocracy in New York Politics, 1765–1790" (Ph.D. diss., University of Wisconsin, 1960), 392; RRL to RRL, Jr., May 5, 1775, James Duane to RRL, Jr., Mar. 20, 1776, Livingston Family Papers, NYPL; *American Archives*, 4th ser., 2:510–512.

19. *American Archives*, 4th ser., 2:1534; Tryon to Dartmouth, July 4, Aug. 7, 1775, C.O. 5/1106; Smith, *Memoirs* 1:240.

20. Larry R. Gerlach, *Prologue to Independence: New Jersey in the Coming of the American Revolution* (New Brunswick, N.J., 1976), 327.

21. Kriesberg, *Social Conflicts*, 133–134. What was happening in New York was not unique. John M. Head, *A Time to Rend: An Essay on the Decision for American Independence* (Madison, Wisc., 1968), 19, xiii–xiv, argued that New York, New Jersey, Pennsylvania, Delaware, Maryland, and South Carolina, which "were populated by an explosive mixture of cultural groups" and had experienced stable or rapid economic development in the decade before 1774, suffered from "the absence of unifying institutions" and were "comparatively hesitant about or . . . strongly opposed" to independence. Although the various groups had managed to live in relative harmony, he said, the imperial crises of the 1760s and 1770s affected them all so differently that they lacked the internal unity needed to develop a united front against Great Britain.

22. For an alternate view of New York's political parties and their leaders, see Edward Countryman, *A People in Revolution: The American Revolution and Political Society in New York, 1760–1790* (Baltimore, 1981), 78.

23. "Candidus," *Constitutional Gazette*, Mar. 16, 1776; Samuel Seabury, *Free Thoughts on the Proceedings of the Continental Congress*, in Samuel Seabury, *Letters of a Westchester Farmer*, ed. Clarence H. Vance (White Plains, N.Y., 1930), 43–68. Concerning the spirit of materialism in New York, see Michael Kammen, *Colonial New York: A History* (New York, 1975), 230; and William Livingston and Others, *The Independent Reflector*, ed. Milton M. Klein (Cambridge, Mass., 1963), 33.

24. RRL, Jr., to Duane, Feb. 16, 1776, Livingston Family Papers, NYPL. Also see Milton M. Klein, "New York Lawyers and the Coming of the American Revolution," *NYH* 55 (1974): 383–408.

25. CC to Dartmouth, Dec. 7, 1774, *CC Letter Books* 2:373; John Holt to Joseph Reed, Aug. 24, 1775, Reed Papers, Reel 1, NYHS; "A Sober Citizen," *To the Inhabitants of the City and County of New York*, Apr. 16, 1776 [New York, 1776], Evans, 15110.

26. CC wrote Gage on May 4 that the committee "has assumed the whole Power of Government"; *CC Letter Books* 2:406. For its activities, see *American Archives*, 4th ser., 2:468–470, 509, 522, 529-535, 636, 727. Address of the New York Association to Lt. Gov. Cadwallader Colden, May 11, 1775, *DCHNY* 8:585.

27. For Congress's activities, see *American Archives*, 4th ser., 2:845–846, 934, 1046, 1242, 1245, 1254, 1255, 1262, 1265–1270, 1275–1286, 1292-1299, 1301, 1310,

1333–1338, 1793, 1800, 1806, 3:15, 20-25, 133, 139, 150, 213, 223, 235, 238, 262, 438, 445, 459, 466, 543, 625, 627, 644, 653, 660, 681, 690, 708, 726, 737, 750, 774, 778, 851, 936, 983, 988, 1118, 1150, 1181, 1206. CC to Capt. George Vandeput, May 27, 1775, *CC Letter Books* 2:413.

28. *American Archives*, 4th ser., 2:1265, 1271, 1326–1327. Isaac Sears was elected to Congress on June 8, 1775, when George Folliot refused to serve; *Journals of the Provincial Congress, Provincial Convention, Committee of Safety, and Council of Safety of the State of New York*, 2 vols. (Albany, 1842), 1:36. Kriesberg, *Social Conflicts*, 6–9, 179. The report presented on June 24 was apparently based on a proposal John Dickinson had made to the Continental Congress in May. Nonetheless, the document adopted on June 27 contained significant changes, which reflected public opinion in New York: the call for a permanent Continental Congress and the denial of Parliament's right to interfere with religion as practiced in the colonies. John A. Neuenschwander, *The Middle Colonies and the Coming of the American Revolution* (Port Washington, N.Y., 1973), 93–95.

29. *American Archives*, 4th ser., 2:1341; Tryon to Dartmouth, July 7, 1775, *DCHNY* 8:593; Gage to Tryon, July 18, 1775, Military Papers of Gen. Thomas Gage, Clements Library, Ann Arbor; Philip Ranlet, *The New York Loyalists* (Knoxville, 1986), 61.

30. *Extract of a Letter from Philadelphia to a Gentleman in This City*, May 8, 1775 [New York, 1775], Evans, 14341; Christopher Smith to John Alsop, May 12, 1775, Misc. Mss., NYHS; *American Archives*, 4th ser., 2:618; *Journals of the Continental Congress* 2:60.

31. Isaac Hamilton to CC, May 26, 1775, *The Letters and Papers of Cadwallader Colden*, 8 vols. (NYHS, *Collections*, vols. 50-56, 67 [New York, 1917–1923, 1937]), 7:297–298; and CC to Hamilton, May 27, June 5, CC to Gage, May 31, 1775, *CC Letter Books* 2:413–414, 417–418; *American Archives*, 4th ser., 2:1274; *In Provincial Congress*, June 7, 1775 [New York, 1775], Evans, 14304; Champagne, *Alexander McDougall and the American Revolution* (Syracuse, 1975), 89, 116. *New York in the Revolution*, 57–65; the quotes are from pp. 57, 58, 59, and 65.

32. *American Archives*, 4th ser., 2:1257.

33. Vandeput to Tryon, July 13, John Watts, Jr., David Matthews, and George Brewerton to Vandeput, July 13, 1775, C.O. 5/1106. *American Archives*, 4th ser., 2:1305–1306, 1645, 1785-1786, 1792; the last quote is from p. 1792.

34. Tryon to Vandeput, July 30, 1775, C.O. 5/1106; *American Archives*, 4th ser., 2:1820, 3:533; Elaine Forman Crane, *A Dependent People: Newport, Rhode Island in the Revolutionary Era* (New York, 1985), 121–123.

35. Vandeput to Graves, Aug. 24, 1775, Kenneth G. Davies, ed., *Documents of the American Revolution, 1770–1783*, 21 vols. (Kill-o'-the-Grange, Ireland, 1972–1981), 11:82–83, herein cited as *Documents of the Revolution*; *American Archives*, 4th ser., 3:259–260, 535, 541–542, 5:1449; Holt to Reed, Aug. 24, 1775, Reed Papers, Reel 1.

36. Vandeput to the Mayor and Magistrates of the City of New York, Aug. 24, Vandeput to the Mayor and Magistrates of New York, Aug. 24, Whitehead Hicks to Vandeput, Aug. 24, the Mayor and Magistrates to Vandeput, Aug. 25, Vandeput to the Mayor and Magistrates, Aug. 25, 1775, C.O. 5/1106.

37. *American Archives*, 4th ser., 3:261; Extract of a Letter from New York, *Pennsylvania Journal*, Aug. 30, 1775; Tryon to Dartmouth, Sept. 5, 1775, *DCHNY* 8:632.

38. *American Archives*, 4th ser., 3:558, 564–565; *In Provincial Congress*, Sept. 1, 1775 [New York, 1775], Evans, 14311; *Constitutional Gazette*, Sept. 6, 1775; Morgan Lewis to Samuel Blachley Webb, Sept. 4, 1775, Worthington C. Ford, ed., *The Correspondence and Journals of Samuel Blachley Webb*, vol. 1 (New York, 1893), 102.

39. Graves to Vandeput, Sept. 10, 1775, *Documents of the Revolution* 11:104; *American Archives*, 4th ser., 3:902.

40. *American Archives*, 4th ser., 3:261; Extract of a Letter from New York, *Pennsylvania Journal*, Aug. 30, 1775; Tryon to Lord George Germain, Apr. 6, 1776, *DCHNY* 8:674; Lewis to Webb, Sept. 4, 1775, Ford, ed., *Correspondence of Webb* 1:102; Smith, *Memoirs* 1:265. Also see Kriesberg, *Social Conflicts*, 172; and Champagne, "New York's Radicals and Independence," *JAH* 51 (1964): 31.

41. Tryon to Dartmouth, Aug. 7, 1775, C.O. 5/1106; Smith, *Memoirs* 1:239.

42. The quotes are from Countryman, *People in Revolution*, xiii.

43. Germain to [Lord Suffolk], [June 16 or 17, 1775], Richard Lord Howe to Germain, Sept. 25, 1775, *Report on the Manuscripts of Mrs. Stopford-Sackville, of Drayton House, Northamptonshire*, vol. 2 (Historical Manuscripts Commission, *Fifteenth Report* [London, 1910]), 3, 9; Dartmouth to Gage, July 1, Aug. 2, 1775, Gage to Dartmouth, Aug. 20, 1775, Dartmouth to Gen. William Howe, Sept. 5, 1775, General Howe to Dartmouth, Oct. 9, 1775, C.O. 5/92; [Extract of a letter from Maj. Gen. John Burgoyne], John W. Fortescue, ed., *The Correspondence of King George the Third . . .*, 6 vols. (London, 1927–1928), 3:242–245; Gen. Henry Clinton to Gage, Aug. 7, 15, Oct. 7, 1775, Sir Henry Clinton Papers, 1750–1812, Clements Library.

44. *American Archives*, 4th ser., 1:170-171, 172-173; William Tryon, *Proclamation*, Nov. 14, 1775 [New York, 1775], Evans, 14068; Richard B. Morris, ed., *John Jay, The Making of a Revolutionary: Unpublished Papers, 1745-1780* (New York, 1975), 1:172, n. 3; Smith, *Memoirs* 1:256; Paul H. Smith et al., eds., *Letters of Delegates to Congress, 1774–1789*, 14 vols. (Washington, D.C., 1976–), 3:26; Carl Lotus Becker, *The History of Political Parties in the Province of New York, 1760-1776* (Madison, Wisc., 1909), 228. Bernard Mason, *The Road to Independence: The Revolutionary Movement in New York, 1773-1777* (Lexington, Ky., 1966), chap. 4; the quotes are on pp. 115, 113.

45. McDougall to John Jay, Oct. 30, Nov. 15–16, 26, Dec. 24, 1775, Morris, ed., *John Jay* 1:174, 179–180, 181-182, 214-217; Gerlach, *Prologue to Independence*, 287, 294–295, 296,303. For the situation in Bergen County, New Jersey, see Adrian C. Leiby, *The Revolutionary War in the Hackensack Valley: The Jersey Dutch and the Neutral Ground* (New Brunswick, N.J., 1962), 29–34.

46. "The Intelligencer" [or Hugh Hughes] to Samuel and John Adams, Feb. [4], 1776, Samuel Adams Papers, 1635–1827, NYPL; Smith, *Memoirs* 1:260-261.

47. McDougall to Philip Schuyler, Nov. 14, 1775, McDougall Papers; McDougall to Jay, Dec. 24, 1775, Morris, ed., *John Jay* 1:214-215.

48. "Declaration of the Inhabitants of Queens County, New York," Dec. 6, 1775, *Calendar of Historical Manuscripts* 1:200–201; *American Archives*, 4th ser., 2:321-322; Tryon to Dartmouth, Nov. 11, 1775, C.O. 5/1106; Memorial of James Leadbetter, n.d., Testimonial of Tryon for Leadbetter, n.d., Audit Office 13/65, 44, 53, Public Record Office, London [Library of Congress microfilm]; Paul David Nelson, *William Tryon and the Course of Empire: A Life in British Imperial Service* (Chapel Hill, N.C., 1990), 137–138; Tryon to General Howe, Dec. 13, 1775, C.O. 5/93; General Howe to Tryon, Jan. 11, 1776, England and America, 1620–1782, vol. 14, George Bancroft Collection, NYPL.

49. "An Occasional Remarker," *American Archives*, 4th ser., 3:1552-1553; *Pennsylvania Journal*, Dec. 6, 1775; Rivington to Tryon, Dec. 4, 1775, C.O. 5/1107; Jones, *History* 1:66–67; Vandeput to Capt. Hyde Parker, Dec. 18, 1775, *Documents of the Revolution* 11:212-213; *Journals of the Provincial Congress* 1:210, 213-214; Jay to McDougall, Dec. 22, 1775, Morris, ed., *John Jay* 1:210. The Sears quote is from Christen, *King Sears*, 411.

50. Smith, *Memoirs* 1:244–251; the full plan is on pp. 245–246. McDougall to Jay, Dec. 8, 1775, Morris, ed., *John Jay* 1:193; *Journals of the Continental Congress* 2:224–234. For a whig critique of North's plan, see "Monitor," No. VI, *NYJ*, Dec. 14, 1775. For the best discussion of William Smith's plan, see Mason, *Road to Independence*, 118–129. A peace initiative coupled with military preparations or overt hostilities is rarely convincing and often ends in a conflict's escalation; Kriesberg, *Social Conflicts*, 195.

51. Mason, *Road to Independence*, 120–121; *Address of Governor Tryon to the Inhabitants of New York*, Dec. 4, 1775 [New York, 1775], Evans, 14297; Smith, *Memoirs* 1:253–254. *American Archives*, 4th ser., 4:394–395, 406; the quote is from pp. 411–412.

52. Klein, "Failure of a Mission: The Drummond Peace Proposal of 1775," *Huntington Library Quarterly* 35 (1970): 343–380; Smith, *Memoirs* 1:254, 255; Smith to Tryon, Dec. 17, 1775, *DCHNY* 8:653–654; *American Archives*, 4th ser., 4:542, 1028; "Philo-Demos," *Constitutional Gazette*, Jan. 6, 1775; "Publicola," *To the Electors of New York*, Jan. 6, 1775 [New York, 1775], Evans, 15039; Becker, *History of Political Parties*, 242; Mason, *Road to Independence*, 130–131; *NYGWM*, Feb. 19, Mar. 18, 1776.

53. Smith, *Memoirs* 1:241–242; Tryon to Vandeput, Oct. 10, 1775, C.O. 5/1106; Francis Rhinelander to P. Van Schaack, Oct. 2, 1775, Peter Van Schaack Papers, Columbia University, New York City; *Secret Journal of the Acts and Proceedings of Congress from the First Meeting Thereof to the Dissolution of the Confederation, by the Adoption of the Constitution of the United States* (Boston, 1820), 31; Champagne, "Sons of Liberty," 414–415.

54. *American Archives*, 4th ser., 3:1314–1315; McDougall to Charles Lee, Dec. 20, 1775, McDougall Papers.

55. J. Adams, "Notes of Debate," Oct. 6, [1775], Smith, ed., *Letters of Delegates to Congress* 2:125; Lyman H. Butterfield et al., eds., *Diary and Autobiography of John Adams*, 4 vols. (Boston, 1961), 2:195. The quotes are from *American Archives*, 4th ser., 3:1052, 1053, 1054.

56. Harris Cruger to Henry Cruger, Nov. 3, 1775, *Calendar of Home Office Papers of the Reign of King George III, 1760–1775*, 4 vols. (London, 1878–99), 4:481. The quote is from "Intelligencer" [or Hughes] to S. and J. Adams, Oct. 17, 1775, S. Adams Papers.

57. *American Archives*, 4th ser., 3:1308–1309; V. Pearse Ashfield to Isaac Wilkins, Nov. 4, 14, 1775, *Calendar of Home Office Papers* 4:482, 487.

58. John Patterson to Robert Livingston, Nov. 6, 1775, Livingston Family Papers, Johnson Redmond Collection, Reel 6, NYHS (microfilm); "The Intelligencer" [or Hughes] to J. Adams, Oct. 16, 1775, Robert J. Taylor et al., eds., *Papers of John Adams*, 8 vols. (Cambridge, Mass., 1977–), 3:205–207; "The Intelligencer" [or Hughes] to J. Adams, Oct. 17, 1775, S. Adams Papers; *Journals of the Continental Congress* 3:300; *American Archives*, 4th ser., 3:1314; C. Lee to McDougall, Oct. 26, 1776, *The Lee Papers*, 3 vols. (NYHS, *Collections*, vols. 4–7 [New York, 1872-1875]), 1:214–215, herein cited as *Lee Papers*.

59. C. Lee to George Washington, Jan. 5, 24, Committee of Safety to C. Lee, Jan. 21, C. Lee to President of Congress, Jan. 22, 1776, *Lee Papers* 1:235, 242–244, 247–248, 259–260; J. Adams to Washington, Jan. 6, 1776, Taylor et al., eds., *Papers of John Adams* 3:395–396; Washington to Committee of Safety, Jan. 8, 1776, Instructions to Maj. Gen. Charles Lee, Jan. 8, 1776, George Washington, *The Writings of George Washington*, ed. Worthington C. Ford (New York, 1889–1893), 4:220–222; Committee of Congress to Committee of Safety, Feb. 1, Thomas Nelson to Thomas Jefferson, [Fe]b. 4, 1776, Smith, ed., *Letters of Delegates to Congress* 3:181–182,193; Smith, *Memoirs* 1:260; *American Archives*, 4th ser., 4:1096, 1100.

60. Andrew Allen to Sarah Allen, Feb. 5, 1776, Smith, ed., *Letters of Delegates to Congress* 3:196–197; Extract of a Letter from New York, *Pennsylvania Journal*, Feb. 7, 1776; Smith, *Memoirs* 1:263; *American Archives*, 4th ser., 4:942; Champagne, *Alexander McDougall*, 103–104; C. Lee to Washington, Feb. 14, 1776, *Lee Papers* 1:295.

61. *Journals of the Provincial Congress* 1:284; *American Archives*, 4th ser., 5:272, 274, 281, 287, 308–309, 332, 337; Neuenschwander, *Middle Colonies*, 166; Joseph S. Tiedemann, "A Revolution Foiled: Queens County, New York, 1775–1776," *JAH* 75 (1988): 430.

62. *American Archives*, 4th ser., 5:354; John Jones to Duane, Apr. 14, 1776, James Duane Papers, 1680–1853, NYHS.

63. *American Archives*, 4th ser., 5:1451, 1453; *Constitutional Gazette*, Apr. 20, 1776.

11. Independence

1. *NYJ*, Nov. 9, 1775. For the development of sentiment for independence, see Bernard Mason, *The Road to Independence: The Revolutionary Movement in New York, 1773–1777* (Lexington, Ky., 1966), 134–177.

2. *NYJ*, Nov. 23, 30, Dec. 7, 21, 1775.

3. "Philo Patriae," "Patriotism," *NYJ*, Nov. 2, 1775; Peter Force, ed., *American Archives . . . A Documentary History of . . . the North American Colonies*, 4th ser., 6 vols. (Washington, D.C., 1837–1846), 3:1553, herein cited as *American Archives*; "A Poor Man," *Constitutional Gazette*, Nov. 25, 1775.

4. *NYJ*, Jan. 25, 1776.

5. *NYJ*, Nov. 2, 1775.

6. *American Archives*, 4th ser., 3:1106.

7. *Constitutional Gazette*, Sept. 27, 1775.

8. *NYJ*, Sept. 21, 1775.

9. *NYJ*, Dec. 21, 1775; *The New York Packet and the American Advertiser*, Jan. 25, 1776. For the struggle in Pennsylvania over independence, see Richard Alan Ryerson, *The Revolution Is Now Begun: The Radical Committees of Philadelphia, 1765–1776* (Philadelphia, 1978), 149–176.

10. *NYJ*, Feb. 22, 1776. Also see A. Owen Aldridge, "The Influence of New York Newspapers on Paine's *Common Sense*," *NYHSQ* 60 (1976): 53–60.

11. *Constitutional Gazette*, Mar. 16, 1776.

12. *NYJ*, Feb. 1, 1776.

13. *American Archives*, 4th ser., 5:854–856.

14. *New York Packet*, Mar. 3, Apr. 18, 1776; *Constitutional Gazette*, Mar. 9, 30, 1776; *NYGWM*, Apr. 8, 15, 1776; *NYJ*, Apr. 18, 1776; "The Intelligencer" [or Hugh Hughes] to Samuel and John Adams, Feb. [4], 1776, Samuel Adams Papers, 1635–1827, NYPL.

15. *American Archives*, 4th ser., 5:438–440, 1389, 1441–1442. The quote is from Letter from New York, Mar. 22, 1776, John Almon, ed., *The Remembrancer or Impartial Repository of Public Events*, 17 vols. (London, 1775–1784), 3:85.

16. RRL, Jr., to James Duane, Feb. 16, 1776, Livingston Family Papers, NYPL. Duane, too, was very hesitant to seek independence; Duane to RRL, Jr., Mar. 20, 1776, Livingston Family Papers, NYPL. "To the Inhabitants of New York," *American Archives*, 4th ser., 5:854–856; "Salus Populi," *Constitutional Gazette*, Feb. 14, 1776.

17. *Constitutional Gazette*, Feb. 14, 1776; *NYJ*, Feb. 29, Mar. 14, 1776. A "Salus Populi" had already indirectly supported independence in the Dec. 27, 1775, issue of the *Pennsylvania Journal*.

18. "A Free Citizen," *To the Honourable Committee of Safety of the Colony of New York* [New York, 1776], Evans, 14384.

19. John Jay to Alexander McDougall, Apr. 11, 1776, Richard B. Morris, ed., *John Jay, The Making of a Revolutionary: Unpublished Papers, 1745–1780* (New York, 1975), 1:254; *American Archives*, 4th ser., 6:395; Worthington C. Ford et al., eds., *Journals of the Continental Congress, 1774–1789*, 34 vols. (Washington, D.C., 1904–1937), 4:342, 351, 357–358, herein cited as *Journals of the Continental Congress*; RRL, Jr., to Jay, May 17, 1776, Livingston Family Papers, NYPL; Duane to Jay, May 18, Jay to Duane, May 29, 1776, Morris, ed., *John Jay* 1:266, 269–270.

20. *American Archives*, 4th ser., 6:1332; Mason, *Road to Independence*, 151–152.

21. *American Archives*, 4th ser., 6:1338.

22. *American Archives*, 4th ser., 6:895–898.

23. The quote is from *American Archives*, 4th ser., 6:614–615. *NYGWM*, June 3, 1776; Hughes to John Adams, May 29, 1776, Robert J. Taylor et al., eds., *Papers of John Adams*, 8 vols. (Cambridge, Mass., 1977–), 4:219–220.

24. *American Archives*, 4th ser., 6:1362–1363, 1377; *Journals of the Continental Congress* 5:425; Thomas Jefferson, "Notes of Proceedings in Congress," [June 7–28, 1776], Paul H. Smith et al., eds., *Letters of Delegates to Congress, 1774–1789*, 14 vols. (Washington, D.C., 1976–), 3:158–164; Edward Rutledge to Jay, June 29, 1776, Morris, ed., *John Jay* 1:280–281.

25. *American Archives*, 4th ser., 6:1395–1396.

26. On June 16, for instance, Congress learned of the "Hickey Conspiracy," a plot to kidnap Washington when the British invaded New York; Philip Ranlet, *The New York Loyalists* (Knoxville, 1986), 156–157.

27. William Smith, *Historical Memoirs of William Smith, Historian of the Province of New York, Member of the Governor's Council . . .*, ed. William H. W. Sabine, 2 vols. (New York, 1956–1958), 1:257, herein cited as Smith, *Memoirs*; Jacob Walton to Henry Cruger, Nov. 1, Harris Cruger to Henry Cruger, Nov. 3, 1775, *Calender of Home Office Papers* 4:480, 481; RRL, Jr., to Jay, [July 6, 1776], Morris, ed., *John Jay* 1:282–283; RRL, Jr., to Edward Rutledge, Oct. 10, 1776, Livingston Family Papers, NYPL.

28. Vice Adm. Samuel Graves to Philip Stephens, July 16, V. Pearse Ashfield to Isaac Wilkins, Nov. 4, 1775, *Calendar of Home Office Papers of the Reign of King George III, 1760–1775*, 4 vols. (London, 1878–99), 4:394, 482; RRL, Jr., to Jay, July 17, 1775, Morris, ed., *John Jay* 1:158–160; Gov. William Tryon to Lord Dartmouth, Apr. 12, 1775, C.O. 5/1106; Roger J. Champagne, "New York Politics and Independence, 1776," *NYHSQ* 46 (1962): 286; William A. Benton, *Whig-Loyalism: An Aspect of Political Ideology in the American Revolutionary Era* (Rutherford, N.J., 1968), 176.

29. Seabury played on these fears in *Free Thoughts on the Proceedings of the Continental Congress*, Samuel Seabury, *Letters of a Westchester Farmer*, ed. Clarence H. Vance (White Plains, N.Y., 1930), 43–68.

30. *American Archives*, 4th ser., 6:897.

31. *NYJ*, June 20, 1776. Concerning "the Assault on Aristocracy" throughout America, see Gordon S. Wood, *The Radicalism of the American Revolution* (New York, 1992), 271–286.

32. Champagne, "New York's Radicals and the Coming of Independence," *JAH* 51 (1964): 39–40. By February 1776 only 16,000 people lived in town; Smith, *Memoirs* 1:264. By August the number was down to about 5,000; Oscar Theodore Barck, Jr., *New York City during the War for Independence* (New York, 1931), 76.

33. New York delegates to the Provincial Congress, July 2, 1776, Smith, ed., *Letters of Delegates to Congress* 3:371–372; *Constitutional Gazette*, July 3, 1776; *American Archives*, 4th ser., 6:1443–1444.

34. Peter Force, ed., *American Archives . . . A Documentary History of . . . the North American Colonies*, 5th ser., 3 vols. (Washington, D.C., 1848–1853), 1:1387–1388, 1394, 1410, 1466; Mason, *Road to Independence*, 230; Edward Countryman, *A People in Revolution: The American Revolution and Political Society in New York, 1760–1790* (Baltimore, 1981), 163–166.

35. William Duer to Jay, May 28, 1777, Morris, ed., *John Jay* 1:406; William Smith to Philip Schuyler, Aug. 17, 1776, Smith, *Memoirs* 2:2–3; and RRL, Jr., to William Duer, June 12, 1777, Robert R. Livingston Papers, NYHS (microfilm).

36. Countryman, *People in Revolution*, xiii, 72–98.

Epilogue

1. William Howe to Lord George Germain, Sept. 3, 21, 1776, C.O. 5/93; George R. Barnes and J. H. Owen, eds., *The Private Papers of John, Earl of Sandwich, First Lord of the Admiralty, 1771–1782*, 4 vols. (London, 1932–1938), 1:156–157.

2. The first and last quotes are from *NYGWM*, Sept. 30, 1776; the middle quote is from Extract of a Letter from New York, Sept. 23, 1776, John Almon, ed., *The Remembrancer or Impartial Repository of Public Events*, 17 vols. (London, 1775–1784), 4:119. Frank Moore, comp., *The Diary of the American Revolution, 1775–1781* (New York, 1967), 163; Gen. George Washington to New York Legislature, Sept. 8, 1776, George Washington, *The Writings of George Washington*, ed. Worthington C. Ford (New York, 1889–1893), 6:35; Oscar Theodore Barck, Jr., *New York City during the War for Independence* (New York, 1931), 79–81.

3. Extract of a Letter from New York, Sept. 23, 1776, Almon, ed., *Remembrancer* 4:119.

4. *NYGWM*, Sept. 30, 1776; Tryon to Germain, Sept. 24, 1776, C.O. 5/1107; Worthington C. Ford et al., eds., *Journals of the Continental Congress, 1774–1789*, 34 vols. (Washington, D.C., 1904–1937), 5:733; Barck, *New York during the War for Independence*, 81.

5. Tryon to Germain, Sept. 24, 1776, C.O. 5/1107; Barck, *New York during the War for Independence*, 48.

Historiographical Essay

1. Carl Lotus Becker, *The History of Political Parties in the Province of New York, 1760–1776* (Madison, Wisc., 1909), 1, 22, 10–11, 21, 35, 50. For a discussion of how Becker's ideas evolved, see Bernard Mason, "The Heritage of Carl Becker: The Historiography of the Revolution in New York," *NYHSQ* 53 (1969): 127–147; and Milton M. Klein, "Detachment and the Writing of American History: The Dilemma of Carl Becker," in Alden T. Vaughan and George Athan Billias, eds., *Perspectives on Early American History: Essays in Honor of Richard B. Morris* (New York, 1973), 120–166.

2. Edmund S. Morgan, "The American Revolution: Revisions in Need of Revising," *WMQ* 14 (1957): 3–15; the quote is from p. 10. "A Freeman" to Printer, *WPB*, Nov. 28, 1765; "Freeman," "Liberty, Property, and No Stamps," *New York Mercury*, Dec. 23, 1765. Also see Michael Kammen, *Colonial New York: A History* (New York, 1975),

351; and John Phillip Reid, *Constitutional History of the American Revolution: The Authority of Rights* (Madison, Wisc., 1986), 31–33.

3. Klein, "Democracy and Politics in Colonial New York," *NYH* 60 (1959): 221–246; Nicholas Varga, "Election Procedures and Practices in Colonial New York," *NYH* 61 (1960): 249–277; Roger J. Champagne, "Liberty Boys and Mechanics of New York City, 1764–1774," *Labor History* 8 (1967): 115–135; and Staughton Lynd, "The Mechanics in New York Politics, 1774–1785," in his *Class Conflict, Slavery, and the United States Constitution* (Indianapolis, 1967), 79–108.

4. Becker, *History of Political Parties*, 50, 161, 219–220, 267, 272; the quotes are from pp. 220, 228, 116, 10, 32, 136, 82. Alexander Clarence Flick, *Loyalism in New York during the American Revolution* (New York, 1901), 180–182.

5. Gary B. Nash, "Social Change and the Growth of Prerevolutionary Radicalism," in Alfred F. Young, ed., *The American Revolution: Explorations in the History of American Radicalism* (De Kalb, Ill., 1976), 3-36; the first quote is from p. 6. Nash, *The Urban Crucible: Social Change, Political Consciousness, and the Origins of the American Revolution* (Cambridge, Mass., 1979), 362–374; the remaining quotes are from pp. 383, 371, 372.

6. Edward Countryman, *A People in Revolution: The American Revolution and Political Society in New York, 1760–1790* (Baltimore, 1981), xi, xiii, 296, xiii, 4, 102, 153, 132. For an alternate view of political society in New York, see Klein, "The Cultural Tyros of Colonial New York," *South Atlantic Quarterly* 66 (1967): 218–232; and Klein, "Shaping the American Tradition: The Microcosm of Colonial New York," *NYH* 59 (1978): 173–197.

7. Countryman, *People in Revolution*, chap. 2; the riots are listed on pp. 37–45, and the quote is from p. 36.

8. Louis Kriesberg, *Social Conflicts*, 2d ed. (Englewood Cliffs, N.J., 1982), 93, 136.

9. Countryman, *People in Revolution*, 71, 56; Kriesberg, *Social Conflicts*, 125; Dirk Hoerder, *Crowd Action in Revolutionary Massachusetts, 1765–1780* (New York, 1977), 386; Gordon S. Wood, *The Radicalism of the American Revolution* (New York, 1992), 89.

10. Champagne, "The Sons of Liberty and the Aristocracy in New York Politics, 1765–1790" (Ph.D. diss., University of Wisconsin, 1960), 10, 2, 439.

11. Champagne, "New York and the Intolerable Acts, 1774," *NYHSQ* 45 (1961): 196; Champagne, "New York Politics and Independence, 1776," *NYHSQ* 46 (1962): 303. For a new study that nicely restates the Consensus argument but that was published too recently to inform this study, see Mary Lou Lustig, *Privilege and Prerogative: New York's Provincial Elite, 1710–1776* (Madison, N.J., 1995), esp. p. 180. For yet another new study that emphasizes the opportunism of New York's political leaders in this period, see Alan Tully, *Forming American Politics: Ideals, Interests, and Institutions in Colonial New York and Pennsylvania* (Baltimore, 1994), esp. pp. 249–256.

12. Champagne, "New York's Radicals and the Coming of Independence," *JAH* 51 (1964): 27, 28, 29. Mason, *The Road to Independence: The Revolutionary Movement in New York, 1773–1777* (Lexington, Ky., 1966), 42–61, 172–177; the quotes are from pp. 113, 177. Philip Ranlet, *The New York Loyalists* (Knoxville, 1986), 7, singled out the whig leadership's fear of mob violence to explain its caution. In 1973, John A. Neuenschwander advanced a sectional interpretation for what happened in the Middle Colonies between 1763 and 1776, yet his explanation for why New Yorkers were reluctant to rebel was compatible with the Consensus approach. Pennsylvania, Delaware, New Jersey, and New York, he said, were united by "two fundamental principles." One

was a mistrust of New England expansionism, which residents of these four colonies considered largely responsible for the troubles with Britain. The other was the need to preserve the empire. Not only did they fear that New England would seek to dominate them if the empire was sundered, but they realized that they had prospered economically in the 1760s and 1770s from their membership in the empire, and that the imperial government had favored their interests over those of the other two sections. As promising as Neuenschwander's approach is, it is not without problems. First, he treated "the merchants and landed gentry of New York" (that is, the De Lanceys and the Livingstons) as if they thought alike about the imperial crises. Second, he conceded in a footnote that New York City's economy was not as prosperous as Philadelphia's, but "somewhat depressed" between 1763 and 1770. Third, he took no account of the role that religious and ethnic pluralism might have played in determining how the Middle Colonies saw imperial affairs. Finally, to explain why New York was the most reluctant of the colonies to rebel, Neuenschwander offered a variation of the Consensus interpretation. "New York's behavior since the 'Intolerable Acts' had been marked by a high degree of opportunism." In 1775, "with the Indian menace on the frontier, the British threat to New York City, a substantial Tory party within and the New England radicals fulminating to the north, it is no wonder that New York Whigs acted like men in a trance." In 1776, "with their property and even their lives at stake the New York Whigs did not abandon their opportunism; they only clutched to it more tightly." John A. Neuenschwander, *The Middle Colonies and the Coming of the American Revolution* (Port Washington, N.Y., 1973), 6–8, 28–30, 128–129, 204–205; the quotes are from pp. 7, 216, 211, 204, 128, and 205. For a study that recognizes the significance of ethnic and religious pluralism in the Middle Colonies, see Larry R. Gerlach, *Prologue to Independence: New Jersey in the Coming of the American Revolution* (New Brunswick, N.J., 1976), chap. 1, esp. pp. 6, 11, 33.

13. Arthur M. Schlesinger, *The Colonial Merchants and the American Revolution, 1763–1776* (New York, 1918), 92. Champagne, "Sons of Liberty," 84, 92; the quotes are from pp. 507 and 307–308. In *Alexander McDougall and the American Revolution* (Syracuse, 1975), 1, Champagne's argument was much the same: Of modest birth and "middling social rank," McDougall "was an ambitious man" who saw his own political career as a Liberty Boy as "a measure of his status and a means to greater fulfillment. Christen's dissertation was published posthumously in 1982 as Robert J. Christen, *King Sears: Politician and Patriot in a Decade of Revolution* (New York, 1982), 29–31; the quote is from p. 33. Pauline Maier, *The Old Revolutionaries: Political Lives in the Age of Samuel Adams* (New York, 1980), 99, 100. Also see Edmund S. Morgan and Helen M. Morgan, *The Stamp Act Crisis: Prologue to Revolution*, rev. ed. (New York, 1963), 236. Even some Progressive historians have made this same argument; see Herbert M. Morais, "The Sons of Liberty in New York," in Richard B. Morris, ed., *The Era of the American Revolution: Studies Inscribed to Evarts Boutell Greene* (New York, 1939), 272–73, 269.

14. Bernard Friedman, "Hugh Hughes, A Study in Revolutionary Idealism," *NYH* 64 (1983): 236, n. 19, 237. Friedman, "The New York Assembly Elections of 1768 and 1769: The Disruption of Family Politics," *NYH* 46 (1965): 3–24; the quote is from p. 5. Christen, *King Sears*, 42–43; Champagne, *Alexander McDougall*, 13–14. In 1961, Champagne had stated that Isaac Sears, John Lamb, and Alexander McDougall had "enjoyed decisive influence during the fights against the Stamp Act and the Townshend Acts prior to the repeal of 1770"; Champagne, "New York and the Intolerable Acts," *NYHSQ* 45 (1961): 196. In a 1962 dissertation, L. Jesse Lemisch argued that

New York's seamen played a significant role in the Stamp Act riots. Livingstonite lawyers "were not pulling the strings at the time"; rather, the mariners were led by Sears and probably also by McDougall and Marinus Willett. See Jesse Lemisch, "Jack Tar vs. John Bull: The Role of New York's Seamen in Precipitating the Revolution" (Ph.D. diss., Yale University, 1962), 108; the quote is from p. 105.

15. Leopold S. Launitz-Schürer, *Loyal Whigs and Revolutionaries: The Making of the Revolution in New York* (New York, 1980), 23, 35–36; William Smith, *Historical Memoirs of William Smith, Historian of the Province of New York, Member of the Governor's Council, and Late Chief Justice of That Province under the Crown, Chief Justice of Quebec*, ed. William H. W. Sabine, 2 vols. (New York, 1956–1958), 1:95, herein cited as Smith, *Memoirs*; Sears to John Holt, *NYJ*, May 10, 1770.

16. Launitz-Schürer, *Loyal Whigs*, 129, 197; Patricia U. Bonomi, *A Factious People: Politics and Society in Colonial New York* (New York, 1971), 239, 277, 278; Morton Deutsch, *The Resolution of Conflict, Constructive and Destructive Processes* (New Haven, 1973), 351–352, 356–359.

17. Cynthia Anne Kierner, *Traders and Gentlefolk: The Livingstons of Colonial New York, 1675–1790* (Ithaca, N.Y., 1992), 143–144, 161, 167; Robert Kelley, "Ideology and Political Culture from Jefferson to Nixon," *AHR* 82 (1977): 537. Concerning Kelley's comment, also see Howard Miller, *The Revolutionary College: American Presbyterian Higher Education, 1707–1837* (New York, 1976), 7, 112–116. Launitz-Schürer, *Loyal Whigs*, 179. For the role that Anglicization and trade played in making many in the "cosmopolitan merchant and financial elite" of New York City loyalist, see Kelley, "Ideology and Political Culture," *AHR* 82 (1977): 538.

18. Smith, *Memoirs* 1:88–91, 94–97, 128; Richard Hofstadter, *The Idea of a Party System: The Rise of Legitimate Opposition in the United States, 1780–1840* (Berkeley, 1970), 1–40; CC to [Lord Hillsborough], July 7, 1770, *The Colden Letter Books*, 2 vols. (NYHS, *Collections*, vols. 9–10 [New York, 1877–1878]), 2:223–224; William Livingston and Others, *The Independent Reflector*, ed. Klein (Cambridge, Mass., 1963), 143–150, 215–220, herein cited as *Independent Reflector*. Also see Robert Kelley, *The Cultural Patterns of American Politics: The First Century* (New York: 1979), 50, 63–70. For a recent work that emphasizes party development, not opportunism, as the key to understanding political developments in the Middle Colonies in this period, see Benjamin H. Newcomb, *Political Partisanship in the American Middle Colonies, 1700–1776* (Baton Rouge, 1995), esp. pp. 6–7.

19. Mason, *Road to Independence*, 6; Champagne, *Alexander McDougall*, 3. Also see Launitz-Schürer, *Loyal Whigs*, 16, 40; and Bonomi, *Factious People*, 239, 279–280. For the argument that ideas and constitutional principles mattered in this period, see Klein, "Democracy and Politics," *NYH* 60 (1959): 221–246; Klein, "Prelude to Revolution in New York: Jury Trials and Judicial Tenure," *WMQ* 17 (1960): 439–462; and Klein, "Politics and Personalities in Colonial New York," *NYH* 47 (1966): 3–16.

20. Bernard Bailyn, *The Ideological Origins of the American Revolution* (Cambridge, Mass., 1967), 95, 57, 117; Donald E. M. Gerardi, "The King's College Controversy 1753–1756 and the Ideological Roots of Toryism in New York," *Perspectives in American History* 11 (1977–1978): 148–149; Janice Potter, *The Liberty We Seek: Loyalist Ideology in Colonial New York and Massachusetts* (Cambridge, Mass., 1983), 84–106.

21. Kierner, *Traders and Gentlefolk*, 143–144, 161, 167; Maier, *Old Revolutionaries*, 3–50, 51–100. Also see Klein's discussion of the influence that British Real Whig writers, such as Thomas Gordon and John Trenchard, had on the party's Whig "triumvirate"; *Independent Reflector*, 20–21.

22. Potter, *Liberty We Seek*, 18, 21.

23. Marc Egnal has recently offered a new interpretation of the American Revolution: Livingston "expansionists"—upper-class colonists who shared the "heartfelt conviction that America could and should aspire to greatness" and "who were actively committed to promoting the rise of the New World"—were arrayed against De Lancey "nonexpansionists," "well-to-do citizens" who had "little faith in America's ability to assert itself in a world of hostile nations" and who "were unwilling to support the bold steps needed to strengthen the sovereignty of the colonies." At least for New York, however, this argument has important similarities with the Consensus approach. Like Champagne, Egnal believes that the real fight was among patricians, that the Livingstons were the key actors in the anti-British protest movement, and that the Liberty Boys played only a secondary role. Neither Sears nor Lamb appears on the list of expansionists printed in the appendix. And Egnal claims that in the Stamp Act crisis the Livingstons "spearhead[ed] the protests," though they "grew increasingly more cautious," especially after November 2, 1765. Despite the fact that Sears and James De Lancey allied with one another on December 6, Egnal argues without tangible evidence that "until the very end of the year the Sons of Liberty, despite the buffets they received, felt more comfortable working with the Livingstons than with the De Lanceys." Indeed, if it had not been for the Hudson Valley land riots of 1766, Egnal believes, "this balance of forces between a cautious but patriotic Livingston faction leading the protests and a De Lancey faction playing a distinctly subordinate role in the resistance movement might have continued in 1766." Marc Egnal, *A Mighty Empire: The Origins of the American Revolution* (Ithaca, N.Y., 1988), 168–190; the quotes are from pp. xiii-xiv, 170, 173, 174.

Index

Huguenots, 22, 32, 39, 169
"Humanus," 201
Hunter, Robert (New York governor), 49
Hutchinson, Thomas (Massachusetts), 3,
    50, 71, 138, 192

Illick, Joseph E., 225
"Impartial," 217
Imperialism (British), opposition to, 25, 48,
    62, 81–82, 124, 149, 170, 176, 181, 190,
    196, 225–226, 267
Impressment, 46, 58
Independence, 1, 5–6, 9, 69, 92, 114, 124,
    153, 207, 215, 236, 238, 253, 256; British
    fears about, 221; declared, 226, 251;
    movement for, 245–251; opinions on,
    227–228
"Independent Whig, An," 245
Inglis, Charles, 133, 208, 237

James, Maj. Thomas, 1, 17, 45, 75
Jardine, Charles, 169
Jauncey, James, 125–128, 132–133, 142,
    168
Jay, John, 20, 37, 132, 198, 236, 239, 248,
    252; and Committee of Fifty-one, 190;
    election to First Continental Congress,
    193–196; and emergence of loyalists,
    208, 219; and whig party, 208, 219, 228
Johnson, Sir William, 55, 158
Jones, David, 52
Jones, Thomas, 3–4, 92, 141, 152, 202, 206,
    267; on Anglicanism, 22–23; on First
    Continental Congress, 196; on Lexington
    and Concord, 221–222

Kalm, Peter (European visitor), 16
Kelley, Robert, 265
Kelly, William, 105–106, 179
Kempe, John Tabor, 211, 213
Kennedy, Capt. Archibald, 20, 76–77,
    80–81
King, David, 237
King's College (New York City), 3, 17, 23,
    207, 256, 266
Kissam, Benjamin, 229
Klein, Milton M., 25
Knollenberg, Bernard, 66
Kriesberg, Louis, eight-stage model of, 8–9.
    See also Social-conflict theory

Lamb, Catherine (née Jardine), 169
Lamb, John, 39, 72, 84, 169, 227, 233, 251,
    264; and balloting bill, 146; and Coercive
    Acts, 188, 198; Thomas Jones on, 92; and
    Liberty Pole, 148; and Alexander McDou-

gall, 143–145; and Quartering Act, 144;
    and Tea Act, 181–182
Landowners (New York Colony), 27, 35–36,
    49–54, 65–66, 118, 121, 126, 133
Laqueur, Walter, 6
Lasher, Col. John, 3, 232
Launitz-Schürer, Leopold, 264–265
Lawyers (New York City), 22, 27, 36, 43, 49–
    54, 58, 89, 95, 180, 227, 264; and 1768
    elections, 125–127; and 1769 elections,
    133; and Stamp Act, 65, 68, 78–81
Leach, Catherine, 207
Leadbetter, James, 237
Lee, Maj. Gen. Charles (Virginia), 240–242
Lee, Richard Henry (Virginia), 249
Lee, William, 211
"Legion," 177–179
Lewis, Francis, 188–191, 194
Lexington, Battle of, 21, 216, 220–221, 243
"Libertas," 71
Liberty Pole, 17, 21, 66, 97, 166, 217–219;
    efforts to cut down, 110–112, 147–149
Lispenard, Leonard, 3, 193, 195, 222
Livingston, Peter R., 115, 136, 138
Livingston, Peter Van Brugh, 132, 139, 250
Livingston, Philip, 70, 141, 198, 223, 236,
    239; and 1768 elections, 125–128; and
    1769 elections, 132–134; and Committee
    of Fifty-one, 188; ejected from Assembly,
    136–138; and First Continental Congress,
    193; and Massachusetts Circular Letter,
    130; and Tea Act, 180–181
Livingston, Philip (son of Peter Van Brugh
    Livingston), 139, 250
Livingston, Robert, 136
Livingston, Robert, Jr., 125
Livingston, Robert R., 20–23, 36–37, 46,
    52, 128, 167–168, 193; and Assembly
    seat, 137–138, 146; and Stamp Act, 64,
    70, 76–77, 80, 86, 89
Livingston, Robert R., Jr., 252; and indepen-
    dence, 246–250
Livingston, William, 36–38, 53, 133, 193,
    208, 267; and Stamp Act, 65–66, 69–72,
    79
Livingston family, 20, 35–37, 76, 151, 190
Livingston Manor (New York), 30, 125,
    136–138
Livingston party, 24, 100, 164, 180, 188,
    193, 203, 207, 214; in 1768 elections,
    125–128; in 1769 elections, 131–135; in
    1770 elections, 166; and Anglican
    church, 21, 133; in Assembly, 136–137;
    coalition with Liberty Boys, 178, 188,
    196, 206, 223, 227; and Cadwallader Col-
    den, 51–55, 139; discussed, 35–41, 146;